A PURELY AMERICAN INVENTION

INVENTION

The U.S. Open-End Mutual Fund Industry

A PURELY AMERICAN INVENTION

The U.S. Open-End Mutual Fund Industry

LEE GREMILLION

The National Investment Company Service Association

Published by The National Investment Company Service Association
Printed in the United States of America

Library of Congress Cataloging-in-Publication Data

Gremillion, Lee L. (Lee Louis)
   A purely American invention : the U.S. open-end
mutual fund industry / Lee Gremillion. -- 1st ed.
      p. cm.
      Includes bibliographical references and index.
      LCCN: 00-110215
      ISBN: 0-9705845-0-4

   1. Mutual funds--United States. I. Title.

HG4530.G74 2000   332.63'27
                             QBI00-862

By providing shareholders with ready liquidity, redemption on demand made open-end funds more secure in an era of insecurity. There is no precedent for the open-end structure in Britain. *It is a purely American invention, and one of the great innovations of the U.S. capital markets.*

— Max Rottersman and Jason Zweig, "An Early History of Mutual Funds," *Friends of Financial History*, spring, 1994.

To Kathy, Andrew, and Christine

Foreword

It was a bit more than a half-century ago when I opened the December 1949 issue of *Fortune* magazine and discovered the mutual fund industry. An Economics major at Princeton University, I was seated in the reading room of the then-brand-new Firestone Library, considering the choice of a topic for my senior thesis, which was due to be submitted some 16 months later. Determined to write on a subject never before explored in a Princeton thesis (there went Adam Smith, Karl Marx, and Lord Keynes!), I quickly realized that I had found my subject. As it turned out, I had also found a wonderfully rewarding career, the focus of my life-long vocation, and the mission I would pursue to this day: Serving the mutual fund shareholder.

The title of the article that I read all those years ago was "Big Money in Boston." It focused on Massachusetts Investors Trust (MIT), the industry's oldest fund (founded in 1924), its then-largest fund ($280 million in assets) and its lowest-end fund (0.33 percent expense ratio). It is hardly a coincidence that it is MIT that leads off: "A Brief History of Mutual Funds in the United States," the title of Chapter 2 of the sweeping and comprehensive compendium of the mutual fund industry that you are holding in your hands as you read these words.

A Purely American Invention is a remarkably important work. Sponsored by The National Investment Company Service Association and ably and authoritatively written by PricewaterhouseCoopers lead Partner Lee Gremillion, it is a book whose time has come at the perfect moment. If it had been written a quarter-century earlier, it would have been regarded as a death knell, for fund industry assets were then a miniscule $34 billion—and shrinking! Who could possibly have had the ability to foresee the remarkable sea change that would sweep the industry during the ten years that would end as the second millennium ended and the third began.

As I read this book, I was transfixed, and couldn't help reaching back in time to my first exposure to the industry 50-plus years ago. Until I read that *Fortune* article, I had known absolutely *nothing* about mutual funds. Indeed, I don't even recall an understanding of stocks and bonds. But after I'd completed my extensive research—my bibliography cited 23 books; 43 articles; three of the classic *Investment Companies* manuals, published annually by Arthur Wiesenberger & Company to this day—and read the entire 4,217-page report of the U.S. Securities & Exchange Commission that led to the enactment of the Investment Company Act of 1940, I thought I'd gained a pretty solid understanding of the industry.

I chose the title *The Economic Role of the Investment Company*[1] for my thesis. While it explored many possible roles for the industry, it set forth a simple, overarching principle for mutual funds. In the Introduction: "Their prime responsibility must always be to their shareholders." In the Conclusion: "The tremendous growth

---

[1] At the insistence of the publisher, the thesis was recently published in it entirety—along with 25 of my speeches—in *John Bogle on Investing: The First 50 Years*, the first volume of the new McGraw-Hill series "Great Ideas in Finance."

potentiality of the investment company rests on its ability to serve the needs of both individual and institutional investors…to serve them with management operating in the most efficient, honest, and economical way possible…the principal function of investment companies is the management of their investment portfolios." Today, I continue to hold high these very same ideals.

Following my early study of the industry, I spent the next quarter century laboring in the mutual fund vineyards at Wellington Management Company and became its Chief Executive in 1967. Then as now, I was a diligent, determined participant in virtually all aspects of the business—administration, operations, marketing, investment management—and by 1974, I had come to believe that I knew everything about mutual funds that I needed to know. Today, however, with the sweeping changes that have taken place in the past 25 years, I sometimes wonder if I know *anything* that I need to know if I am to remain an active participant in this wonderful business.

A Purely American Invention to the rescue! This book has already played a major role in filling the embarrassing gap in my knowledge. Its subject matter is nothing less than *the way funds work*. It covers the industry's history (please remember, "those who ignore the past are condemned to repeat it"); industry structure; the investment management "front office" (portfolio supervision) and the "back office" (making the system work); the fund accounting, audit, and legal functions; the transfer agency, now handling 200 *million* shareholder accounts; customer service; distribution methods (including the different challenges faced by the broker, direct, bank, and institutional channels, as well as the similar challenges that *all* channels face in advertising and retirement investing); the incipient trend toward globalization; and, of special significance, the dramatic changes now taking place in the industry as a result of the revolution in e-business and e-commerce.

I am profoundly impressed by the broad and comprehensive sweep of information and knowledge that this book makes available to industry participants, college students, and anyone else with a serious interest in this industry. But I am even *more* impressed by the fairness and even-handedness it brings to its discussion of many of the controversial issues that face the industry today. Controversy is hardly surprising in an industry that I've often described as characterized by dog-eat-dog competition, and the multiple ways that various funds compete—in distribution channels, in marketing, in advertising, in fund creation, in portfolio policy, in investment strategy—surely characterize any highly competitive industry.

But *cost* competition remains conspicuous by its absence. Remember MIT's 1949 assets of $280 million and its expense ratio of 0.33 percent? Well, in 1999, despite a 30-fold increase in those assets to $8.5 *billion*, its expense ratio had *risen* to 0.88 percent, generating an 80-fold increase in fund expenses. While the MIT expense ratio last year was nearly 50 percent *below* the equity fund average of 1.61 percent, neither figure suggests that the staggering economics of scale involved in mutual fund management are being adequately shared—if shared at all—with fund owners. One need not agree with that conclusion in order to wonder whether the fine study of fund expenses provided in *A Purely American Invention* (based on limited publicly available information) shouldn't be supplemented by an extensive study of the impact of industry costs—not only management fees and expense ratios, but sales charges, portfolio transaction costs, and opportunity cost—on investor returns.

Since I wrote my thesis in 1951, investment activity in the fund industry has increased in just about every measurable way. Funds themselves come and go at a much higher rate. While some 14 percent of the funds operating during the 1960s no longer existed when 1970 began, fully 55 percent of the funds of the 1990s were gone at the dawning of 2000. Fund portfolio managers (virtually an unknown breed back then, when investment committees ruled the roost) now last on average just five years. Annual portfolio turnover, then about 15 percent, is now near 90 percent. And fund shareholders themselves, joining in this spate of activity, now redeem shares at a 45 percent annual rate, nine *times* the 5 percent rate of 1960. I will not express here the strong opinions I hold about these trends, but I hope that those whose careers depend on the fund industry and those whose careers will shape its future alike will forthrightly consider their implications—specifically, the impact of this frenzied activity on the investment returns of the mutual fund investors whom we are all pledged to serve.

To the author's credit, the final chapters of *A Purely American Invention* vigorously tackle these and other key issues. They include a fine discussion of industry life-cycles, saturation, and alternative products, and jump unhesitantly into three especially contentious issues; First, fees and expenses; second active management vs. passive and third, the state of "the market" in an industry that is, above all, market sensitive. Surely the years ahead hold no shortage of challenges for all of us in the mutual fund field.

There are yet other subtle changes taking place in the U.S. financial markets, and as you begin to read this book I'd like to get you thinking about these three implications of the rise of "People's Capitalism" that this industry has done so much to foster:

- First, with People's Capitalism as the American ethos, what will be the social impact on our political system of the ownership of stocks by the preponderance of our citizenry? With *de facto* control of Corporate America by the public and its stewards, how can the citizenry be *against* "big business" when, by owning stocks, "we the people" are *big* business?

- Second, what are the implications of living in an economy that is becoming ever more *financial-market-dependent*? Clearly, substantial investment risk has been transferred from corporations and financial institutions to individuals. With the financial markets inevitably subject to extreme waves of optimism and pessimism, will these swings be translated into greater volatility in the economy itself?

- Third, what role will government play in the financial markets: even today, as it tries to steer a stable course for our economy, the Federal Reserve focuses on the level of stock prices. But in the long run, stocks cannot be propped-up at unsustainable levels by easy monetary policy or encouraging words. So as common stocks inevitably enter the political arena, will our political authorities have the courage and the wisdom to let the markets take their own course as, finally, they must?

No matter how these issues are resolved, our job, in the final analysis, remains to serve our shareholders, just as it was the job of our founders when this industry began 75 years ago, and just as it was when I wrote my thesis 50 years ago. *No industry can long endure if it fails to effectively serve its clients*. While the booming stock market of the past 18 years—the greatest bull market in all human history—may have concealed whatever shortcomings this industry may have evidenced in delivering its services to investors, those soaring equity trees are unlikely to grow to the sky. So we'd best be prepared to be tested under duress—the *acid test* for an industry. In a book that he wrote 87 years ago, Supreme Court Justice Louis Brandeis expressed it in these timeless words:

> "In business, the earning of profit is something more than an incident of success. It is an essential condition of success. But while loss spells failure, large profits do not connote success. Success must also be sought in the improvement of products, in a more perfect organization, in eliminating friction as well as waste, and in the establishment of right relations with customers and with the community."

You'll get the most out of this book, *A Purely American Invention: The U.S. Open-End Mutual Fund Industry*, if you keep in mind the title of Justice Brandeis' book: *Other People's Money*.

John C. Bogle
Valley Forge, PA
November 9, 2000

Preface

This all started in 1996 when my friend and colleague Kathleen O'Halloran and I were both serving as members of the NICSA East Coast Regional Committee. Each year, the East Coast Committee had to create programs for a half dozen or so NICSA meetings, each of which contained several hours of seminars, panel discussions, and presentations designed to educate the mutual fund industry employees who attended. The committee continually wrestled with the challenge of identifying new and relevant topics for which qualified and interesting presenters could be mustered.

Kathleen, the director of training for Pioneering Services Corporation, and I had an idea as we searched for NICSA meeting topics. Within the fund companies, or companies that provided services to fund companies, both of us knew many people whose knowledge of the industry was deep but not broad. These individuals knew a great deal about the particular function they performed—fund accounting, transfer agent operations, internal wholesaling, fund audit, and so on—but not very much about the other parts of the fund company, or how they all fit together. Both of us remembered how in the course of our own careers we had started in one functional area (the transfer agent), and only gradually learned about the other things a mutual fund company did. Sometimes this learning involved real eye-openers. For example, when I learned about fund accounting entries for mortgage-backed securities, I finally understood why, years earlier, I had had to write programs to make our shareholder accounting system (a transfer agent function) pay dividends a certain way. We suspected that many people had similar gaps in their overall understanding of the industry.

Kathleen and I concluded that NICSA could present a *tutorial*—a broad discussion of the functions of a mutual fund company, and how these functions operated together—that would help people close these gaps. We proposed such a session, had it approved, and prepared the materials. We scheduled the first offering—a three hour session—for the September 1996 NICSA meeting in Boston, wondering whether we could fill all that time. When we ran the session, to a packed roomful of students, we found that we had to talk as fast as we possibly could to complete the material. We also found that the tutorial had struck a chord—the attendees loved it and wanted more of the same. Over the next few years, NICSA ran the tutorial—entitled *Introduction to Mutual Funds*—repeatedly, both on the East Coast and in other regions, and expanded its offerings to other tutorials as well.

The continuing demand for these tutorials, along with the lack of published materials describing fund company operations, eventually convinced me that a book about the industry would serve the needs of several target audiences. By that time I had been associated with the mutual fund industry for almost fifteen years, first as an employee of a fund company, and then as a consultant. My consulting work in particular had covered the broad range of mutual fund functions, and I had worked with many of the industry's leading firms. My employer, PricewaterhouseCoopers, provided unparalleled access to research materials, in part because of their position as the leading auditor of mutual funds in the United States. So, after some discussions with NICSA President Bob Goldberg, who enthusiastically supported the idea, I decided to write a book about the U.S. open-end mutual fund industry and how it works.

In writing this book, I have attempted to address the needs of three target audiences. First, it is aimed at employees of organizations involved in one or more aspects of the mutual fund industry, the same audience the NICSA tutorials serve. These organizations include mutual fund management companies, other asset managers, third-party fund accounting and transfer agent service providers, custody banks, public accounting firms, and a host of smaller service providers. Collectively, these organizations bring in thousands of new employees annually, due to growth and normal turnover. Many of these new employees have not previously worked in the industry. Others may have worked in the industry before, but know only a limited subset of mutual fund functions. This book attempts to help these individuals gain an understanding of both fund operations and the broader context in which they are performed.

Business students studying the mutual fund industry form the second target audience. The mutual fund industry has grown in size and importance to a point where mutual fund operations are taught as a subject in some schools of business. This book is intended to serve as a potential text for such courses, laying out for students what fund companies do and what their management functions and issues are.

Finally, I have tried to address this book to the general reader who seeks an understanding of the industry. Many of us, when faced with an unfamiliar phenomenon, naturally ask the question, *How does this thing work?* This book is intended for those who ask this question about mutual funds and the fund industry. When I surveyed the literature on the industry, I found very little published material to help the lay reader understand what a fund company does and how it does it. While dozens of books have been written to tell potential investors about how to select mutual funds for their personal investment portfolios, very few have addressed themselves to any aspect of how a fund company actually works. Those that do address fund company functions largely limit themselves to the investment management decision-making process.

This lack of information is particularly troubling given the important debates now going on in the industry concerning the level of fund fees, disclosures required of funds, the responsibilities of fund directors, and other policy issues. Even an intelligent investor will find it hard to evaluate the positions being put forth by the various parties without an understanding of the context in which they are made. How can an investor decide, for example, whether fee levels are too high without knowing what those fees are used to pay for? (To help with this issue, I have attempted to discuss not only the functions fund companies perform, but also how much these functions cost, both for individual funds and for the industry as a whole.) In general, where there are controversies, I have tried to present both sides of the argument, as well as the context in which the argument occurs. I have tried to provide the reader with the information he or she needs to become a better-educated consumer of the services provided by the U. S. mutual fund industry.

Edina, Minnesota
September 1, 2000

Acknowledgements

First and foremost, I thank NICSA President Bob Goldberg for the essential role he played in the development of this book. Bob enthusiastically supported the project from the very beginning, sharing and reinforcing my belief that a book of this sort would be of value to the industry. Bob provided advice and introductions whenever I needed them to get access to fund company staff for information gathering. He and the staff of the NICSA office relieved me of one of the most obnoxious duties any author has to perform, that of dealing with the publisher, allowing me to concentrate simply on writing the text. And he was a constant source of encouragement. It is no exaggeration to say that without Bob's help, this book would not have been written.

Along the way I had three individuals who read each and every draft chapter and offered invaluable suggestions on both style and content. Lisa von Biela, an investment management consulting specialist with PricewaterhouseCoopers, focused on the clarity and precision of the text, improving it in numerous instances. Margaret Symington, formerly of PricewaterhouseCoopers, reviewed the contents and offered suggestions from her point of view as an investment operations expert. Finally, Linda Johnson of PricewaterhouseCoopers was my *de facto* editor. She rigorously applied the standards of a professional journalist to make the style crisp, correct, and consistent. Her efforts in particular contributed materially to the quality of the text.

A number of PricewaterhouseCoopers staff deserve thanks for their help with various aspects of the subject. Many consulting professionals reviewed and offered suggestions on segments of the manuscript that addressed their specific areas of expertise. These included William Downey, Sally Staley, Ellen Stulb, Shelley Hartman, Christina Mans, Claire Ingwersen, Lisa Carlson, Roger White, Amy Hockman, and Claudia Johnson. Their helpful comments strengthened discussions of many topics. Jean Scanlan, PricewaterhouseCoopers' head of Investment Management Research provided invaluable assistance in finding reference material. I learned from this process that if Jean can't find it, then it doesn't exist. Finally, Judy Driscoll applied her desktop publishing expertise to transform ugly, typed manuscript pages into attractive camera-ready copy. The format of the finished product you have in your hands is Judy's creation.

Many industry professionals also contributed their knowledge by participating in interviews or otherwise providing data. Some of them are identified within the chapters; others contributed background information. These individuals (in roughly the order in which I interviewed them) include Kathleen O'Halloran, Roger Rainville, Mary Mosher, and Bob Mandile of Pioneer; Richard Grueter, Chris Cornwall, and Allen Goldstein of PricewaterhouseCoopers (U.S.); Jan Clifford and Phil Meltzer of MFS; Anne Collins of Liberty Financial; Alan Greene and Russell Donohoe of State Street Bank; Bill Galvin, Sean Katoff, Chris Bedowitz, Peter Lovell, and Pat Johnston of INVESCO; Dan Wright, Joanne Yetka, Brandi Peachey, Rachel Ventresca, Susan Fowler, and Greg Volpe of David L. Babson; Jim Walline and Mike Swendsen of Lutheran Brotherhood; John Deane and Margaret Reilly of AIM; Joseph Greene of American Century; Matthew Thompson of Faegre & Benson, LLP; and Kavita

Savur of PricewaterhouseCoopers (U.K.). To these individuals, and to any whom I have inadvertently overlooked, I give sincere thanks.

All of these individuals have contributed to the information contained in this book. However, any errors it contains—whether of commission or omission—remain my responsibility alone.

Like most authors, I owe a particularly heavy debt of gratitude to my family for cheerfully enduring the long hours that I had to take from my time with them to complete this project. Much of the writing was a nights-and-weekends effort, which meant it came at their expense. For their unwavering support, I am deeply grateful.

Contents

CHAPTER 1
Introduction to the Industry

As recently as 1980, only one in 16 households invested in mutual funds; today that number is more than one in three, as we have evolved from a nation of savers into a nation of investors.
— Arthur Levitt (1997)[1]

Mutual Funds—Big Business by Any Standard

Open any issue of the *Wall Street Journal,* or the business section of any major newspaper, and you will find several pages of densely packed print labeled "Mutual Funds." These pages list the names, prices, yields, and other key attributes of over 7,700 funds, each a separate company representing an investment pool in which individuals or institutions can participate. At the end of 1999, there were more of these funds than there were common stocks on the New York or American Stock exchanges. Collectively, these 7,700 or so funds represented over $6.5 trillion dollars of assets, about 10 percent of the total financial assets of the U.S. population. At the start of the twenty-first century, almost 25 percent of U.S. retirement funds were invested in mutual funds.[2]

These funds give over 80 million people a way to participate in the securities markets, without having to become money managers themselves. They are professionally-managed, pooled investment vehicles. A mutual fund allows individuals (you, me, anyone with some money to invest) and institutions (corporations, foundations, pension funds) to pool smaller amounts of money into a larger amount for investment. Investment management professionals then manage this larger amount, to allow:

- investment strategies that would not otherwise be feasible (such as buying bonds that only sell in very large denominations);
- achieving economies of scale (such as paying very low broker commissions) that are not attainable when investing smaller sums; and
- making it easy to reduce risk by holding a diversified basket of securities.

As we will see below, mutual funds offer the investor a number of significant advantages compared to investing in individual securities.

Because of these advantages, mutual funds have gained an increasing share of the nation's investable assets. In 1999, mutual funds attracted almost 65 percent of the total amount of money that Americans put into investments or savings that year. During 1999, the total assets invested in mutual funds grew from $5.5 to $6.8 trillion. About two-thirds of that growth can be attributed to investment performance—that is, to dividends that shareholders reinvested in the funds, and to the increase in value of the stocks, bonds, and other securities the funds held. But, almost one-third of the increase was new money, assets that Americans chose to put into mutual funds instead of bank savings, individual stocks, or other investments.

To a large extent, the mutual fund industry is a recent, American phenomenon. While mutual funds or similar investment vehicles exist in other countries, they are nowhere so popular as in the United States. At the end of 1999, the U.S. assets invested in mutual funds represented almost 66 percent of the worldwide total of open-end, pooled investment funds. France has the next largest mutual fund industry after the United States, with French funds holding the equivalent of about US$700 billion in assets—an order of magnitude smaller than U.S. fund holdings. And the U.S. industry has exploded in the past twenty years. At the end of 1979, U.S. funds managed a total of about $100 billion. Over the next twenty years, this figure grew by almost two orders of magnitude.

By 2000, the mutual fund industry had become a significant component of the U.S. financial services sector. In 1999, the almost 8,000 funds generated over $60 billion in revenue and provided employment for over a quarter of a million people, with fund management companies, investment advisers, custodial banks, distributors, transfer agents, and other third-party service providers. Collectively, U.S. mutual funds owned about 20 percent of the equity of publicly held U.S. corporations, about 10 percent of the debt securities issued by the U.S. Treasury and various federal agencies, and about 30 percent of the bonds issued by municipalities (states, cities, counties). In the past few years, authors have penned over 200 books advising investors how to use mutual funds to help them meet their financial goals. A number of universities have recently established courses in mutual fund management.

Mutual Fund Defined

Before going any further, a few definitions are needed. All the funds listed in the Mutual Funds section of the newspaper fall into one particular category: they are open-end mutual funds. Open-end funds are ones that will always sell new shares to investors wanting to invest money, or redeem shares from investors wanting their money back, at a price dependent on the net asset value (NAV) of the fund. (Well, almost always—there are exceptions, which we will describe as we go along.) In addition, each fund in the paper is a separate company— corporation or business trust—registered with the Securities and Exchange Commission (SEC) pursuant to the Securities Act of 1933, and, therefore, available for sale to the public. By and large, when someone says "mutual fund" in the United States today, this is what he or she is talking about—a registered, open-end investment company.

This book focuses on open-end mutual funds. There are other types of funds and pooled investment vehicles, described briefly in the following paragraphs, but none approach the stature of open-end funds in today's economy.

Closed-end funds were more popular than open-end funds during the early years of the industry. Closed-end funds do not purchase and redeem shares at a price dependent on NAV. Instead, they collect a pool of money, issue shares once to the investors who contributed that money, and neither issue nor redeem thereafter.

The shares of a closed-end fund trade on the secondary market, such as the New York Stock Exchange, just as does the common stock of a corporation. The market determines the share price one gets when buying or selling shares, and this price may be very different from the net asset value.

Today, closed-end funds have declined in popularity (for reasons discussed in the next chapter), to the point that their assets in 1999 represented just 3 percent of those of open-end funds. We will not focus on closed-end funds in this book, except on occasion to contrast them with open-end funds.

Unit investment trusts (UITs) resemble mutual funds, but the portfolio of securities of a UIT is fixed at inception and not actively managed. The sponsor of a UIT assembles a pool of money, purchases a basket of securities, and sells securities only in special cases, such as when a bond is called earlier than its maturity date. Most UITs invest in debt securities. They are set up with a specified life span, after which they are liquidated. In general, holders of UIT shares purchase them to get a stable investment with a stated life span, although they usually can redeem their shares at any time at the current net asset value. At the end of 1997, Americans had UIT investments of less than $100 billion, a small fraction of the amount held in open-end mutual funds.

Variable annuities (VAs) are contracts sold by insurance companies. The investor pays a lump sum or makes periodic payments; the insurance company invests this money in a portfolio of securities, often mutual funds. The value of this invested money goes up or down as the prices of the underlying securities rise or fall. After a specified period of time, often when the purchaser reaches age 65, the insurer starts paying the investor an annuity. The amount paid out—either a lump sum or individual payments as elected by the contract holder—varies according to the performance of the underlying securities.

The insurance contract allows the investor to defer the tax on the income earned from the investment until the money is withdrawn. This feature of VAs appeals to investors looking for ways to invest for retirement. On the other hand, variable annuities come with a cost—sales charges, administrative charges, and asset charges, all tacked on top of the costs required to manage the underlying investments. The magnitude of these costs varies from one contract to another and from one insurance company to another. At the end of 1998, Americans had about $500 billion invested in VAs for which the underlying securities were mutual funds.

Hedge funds, another type of pooled vehicle, differ from mutual funds mainly because they are not aimed at the general public, but rather at the sophisticated and large investor. Hedge funds are private, unregistered pools bound by contracts between the investors and the sponsors of the fund. The SEC does not regulate them beyond enforcing general standards of behavior aimed at preventing fraud. Whatever the sponsors and investors agree upon, goes. Typically, these funds require a minimum investment of $1 million or more, and typically pursue riskier investment strategies than do mutual funds.

Hedge funds represent just one variation on a much wider theme—the private investment pool. Many investment management organizations will pool assets from among their clients to achieve economies of scale. For example, banks often create collective trust funds into which they put the individual assets of trust customers, instead of attempting to manage each trust account separately. Insurance companies managing investments for other institutions (typically retirement plans), often do much the same thing. While these pools share some attributes with mutual funds, they are not offered to the general public, nor are they bound by the same regulations as are registered funds.

Private investment pools vary endlessly. At the small and simple end of the range lie investment clubs like the famous Beardstown Ladies. At the other end, we find such entities as limited partnerships, requiring investments of $1 million or more, formed to invest in arcane instruments or special economic sectors. The infamous Long Term Capital Management, a hedge fund, serves as an example. Each kind of investment pool has its place in the U.S. financial landscape, but none looms nearly so large in that landscape today as the mutual fund.

Who Invests in Funds, and Why

Who owns these trillions of dollars' worth of mutual funds? Individual U.S. citizens own the lion's share—81 percent at the end of 1999. Institutions of various sorts—bank trust departments, pension plans, corporations—own the remaining 19 percent. The Investment Company Institute (the ICI, described in Chapter 3) has published a profile of the average mutual fund investor in 1998, some of the attributes of which are shown in the following table. As the table suggests, the typical mutual fund investor is solidly entrenched in the American middle class.

The growth in mutual fund assets over the past twenty years has been paralleled by the growth in the number of investors. In 2000, more than one in three American households owned one or more mutual funds. So why do so many Americans keep a large part of their investments in the form of mutual funds? Different investors will have different reasons, but the major ones include professional management, easy diversification, liquidity, convenience, a wide range of investment choices, and regulatory protection.

Professional management. Mutual funds provide access to professional investment management for individuals who otherwise could not afford it. Trust departments of banks and private investment counsel firms have long offered professional management, but the minimum threshold for these services is typically $1 million or more in assets. Except in a few special cases, mutual funds require minimum investments in the $500 to $5,000 range, making them much more accessible.

Diversification. In general, an investor reduces risk by investing in a larger number of securities, reducing the impact of a decline in value of any one of them. A mutual fund, with its large pool of assets, can economically hold a much larger portfolio of securities than any but the wealthiest individual investor could. Funds can hold a wider range of security types than individuals as well. Individual

HOUSEHOLD OWNERS OF MUTUAL FUNDS DEMOGRAPHIC AND FINANCIAL CHARACTERISTICS, 1998	
Demographic Characteristics	
Median age	44
Percent of households:	
Married	68
Employed full- or part-time	82
Retired	17
Four-year college degree or more	50
Financial Characteristics	
Median household income	$55,000
Median household financial assets	$80,000*
Percent of households owning:	
Individual stocks, bonds, or annuities	73
IRAs	57
Defined contribution plan	77

Source: ICI Mutual Fund Fact Book, 1999.

* Excludes the value of the respondent's primary residence, but includes assets in any employer-sponsored retirement plans.

securities of some types cost tens or hundreds of thousands of dollars each to purchase, putting them out of the reach of most individuals, but not of mutual funds. Individual citizens find it difficult or impossible to purchase foreign securities, but can easily buy shares in mutual funds that hold foreign securities.

Liquidity. Mutual funds must determine a net asset value (NAV) every business day, and redeem all shares offered for liquidation that day at that NAV. Shareholders are assured of being able to convert their holdings to cash whenever they want, through a well-defined and fair process, which is described in Chapter 7.

Convenience. Mutual funds are easy to buy and sell, both directly from fund groups, and through intermediaries such as brokers. They offer a wide range of attractive features for their shareholders, such as check writing, automatic purchase and redemption programs, and twenty-four hour access to information.

Choice. An investor today can find a mutual fund to fit any investment goal he or she may have, from conservative to aggressive. In later chapters, we will see some of the types of mutual funds that provide this wide range of choices.

Regulation. U.S. mutual funds are subject to regulation and oversight by the Securities and Exchange Commission (SEC). Each fund must provide each potential investor with a prospectus, a document that discloses its goals, fees and expenses, and investment strategies and risks. Funds must provide periodic reports showing the fund's actual activity and performance.

There's No Free Lunch, However

Of course, the flip side of this coin is that investors pay for all these benefits. In 1999 specifically, they paid an average of about two-thirds of 1 percent of the value of their fund assets for basic management services—investment management, administration, and the like.[3] Some shareholders paid commissions to intermediaries as they purchased shares of the fund. Many funds paid commissions to brokers as they bought and sold securities, commissions that are paid from the shareholder's assets. The specific amount any one shareholder paid depended on the fund (where fees range from a few one-hundredths of a percent to over 1 percent of assets), and the distribution method (zero for funds that have no sales commissions to several percent for some funds that do involve commissions).

These fee amounts have been a source of controversy for decades. Almost every year brings shareholder litigation against management companies over fees, and arguments back and forth between attackers and defenders of the industry. The courts have largely sided against plaintiffs in these excessive fee complaints, and several econometric studies have concluded that competition has been effective in controlling fees. The ICI has published studies showing that increasing competition in the industry has driven fees down over the past seventeen years.[4] Industry critics have claimed exactly the opposite. The U.S. General Accounting Office

> **Speaking of Costs: Basis Points**
>
> A *basis point* is one one-hundredth of a percent (.0001). Since many fee and cost amounts are fractions of a percent, they are often described in terms of basis points. For example, the .35 of one percent of average assets that Charles Schwab charges funds to belong to its OneSource program is typically described as a "thirty-five basis points fee."

WEIGHING IN ON MUTUAL FUND FEES – SOME COMMENTS FROM INDUSTRY FIGURES

Strategic Insight, a mutual fund industry research and consulting firm
"As industry critics continue to call attention to mutual fund fees, an SI study calculates that fund managers receive advisory fee revenues of under $100 annually per average account… [this] leaves $30 or less in profits per average-fund account, net after expense and taxes; hardly an excessive amount."[5]

Jack Dreyfus, an industry pioneer
"Unless you have made a study of the market and have time to continue to study it, and have confidence in your judgement, it's well worth a half a percent or one percent to put your money in the hands of professionals."[6]

John Bogle, another pioneer
"…enormous amounts of the expenses paid by fund shareholders are not benefiting those very same shareholders. In effect, high fees are paying for huge profits to fund managers…"[7]

studied the issue in 1999–2000 at congressional request, but failed to come to a conclusion about the propriety of fee levels. The battle rages on, and will surface in many subsequent chapters of this book.

In any event, fee amounts obviously have not deterred the majority of American investors who in recent years have poured money into mutual funds. In particular, they have turned to mutual funds as their preferred way of buying into the stock market. As Figure 1 shows, over the past fifteen years U.S. households have become net buyers of equities (stocks) via mutual funds, at the same time as they have become net sellers of individual equity securities.

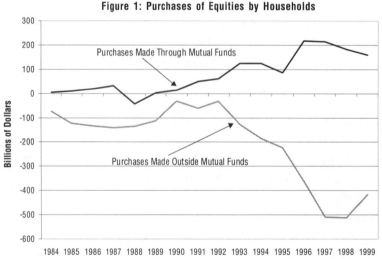

Figure 1: Purchases of Equities by Households

Source: Investment Company Institute

The Structure of a Mutual Fund

Mutual funds have shareholders, directors, assets (cash and securities) and contracts, and not much else. They differ significantly from most business organizations in that they have neither employees nor plant and equipment. (The reasons for this will be explained in the next chapter.) Instead, each fund, as represented by its board of directors, contracts with other organizations to provide the functions it needs. Figure 2 shows the ICI's depiction of the structure of a fund and its supporting organizations.

Board of Directors. Mutual funds are typically organized as corporations or trusts, and each fund has a board of directors to oversee the way the business operates and to ensure that corporate policies are followed. A fund's board differs from the normal corporate board of directors in that the Investment Company Act of 1940 requires fund directors to look out for the investor. The '40 Act, which defines much of the regulatory environment for mutual funds, is discussed in detail in the next chapter. Specifically, the board must oversee matters where the interests of the fund and its shareholders differ from the interests of its investment adviser or management company. To make this work, the Act requires at least 40 percent of the board to be unaffiliated with the management company.

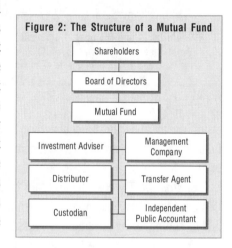

Figure 2: The Structure of a Mutual Fund

Management Company. The management company typically performs the administrative functions at the core of a fund complex—a family of related funds, all contracting with the management company for some or all of the services they need. In addition to administration, a management company may provide investment management, distribution, and transfer agent functions. The configurations of management companies—which functions they perform internally and which they turn over to third parties—vary endlessly. Management companies themselves can take any of the many organizational forms available to American businesses.

Throughout the course of our discussions we will see examples of management companies, the way they are organized, and the functions they perform. For most fund families, the management company performs at least the basic administrative services, including overseeing the performance of other companies providing service to the fund and ensuring that the fund complies with federal requirements.

Investment Adviser. The investment adviser does the actual picking of securities to buy and sell to maintain an investment portfolio that meets the fund's objectives. The fund contracts with one or more advisory firms to provide this service in return for an investment management fee, usually a percentage of the assets under management.

Distributor. A mutual fund usually distributes its shares through a principal underwriter or distributor, which may be part of the management company, or may be a separately contracted third party. The principal

---

MUTUAL FUND MANAGEMENT COMPANIES – A VARIETY OF FORMS

- Some management companies are private corporations, owned by a small group of individuals. The most striking example of this is *Fidelity Management and Research*, which is owned mostly by members of the Johnson family of Boston.

- Some are subsidiaries or components of larger companies, such as *Colonial Management Associates,* a subsidiary of The Liberty Financial Companies, and *Putnam Investments*, a subsidiary of Marsh MacLennan.

- A number of management companies are independent, publicly-traded corporations, such as *T. Rowe Price* (NASDAQ: TROW) and *Eaton Vance* (NYSE: EV).

- One management company is a singularity: *The Vanguard Group, Inc.* The Vanguard funds themselves own the management company, lock, stock, and barrel. This mutual ownership structure aims at keeping costs to the fund at a bare minimum by eliminating any need for the management company to make a profit.

---

distributor then sells the shares directly to investors, or to investors via other intermediaries, such as brokers or financial advisers. Distributors receive commission payments from shareholders, either as part of transactions, or in the form of asset-based fees.

Custodian. The custodian actually holds the inventory of securities that the fund owns. The Investment Company Act of 1940 requires that funds place their holdings in custody as a means of protecting the investors, and most funds today use qualified banks to do this.

Transfer Agent. The transfer agent keeps the shareholder records, executes the buy, sell, and other transactions the shareholders request, calculates and disburses dividends, and provides a range of reporting and other services. Many management companies provide complete transfer agent services themselves; others completely outsource these functions to third-party providers; and still others employ a mix—they perform some transfer agent functions internally and outsource some.

Independent Auditors. The various Acts governing the industry require that financial statements be certified by independent auditors. A mutual fund audit involves procedures unique to the nature of open-end funds, such as verification of the security prices that underlie the fund's net asset value.

There are a number of organizations that provide other, more specialized services for mutual funds—printing and mailing, literature fulfillment, escheatment, cash handling, legal services, and so on. All of these organizations—what they do, how much they cost, how they evolved, what issues and controversies attend them—form the subjects of the chapters that follow.

CHAPTER 2
A Brief History of Mutual Funds in the United States

*The prosperity of the investment company industry may be easily
contrasted with the unhealthy condition of other financial services.
It is not without irony, however, that much of this success is the
result of an early history that included an era of widespread abuses
and the reasonable legislation that was to follow.*

— William A. Campbell (1994)[1]

A review of the history of mutual funds in the United States explains much of why the industry is structured as it is today. This history lies largely within the twentieth century, and runs through several distinct periods:

- the beginning, which includes the years from the turn of the century through the early 1920s;
- the boom years of the twenties—the era of widespread abuses—culminating in the Crash of 1929;
- the Depression years, during which reasonable legislation, including the Investment Company Act of 1940, was developed and passed;
- the slow but steady growth period from 1940 through the late 1970s; and
- the explosive growth period of the 1980s and 1990s.

This chapter examines each of these periods, particularly focusing on the events and legislation that have shaped the industry into what it had become by 2000.

In the Beginning

As with most industries, the mutual fund industry's family tree and moment of birth defy precise specification. Most observers trace the earliest predecessors of today's U.S. investment companies to various types of pooled investment vehicles formed in the 1800s, mostly in Europe. The Foreign and Colonial Government Trust, founded in London in 1868, may have been the first to pool money from smaller investors specifically to achieve investing economies of scale.[2] The Foreign and Colonial most resembled what we would call a unit trust today, and it invested primarily in government debt (permitting no more than £100,000 in the securities of any one government). A number of its features hinted at those of modern funds, such as its 3 percent sales charge, and its 25 basis point management fee.

British law of the late 1800s provided a favorable environment for pooled investment funds, and by 1875 eighteen trusts similar to the Foreign and Colonial had been formed, with total paid-in capital of over £6.5 million. Some trusts, notably the Scottish American Investment Trust formed in 1873, aimed specifically at investing in the United States. (For reasons mostly associated with the happenstance of personalities, two Scottish cities, Edinburgh and Dundee, became trust centers along with London.) These English and Scottish investment trusts resembled closed-end funds, and generally emphasized income generation for their participants.

Most investment funds of this era were European, because before World War I the United States was a debtor nation, with little domestic investing beyond that done by wealthy individuals.[3] Nevertheless, a few vehicles similar to the British and Scottish investment trusts were established in the United States around the turn of the century. The New York Stock Trust (1889), the Boston Personal Property Trust (1893), and the Railway and Light Securities Company (1904) contend for the title of first American investment trust. The facts needed to establish which of these has best claim to the title, however, "have been lost in the haze of the years."[4] In any event, the proportion of American investing represented by these various investment funds was miniscule—a small fraction of a percentage point of the value of U.S. household financial assets.

The Roaring Twenties and The Crash

World War I changed the debtor/creditor relationship between the United States and Europe. The war destroyed much of Europe's industrial base, providing an opportunity for U.S. industry to expand dramatically into new markets. After a post-war correction from 1920 to 1921 during which commodity prices declined from their war-inflated price levels, the American economy entered a strong growth phase. In the twenties Americans had money to spend and money to invest. Just as important for the fund industry, 20 million Americans had learned something about investing during the war, when the United States government had sold them Liberty Bonds, some with denominations as small as fifty dollars.[5]

The bull market of the twenties drew many Americans into investing directly in common stocks. Many, however, were attracted to the advantages of professional management, diversification, and economies of scale that an investment trust offered (at least in theory). The result, as one study of the industry states, was that "...trusts came thick and fast. Investment trusts were formed by investment bankers, by brokers, by industrialists, by banks, and by trust companies."[6]

While the organizational details varied from trust to trust, the investment trusts of the twenties fell into two basic types. The first, and most popular, type resembled the British and Scottish investment trusts, or what we today call closed-end funds. The organizers established a company and sold shares (and sometimes bonds) to raise money to form the investment pool. Once the pool was formed, the company's shares traded on a secondary market, just like the stock of any other company. In the five years leading up to 1929, fifty-six of these closed-end investment trusts were formed. At the time of the Crash, the eighty-nine closed-end investment trusts open to the public held assets valued at about $3 billion.[7] By way of comparison, the total value of stocks on the New York Stock Exchange at the same time was $87 billion.

The other major type of investment company structure appeared for the first time in the twenties: the open-end fund, sometimes called the "Boston-type" investment trust.[8] A few open-end trusts had actually been formed before the twenties, but these had not been made available to the public. For example, the Alexander Fund, established in 1907, began as an investment for a small circle of friends—although it was eventually opened to the public. The Alexander Fund was open-end because its bylaws provided that participants could withdraw their units at any time and receive the net unit value as of that date.

SHAPERS OF THE INDUSTRY: EDWARD G. LEFFLER

Edward Leffler, a Midwesterner of Swedish descent, was working as a securities salesman in Boston in 1924 when he became the catalyst for one of the most important developments in the industry. During his six years of selling securities, Leffler had never been satisfied with the way small investors were treated, and believed that Americans needed a mechanism via which Wall Street could help them get ahead financially. After studying the investment trusts of the day, he came to believe that the ideal vehicle would be a pooled fund with four key attributes:

- it would be professionally managed;
- it would diversify its holdings to reduce risk;
- it would keep costs within tolerable limits; and
- it would redeem its customers' shares at any time.

This last feature, redemption on demand, became the hallmark of the American open-end fund.

Leffler promoted his ideas for three years, finally interesting the Boston brokerage firm of Learoyd, Foster, & Company enough that they hired him and formed the Massachusetts Investment Trust on March 21, 1924. Leffler soon left the fund because its management did not initially allow redemption on demand, although they changed their minds shortly after Leffler departed.

In 1925 Leffler, who had started his own firm, launched a new fund called Incorporated Investors. For the next few years Leffler traveled the country selling both Incorporated Investors and the concept of the open-end fund. Leffler sold mutual funds on and off for the rest of his career, ending up in the 1930s selling the shares of another pioneering fund, State Street Research Investment Trust. He testified at the SEC hearings in 1936, where he continued to demonstrate his concern for the welfare of the individual investor, concern which had done much to shape the industry itself.

The first open-end fund to be offered to the public at its inception was the Massachusetts Investors Trust, founded in 1924. Within a year it had attracted 200 investors, whose 32,000 shares were worth $392,000.[9] MIT today would be called a large cap equity fund—it started out by investing in nineteen blue chip industrial firms, fourteen railroads, ten utilities, and two insurance companies. It sold at an effective sales charge of 5 percent. Other open-end funds followed, but they lagged the closed-end funds in popularity—only nineteen open-end funds had been established by 1929, with assets totaling a mere $140 million.[10]

The crash of 1929 changed everything. Many of the closed-end funds had indulged in risky, even abusive, practices that magnified the effect of the stock market crash on their investors. A few trusts were nothing more than Ponzi schemes, outright frauds. Many of those that operated legally did things that today are illegal for good reason, including:

- failing to disclose the holdings in the portfolio (so that the securities, and therefore the fund, could be valued at whatever price the fund managers wanted);
- borrowing money to inflate the size of the fund and enhance the investor's return via leverage (but exposing the shareholders to the loss of their stake to senior debt-holders); and
- purchasing securities not via arms-length transactions, but rather as favors to help insiders unload undesirable stocks.

The speculation of the late twenties had driven up the prices of the closed-end funds even higher than it did the prices of the underlying stocks and bonds. By mid-1929, the average closed-end trust was selling at a premium of almost 50 percent of the value of its portfolio of holdings.[11]

This combination of speculation, unsound practices, and leverage made the stock market crash even harsher for closed-end trust holders than it did for holders of common stock. Between the end of 1929 and the end of 1930, the stock market, as reflected by the Dow Jones Industrial Average (DJIA), fell from 248 to 164, a 34 percent drop. At the same time, the closed-end funds declined from an average premium of 47 percent *above* net asset value to an average discount of 25 percent *below* net asset value—a drop of 72 percent (not counting the simultaneous drop in the net asset value itself). As a result, closed-end funds became poison to investors—not a single new one opened during the 1930s.

While the crash deflated the value of the open-end funds as well, it also demonstrated their strengths. The open-end funds' own policy of redemption upon demand at net asset value safeguarded them against many of the problems that devastated the closed-end funds. They couldn't hold any large proportion of their portfolios in unmarketable securities, because they might have to sell them at any time to meet investor redemptions. They couldn't borrow heavily for the same reason. And because their share price was always set at net asset value, speculation could not inflate the price of fund shares to extravagant levels beyond what it was doing to the prices of the underlying securities. As a result of these factors, open-end funds fared much better than closed-end funds. For example, MIT lost 83 percent of its value between September 1929 and July 1932—as opposed to an 89 percent decline in the DJIA—but it gained investors and new money during that same period.

The crash of 1929, traumatic as it was for so many people, served as a crucible for the fledgling mutual fund industry. It exposed the structural flaws that the roaring twenties mentality had fostered, and confirmed the utility of properly managed and controlled funds. In particular, it demonstrated the fundamental value of the open-end structure. As one historian has put it,

> *By providing shareholders with ready liquidity, redemption on demand made open-end funds more secure in an era of insecurity. There is no precedent for the open-end structure in Britain. It is a purely American invention, and one of the great innovations of the U.S. capital markets.*[12]

PRESENT AT THE BEGINNING: THREE FUNDS THAT PRE-DATE THE CRASH OF 1929

The recent explosive growth of the industry means that the vast majority of mutual funds today are veritable infants. Of the 7,000+ funds registered at the end of 1998, two-thirds were less than ten years old, and almost half were less than five years old. But the history of a handful of funds stretches back to the early days, before the Great Depression.

Massachusetts Investors Trust—Most industry historians credit this fund, established in 1924, as being the first open-end mutual fund offered to the public in America. It devoted its portfolio exclusively to common stocks, and, unlike many funds of the time, fully disclosed the portfolio holdings to the shareholders. For the first eight years of the fund's existence, the trustees ran it out of their back pockets, meeting whenever needed in each other's offices to decide what stocks to purchase or sell. In 1932, with fund assets at $20 million, the fund opened its own offices, hired its first full-time employee, and switched from simply holding well-known blue chip stocks to an explicit value style of investing.

MIT survived the Depression, was the first fund to register under the Securities Act in 1933, and by 1959, when *Time* magazine featured it in a cover story on mutual funds, was the biggest fund in the industry at $1.5 billion. Today, MIT is part of the MFS family of funds, and its prospectus describes its investment objective as "reasonable current income and long-term growth of capital and income." As of the end of 1998, the fund held assets valued at around $11 billion.

State Street Research Investment Trust—State Street Research Investment Trust contends with MIT for the title of the first open-end fund. Three Boston friends, Paul Cabot, Richard Saltonstall, and Richard Paine, had formed an informal investment account into which they pooled their own money for buying stocks. In July 1924, shortly after MIT was founded, they incorporated this fund and opened it to other investors. In 1932, with fund assets evaporating in the wake of the crash, State Street Research hired salesman Ed Leffler as one of the industry's first dedicated distributors. Leffler succeeded in tripling the funds assets in 1933 to $21 million, and grew them to $27 million in 1934.

Today the State Street Research Investment Trust is characterized as a growth and income fund, and its prospectus describes its investment objective as "provid[ing] long-term growth of capital and, secondarily, long-term growth of income." At the end of 1998, the fund held assets totaling about $2.5 billion.

The Pioneer Fund—In 1928 Philip Carret, then a journalist working for *Barron's*, started a small, family-funded investment trust that he named the Fidelity Investment Trust. He managed the fund for 23 years, pursuing an investment philosophy he described as "find[ing] things that made sense and gave a reasonable return." In 1951, Carret changed the name to The Pioneer Fund, another name he claims to have "dreamed up."[13] Carret remained president of Pioneer until 1963, when he relinquished the post to Jack Cogan.

Today's Pioneer Fund pursues "reasonable income and capital growth" primarily through a value approach to investing in U.S. equity securities. At the end of 1998, the fund held total assets valued just under $6 billion. According to the prospectus, the average annual total return for the fund (class A shares) since inception in 1928 has been 13.41%, as compared to the S&P 500 index return of 10.91% over the same period. A hypothetical investor who put $10,000 into the original Fidelity Investors Trust in 1928, reinvested all dividends and capital gains, and held the shares until 1998 would have seen the $10,000 grow to $67 million!

The Thirties: Depression and Regulation

In 1932 the U.S. electorate voted in Franklin Roosevelt and his promise to replace the Republican *laissez faire* approach to government oversight of business with a more active regulatory approach. Not surprisingly, seven years of regulation followed the decade of excess, as the federal government attempted to enact safeguards against the practices that had led to so many of the problems in the financial services industry. Along with much legislation addressing other industries, Congress passed four major acts that affected mutual fund industry practices.

The Securities Act of 1933

The Securities Act of 1933 addressed a much broader arena than just mutual funds—it set rules for any public offering of securities. It required that anyone who wanted to offer securities to the public must register those securities, and provide any prospective investors with a prospectus that adequately disclosed the nature of the offering. It also explicitly prohibited deceit, misrepresentation, and other fraudulent practices in the sale of securities, and regulated the types of advertisements that could be made for securities offerings.

Since the shares of open-end mutual funds are publicly traded common stock, they fall under the provisions of the Securities Act of 1933, and its subsequent rules. Consequently each fund must prepare a comprehensive registration statement for approval by the appropriate regulatory body, and each must be described by a prospectus that must be delivered to the investor before he or she can purchase fund shares. The regulations pursuant to the Act also require that a fund be prepared to provide additional details in a Statement of Additional Information whenever an investor requests.

The Securities Exchange Act of 1934

The Securities Exchange Act also broadly addressed the exchange of publicly-traded securities. It created the Securities and Exchange Commission (SEC) to enforce federal securities laws. It further required securities exchanges and broker dealers to register with the SEC, and established a number of requirements for record keeping, reporting, financial responsibility, staff qualifications, and business practices that broker dealers must meet to sell securities.

For mutual funds, the 1934 Act established rules that the distributors and transfer agents must follow. Transfer agents must register with the appropriate regulatory agency—the Federal Reserve Board for banks, the SEC for almost anyone else. Failure to follow the rules of conduct would result in an agent's de-registration.

In addition to the 1933 and 1934 Acts, which addressed the securities industry broadly, Congress passed two acts in 1940 that specifically addressed the fund industry.

The Investment Company Act of 1940

After dealing with regulations for a variety of sectors of U.S. business, Congress finally focused its attention squarely upon the investment companies. In the Public Utility Holding Company Act of 1936, Congress directed the SEC to make a study of investment companies and report its findings. The SEC did so, and began public hearings on investment company regulation in 1938. From its research and public hearings, the SEC originated a first draft of legislation that was introduced by Senator Wagner of New York in March 1940. This version was so harsh in the measures it adopted to prevent abuses that one industry figure stated, "The cure they suggested was a bill that would burn down the barn to kill the rats."[14]

Since it was clear that Congress would not pass the SEC's initial version of the bill over the objections of the industry, SEC and industry representatives worked over the next few months to hammer out a bill that provided enough investor protection to satisfy the regulators, but still gave the investment companies the freedom they needed to operate. With Congressional attention increasingly diverted toward impending war, this compromise passed easily, and the Investment Company Act of 1940 became effective on November 1.

The 1940 Act specifically took aim at eight troublesome practices that had "adversely affected" the "national public interest and the interest of investors."[15] These eight types of abuses, and the salient points of the approach the Act took to dealing with each, are shown in Table 1. Subsequent chapters discuss the operational implications of the Act's provisions for the various components of the industry. Fundamentally, however, the 1940 Act formed the foundation upon which all regulation specific to the mutual fund industry regulation has been based.

The Investment Advisors Act of 1940

Finally, the Investment Advisors Act of 1940 required that any organization (other than a bank, which would be regulated under banking statutes) that provides investment advisory service to mutual funds must register with the SEC. The Act also imposed restrictions on the contracts between investment advisers and funds. Advisory contracts could not extend beyond two years, must provide the fund the ability to terminate without penalty upon 60 days' notice, and must receive the approval of a majority of the fund's outside directors to be renewed.

The industry won an important tax concession when the Revenue Act of 1936 established that mutual investment companies—arguably the first official use of the term "mutual" to apply to the industry—could avoid paying federal tax on their income if they met a number of requirements, including distributing all taxable income to their shareholders, and redeeming their shares upon demand. Because this latter requirement limited the pass-through tax status to open-end funds, it gave them a clear advantage over the closed-end funds, and accelerated their growing popularity. In 1929, closed-end funds had accounted for over 95 percent of the industry's total assets of about $3 billion. By 1940, the closed-end funds' share of a much smaller pie ($1.1 billion) had declined to 57 percent. In 1943, open-end funds' share of the market exceeded that of closed-end funds for the first time, and their relative share has increased ever since.

During this period, the mutual fund industry took on more of its modern shape. A number of new open-end funds were established, and all of those established during or after 1932 had the attributes we now associate with open-end mutual funds: they eschewed leverage, they stood ready at any time to redeem at a price based on NAV, and they issued only common stock with full voting rights. In fact, some observers contend that the 1940 Act merely set into law the practices that the open-end fund industry had already adopted.[16]

Table 1

SUMMARY OF PROVISIONS OF THE INVESTMENT COMPANY ACT OF 1940

Issue or Abuse Targeted by the Act	1940 Act Provisions
Inadequate disclosure to shareholders of the nature of the investment company, its objectives, activities, holdings, or other relevant information	• An investment company must register with the SEC, providing an extensive statement of its policies and structure (§10). It must file annual reports with the SEC (§30), and maintain specified accounts and records (§31).
Investment company management pursuit of their own interests at the expense of shareholder interests	• An investment company's board of directors must include no more than 60 percent of its membership from individuals affiliated with the management company (§10). • The fund must have a written contract, approved by the shareholders, with its investment adviser and principal underwriter (§15). • Persons affiliated with the adviser or other service providers to the fund may not conduct financial transactions with the fund (§17).
Issue of securities that is inequitable for current shareholders or fails to protect their interests	• All shares of stock issued by an investment company must have equal voting rights (§18). Shareholders are entitled to vote on specified provisions, such as changes in investment policy (§13), and appointment of independent auditors (§32).
Mismanagement of the investment company or concentration of control via pyramiding or other abuses	• Fund investment in other funds is restricted (§12). [This has since been relaxed.] • Securities must be held in custody by a specified organization, or in accordance with specified procedures (§17). • Officers and employees who have access to cash or securities must be bonded (§17). • Dividends may be paid only from undistributed income, unless a written statement is provided disclosing the source (§19).
Unsound or misleading accounting practices that are not subject to independent review	• The fund's annual reports are required to be audited by independent auditors (§30, supplementing provisions of the 1934 Act).
Restructuring without approval of the shareholders	• Shareholders must vote on any major change in the fund's structure or operations (§several).
Excessive borrowing and issue of senior securities, making the junior securities speculative	• An open-end company is prohibited from issuing senior securities (§18), and investment practices that are equivalent to borrowing are severely limited (§12).
Operation without adequate assets or reserves	• An investment company must have a net worth of $100,000 (§14).

The Slow-but-Steady Growth Years: 1940 to 1980

For the next four decades, the U.S. fund industry grew steadily but slowly, as illustrated in Figure 1. Assets under management grew at a rate of about 13 percent per year, fueled both by the appreciation in value of the securities held and by incremental purchases by investors, so-called "new money." The formation of new funds also proceeded at a modest rate. From sixty-eight funds in 1940, the number increased to 103 in 1951, to 204 in 1967, and was still under 500 in 1980.

Figure 1 also shows the size of fund assets compared to the total deposits in FDIC-insured commercial banks in the United States. The bank deposit total puts the mutual fund figures in perspective relative to the size of the economy. Not only did the funds grow slowly in absolute terms between 1940 and 1970, but they also made little headway relative to what Americans put in banks. At around $55 billion in total assets in 1978 (in a U.S. economy whose gross domestic product that year was $2.3 trillion), mutual funds remained distinctly a side show.

Nevertheless, growth had proceeded at a sufficient pace by 1960 to induce Congress to call for new studies of the industry. Three reports prepared or commissioned by the SEC in 1962, 1963, and 1966 raised concern regarding potential conflicts of interest between fund shareholders and fund management companies. Industry critics claimed that a fund had no recourse when its adviser charged excessive fees, since the adviser effectively

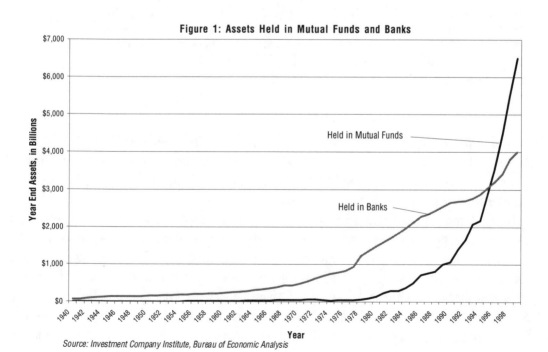

Figure 1: Assets Held in Mutual Funds and Banks

Source: Investment Company Institute, Bureau of Economic Analysis

SHAPERS OF THE INDUSTRY: JACK DREYFUS

Jack Dreyfus is certainly one of the most colorful individuals to grace the halls of mutual fund history. His autobiography[17] starts with a scenario in which an angel attempts to convince Jack's skeptical mother (now in heaven) that her inept, lazy son had in fact become a success along several dimensions. The major part of the autobiography deals not with Wall Street, but with Dreyfus' second life during which he led a crusade to convince the medical world of the value of the psychiatric drug Dilantin. But between his unpromising boyhood and his career as medical crusader, Dreyfus did make his fortune on Wall Street and in the process introduced advertising to the mutual fund industry.

In 1952, Dreyfus & Company, a Wall Street brokerage firm, took over management of the Nesbett Fund. Its founder, John Nesbett, had only been able to attract $500,000 in assets after three years of managing it, so the fund did not generate enough revenue for him to make a living. They changed its name to the Dreyfus Fund, and slowly attracted new money. In 1957, Dreyfus decided to stimulate sales and commissioned a television ad for the fund. The ad featured a lion that strolled out of the subway, past a newsstand on Wall Street, and into the Dreyfus office, where it transformed into the Dreyfus Company logo. As Dreyfus put it,

> The advertisement was a great success. Nobody got tired of the lion, or the music. That was fortunate because we had to run the same ad thousands of times—shortly after it was approved the SEC put restrictions on TV commercials.

Dreyfus also wrote the fund prospectus himself, drawing a comment from *Barron's* about its pleasantly surprising lack of legalese. In 1958, he published the entire prospectus as a supplement in the Sunday *New York Times*. He then proceeded to use reprints of the supplement as the official prospectus because he could buy them for three cents apiece, which was cheaper than the normal cost of printing the prospectus.

The mutual fund world lost one of its most imaginative figures in 1970, when he retired from management to devote himself full time to promoting Dilantin. Dreyfus believed that Dilantin was an underappreciated wonder drug, and he spent the next thirty years of his life sponsoring research and working towards getting the medical establishment to accept it.

controlled all the fund's options. Of the reports that examined this issue, the one prepared by the Wharton School of Finance and Commerce in 1962 contended that the allegation had merit. These reports prompted Congress to draft the 1970 Amendments to the Investment Company Act of 1940, to tune mutual fund regulation, specifically to increase shareholder protection against excessive management fees.

The 1970 Amendments addressed the imbalance of power between shareholders and management company by requiring that the independent directors on the fund board be disinterested, i.e., not connected in anyway with the interests of the management company or investment adviser. The amendments also explicitly stated that the investment adviser to a fund has a fiduciary duty in regard to fees and other compensation received from the fund. The seventy Amendments did have the effect of encouraging litigation over fees—in the 1960s, fourteen suits were brought against fund advisers claiming excessive fees; during the period from 1975 through 1985, fifty-four suits were filed. However, very few cases went to trial, and when they did, the court almost always ruled in favor of the adviser, holding that the plaintiff had not met the burden of proof in establishing that fees had been excessive.

In 1979, the SEC adopted Rule 12b-1, a rule that has had a significant impact on industry operations. Rule 12b-1 simply stated that it was legal for a fund to use some amount of shareholder assets to finance distribution, so long as a number of specified conditions were met. Heretofore, all distribution expenses (advertising, sales commissions, and any other marketing expense) were paid by the management company out of the fee the fund paid for administrative and advisory services. The various avenues of distribution that Rule 12b-1 helped open up are discussed in more detail in Chapter 8.

SHAPERS OF THE INDUSTRY: NED JOHNSON

The Johnson family's pedigree in the mutual fund industry dates from the beginning. Edward C. Johnson, II (Ed) first got into the industry during the 1920s, as general counsel for Incorporated Investors (one of the first open-end fund companies), and later became a senior executive of the management company. In 1943, Johnson took control of a small, troubled fund known as the Fidelity Fund. In 1946, he incorporated his own firm to manage it: Fidelity Management and Research (FMR). For the next thirty-plus years Ed Johnson built FMR until by 1970 the Fidelity funds it managed accounted for almost 10 percent of industry assets.

In 1957, Ed's son Edward C. Johnson, III (Ned) joined FMR as an assistant vice president and stock analyst. In 1961, Ned Johnson began managing the Fidelity Trend Fund, and outperformed all his growth fund competition for the next four years. His role in FMR expanded steadily and in 1972, with fourteen funds in the Fidelity complex, he took over control of the management company from his father. During Ned Johnson's tenure the Fidelity funds grew to be the colossus of the industry. By the late 1990s, every fourth or fifth dollar flowing into U.S. stock funds was flowing into a Fidelity fund. At the end of 1999, the Fidelity open-end funds totaled $800 billion in assets, about 13 percent of U.S. open-end fund assets.

Ned Johnson, more than any other single individual, can be credited with the transformation of the U.S. mutual fund from a service to a product. During the 1970s and 1980s, the management team he assembled at Fidelity either pioneered or popularized a long list of new features and services, such as check writing against money market funds, superior telephone customer service, and enhanced reporting. The Fidelity family grew to include a fund for every investing fancy: sector funds, high-yield bond funds, tax-exempt funds, international funds, you name it. Fidelity's advertising emphasized the Fidelity brand, much as consumer product firms used branding to sell shoes or soap. While many fund complexes today do most or all of these same things, it was Fidelity under Ned Johnson that led them to it. As one Fidelity executive put it, "If Ned thought it would sell, he would do it."[18] In recognition of the revolutionizing effect Johnson had on the industry, in 1999 the *Los Angeles Times* made Johnson the only mutual fund executive on its list of individuals who have had the most effect on business in the twentieth century.[19] Johnson ranked 45 on the list, between Rachel Carson (44) and Milton Friedman (46).

Fidelity may well remain under Johnson family management for a third generation. In 1988, Abigail Pierrepont Johnson joined FMR as a stock analyst. She became a member of the FMR board in 1994, and in 1996 took over management of the Fidelity Trend Fund, the fund her father had first managed in the 1960s. She is a major owner of the voting stock, and widely viewed as the heir apparent.

The Modern Industry Takes Off: Explosive Growth in the 80s and 90s

As shown in Figure 1, the dramatic acceleration of growth in the mutual fund industry started in the early 1980s, and continued through 2000. The late 1970s and early 1980s also saw a change in the nature of funds, as shown in Figure 2. Until the mid-1970s, mutual funds were primarily seen as a way for the modest investor to get the aid of professional management for participating in the stock market. Some funds were balanced between stocks and bonds, and there were a few bond funds, but by and large mutual fund meant stock fund. Few industry statistics gathered before the 1970s even differentiate between types of funds.

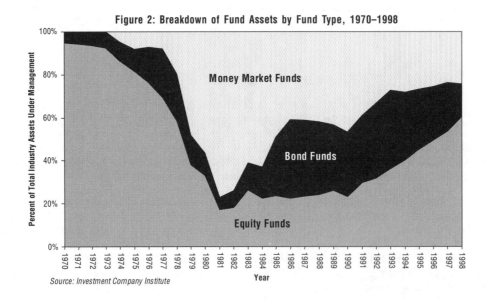

Figure 2: Breakdown of Fund Assets by Fund Type, 1970–1998

Source: Investment Company Institute

In the late 1970s, a number of economic factors drove interest rates up to unprecedented levels. Between late 1978 and late 1982, the Fed Funds rate was usually in double digits, and once even topped 20 percent. At the same time, banking regulations (specifically Regulation Q of the Federal Reserve Act) capped the interest that a bank could pay on deposit accounts, the traditional savings vehicle for individuals of modest means. This spread opened a gap for money market mutual funds, and innovators in the industry were quick to drive through it.

Money market mutual funds gave small investors access to high yielding short-term instruments that were generally beyond their means to buy individually. In 1970, the Federal Reserve removed interest rate restrictions on certificates of deposit greater than $100,000, but few Americans could afford to invest that amount. Money-market mutual funds, which invest in high-quality, short-term instruments, could trade in such large denominations. As a result, investors could move their money from bank deposits that earned less

SHAPERS OF THE INDUSTRY: JOHN BOGLE

John Bogle has led a life-long crusade as an advocate for the investor by fighting against excessive cost in asset management that erodes investors' returns. The second largest fund complex in the industry, The Vanguard Group, stands as a monument to his determination.

Bogle came to the industry early in his career. His senior thesis at Princeton covered the mutual fund industry and attracted the attention of Wellington Management executives, who interviewed and hired him in 1951. Over the next twenty years he worked his way to the top at Wellington, becoming CEO in 1967. But he never came to terms with a group of partners that Wellington had acquired in 1967, and in early 1974 they maneuvered the Wellington board into calling for his resignation.

Bogle refused to go quietly, and instead struck a compromise that gave him a new organization to handle fund administration, while Wellington retained the investment advisory role. He named this administrative organization The Vanguard Group, Inc., after Nelson's flagship at the Battle of the Nile. (This nautical theme continues to pervade Vanguard today, as any visitor to its Malvern, Pennsylvania campus will readily see.) With Vanguard, Bogle did something that he had suggested at Wellington but could never get approved—he organized it as a mutual company, owned by the funds themselves. He believed that this type of organization would minimize the cost to the funds and, therefore, to the investors, because it removed the need to provide a profit.

In 1979, Bogle got approval from the SEC to use fund assets to pay for distribution. Heretofore distribution costs had always been paid by the advisory firm, out of their fee. Bogle believed that this practice tied the fund to the adviser, since breaking the advisory contract would leave the fund with no means of distribution. If the funds could pay for their own distribution, they could lower their costs by shopping around for the best deals in advisory services. Ironically, shortly after Bogle won his three year battle for SEC approval of his proposal, the SEC issued Rule 12b-1, which allowed anyone to use fund assets to pay for distribution.

Bogle has also been the mutual fund industry's most vocal and persistent advocate of indexing, or passive management. In two books and countless articles, speeches, and appearances, he has argued that most active management costs the investor more money over the long term than it returns in increased performance. His ideas, which were widely rejected in the seventies, have been vindicated in recent years by the phenomenal success of the Vanguard indexed funds.

Throughout his career, Bogle has battled heart problems that have required medication, pacemakers, and in 1996, a heart transplant. Although retired from active management of The Vanguard Group, Bogle has returned after his transplant to carry on as a passionate spokesman for the ideas that he has advocated for the past fifty years.

than 5 percent to money-market mutual funds, which at that time provided double digit yields. In return, they gave up the protection of FDIC deposit insurance on their assets. James Benham, a money market fund pioneer, explained the lure:

> *In 1970, when I conceived the idea for Capital Preservation Fund, the open market rate was 8 percent on T-bills, and you could only earn 5 percent on a passbook savings account. There was a differential of three full percentage points available for those who could capture it. Well, the little people couldn't capture it. The average balance in a passbook account in those days was something like $2,700 and they raised the minimum on T-bills in January 1970 from $1,000 to $10,000. With a fund, you could let people in for $1,000.*[20]

In the 1970s investors began to take this option in droves: between 1974 and 1982 the total assets held by money market funds grew by two orders of magnitude, from less than $2 billion to over $200 billion. In 1982, three-fourths of the mutual fund industry's assets were in money market funds. That year Congress removed the banks' regulatory handicap with an act that enabled banks to offer deposit accounts—negotiable order of withdrawal (NOW) accounts—that paid interest rates similar to those of money market funds. This slowed the large scale flow of money from banks to mutual funds, but little money flowed back to the banks. Investors had tried mutual funds and liked what they found.

The brief money market boom had an important effect in bringing investors back into the world of mutual funds. The prolonged bear market of the 1970s had caused industry assets to shrink and the number of shareholder accounts to decline, from almost 11 million in 1971 to 8.5 million in 1978. Starting in 1979, the rapid growth of the money market funds boosted the shareholder account total to over 21 million in 1983. Then, when growth in money market funds slowed, the bull market of the 1980s made long-term funds attractive again, and growth resumed across the board.

The figures in Table 2 illustrate the growth of the industry since 1980. Total assets, assets in each fund category, the number of funds, and the number of shareholder accounts have all grown at compound annual

Table 2: U.S. Mutual Fund Statistics (all figures as of year end)

Year	Assets Under Management ($ billions)				No. of Funds	No. of Shareholder Accounts
	Total	Equity Funds*	Bond Funds	Money Market Funds		
1981	241	41	14	186	665	17,500,000
1982	297	54	23	220	857	21,400,000
1983	293	77	37	179	1,026	24,600,000
1984	371	91	46	234	1,241	28,700,000
1985	495	129	123	244	1,527	34,800,000
1986	716	180	243	292	1,835	46,000,000
1987	769	205	248	316	2,312	54,400,000
1988	809	216	256	338	2,708	54,700,000
1989	981	281	272	428	2,900	58,100,000
1990	1,066	283	284	498	3,086	62,000,000
1991	1,393	465	385	543	3,408	68,300,000
1992	1,643	601	495	546	3,830	79,900,000
1993	2,070	891	614	565	4,537	93,200,000
1994	2,155	1,022	522	611	5,329	114,400,000
1995	2,812	1,472	587	753	5,729	131,300,000
1996	3,526	1,979	645	902	6,254	150,200,000
1997	4,468	2,685	724	1,059	6,684	170,500,000
1998	5,525	3,343	831	1,352	7,314	193,900,000
1999	6,846	4,425	808	1,613	7,791	227,700,000
CAGR	20%	30%	25%	13%	15%	15%

Source: Investment Company Institute
*For the years 1984 on, this figure includes funds categorized as either equity or hybrid funds,
  to be consistent with the categorization scheme used earlier

rates (CAGR) in double digits. Some of the growth in assets results from appreciation in securities prices, but much of it reflects new money flowing into the funds. This raises the question: where did all this money come from? Economists studying the industry have concluded that it mostly came from investors reallocating their portfolio of investments from other vehicles to mutual funds.[21] Several factors played a role in inducing this shift.

Retirement Savings

Much of the flow of money into mutual funds in this period resulted from Americans' increasing tendency to use funds for retirement savings. In the late 80s, the vanguard of the baby boom generation turned 40, and for many boomers the question of retirement financing took on immediate and personal interest. Two acts of the federal government served both to spur retirement savings and to help channel much of it into mutual funds.

The Employee Retirement Income Security Act (ERISA) of 1974 attempted to reform pension practices in the United States by mandating that employees be vested in their pensions within ten years, and that the employees be able to retain their pension rights as they move from one employer to another. These requirements, coupled with a mobile U.S. workforce whose longevity was increasing, made many employers choose to provide defined contribution rather than the traditional defined benefit plans. Chapter 10 covers this in more detail. Over the course of the late 1980s and into the 1990s, these defined contribution pension plans turned more and more to mutual funds to provide the investment vehicles for their participants' contributions. In 1998, employer-sponsored plans accounted for 10 percent of the net cash flow into U.S. mutual funds.

The Tax Reform Act of 1981 allowed each American with earned income to set up an individual retirement account (IRA), and, in many cases, fund an annual contribution to it with pre-tax money. IRAs have also provided a significant flow of new money into mutual funds. This flow was strong in the years leading up to 1986, weaker after 1986 when the Tax Reform Act restricted the tax benefits of IRAs, and has strengthened again in the wake of 1997 legislation liberalizing IRA provisions. As of the end of 1999, 38 percent of mutual fund assets represented retirement savings, about evenly split between IRAs and employer-sponsored defined contribution plans.

New Distribution Channels

Until the late 1970s, mutual funds came in one of two types: load funds, sold by broker dealers who received a commission on the transaction, and no-load funds, sold directly to the public by the management company. In 1979, Rule 12b-1 allowed funds for the first time to pay for distribution directly out of fund assets. This opened the door for new distribution channels, and the growing size and profitability of the industry encouraged innovators to develop them. In the 1980s and 1990s, several emerged as important supplements to the traditional channels. These new distribution channels, discussed in detail in later chapters, include mutual fund supermarkets, wrap programs, financial advisers, banks, and, most recently, the Internet.

Product Development

In its 1997 report on money management in America, Bernstein Research pointed out that mutual funds had evolved over the previous fifteen years from being a service to being a product.[22] Until the late 1970s, an investor buying mutual fund shares bought professional management to help produce income and/or capital appreciation—period. During the 1980s and 1990s, competition drove fund management companies to turn their offerings into products along several dimensions. First, they tremendously diversified the types of funds available to more closely fit the objectives of the investor. From the five categories of funds tracked by the ICI in 1970, funds grew to thirty-three categories tracked in 2000, as discussed in Chapter 4. Second, they developed a wide range of features and services for fund shareholders: check writing, electronic funds transfers, automatic investment or redemption plans, automatic investment reallocation plans, and tax cost reporting, to name a few. Finally, the management companies turned increasingly to the same marketing techniques, such as advertising and branding, that corporate America used to sell cars, soap, and other consumer products.

SHAPERS OF THE INDUSTRY: PETER LYNCH

From Michael Jordan pushing Nike to Geraldine Ferraro pushing Coke, from John Housman pitching E.F. Hutton to Jimmy Dean pitching sausage, American consumer marketing has always loved the celebrity endorsement. For the mutual fund industry, the celebrity delivering the endorsements has been Peter Lynch.

Lynch surely has earned his celebrity status. Between 1977 and 1990, he managed the Fidelity Magellan Fund to become the industry's largest. When he took it over, it held less than $26 million; when he relinquished its management in 1990, it held assets valued at $14 billion. Throughout the period, Lynch's annual performance regularly beat the fund's benchmark, the S&P 500 Index, often by over 20 percent.

This performance not only attracted investors, it also attracted media attention. He appeared on television and on the covers of magazines. He wrote two best-selling books. Financial writers quoted him widely. His obvious love for what he did and his folksy good humor made him a natural. His approach to stock picking, on which he expounded regularly, was commonsensical and appealing: keep it simple; focus on what *you* understand to be good.

Lynch retired in 1990 from his all-consuming job as manager of the Magellan Fund to spend more time with his family. He was too valuable an asset for Fidelity to allow to lay fallow, however. A few years later they induced him to return to a part-time position in the firm. Since his return, he has appeared in Fidelity advertising in all media, and one can hardly open a financial magazine, walk through an airport, or even drive down the highway without seeing Peter Lynch, the mutual-fund industry's leading celebrity, smiling from one or more advertisements.

The result has been to entrench mutual funds firmly in the American financial services landscape—from 1980, when 1 in 20 Americans owned mutual fund shares, the industry grew until over 1 in 3 Americans was a mutual fund shareholder in 2000. Where will we go next? A number of interesting questions remain open. When will demographics turn against the industry? How competitive is it? How concentrated? Is it becoming more or less competitive and concentrated? Where are the new opportunities? What are the challenges? Chapter 16 picks up the mutual fund industry story with a discussion of these and other questions that will influence where the industry goes from here.

SHAPERS OF THE INDUSTRY: CHARLES SCHWAB

Charles Schwab, "Chuck" to his friends and employees, has never shied away from eccentric ideas. As a student, he proposed such innovations as drive-through animal parks and rock and classical music rodeos. As a businessman, he pioneered the discount brokerage business when no one thought it would work. And as a successful CEO, he sponsored an innovation that has enormously impacted mutual fund distribution: the fund supermarket.

Schwab founded his firm in 1971 as a traditional brokerage, but soon saw that the SEC's decision to end fixed stock commissions created an opportunity to exploit a discontinuity in the economic landscape. The old commission structure had left an entire market segment unserved—that of independent-minded investors who needed transaction execution but not advice. Schwab quickly transformed his firm into a discount brokerage that served this group of investors. By 1993, the success of this approach had made Schwab a member of Forbes' list of the 400 richest people in America.

In the early 1990s, as America was falling in love with mutual funds, Schwab and his team of executives saw another opportunity to exploit a niche that no one yet occupied: super-distributor of no-load funds. He sent his executives around to the no-load fund complexes with a proposition: for a small fee tagged to the size of investor assets the program brought to the fund, Schwab would sell the complex's funds and handle shareholder record keeping. This gave investors one point at which they could buy, sell, and exchange funds from multiple families, with no transaction fees to pay. It allowed the funds to enter a new distribution channel with no large fixed outlay of money. The smaller fund groups, for which the expense of retail distribution was daunting, found this particularly attractive. So in 1992, Schwab launched OneSource with 86 funds from eight fund complexes.

OneSource was immediately successful, as many investors found that this approach was exactly how they wanted to deal with mutual funds. Shareholder dollars attracted new funds to the program, which attracted more shareholders, in an ever increasing spiral. By the end of 1998, Schwab's mutual fund market included over 1,000 funds, and had collected $80 billion in assets. It had also attracted the ultimate, if unwanted, compliment: a dozen or more competitors had imitated it, and started their own mutual fund supermarkets.

Charles Schwab learned while working with his 8-year-old son's school psychologist that he, like his son, was dyslexic. Suddenly, he said, all his struggles with reading and spelling made sense. But this cloud had an exceptional silver lining. Schwab attributes much of his success as an innovator to his particular and unconventional learning style and the vision it allows him.

CHAPTER 3

Overview of Industry Structure

The typical open-end mutual fund has very limited internal resources, contracting out almost all of its activities. Thus an open-end mutual fund can be seen as a set of contracts between the trustees and other organizations which provide specialized services.

— Peter Fortune (1997)[1]

The mutual fund industry includes not only 80+ million individual and institutional investors who supply capital to be invested and almost 8,000 funds that invest it, but also thousands of other organizations.[2] Most of these organizations provide required services—investment advice, distribution, customer service, custody, auditing, consulting, legal representation, securities prices, and other information—to either investors or funds. Some are subcontractors, providing services to other service organizations. Some regulate the activities of the funds and their service providers. Finally, the funds and service providers have organized themselves into industry associations that educate and represent their membership. Collectively, these organizations make up the mutual fund industry.

Most of the organizations that comprise the industry are covered in detail in the chapters that describe the services they provide. This chapter sets the context for those more detailed discussions. It covers the funds themselves, and briefly identifies what the other entities in the industry do, how they relate to the fund, and, when available, the magnitude of their participation in industry revenues.

Figure 1 shows these major groups of players and the flows of money that connect them. Investors supply the money that drives the entire industry when they purchase mutual fund shares. The funds use most of this money to purchase securities in accordance with the stated investment objectives. As the funds purchase and sell securities, they exchange money in the capital markets with counterparties, i.e., the organizations from which they purchase securities, and to which they sell them. The issuers of these securities send money to the funds when they pay dividends or interest and when certain types of securities mature. Investors remove money from the funds when they redeem shares, and when they elect to take dividend and capital gains distributions from the funds in the form of cash.

The growth of the industry—measured by the value of assets under management—is fueled by three sources. First, to the extent that investors purchase more than they redeem, they provide a net inflow of funds. In fact, investors did exactly that for fourteen of the last fifteen years of the twentieth century (1988 saw a net negative flow of $23 billion).[3] Second, many of the securities the funds hold appreciate in value, providing

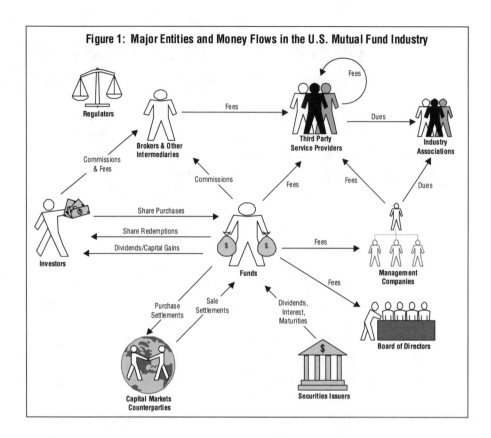

Figure 1: Major Entities and Money Flows in the U.S. Mutual Fund Industry

unrealized capital gains, or market appreciation. As Table 1 shows, during 1998, the increase in the value of mutual fund assets—from $4.5 trillion to slightly over $5.5 trillion—stemmed approximately one-half from net inflow of new money and one-half from market appreciation. Finally, the fixed-income securities held by the funds pay interest income, some of the equity securities pay dividends, and the funds realize net capital gains when they sell securities. The funds distribute almost all of these to the shareholders, to avoid having them taxed at the fund level. While shareholders typically take about one-third of these dividends and gains distributions in cash, they return two-thirds to the funds in the form of reinvestments.

Most of this increase in the value accrues to the fund shareholders. Some of it, however, is used to generate revenue for those organizations that provide service for the funds.

- *Management companies* receive fees for the fund administration, investment advisory, distribution, customer servicing, and other services that they provide.
- *Directors* are compensated by the funds for their services in looking after the interests of the shareholders.
- *Third-party service providers* of many sorts receive fees, either directly from the funds or indirectly through the management companies.

Table 1: Change in Asset Value of U.S. Mutual Funds in 1998 (figures in billions)

Value of Assets as of January 1, 1998		$4,470
Net of Purchases and Sales by Investors in 1998		
Stock Funds	$159	
Hybrid Funds	$116	
Fixed-Income Funds	$74	
Money Market Funds	$235	
Total Net Purchases		$574
Fee and Expense Outflows (estimated)		
Service Fees	($32)	
Distribution Charges	($20)	
Portfolio Transactions	($14)	
Total Fee and Expense Outflows		($66)
Dividends, Interest, and Net Capital Gains		
Earned on Investments	$697	
Paid in Cash to Investors	($145)	
Net Appreciation		$552
Value of Assets as of December 31, 1998		$5,530

Source: Investment Company Institute, calculations explained within the chapter.

- *Brokers and other financial intermediaries* receive fees in several different ways. They may be compensated for the activities they carry out in distributing the funds to investors, either directly by the investors, or indirectly by the funds. The funds also employ intermediaries to execute securities trades, for which they are compensated with commissions or spreads.
- *Industry associations* receive membership fees, or dues, from the funds or management companies.

Many of these service providers pay fees in turn to organizations that provide service to them, for example, when fund accounting organizations pay information vendors for transmissions of securities prices.

One group in Figure 1 is not connected to the funds by money flows, at least not directly. The *regulators*, primarily the Securities and Exchange Commission (SEC) and the National Association of Securities Dealers (NASD), are funded in other ways. The SEC's funding derives from the general appropriations of the federal government. Member firms fund NASD, but the funding is unrelated to any particular segment of the securities industry in which firms participate.

The Funds

At the heart of the industry are the 8,000 or so open-end funds, or investment companies, each of which is a separate legal entity. An investment company can organize under the laws of any state, and may be a corporation, business trust, or limited partnership. Most open-end funds have been set up as either Massachusetts business trusts or Maryland corporations. These particular choices stem from convenience. In the past the requirements for obtaining shareholder approvals or holding shareholder meetings imposed by these two forms have not added significantly to the governance requirements already imposed by the 1940 Act.[4]

In recent years, other states have changed their laws to offer similar flexibility to accommodate mutual funds. Delaware, for example, has adopted a business trust statute more attractive along some dimensions than that of Massachusetts. In 1998, The Vanguard Group called a shareholder meeting to get approval to convert all the funds from their current organization as Maryland corporations to that of Delaware trusts. Vanguard calculated that this would result in savings of $18 million per year, primarily in state taxes.[5]

The 1940 Act imposes a number of very specific requirements for any open-end investment company offered to the general public in the United States.

- It must register pursuant to the Securities Act of 1933, and provide notice filings for those states in which it intends to sell shares.
- Its name must be consistent with its investment objective.
- It must declare its investment objective and how it will pursue that objective, and then operate accordingly.
- It must prepare a prospectus and statement of additional information, as discussed in Chapter 4, to inform potential investors of every relevant aspect of its operation.
- It can issue only one class of stock, every share of which must have equal voting rights, and each of which must be redeemable upon demand.
- It must establish a board of directors or trustees, approved by vote of the shareholders. A specified percentage of the directors or trustees must be independent, i.e., unaffiliated with the fund's management company.
- It may not issue debt securities, nor borrow money beyond 5 percent of total assets.
- It must have a net worth of at least $100,000 in assets before offering shares to the public.
- It must execute agreements, subject to approval of the directors (and, in some cases, the shareholders) for investment advisory, distribution, custody, audit, shareholder service, and other services.
- It must calculate its net asset per share value daily.
- It must report to regulators and shareholders in accordance with regulations, and submit these reports to the SEC for review.

All this creates cost thresholds both for setting up a fund and for operating it economically. Experience indicates that fund setup can easily cost over $150,000, and that a fund must quickly reach a level of $50 to $100 million under management to cover ongoing expenses at acceptable fee rates.[6]

WHAT'S IN A NAME?

Perhaps a rose would smell just as sweet with another name, but the SEC won't tolerate anything but precision when it comes to the names applied to mutual funds. Section 35(d) of the 1940 Act provides that a fund cannot use a name that may be deceptive or misleading. In interpreting this section, the SEC has laid down a number of specific rules. For example:

If the fund's name...	Then the fund *must*...
...contains "Tax-Exempt" or "Tax-Free"	...hold mostly tax exempt securities. Specifically, it must get 80 percent of its income from and have 80 percent of its holdings in tax exempt securities.
...represents it as "balanced"	...hold a mix of equities and fixed-income assets. Specifically, it must have at least 25 percent of its assets in fixed-income senior securities.
...implies that it will invest in a particular type of securities	...do so. Specifically, it must keep 65 percent of its assets invested in the indicated type of securities.
...says it's a money market fund	...limit its risk as appropriate to a money market fund. Specifically, it must comply with all the provisions of Rule 2a-7 concerning maturity, quality, and diversification.
...says it specializes in a particular country	...actually specialize in that country. Specifically, 65 percent of its assets must be securities issued in that country.
...characterizes the fund's maturity (e.g., as short-term, long-term, etc.)	...maintain a dollar-weighted average portfolio maturity as prescribed. The SEC prescribes the acceptable maturity limits for each term; e.g., short-term means no more than 3 years.

Fund Directors

Mutual funds organized as corporations have directors; those organized as business trusts have trustees. In practice, they do exactly the same thing, and people in the industry use the two terms synonymously. A fund's board of directors or trustees is subject to the same laws as that of any other corporation or trust, as well as to additional requirements laid down by the 1940 Act. Table 2, from the Investment Company Institute's 1999 Mutual Fund Fact Book, summarizes the duties of a mutual fund director or trustee, highlighting those duties unique to mutual fund directors.

A fund's directors are intended to be fiduciaries, ensuring that the fund's service providers, particularly the management company, act in the best interest of the shareholder. Recognizing that directors affiliated with the management company have a built-in conflict of interest, the 1940 Act required that at least 40 percent of the board consist of "independent" directors—defined to exclude affiliates of the management company, investment adviser, principal distributor, legal counsel, or any member of a broker dealer. The Investment Company Amendments Act of 1970 strengthened this independence. It created a category called disinterested director, provided a set of rules defining the disinterested director, and required a separate majority vote of disinterested directors for provisions such as approval of advisory contracts and distribution agreements. By the late 1990s, many fund groups had a majority of disinterested directors on their fund boards, and the SEC proposed to make this a universal rule, although at this writing, the rule has yet to be adopted.

The U. S. Supreme Court has clearly confirmed the role of the independent or disinterested fund directors:

> *Congress' purpose in structuring the Act as it did is clear. It "was designed to place the unaffiliated directors in the role of 'independent watchdogs'" who would furnish an independent check upon the management of investment companies... In short, the structure and purpose of the [Investment Company Act] indicate that Congress entrusted to the independent directors of investment companies, exercising the authority granted to them by state law, the primary responsibility for looking after the interests of the funds' shareholders.*[7]

By and large, how well one believes fund directors discharge their responsibilities correlates with one's judgement about the level of fund fees. Some industry critics do not believe that boards are truly independent and concerned with the shareholder's interest. Legendary investor Warren Buffett, for example, has likened fund directors to cocker spaniels in a watchdog situation that

Table 2: Duties of Directors or Trustees

Description of Duty	Corporate Director	Fund Director
Authorize issuance of securities	X	X
Declare dividends	X	X
Elect officers	X	X
Appoint committees	X	X
Serve on committees:		
Audit committee	X	X
Nominating committee	X	X
Call shareholder meetings	X	X
Adopt and amend bylaws, if necessary	X	X
Select independent public accountants	X	X
Approve mergers or other transactions	X	X
Review registration statement (including prospectus)	X	X
Review proxy statements	X	X
Review financial reports	X	X
Handle extraordinary situations:		
Takeovers	X	X
Regulatory problems	X	X
Approve investment advisory and subadvisory contract		X
Approve underwriting or distribution contract		X
Approve service contracts:		
Transfer agent		X
Custodian		X
Handle disputes or claims arising under the company's contracts with service providers		X
Approve foreign custodian arrangements		X

Source: Investment Company Institute

called for dobermans, implying that the management companies populate the boards with individuals who will comply with their wishes.[8] On the other hand, SEC Chairman Levitt, in describing in 1999 the SEC's proposals to strengthen fund boards, frankly admitted the lack of any urgent problem with fund governance that needed to be fixed.[9]

Boards of directors or trustees come in various sizes (the regulations are silent on this point). The typical board has between six and twelve members. They are often organized for an entire series of funds, rather than for individual funds, with a single board for all members of a fund family. Many directors, therefore, prepare for and attend dozens or even hundreds of meetings each year. Funds compensate their directors for exercising these duties. Director compensation ranges widely, with the highest paid directors receiving over $150,000 per year. A 1999 study found median compensation for directors in large fund complexes to be $75,000.[10] A fund's Statement of Additional Information (SAI) must disclose the amounts paid to directors by the individual fund and the fund complex as a whole. Directors' fees made up an unspecified part of the $1.5 billion of "other operating expenses" for the industry in 1998 (see Table 4).

The Management Companies

Most funds do not stand alone, but rather form part of a family of funds that have been organized by and receive a common set of services from an organization that specializes in running mutual funds—a *management company*. The management company (which itself may be divided into several separate legal entities each performing a different function) and the group of funds it controls are often known as a fund complex. As Chapter 1 mentioned, management companies can have a variety of organizational forms as privately or publicly held corporations, or subsidiaries of other organizations.

In May 1999, Financial Research Corporation data indicated that 651 separate organizations managed open-end fund families with total assets ranging from as low as $100,000 to over $600 billion. Of these, forty-nine had entered the industry within the previous two years. During the same two year period, twenty-five entities had left the list, mostly small firms that had been acquired. Table 3 shows a breakdown of management companies by size of the assets managed within their fund complexes.

Table 3 clearly shows that the industry is characterized by a large number of small management companies (578 companies each managed under $10 billion in mid-1999), along with a relatively small number of very large companies. For example, at the end of 1999, the dozen largest fund complexes—Fidelity, Vanguard, American Funds, Putnam, Merrill Lynch, Janus, Franklin Templeton, AIM Management, Dean Witter, Federated, T. Rowe Price, and Dreyfus—accounted for just over 50 percent of the industry's total assets under management. Analysts have argued at length about whether the industry is becoming more or less concentrated; Chapter 16 analyzes this topic.

Table 3: Distribution of Management Companies, U.S. Open-End Funds

AUM Range	Number of Management Companies, by Primary Distribution Method*						Total AUM
	Bank	Captive	Direct	Institutional	Wholesale	Total	
< $1 billion	41	13	238	22	97	411	$70
$1 - $10 billion	42	22	58	16	29	167	$583
$10 - $25 billion	9	5	6	6	10	36	$641
$25 - $50 billion	3	1	3	2	2	11	$393
$50 - $100 billion	2	3	3	0	7	15	$1,100
> $100 billion	0	3	4	0	4	11	$2,519
Total	97	47	312	46	149	651	
Total AUM	$559	$869	$2,009	$231	$1,638		$5,306

*Primary Distribution Methods:

Bank – funds sold through brokers or other intermediaries through the auspices of banks, in bank branch offices
Captive – funds distributed through a sales force that works directly for the same organization as the management company
Direct – funds sold directly to the investor by the distribution arm of the management company, typically with no load
Institutional – funds sold to institutions (corporations, foundations, etc.) rather than to individuals
Wholesale – funds sold to individual investors via third-party (i.e., non-captive) brokers, typically load funds

Source: Financial Research Corporation (assets under management figures in billions, as of May 31, 1999)

The typical management company provides or oversees a core set of services that includes fund adminis-tration, investment advisory, principal distribution, and transfer agent processing, including customer service. Often each service unit is organized as a separate subsidiary of the management company. The variety of fee arrangements through which the funds compensate the management companies for these services is endless. These fee arrangements have been the source of controversy and even litigation throughout the life of the industry. The current level of fees in the industry, and whether they are increasing or declining, is related to the issue of concentration, and is likewise discussed in Chapter 16.

Table 4 summarizes the fee expenses paid by funds, which provided the revenue earned by fund service providers in 1998. Management companies earned the major part of the over $32 billion of fee revenue, although some significant part of it was passed on to third-party service providers. Mutual fund management has been a profitable business in the recent past: Strategic Insight, an industry research firm, studied the 1998 financial reports of eighteen publicly held management com-panies that collectively managed over $1 trillion in assets, and found their operating margin averaged about 36 percent. They further estimated that the management companies earned 0.23 percent pre-tax and about 0.15 percent after-tax on the assets under management.[11] If these ratios are representative for the industry as a whole, then management companies collectively made about $7.5 billion in after-tax profit in 1998.

Table 4:
Mutual Fund Industry Fee Expenses in 1998

Category	As a % of AUM	$billions*
Advisory and Fund Administration	.467	23.35
Shareholder Servicing	.115	5.75
Custody	.023	1.15
Audit	.004	.2
Legal	.004	.2
Other operating expenses†	.030	1.5
Total	.643	32.15

*Based on average assets under management for the year of approximately $5 trillion.

†Other operating expenses includes bookkeeping, directors, interest, postage, printing, registration, salaries, shareholder meetings, and taxes.

Source: Strategic Insight, *Money Management Financial Comparisons, 1998.*

Third-Party Service Providers

While management companies provide much of the support for U.S. mutual funds, nearly every function can be, and in some cases is, contracted out to third parties. Some functions, such as fund accounting and transfer agent processing, are performed internally in some fund complexes, and outsourced in others. Some functions fall to third-party providers because of regulations (e.g., custody, audit) or economies of scale (e.g., high volume printing). Thus the industry has developed a robust set of service providers.

Investment Advisers. For most fund groups, the management company provides investment advisory service, as well as fund administration. Thus the majority of the $23 billion spent in 1998 on these functions was earned by the management companies. Some groups, particularly smaller ones, turn to external providers for these functions. Also, even some larger fund groups use sub-advisers for management of certain types of assets that require special expertise, such as foreign securities.

Transfer Agents. Transfer agent processing and customer service may be done by either the management company or by one of a number of third-party transfer agents. Chapters 11 and 12 cover these functions and the organizations that perform them. Strategic Insight estimates that $5.75 billion was spent on these functions in 1998, as shown in the shareholder servicing category in Table 4. Most of this money goes to the management companies, and a smaller amount to third-party transfer agents.

Fund Accountants. Fund accounting keeps the books of the funds—assets, liabilities, income and expenses—in accordance with the provisions of the 1940 Act and subsequent regulations. It calculates the daily net asset value per share on which all shareholder activity is valued. As with transfer agent functions, management companies sometimes perform fund accounting internally and sometimes contract with third parties for the service. Fund accounting is also one of the services some management companies cover under their unitary fee. The Tower Group estimates that the industry spent about $500 million on fund accounting services in 1998, an amount that is divided between management companies and third-party fund accounting organizations.[12] Chapter 7 covers fund accounting functions and the organizations that perform them.

Custodians. The 1940 Act imposes very specific requirements on funds regarding the safekeeping, or custody, of their assets. They must place their securities with a "qualified custodian," defined as either (1) a bank; (2) a member of a national securities exchange; (3) the company itself; or (4) a central clearing system. A number of 1940 Act sections and subsequent rules prescribe requirements that must be met in each case. As a practical matter, most fund complexes today use banks for the bulk of their custody service. As Table 4 indicates, mutual fund custody was about a $1.15 billion business in 1998. Chapter 6 discusses what the custodian does and how it interacts with the investment manager.

Auditors. The Securities Act of 1933 requires that any corporation offering its stock to the public engage independent accountants to attest to the propriety of its accounting practices. Section 32(a) of the 1940 Act further requires that an investment company's board of directors vote annually to select its independent accountants, and that this selection generally be ratified by the vote of the shareholders. Investment company audit is a specialized practice, requiring that the auditors be familiar with the arcane rules established for mutual funds. As Figure 2 shows, a handful of large accounting firms audit almost the entire universe of U.S. mutual funds. Investment company audit fees amounted to about $200 million in 1998.

Consulting and Legal Firms. Most of the large consulting and legal firms and many smaller ones provide service to the other players

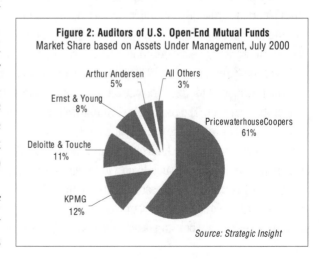

Figure 2: Auditors of U.S. Open-End Mutual Funds
Market Share based on Assets Under Management, July 2000

Arthur Andersen 5%

All Others 3%

Ernst & Young 8%

PricewaterhouseCoopers 61%

Deloitte & Touche 11%

KPMG 12%

Source: Strategic Insight

in the industry, particularly the management companies. For example, consulting firms often engage in large system integration projects to support the information technology needs of investment advisers, brokers, and transfer agents. They are compensated from the fee revenue earned by the management companies or other service providers.

Analysts and Rating Agents. A number of very specialized firms concentrate on observing and analyzing the industry and its players. Lipper Analytical Services, now a subsidiary of Reuters, and Morningstar, Inc. have been leaders in the field of rating mutual funds according to their historical performance adjusted for risk. DALBAR, FRC, and Strategic Insight take measurements of the industry—fund characteristics, assets and flows, expenses—and sell this information and the analyses they perform upon it. Some portion of their revenue comes indirectly from the funds through management companies, service providers, and financial intermediaries who purchase their services.

Brokers and Other Intermediaries

Brokers play two different roles for the industry. When a fund's portfolio manager makes a securities trade, brokers and other intermediaries help execute that trade. A senior vice president at American Century Investments describes how this might go: "My trading desk calls a sales trader, who calls the position trader, who calls the floor broker, and then the floor broker goes to the specialist."[13] The fund compensates this chain of intermediaries for their services in one of two ways, depending on the type of security. Often, particularly when the security is a stock listed on the New York Stock Exchange, the broker receives an explicit commission based on the amount of the trade, just as an individual investor would. In other cases, the brokerage firm makes its money through the spread—the difference between the bid and ask price for the security, or what it bought the security for and the selling price. Chapter 5 discusses the fund's interactions with these sell-side brokers.

The amount of money funds spend on brokerage services in executing trades is difficult to determine. Funds report the brokerage commissions they have paid in recent years in their SAIs. Livingston and O'Neal, studying this data for a sample of equity funds, determined that these brokerage commissions average about .28 percent of average net assets under management annually.[14] Applying this .28 percent rate to the $2.5 trillion of equity fund assets in 1998 yields a total of $7 billion in commissions.

The trading cost for fixed-income securities is more difficult to determine, since it is often hidden in the price of the securities. The brokerage firm may sell from its inventory, without explicit commission, instead making a profit by selling the security at a higher price than it paid. While some investment managers calculate an imputed commission for fixed-income trades, others do not, and commissions of this type are generally not believed to be precise enough to post to the accounting ledger. Thus the magnitude of what the funds pay for fixed-income securities transactions is obscure. If we assume that the hybrid, fixed income, and money market segments of the industry incur costs similar in magnitude to the equity segment, then the total for the industry in 1998 might be estimated at about $14 billion.

John Bogle takes a high-level stab at estimating these costs, stating that "a variety of studies suggest that [transaction costs] approximate 0.5 percent to 2 percent of fund assets per year, with higher costs for smaller funds with high rates of portfolio turnover and lower costs for larger funds with lower turnover rates."[15] As a rule of thumb, he suggests calculating this cost for a fund as 0.6 percent of the total annual portfolio turnover value (purchases plus sales). This formula, applied to the industry as a whole for 1998, yields an estimate of around $30 billion for what executing securities transactions cost the industry. Bogle's rule-of-thumb figure includes the cost of market impact (i.e., the amount that the transaction itself changes the market price for the security), an item researchers have found great difficulty in quantifying.[16] Market impact is already reflected in either the ending value of securities held by the funds or the value of realized gains. Therefore, Table 1 uses the $14 billion figure derived by extrapolating from the Livingston and O'Neal study for the cost of brokerage services. (However, Bogle's overall estimate appears to be correct. Researchers in 1999[17] and 2000[18] studies of fund expenses found that the mostly equity funds in their samples incurred annual transaction costs of around 80 basis points, including both brokerage commissions and market effect.)

The brokerage firms don't keep all of this money, however. They return a significant amount to the investment advisers in the form of soft dollar arrangements—effectively, rebates that the brokers give the advisers in the form of research and other services. A recent SEC study found that the brokers in the sample it studied returned, on the average, 12 percent in commissions the investment adviser paid the broker.[19] However, the investment advisers typically consume the soft dollar services, so they do not decrease the net flow from the funds. Chapter 5 discusses soft dollar arrangements in more detail.

The brokerage industry, which includes broker dealers and other intermediaries such as financial planners and bank trust departments, also earns revenue by selling the shares of some mutual funds to investors. Investors compensate these brokers either on a transaction basis (e.g., a front-end commission calculated as a percentage of the purchase amount), or on an asset basis (e.g., a trail commission calculated as a percentage of assets held), or both. Chapter 8 discusses brokers and other intermediaries and their roles in distributing mutual funds.

Commissions paid to brokers for fund share sales or asset retention fall into three categories.

1. *Front-end sales charges on purchase transactions.*
   Most load funds compensate the intermediary that sells their shares via a front-end load, a commission that is deducted from the amount that the investor pays. The magnitude of the commission differs from trade to trade, depending on the commission rate structure of the fund, and any commission discounts the investor might receive due to volume.

2. *Ongoing, asset-based commissions (12b-1 commissions).*
   Rule 12b-1 allows funds to use fund (i.e., shareholder) assets to pay for distribution activities. In practice, funds that have 12b-1 fees assess a charge that typically ranges between .25% and 1.00% per year of asset value, and distribute most of this to the intermediaries that sold the shares on which the commission is assessed. "Pure" no-load funds do not assess the 12b-1, or any other, sales charge.

3. *Sales charges paid upon redemption.*

Some funds levy charges when an investor redeems shares. In some cases, these redemption fees merely compensate the fund for expenses incurred due to the redemption. Such fees are not sales charges and do not become revenue for anyone. Other redemption charges, notably contingent deferred sales charges, are commissions assessed against the investor at the time of redemption instead of time of purchase. These typically reimburse the fund's principal distributor for commission payments that were given to the intermediary at the time of purchase ("fronted" by the distributor), but not deducted at that time from the investor's payment. Chapter 8 describes these and other commission schemes in detail.

The ICI, in studies of the ownership of fund shares, determined that the average cost of ownership resulting from distribution expenses in 1997 was 0.61 percent for equity funds, and 0.53 percent for bond funds (money market funds are mostly no load).[20] Extending these figures by the average assets in equity and bond funds in 1998 results in about $20 billion for total distribution expenses.

Thus the brokerage industry, broadly defined to include any firm that (1) sells mutual fund shares to investors, or (2) helps execute portfolio security transactions for funds, received revenues from the funds and investors in 1998 somewhere in the neighborhood of $35 billion.

The Industry Associations

A number of non-profit, member-supported associations address various aspects of the securities industry. Two in particular focus on the mutual fund segment.

The Investment Company Institute (ICI)

Shortly after the passage of the 1940 Act, the mutual fund executives who had worked together to help influence the legislation formally organized the National Association of Investment Companies. This organization would "avail itself of any opportunity to be of constructive assistance" to the SEC as it developed mutual fund regulation.[21] In 1961, it changed its name to the Investment Company Institute, and claims as its mission today

> to advance the interests of investment companies and their shareholders, to promote public understanding of the investment company business, and to serve the public interest by encouraging adherence to high ethical standards by all elements of the business.[22]

Mutual funds operated by virtually all of the management companies in the U.S. belong to the ICI. With headquarters in Washington, D.C., it is the industry's national trade association, and represents the industry frequently in hearings before Congress. Regular membership in the ICI is limited to SEC-registered investment companies, their investment advisers, and principal underwriters. Broker dealers and investment advisers to non-registered funds may become associate members. The ICI staff gathers data and analyzes a wide variety of issues pertinent to the industry. The ICI publishes much of the data it gathers and the analyses it conducts on its web site (www.ici.org), one of the richest and most useful sources of mutual fund industry information.

Members fund the ICI via an asset-based charge, the rates for which the ICI has been able to reduce in recent years as the growth of the industry has swelled fund asset values. In the year ended September 30, 1998, these dues amounted to about $30 million, while investment income and other revenues added about $8 million, and expenses amounted to $36.3 million. The ICI had about 160 employees in 1998.[25] ICI dues form a small part of the "other" fees shown in Table 4, earlier in this chapter.

LOBBYING FOR THE FUNDS

The Lobbying Disclosure Act of 1995 defines lobbyists as individuals who (1) spend at least 20 percent of their time for a particular client on lobbying activities, (2) have multiple contacts with legislative staff, members of Congress, or high-level executive branch officials, and (3) work for a client paying more than $5,000 over six months for that service. The ICI employs lobbyists on behalf of the mutual fund industry. In 1998, it spent about $3.4 million on lobbying, and employed seven in-house staff in lobbying activities, according to the Center for Responsive Politics' web site (www.opensecrets.org). In addition, it gave almost $700,000 in political contributions, 60 percent to Republicans and 40 percent to Democrats. Overall, the ICI's spending on lobbying represented about 12 percent of the $31 million spent by the securities and investments industry as a whole. In 1998, the ICI ranked 77th in lobbying expenditures, just behind Atlantic Richfield and United Services Automobile Association, and just ahead of Sallie Mae and FedEx.

The list of big spenders among securities and investment industry lobbyists in 1997 included a few other associations: the Bond Market Association spent $2.4 million; the Securities Industry Association, $5 million; and the Uniform Standards Coalition, $1.8 million. Among securities industry firms, the leaders in spending were Bear, Stearns & Company ($1.3 million), Morgan Stanley Dean Witter ($1.8 million), and Merrill Lynch ($2.9 million). Few pure mutual fund management companies made the list—Eaton Vance at $120,000 stands out as the leader. Presumably most fund companies let the ICI do the lobbying for them.

What do these lobbyists do? A lobbyist for DuPont explained it succinctly: "My mission is to get favorable decisions from the U.S. government on key public policy issues."[23] Along these lines, the ICI's lobbying mission is to ensure adequate representation of the mutual fund industry's point of view about any regulatory or legislative question that arises. This means making speeches, writing letters, arranging for and delivering congressional testimony, and above all, canvassing members of Congress and their staffs to present the industry argument.

For example, in 1998 the AICPA issued a rule to require companies to immediately write off start-up costs, such as those incurred in opening a new facility, introducing a new product or service, or expanding into a new territory. The ICI, along with Alliance Capital Management and Federated Investors Inc., lobbied for new fund start-up expenses to be exempt from this rule. Their lobbying resulted in a compromise, under which fund companies could continue to gradually write off any start-up costs sitting on their books as of June 30, 1998, but had to immediately write off new start-up expenses incurred after that date.[24]

The National Investment Company Service Association (NICSA)

While the ICI represents the funds, NICSA represents the fund service providers. NICSA's membership includes about 400 companies that serve mutual funds as investment advisers, transfer agents, custodians, and providers of specialized services. Established in 1962 as an informal forum for operations and shareholder servicing professionals in the mutual fund industry, it remains a much smaller organization than the ICI. NICSA's annual budget of over $2 million is funded by membership dues and proceeds from the conferences and seminars it sponsors.

The Regulators

As the ICI never tires of pointing out, mutual funds form the most strictly regulated segment of the U.S. securities industry. Chapter 2 described the four principal securities laws that govern funds. Today, two national entities have primary oversight responsibility for the funds' compliance with these acts and subsequent regulations—the Securities and Exchange Commission (SEC) and the National Association of Securities Dealers (NASD). In addition, each state maintains securities regulatory bodies, although their scope of responsibility for mutual funds has been much reduced since 1996.

The SEC

The Securities Exchange Act of 1934 authorized the creation of the SEC as the primary agency responsible for administering federal securities laws. The SEC describes itself as "an independent, nonpartisan, quasi-judicial regulatory agency," and describes its mission as ensuring that "publicly held companies, broker dealers in securities, investment companies and advisers, and other participants in the securities markets comply with federal securities law."[26] The president of the United States appoints the five SEC commissioners to fixed, five-year terms, one of which expires each year. To ensure bipartisanship, no more than three serving commissioners may be of the same political party.

The SEC's Division of Investment Management administers the Investment Company Act of 1940, as well as the Investment Advisers Act of 1940 and the Public Utility Holding Company Act of 1936. Like the rest of the SEC, it is staffed by lawyers, accountants, financial analysts, examiners, investigators, economists, and other professionals. In early 1999, the Division had about 150 employees, and accounted for roughly 5 percent of the SEC's annual budget.[27]

The Investment Management Division's staff reviews and processes registration statements, proxy statements, and other reports the funds are required by law to file. It also monitors industry activity to ensure compliance with regulations concerning registration, financial responsibility, sales practices, and advertising. When SEC management deems it appropriate, the Division sponsors or conducts studies of particular issues in the industry as a basis for recommendations for regulation or legislation. For example, the SEC conducted a study of state regulatory practices and their effect on the industry in the early 1990s that influenced the reforms included in the National Securities Markets Improvement Act of 1996. In early 1999, SEC Chairman Levitt

NO-ACTION LETTERS

Management companies and other industry firms can seek informal interpretive advice from the SEC in the form of "no-action" letters. The requesting organization writes a letter to the SEC, essentially asking "will you take any action if we do so-and-so?" describing some activity they would like to undertake, but aren't sure is permitted. The SEC staff studies the proposed action, and, if they feel that it does not violate a statute or rule, the Office of General Counsel issues a "no-action" letter. The letter generally says that the staff "will not recommend to the Commission that it take enforcement action" related to the proposed activity.[28] These letters, while not legally binding, serve to alleviate concerns on the part of requesting organizations that their proposed action might lead to enforcement activity.

For example, in a few of the no-action letters it has issued, the SEC has stated that its staff would not recommend enforcement action if...

- investment advisers and their representatives use in their advertisements the service quality ratings compiled by DALBAR, an industry consultant, provided they meet stated criteria designed to ensure the integrity of the ratings;
- a money market fund acquires a note designed by Goldman Sachs with an extensible maturity and quarterly rate reset, provided they treat each extension of the note's maturity as a separate acquisition and treat the note as a short-term variable rate security;
- the John Hancock Funds uses a greatly simplified and more readable prospectus as a prototype for simplified prospectuses across the fund complex;
- Nicholas Applegate includes in each of its funds' prospectuses information concerning the performance of the investment adviser's similarly-managed non-investment company accounts, as long as they meet a number of rules about how the information is presented;
- Munder Capital Management provides information via the Internet reflecting all new portfolio positions added or eliminated during the month, information about each portfolio company's business, and why the adviser made its recommendation regarding securities purchased or sold;
- a partner in a law firm serves as one of a fund's unaffiliated directors, even though one of his partners rendered legal advice to a bank that was a subsidiary of the parent company of the fund's investment adviser.

These summaries oversimplify letters that are usually several pages long, and filled with detailed provisions and references to statutes and regulations. Most no-action letters address such subtle or arcane issues in the interpretation of the regulations that they defy easy summarization. Nevertheless, no-action letters provide the industry and the SEC with a valuable tool for resolving the inevitable ambiguity associated with complex securities laws.

advised the industry that the SEC planned to aggressively pursue studies leading to regulation to improve various industry practices.[29]

NASD

The Securities Exchange Act of 1934 only empowered the SEC to regulate the exchange markets. The Maloney Act of 1938 amended the 1934 Act to authorize the registration of national securities associations to regulate the activities of their broker dealer members in other markets. NASD, the only national securities association registered in accordance with these provisions, now regulates all broker dealers that do business with the U.S. public.

For mutual funds, NASD regulates much of the distribution activity. It regulates all brokers, including licensing those that sell only mutual funds (Series 6), those that sell mutual funds and other securities (Series 7), and the supervisors of the selling brokers. NASD reviews almost all sales and advertising materials produced by the funds, and may bring disciplinary proceedings against firms or individuals for violations of fund advertising or sales rules. NASD also has authority to establish a maximum limit on sales charges on securities that its broker dealer members sell, which effectively enables it to set maximum limits for the sales loads the funds levy.

State Regulatory Bodies

Until 1996, state level regulation of mutual funds was far from uniform. In testimony to Congress in 1995, the ICI stated that it had identified 18 variants on mutual fund regulation at the state level, which it termed "a crazy-quilt of inconsistent regulation."[30] In 1996, Congress enacted the National Securities Markets Improvement Act (NSMIA), which preempted state authority in three areas of regulation of investment companies.

1. *Registration.* Mutual funds need only comply with SEC registration requirements—all state specific requirements are invalidated. The states can still require funds to submit copies of the documents they file with the SEC, and they can still levy fees on the funds for selling within the state, but they cannot impose any requirements concerning the format or content of the registration documents.

2. *Regulation of various offering documents.* States are precluded from directly or indirectly prohibiting, limiting, or imposing any conditions on various fund documents, including prospectuses, proxy statements, reports to shareholders, and others. The SEC remains the sole arbiter of mutual fund documents through which the funds disclose information to the public.

3. *Merit or substantive regulation.* States cannot regulate the way mutual funds operate, such as by imposing limits on portfolio investments or expenses.

The NSMIA explicitly preserved state law concerning mutual funds in three specific areas: (1) regulations against fraud; (2) requirements for notice filings; and (3) imposition of fees. This Act relieved the funds of a considerable burden in responding to fragmented and conflicting state regulatory requirements, and left the state securities regulatory offices mainly as fee collectors.

CHAPTER 4
The Mutual Fund—Product Definition

The unprecedented flood of cash … has spawned a tidal wave of highly
specialized mutual funds. …One of the most successful new offerings is the
Unpleasant Fund, which currently has stakes in barium enema companies,
privately owned prisons, nuclear-waste disposers, and Yugoslavian cruise
lines. The fund hedges its positions by shorting stocks that sound happy:
Joy Tech, Merry-Go-Round Enterprises, Pep Boys.

—Joe Queenan (1992)[1]

In 1992, the growth of the industry to 3,000 funds prompted Joe Queenan to write his satiric article about the specialized niches many of them filled. Since then, the number of funds has almost tripled. At the end of 1999, it rivaled that of the total number of common stocks traded on the major exchanges—almost 8,000 open-end funds as compared to about 2,700 stocks listed on the NYSE, 700 on the American Stock Exchange, and around 4,900 on the NASDAQ National Market.

Why are there so many funds? Three interrelated factors are responsible.

1. *Investment Objectives*. Investors pursue a variety of objectives in holding mutual funds. For example, some seek current income; some seek capital preservation or appreciation; many seek a combination. They have different horizons for their investments, and varying appetites for risk. Their sensitivities to taxes, federal and state, differ. No fund can be all things to all investors. A fund manager must pick a particular investment objective to pursue—for example, tax-free current income—and operate the fund accordingly. In 2000, the ICI recognized thirty-three broad categories of investment objectives for funds; other observers recognized even more.

2. *Investment Philosophy.* Different investment managers bring different philosophies of investing to their funds. Given an investment objective of aggressive growth, for example, two investment managers can differ dramatically in how they go about picking the securities to get that growth. Active versus passive management, for example, represents one great dichotomy in investment philosophy that has generated, and continues to generate, heated controversy. Among actively managed funds, different managers take widely differing approaches to determining which securities to buy and sell. This yields more variety—multiple funds will address a given objective in multiple ways.

3. *Competition.* The profit to be made in managing mutual funds has attracted many players into the market, and has spurred existing management companies to expand their product line. Banks, insurance companies, brokerage firms, and others entering the industry have swelled the number of fund families from just over 300 in 1988 to over 650 in 1999. While some fund companies are content to occupy a niche, many offer full lines of funds to capture as much of the investor's business as possible. For a given investment objective and philosophy, competing vendors will offer multiple products.

In short, the evolution of investment objectives and investment philosophies, and the increasing competition for investor dollars have fueled a fund explosion. The number of funds on the market grew by more than an order of magnitude during the last twenty years of the twentieth century.

OCCUPYING A NICHE

A universe of almost 8,000 funds does allow for some specialization. Not every fund has to invest in domestic blue chip stocks or AAA-rated corporate bonds. There's room for at least a few distinctive niches, mostly occupied by funds that aim at a narrowly targeted set of investors.

*   A number of funds are religiously oriented. The *Amana Mutual Funds Trust Income Fund*, for example, is managed by Unified Management in Indianapolis with the North American Islamic Trust as a consultant. It invests, according to its prospectus, in a manner "consistent with Islamic principles." These include avoiding any securities that pay interest as well as sticking to companies that make ethical products. Another example, *The Catholic Fund,* keeps 80 percent of its assets invested in companies with products and services that support the teachings of the Roman Catholic Church. And at least two management companies—Lutheran Brotherhood and AAL (Aid Association for Lutherans)—target Lutheran investors.

*   At least one fund—the *Women's Equity Mutual Fund*—attempts to help women try to break through the glass ceiling. WEMF invests only in companies that have records of promoting women into top executive and board positions, actively training them, and paying them fairly. It explicitly avoids companies that repeatedly violate the Equal Employment Opportunity Act or use sexist stereotypes in the workplace.

*   The *Meyers Pride Value Fund* attempts to tap the $800 billion pool of assets that U.S. gays and lesbians are said to control. It screens for pro-gay policies in the firms in whose stock it invests.

*   The *SteinRoe Young Investor Fund* aims small—specifically, at children. It gives its shareholders a quarterly newsletter written in language children can understand, activity books, and wall charts to track their investment growth. It produces a parents' guide explaining how to discuss money issues with children. And, it invests in companies that mean something to most children, such as Walt Disney, McDonald's, and Coca-Cola.

*   Several fund groups serve minorities. For example, the *DEM Equity* and *DEM Index* mutual funds, managed by Baltimore's Chapman Capital Management, focus on what their adviser terms "domestic emerging markets." These include publicly traded companies that are U.S.-based but controlled by African Americans, Asians, Hispanics, and women.

*   One fund plays on regional pride. The *IAI Regional Fund*, managed by Investment Advisors, Inc. of Minneapolis, holds at least 65 percent of its assets in the stock of companies located in the eight states of the upper Midwest. As a benchmark against which to compare its performance, it uses the IAI Midwest 300, a composite index of the stock prices of 300 firms based in those states.

Figure 1 illustrates the relationships among investor objectives and investment philosophy, how the fund ultimately operates, and how it performs. It also illustrates how this book parts company with almost every other book about mutual funds. Most of the hundreds of books that have been published in recent years focus on the left and right sides of Figure 1, ignoring the middle. They address some combination of (1) what the investor's objectives ought to be, (2) what the correct investment philosophy is, and (3) how to evaluate fund performance to pick funds that best meet these criteria. They *prescribe* how to select and use mutual funds, treating the fund operations in the middle as a black box.

Figure 1:
Relationships among Investment Objectives, Philosophy, Policies, and Operations

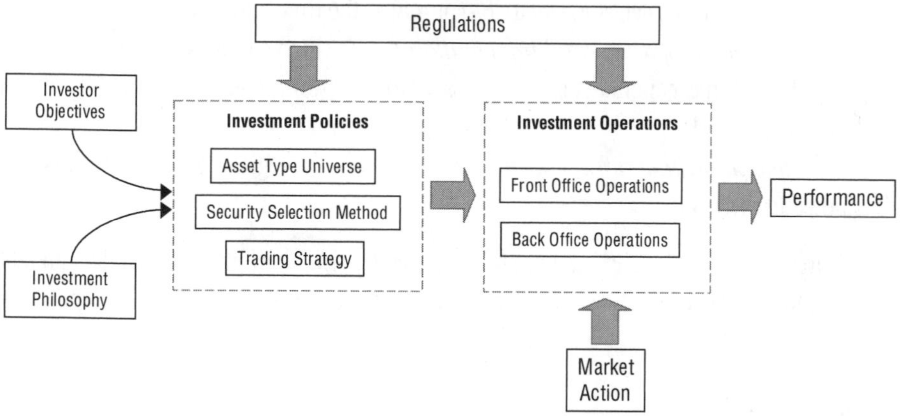

This book opens that box and concentrates on the middle of Figure 1. It acknowledges that investors have differing objectives and fund managers have differing strategies and philosophies. It recognizes that these determine fund investment policies, which then drive investment operations—what asset types the fund holds and the way the manager goes about managing the portfolio. It does not attempt to advise anyone as to how to evaluate a fund's investment strategy or performance. Instead it focuses on what it takes to produce a mutual fund, given target customers, their objectives, an investment strategy, and the regulatory environment. This book *describes* how mutual funds, whatever their objective or style, actually work: how they are produced, how they are sold, how they provide customer service.

This chapter sets the context for the discussion of the manufacturing component of fund management—the process of making and carrying out investment management decisions. It starts by reviewing how funds define themselves via the prospectus and statement of additional information. It illustrates the diversity of funds today by looking at several commonly encountered fund categorization schemes. It uses a sampling of different investment philosophies and styles to illustrate the dimension these add to fund variety. Finally, it discusses how these structural components of the fund drive the operations of the investment advisory and fund administrative organizations.

Defining the Fund

A registered mutual fund must explicitly define the investment objective it seeks to pursue, as well as how it will operate in pursuit of that objective. Registration itself requires the open-end fund to submit and regularly update SEC Form N-1A, which details all aspects of the fund's organization. The instructions for Form N-1A effectively specify how mutual funds define themselves. Form N-1A comprises three parts:

1. Part A, the *prospectus*, which contains information the regulators believe to be essential to an investor making an informed decision whether to purchase the fund's shares;
2. Part B, the *statement of additional information (SAI)*, which contains information the disclosure of which the SEC has concluded is not necessary for investor protection, but which some investors may find useful; and
3. Part C, *further information* the SEC requires to complete the registration, but which is not typically distributed to investors. [2]

In addition, in recent years the SEC has urged companies to prepare simpler, more understandable disclosure documents, and as part of this effort allows funds to prepare a *profile*, a shortened, simplified version of the prospectus.

The Prospectus

The Securities Exchange Act of 1934 requires that any publicly offered security be described by a prospectus, and that the prospectus be delivered to anyone considering purchase of the security. The SEC has expanded upon the 1934 Act requirements to define exactly what goes into an open-end fund prospectus, revising this definition substantially in 1998. Specifically, an open-end fund prospectus must contain the nine items described below. As an example, the Appendix contains the prospectus, as of February 28, 2000, for the series of funds in the C/Funds Group.

1. *Front and back cover pages*. The front cover page must contain the fund's name, the prospectus date, and some standard disclaimer language. The front cover may contain a brief description of the fund's investment objectives. The back cover must explain how to get the SAI and other additional information about the fund. To package the prospectus more attractively, some funds put an additional outside cover on it, with whatever graphics or other information they desire, and the disclaimer "this wrapper is not part of the prospectus."
2. *Risk/return summary: investments, risks, and performance*. The fund must disclose its investment objectives, and summarize how it intends to meet them by identifying its principal investment strategies. It must also discuss the risks the investor incurs in investing in the fund. The regulations

COULD WE SPEAK ENGLISH HERE, PLEASE?

In 1993, Arthur Levitt, incoming chairman of the SEC, had to divest himself of certain stocks that he owned as a requirement of taking the new position. Searching for mutual funds into which to invest his proceeds, he began reading mutual fund prospectuses. What he found appalled him. The language employed made them, as he put it "unintelligible to all but a few lawyers and market professionals."[3] If he, a former investment banker and stock exchange chairman, had trouble understanding them, then what must they seem like to the average investor? Levitt consequently launched the SEC on a crusade to improve investor disclosure by making prospectuses easier to understand. Over the next few years, the SEC's Plain English Project studied the problem, conducted trials, and developed guidelines.

In 1998, the SEC formally adopted rules requiring mutual funds (and other companies) to use plain English in the cover page, summary, and risk factor sections of all prospectuses. The rules require that the writers of prospectuses use simple, clear language to organize, design, and write these prospectus sections. They prescribed six specific practices:
- use active (not passive) voice;
- write in short, declarative sentences;
- use definite, concrete, everyday words;
- whenever possible, employ tabular data presentations or bulleted lists to explain complex material;
- avoid legal jargon and highly technical business terms; and
- avoid multiple negatives.

More generally, the rules require prospectus writers to know their audience, know what information is important and needs to be disclosed, and design and structure the prospectus so that it's easy and inviting to read. The SEC prepared a 28-page manual entitled "The Plain English Handbook: How to Create Clear SEC Disclosure Documents," to provide guidance in plain English practices.

Levitt enlisted Warren Buffett, who has been praised for his clear, understandable letters to Berkshire Hathaway shareholders, to write a preface to the manual. Buffett provided an example of what could be achieved through application of the principles.

> Before (from an actual prospectus):
> *"Maturity and duration management decisions are made in the context of an intermediate maturity orientation. The maturity structure of the portfolio is adjusted in the anticipation of cyclical interest rate changes. Such adjustments are not made in an effort to capture short-term, day-to-day movements in the market."*

> After (as rewritten by Buffett):
> *"We will try to profit by correctly predicting future interest rates. When we have no strong opinion, we will generally hold intermediate-term bonds."*

These SEC efforts have sparked some controversy within the industry. Plain English opponents advance two lines of argument. The first maintains that the prospectus covers complex, subtle issues, and that it is naive to believe that these can be reduced to simple terms. The other focuses more on the liability associated with inadequate disclosure, arguing that funds open themselves to litigation if their efforts to simplify prospectus language result in inadequate descriptions of the fund's investment policies and associated risks. Speaking of prospectus language, a representative of the New York Bar Association pointed out that it has "taken generations of lawyers to make sure that it's all in there and it's all correct."[4] So far, however, the SEC has stood its ground on the issue, and even offered an incentive—cutting by half the time the SEC takes to pass on a registration if the prospectus complies with the plain English guidelines.

require both a narrative description of the nature of the risk and quantitative data, some displayed graphically, on the fund's historical risk/return characteristics. The C/Funds sample prospectus provides this information on a separate set of pages for each of the five funds in the series.

3. *Fee tables.* This section must first specify the fee and expense charges, including commissions and other sales charges, the shareholder incurs as part of holding the fund, and then show the total cost of investing over one, three, five, and ten year periods. While brokerage costs for portfolio trading are not among the items that must be listed among the fund's fees and expenses, the rules do require the prospectus to discuss the consequences of portfolio turnover if they are expected to be significant. As with Item 2, the C/Funds repeats Item 3 for each of the five funds in the series.

4. *Investment objectives, principal investment strategies, and related risks.* This section expands on the summary provided in Item 2. In discussing how the fund intends to meet its investment objectives, the prospectus should describe the principal investment strategies, including the types of securities in which the fund will invest. The prospectus should also explain in general terms how the fund's adviser decides which securities to buy and sell. The SEC has in recent years encouraged funds to write meaningful, plain English prose in this section, with mixed results. The C/Funds prospectus in the Appendix combines Items 2 and 4 into a single discussion.

5. *Management's discussion of fund performance.* The prospectus must discuss factors materially affecting fund performance, provide a line graph illustrating performance, and provide a table showing fund returns over specified periods. A fund may omit this information from the prospectus if it is available in an annual report, and that annual report is delivered along with the prospectus. The C/Funds take this latter approach.

6. *Management, organization, and capital structure.* The prospectus must provide the name and address of the investment adviser(s) and describe how they are compensated. It must also identify the individuals responsible for the day-to-day management of the fund. If there are legal proceedings pending, or unique capital structure arrangements that would expose investors to risk, these must be disclosed in this section of the prospectus. The C/Funds prospectus reveals an item commonly encountered in this area: the management company has agreed to a voluntary limit on the total expenses of the fund.

7. *Shareholder information.* This section includes descriptions of how the fund's shares are priced, how a shareholder purchases and sells shares, the fund's policy on dividends and capital gains, and the tax consequences of investing in the fund. The C/Funds prospectus shows entries typical of a no-load fund family.

8. *Distribution arrangements.* The fund must disclose and describe any sales loads involved in purchasing or selling shares. It must also describe any distribution fees assessed against shareholders under Rule 12b-1. Since the C/Funds are pure no-load funds, with neither transaction commissions nor 12b-1 charges, this section is omitted from their prospectus.

9. *Financial highlights information.* The rules specify a list of financial data the fund must provide in columnar form for each of the preceding five years, or since inception, if the fund is less than five years old. The prospectus must also identify the fund's auditor, and tell how to get the audit report and more detailed financial information.

DISCLOSING THE RISK OF A FUND

How do you best express the risk associated with a mutual fund? The SEC, the funds, the ICI, and the rating agents have been wrestling with this question for years. The SEC has rules embedded in the instructions for Form N-1A, but no one believes that today's rules will be the last word on the subject.

Academics have long defined investment risk as equal to uncertainty in investment return, and generally equated that with variability in those returns.[5] The more an investment's performance varies, the greater the chance that the performance will be down at that particular point in time when the investor happens to need to liquidate the investment. Most often, this variability is measured by the standard deviation of the difference between the fund's return and that of a benchmark—the risk-free returns of U.S. Treasury securities or that of an appropriate index. A fund that tracks closely to the performance of its benchmark is considered lower-risk than one that deviates considerably from it.

Investors themselves define risk much less crisply. In 1996, the ICI released the results of a survey it conducted, exploring what investors thought about risk in mutual fund investing.[6] Most respondents felt that at least two different concepts were appropriate. The top six definitions, along with the percentage of the 648 respondents who selected each of them are as follows:

1. Losing some of the original investment (57 percent);
2. Investment not keeping up with inflation (47 percent);
3. Value of the investment fluctuating up and down (46 percent);
4. Not having enough money at the end of the investing period to meet one's goals (40 percent);
5. Income distribution from the investment is declining (38 percent);
6. Investment not performing as well as a bank CD (30 percent).

Most investors surveyed also preferred both a narrative description of the nature of the fund's risk, as well as a bar graph showing the fund's total return over some period.

The current SEC requirements for prospectus disclosure of risk reflect these investor preferences. They specifically require that a fund disclose the principal risks of investing in the fund in two ways.

1. *Narrative Risk Disclosure*. The fund must summarize the principal risks of investing in the fund, and discuss circumstances reasonably likely to have a negative impact on the fund's NAV, yield, and return. The C/Funds prospectus, for example, which describes an asset allocation investment strategy, talks about how it can be adversely affected by a decline in stock prices when it is primarily invested in equities, and how interest rate risks affect it when it has shifted to fixed-income securities.

2. *Risk/Return Bar Chart and Table*. The bar chart must show the annual total return for the fund for the previous ten years, or since inception. The table must show the fund's average annual return for the past 1, 5, and 10 years, to the extent available, and must show how these compare to a broad measure of market performance. The C/Fund, for example, uses Standard and Poor's Composite Index of 500 Stocks (the S&P 500) as a comparison. The fund must also show the highest and lowest quarterly return it has achieved over the ten-year period. The C/Fund's performance has ranged from a low of -9.7 percent in third quarter, 1990, to a high of 17.1 percent in fourth quarter, 1998.

Finally, to make it absolutely, positively clear that risk is involved in mutual fund investing, the SEC also requires that all funds, except money market funds, state simply and explicitly in this section of the prospectus that losing money is a risk of investing in the fund. The C/Fund's version is representative: on page 1 of the prospectus it states flatly:

"As with all marketable securities, risk of price declines of Fund securities is unavoidable."

While there is evidence that many investors do not actually read and understand a fund's prospectus before investing, the prospectus remains the single most important source of information about a fund.[7] A lively public debate usually ensues from any SEC proposal for significant change to mutual fund prospectus rules.

The Statement of Additional Information

The SAI contains information that the SEC has determined does not need to be in the prospectus to ensure investor protection, but that some investors may find useful. Regulations do not require a fund to provide the SAI unless the investor specifically requests it, and the SAI cannot substitute for the prospectus. Items 10 through 22 of Form N-1A comprise the SAI.

10. *Cover page and table of contents.* In addition to the fund's name and the effective date, the SAI must state on its cover that it is not a prospectus, and tell the reader how to get a copy of the prospectus.

11. *Fund history.* This tells when the fund was organized, in what form, and under what state's jurisdiction. If the fund changed its name—as the C/Funds did, in the example in the Appendix— this must also be disclosed.

12. *Description of the fund and its investments and risks.* This section expands upon the information in the prospectus, discussing fund policies in more detail. For example, the C/Funds prospectus summarizes investment policies and risks in less than one page, while its SAI treats these same subjects in a four-page, detailed discussion. Among other things, the C/Funds' SAI details the investment restrictions under which the funds operate, restrictions that can be changed only by approval of the shareholders.

13. *Management of the fund.* The SAI identifies the members of the fund's board of directors or trustees, their affiliations, and how much compensation they receive, both from the fund and from the fund complex in total. The C/Funds pay their non-affiliated directors the modest sum of $4,300 per year, while their affiliated directors receive no additional compensation beyond what they receive for their duties with the management company.

14. *Control persons and principal holders of securities.* The SAI must disclose who, if anyone, controls the fund by owning more than 25 percent of its voting securities. It also lists any principal holders: individuals or institutions holding 5 percent or more of the shares. The C/Funds example shows some owners of 5 percent or more of some of their funds.

15. *Investment advisory and other services.* The SAI disclosure expands on that contained in the prospectus. It requires the fund to identify the investment adviser and any persons affiliated with both the fund and the adviser; and describe the fee arrangement, and the amount of fees paid to the adviser over the past three years. The fund must provide similar information for its principal underwriter and other service providers.

16. *Brokerage allocation and other practices.* The fund must describe how portfolio transactions are executed, and its policies for selecting brokers. It must also disclose its aggregate brokerage commissions over the past three years, and disclose the specific commission amounts paid to any brokers affiliated with the fund. The C/Funds paid relatively modest brokerage commissions of about $40,000—an effective rate of less than 2 basis points—in 1998, due to their low portfolio turnover.

17. *Capital stock and other securities.* The fund must provide certain information for each class of capital stock of the fund. For most open-end funds that do not issue multiple classes of capital stock with different shareholder rights, this item is as straightforward as that of the C/Funds example in the Appendix.

18. *Purchase, redemption, and pricing of shares.* This section typically repeats and perhaps expands upon the information contained in Item 7 of the prospectus. For example, the C/Funds prospectus merely states that a shareholder may request a certificate in writing, while the SAI describes the request procedure and points out that issuance of certificates is discouraged due to the additional cost involved.

19. *Taxation of the fund.* This item also expands upon the information in the prospectus. The C/Funds, for example, merely state in the prospectus that they are qualified for pass-through status under Subchapter M of the IRS code, whereas they describe in the SAI what actions they take to maintain that status.

20. *Underwriters.* The fund must identify its principal underwriters, and the aggregate amount of underwriting commissions it paid in the past three years. As pure no-load funds, the C/Funds paid no explicit underwriting commissions, since the management company provides that service as part of what it does for its 100 basis point advisory fee.

21. *Calculation of performance data.* The fund specifies exactly how it calculates the performance figures it reports. The C/Funds describe how they calculate total return for their funds, as well as how they calculate 30-day yield for bond funds.

22. *Financial statements.* The funds must provide the most recent annual and semi-annual reports. The C/Funds do as most funds do, and incorporate this information by reference, explaining how one can obtain the two reports.

For the investor attempting to understand the total picture of a fund's investment policies, relationships, and expenses, the SAI contains some essential information that is not available in the prospectus. Getting an SAI isn't always as straightforward as it would appear to be, however. While most funds make the prospectus available for download via the Internet, fewer provide the SAI that way. And Livingston and O'Neal, when conducting their study of fund brokerage costs in the early 1990s, found that it often took repeated requests to get the SAI (and 60 out of the 300 funds they contacted never did send an SAI at all).[8] Today, one can download a roughly-formatted SAI for most funds from the SEC's Electronic Data Gathering and Retrieval (EDGAR) system, via the SEC's web site (http://www.sec.gov).

Other Information

Finally, Part C of Form N-1A requires "Other Information" that becomes part of the public record, but which is not normally distributed to investors. This includes such items as the fund's articles of incorporation, detailed information about personnel employed by the investment adviser or serving as a director or trustee, the location of the fund's accounts and records, and any other relevant information about service contracts not provided in the prospectus or SAI.

The Profile

In 1995, the SEC launched an experiment aimed at improving disclosure to investors by having funds provide a simplified, standardized document called the profile prospectus. Four pages long, the profile prospectus comprised nine specific pieces of information appearing in a standardized sequence. During 1995 and 1996, eight fund groups participated in a trial run. As a result of the trial, the SEC decided to allow funds the option of offering a profile instead of a prospectus to a potential investor, if the investor so chooses.

While some fund groups prepare the profile today, most do not. The profile cannot completely replace the prospectus—an investor may always request to see the full prospectus even if the fund provides a profile. Thus many funds see the profile as a duplication of effort—something else they must keep up-to-date, print, and mail. Also, some fund groups worry that the shorter document might expose them to charges of not adequately disclosing information about their funds.[9]

Categories of Funds

Any sufficiently complex set of objects may be categorized in a number of different ways, and mutual funds are no exception. Most of the schemes one will encounter, however, classify a fund based on some combination of its stated investment objective, the types of assets it holds, and how it selects those assets. Does the fund pursue capital growth, income, or both? Does it hold stocks, bonds, or both, and in what countries or regions are the issuers of those securities? Does it select stocks based on a qualitative evaluation of the issuing company's prospects, or on a technical analysis of stock price patterns? Does it hold corporate or government debt securities? The list goes on and on.

Classification schemes impose a conceptual order upon the otherwise overwhelming mass of detail about individual funds. They also allow for meaningful comparisons among funds. Investors can use them to determine which funds are appropriate for their portfolios, e.g., which funds should be considered for long-term capital appreciation. Ratings organizations can use them to compare funds to indices, e.g., which funds' performance should be evaluated against the performance of the Wilshire 4500. Fund management companies can use them to measure fund performance against peers, e.g., how well has this government long-term bond fund performed as compared to other government long-term bond funds.

There are enough different mutual fund categorization schemes that we could talk about taxonomies of taxonomies. Instead, we will merely review three of the most commonly used categorization schemes—those formulated by the industry trade association, ICI, and two research and rating agencies—Morningstar and Lipper. All three schemes (and, indeed, almost all other fund classification schemes) start with the basic breakdown of equity, long-term fixed income, and money market funds, and extend it to finer categorizations. The three schemes differ slightly from one another, reflecting the different purposes for which they are intended.

The Investment Company Institute

The ICI collects data on mutual fund activity—sales, redemptions, reinvestments, net exchanges, and other items—and publishes this data monthly. For the purposes of publishing this summary data, the ICI groups funds into six major investment categories: stock, hybrid, taxable bond, municipal bond, taxable money market, and tax exempt money market. Within these six broad categories, it recognizes thirty-three specific investment objectives that funds pursue (see Table 1 at the end of this chapter).

A scan of the ICI categories reveals that they primarily reflect what types of securities the funds hold. Within the major asset class breakdowns, funds are further subdivided according to more specific security selection criteria (e.g., from a particular geographic region, from a particular industrial sector, issued by a particular state). The ICI's categorization scheme has changed over time as the number of funds has increased. In 1998, the ICI increased the number of distinct categories it recognized from twenty-one to thirty-three. In its role as the industry association, the ICI offers no comments or analysis on the performance of particular funds. It merely collects and publishes data about fund categories for research purposes. The ICI puts a particular fund into a category based on the prospectus description of the fund's investment objective and policies.

Morningstar

Established in 1984, Morningstar, Inc., provides investors with information, analysis, and research, including ratings and other comparative data for mutual funds. Morningstar does evaluate the performance of individual funds, using its fund categories as the basis for comparing funds to their peers. Morningstar used to classify funds according to their stated objectives, but changed in 1996 to base its scheme on what the funds actually hold.[10] Research had shown that simply using prospectus language resulted in misclassification of a significant proportion of funds, especially among equity funds.[11] Prospectus language allows funds enough latitude that they may drift into patterns of holdings that no longer match those described in the prospectus as they pursue higher returns.

Morningstar divides the long-term mutual fund universe into four basic groups: Domestic stock funds, international stock funds, taxable fixed-income funds, and tax-free municipal-bond funds. (Morningstar does not categorize or rate money market funds.) Morningstar subdivides these broad categories into forty-nine specific categories for publication of group returns. Found at the end of this chapter, Table 2 lists the forty-nine Morningstar fund categories as of late 1999. Morningstar aims primarily at the investor as it categorizes funds. "We wanted to group funds that have meaningful clusters of characteristics," a Morningstar spokesman declared. "Investors should be able to identify a group by a label and then be able to pick a fund from that group."[12]

Morningstar uses twenty-eight equity fund categories to the ICI's nine for three reasons. First, it places U.S. general stock funds into nine groups based on the size of companies whose stocks the funds hold, and the fund's investment philosophy (growth, value, or blend). Second, it identifies nine categories of sector funds, whereas the ICI lumps them all into one category. Finally, it identifies nine categories of international stock funds (based on specific regions in which the fund invests) to the ICI's two. The differences between Morningstar and ICI bond categories are smaller, attributable mostly to Morningstar's recognition of specific New York and California tax-exempt bond fund categories.

Lipper

Lipper Analytical Services started providing fund information in 1973. (Acquired by Reuters in 1998, the firm today simply calls itself Lipper.) Whereas Morningstar aims primarily at investors and financial advisers, Lipper earns the bulk of its revenues from the fund companies. Many management companies base at least part of their portfolio managers' compensation on how well their funds do as compared to their counterparts within the Lipper categories.

Because funds use the categories as a basis for compensation, Lipper employs a relatively large number of narrowly defined categories—eighty-four in all. In 1999, Lipper revised its categories for U.S. stock funds, in recognition that its old approach (based on prospectus language) was not sufficiently precise. Similar to Morningstar, Lipper changed to categories that reflect what the funds actually do. This caused a furor in some parts of the industry, since it resulted in a number of funds being reclassified, potentially affecting how funds stack up against rivals, and, therefore, how managers are compensated.[13] Table 3 shows the Lipper categories as of late 1999.

Approaches to Investment Decision Making

Few issues generate more heated discussion in investment management circles than do approaches to investment decision making. In a sense, this topic resembles religion—men and women of good faith can, and do, consider the same reality and come to diametrically opposed conclusions. Bill Griffeth's 1995 book *Mutual Fund Masters* contains interviews with eighteen well-known and eminently successful investment managers.[14] Reading this book, one is struck by the number of times that one of the masters flatly contradicts a prescription made by one of the other masters. One says you should start analyses of emerging markets with the government econometric reports, another says to ignore those reports. One says to pick common stocks by understanding the fundamentals of the companies themselves, another says to look at the patterns in the prices of companies' stocks. The list of examples goes on and on.

An exhaustive discussion of investment decision making alternatives, if indeed it is even possible, would itself fill a book. This section merely highlights a few of the major, commonly encountered approaches, to illustrate the range of possibilities.

COMBINING RISK AND RETURN: THE MORNINGSTAR STARS

Americans like for critics to sum up their critiques with simple measures of overall goodness. Thus movie reviewers give one or two thumbs up; *Michelin* tells us where the five star restaurants are; *Consumer Reports* summarizes its product analyses with patterns in little circles. We see this reflected even in business to business communications, as when Moody's and Standard and Poor conduct exhaustive analyses of companies, and then summarize them with short letter/number ratings. And ratings can carry great weight—five stars from *Michelin* or an AAA rating from Moody's has large financial ramifications for the organization that receives it.

Morningstar, Inc. has achieved a similar effect with its star ratings for mutual funds. Many investors use this popular fund rating scheme as a navigation beacon marking the channel to good fund investment. One study in 1996 found that 90 percent of the new money that flowed into equity mutual funds in 1995 went to funds with four or five star ratings from Morningstar.[15] In 1997, *SmartMoney* named Morningstar's president Don Phillips as the fourth most influential individual in the industry after Michael Price, John Bogle, and Ned Johnson. "It's no wonder fund companies get so worked up over Morningstar ratings," *SmartMoney* commented. "If a fund can get four or five stars … it's almost assured a big rush of cash. In the five months since Invesco started advertising the five stars earned by Strategic Financial Services, its assets have grown by 37 percent."[16]

The Morningstar stars have become so widely accepted at least in part because they indicate the historical risk-adjusted performance of a fund in a straightforward, easily understood way. Morningstar follows a four-step procedure to determine a fund's star rating.

1. ***Determine the fund's Morningstar return***. First, Morningstar calculates the fund's excess return—that is, the difference between the fund's return (adjusted for sales load) and the 90-day Treasury bill rate, which is considered to be the risk-free benchmark. Morningstar also calculates this excess return figure for the major fund group (domestic stock funds, international stock funds, taxable bond funds, and municipal bond funds) as a whole. Finally, it divides the individual fund's excess return by that of the group. This gives a measure of how well the fund did at generating excess return, as compared to its peers within the group to which it belongs.

2. ***Determine the fund's Morningstar risk.*** Morningstar determines the average underperformance of the fund. For those months in which the fund's excess return was negative, i.e., it did less well than the 90-day T-bill rate, Morningstar adds up these negative returns and averages them over the evaluation period. It does the same for the fund group, and divides the fund's average underperformance by that of the group. This measures how badly the fund underperformed as compared to the group.

3. ***Calculate the fund's raw rating.*** The raw Morningstar rating is simply the risk score subtracted from the return score. Thus a fund is rewarded for outperforming its peers, but penalized for having months in which it underperformed the benchmark.

4. ***Rank funds and assign stars.*** Finally, Morningstar ranks the funds according to their raw scores within the major fund category, and assigns stars. The top 10 percent of funds get five stars; the next 22.5 percent get four stars; the next 35 percent, three stars; the next 22.5 percent, two stars; and the bottom 10 percent get one star. Morningstar does this for three, five, and ten year periods, and then combines the result into an overall rating.

A five-star fund, therefore, has demonstrated a risk-adjusted performance superior to 90 percent of its peers, at least according to the Morningstar methodology. While some observers have argued that the star rating oversimplifies a complex and subtle concept, the consuming public has clearly embraced it, much as it has the *Michelin* restaurant ratings.

Active versus Passive Management

Can any individual or group of individuals, even professional portfolio managers, consistently pick securities that are winners? That is the crux of the question that divides the proponents of active management from those of passive management. The passive management school's argument, made most visibly in Burton Malkiel's *A Random Walk Down Wall Street* contends that financial markets are so efficient* that they make it impossible for active managers to consistently outperform market averages.[17] Passive managers, therefore, do not attempt to select individual securities, but rather match the composition of a segment of the market. Typically, they attempt to match a major benchmark index such as the S&P 500 or the Lehman Intermediate Term Government Bond Index. A passively managed fund (or index fund) can usually operate at a lower expense ratio than an actively managed one, because it requires no expenditures on portfolio manager expertise or research, and it minimizes trading costs.

Active managers attempt to outperform market averages using various investment techniques, succeeding sometimes and failing sometimes. The allure for the investor, of course, is the potential of finding a fund whose manager will succeed in outperforming the market during the period the investor holds the fund. At least one researcher analyzing mutual fund performance has found evidence that (1) some funds consistently outperform the market; and (2) sophisticated investors direct assets to these funds.[18] (Most academic research, however, tends to support the passive management argument.)[19] Actively managed funds typically have higher expense ratios than index funds, for the reasons cited above.

The argument between proponents of active and passive management has continued unabated for over twenty years. It has prompted both scholarly research and emotional name-calling. Any discussion here will certainly fail to resolve it. An interested reader can easily find numerous books and articles weighing in on either side of the argument.

Active equity fund managers employ a variety of investment strategies and styles to select the securities that they believe will outperform the market. They may base their investment decisions on analysis of the issuing companies, on the state of the financial markets, on economic trends, on patterns in stock prices, on combinations of these factors. Active bond fund managers make their selections according to such factors as interest rate forecasts, the impact of securities on the maturity time span of the portfolio, and the credit quality of the issuer. The next few paragraphs describe some of the more prominent methods active managers take to select securities and construct their portfolios.

---

* *Efficient* in this context means that at any point the market has assimilated all the available information about a security and reflected this information in its price. An investor or portfolio manager cannot possibly pick undervalued stocks, since the market has already taken into account any information the investor or manager possesses (except for insider information, which could only be used illegally).

Top-Down Versus Bottom-Up Portfolio Construction

The top-down manager starts the selection process by identifying general economic trends and incorporating them into specific market and economic forecasts. He or she then selects industries and companies that should benefit from those trends. The bottom-up investment manager considers individual stocks before industry, sector, country, and economic factors. This approach assumes that individual companies can prosper, even when the industry or economy is not performing well.

Growth Versus Value Stock Selection

Growth and value managers represent two fundamentally different approaches to selecting common stocks. Growth investing attempts to identify companies that promise dramatic revenue or earnings increases. These companies are typically smaller to medium-sized firms that are expanding into new or existing markets or developing new products. For the most part, growth managers don't mind paying higher prices to get the right stocks and taking more risk to achieve greater return. Growth managers tend to do very well during the advanced stages of a bull market when investors become more aggressive, pushing the markets to new highs.

Value investing attempts to identify out-of-favor companies, whose stock has a good potential to increase in price. These stocks are generally characterized by lower-than-average yields. Value managers usually have a lower turnover of securities in their portfolios and assume less risk than growth-oriented managers. They tend to hold large cash positions at market peaks, when bargains are presumably rarer. In general, value managers do best when the economy is coming out of a slump and undervalued companies begin to recover.

Fundamental Versus Technical Analysis

Fundamental analysis involves study of the issuing company itself—its financial statements and other quantitative data, plus qualitative assessments of factors such as the company's management, physical plant, and market presence. Although different managers have different ways of analyzing these fundamentals, they all attempt to estimate a value for the company's stock that can be compared to the current marketplace. If the manager finds that the current market price is lower than the computed value, then the stock is considered underpriced and a candidate for buying.

Technical analysts, sometimes called chartists, focus on the details of quantitatively measurable data—on changes in the price of particular stocks or of short interest in the market, for example. They attempt to find patterns in past behavior that they can use to match to current patterns and thereby predict future price behavior. In recent years, some researchers have attempted to employ computer artificial intelligence—most often, neural nets—to perform these technical analyses, detect patterns, and predict price movement.

Market Timing

Market timers attempt to predict how the prices will trend for individual stocks, stock groups or the market as a whole. They attempt to determine the right times to buy and sell by analyzing technical factors behind the supply and demand for stocks, such as volume and price, often using charts or computer programs.

Asset Allocation

Asset allocators focus on the anticipated risks and returns of the various asset classes—stocks, bonds, and cash—given certain assumptions about economic growth, interest rates, market valuations, and other fundamental indicators. They continually adjust their portfolio composition among the classes, and individual security selection is accorded secondary importance. The C/Funds, for example, employ an asset allocation strategy, moving holdings between equity and fixed-income securities according to forecasts of economic conditions.

Group Rotation

These managers try to find stock groups that will outperform others at a particular time. They analyze macro-economic trends and how a particular economic cycle may unfold and affect various industrial sectors. For example, they might examine economic forecasts involving unemployment and disposable income to make judgements on how companies producing consumer durable items might fare. They then concentrate their investments in those sectors that the trend should benefit.

Momentum Investing

These investors attempt to find and exploit factors that are currently pushing or about to push a stock's price upward. Some momentum investors focus on the issuing companies—their earnings, cash flow, and other statistics, and especially any surprises about these. Other momentum investors look at the stock prices themselves, emphasizing the degree to which a stock is outperforming, or underperforming, the market index or other stocks in its group.

Every mutual fund is free to select a style that its managers believe will best meet the investment objectives. The fund is obligated, however, to disclose this choice in the prospectus and SAI, and to adhere to its stated principal investment strategies as it operates.

Implications for Operations

The next two chapters will focus on the fund manufacturing process, the investment management front- and back-office operations, as depicted in Figure 1. How a fund company goes about carrying out these functions, particularly those of the front office, is heavily conditioned by the decisions it has made about the fund's investment objectives and philosophy. Two aspects of front-office operations are particularly affected.

1. *Investment Analysis and Decision Making*. The amount and type of research and analysis investment managers carry out vary tremendously from manager to manager. At one end of the scale, passive managers make no attempt whatsoever to analyze individual securities. At the other end, active managers undertake a wide range of quantitative and qualitative analyses to identify particular securities to buy or sell. The nature of these analyses, and therefore the tools and type of information used, depend on the asset types the manager is considering and the investment decision-making style he or she employs.

2. *Trade Order Management.* As we will see in the next chapter, trading in equity securities differs significantly from trading in fixed-income securities. In addition, the investment management philosophy is the primary determinant of the rate at which a fund manager trades. For example, passive managers do relatively little trading, while aggressive active managers may turn their portfolios over several times per year. In another example, the trading pattern for a manager who selects individual stocks based on analyses of company fundamentals will differ greatly from that of a manager who rotates the portfolio into and out of sectors.

Back-office functions are less affected by investment strategy, tending to be more standardized than those of the front office. They differ mostly according to the asset types the fund handles. For example, accounting entries for bonds differ from those of stocks, and foreign securities require different accounting than do domestic issues. Every fund company must perform or arrange for all the basic back-office functions—settlement, custody, accounting, and reporting—regardless of how the portfolio manager makes investment decisions.

Table 1: Investment Company Institute Fund Categories and Descriptions

STOCK FUNDS

1. **Aggressive growth** funds invest primarily in common stock of small, growth companies with potential for capital appreciation.
2. **Emerging market equity** funds invest primarily in equity securities of companies based in less-developed regions of the world.
3. **Global equity** funds invest primarily in worldwide equity securities, including those of U.S. companies.
4. **Growth and income** funds attempt to combine long-term capital growth with steady income dividends. These funds pursue this goal by investing primarily in common stocks of established companies with the potential for both growth and good dividends.
5. **Growth** funds invest primarily in common stocks of well-established companies with the potential for capital appreciation. These funds' primary aim is to increase the value of their investments (capital gain) rather than generate a flow of dividends.
6. **Income equity** funds seek income by investing primarily in equity securities of companies with good dividends. Capital appreciation is not an objective.
7. **International equity** funds invest at least two-thirds of their portfolios in equity securities of companies located outside the United States.
8. **Regional equity** funds invest in equity securities of companies based in specific world regions, such as Europe, Latin America, the Pacific Region, or individual countries.
9. **Sector equity** funds seek capital appreciation by investing in companies in related fields or specific industries, such as financial services, health care, natural resources, technology, or utilities.

BOND FUNDS

10. **Corporate bond – general** funds seek a high level of income by investing two-thirds or more of their portfolios in corporate bonds and have no explicit restrictions on average maturity.
11. **Corporate bond – intermediate term** funds seek a high level of income with two-thirds or more of their portfolios invested at all times in corporate bonds. Their average maturity is five to ten years.
12. **Corporate bond – short-term** funds seek a high level of current income with two-thirds or more of their portfolios invested at all times in corporate bonds. Their average maturity is one to five years.
13. **Global bond – general** funds invest in worldwide debt securities and have no stated average maturity or an average maturity of more than five years. Up to 25 percent of their portfolios' securities (not including cash) may be invested in companies located in the United States.
14. **Global bond – short-term** funds invest in worldwide debt securities and have an average maturity of one to five years. Up to 25 percent of their portfolios' securities (not including cash) may be invested in companies located in the United States.
15. **Government bond – general** funds invest at least two-thirds of their portfolios in U.S. government securities and have no stated average maturity.
16. **Government bond – intermediate** term funds invest at least two-thirds of their portfolios in U.S. government securities and have an average maturity of five to ten years.
17. **Government bond – short-term** funds invest at least two-thirds of their portfolios in U.S. government securities and have an average maturity of one to five years.
18. **High yield** funds seek a high level of current income by investing at least two-thirds of their portfolios in lower-rated corporate bonds (Baa or lower by Moody's and BBB or lower by Standard and Poor's rating services).
19. **Mortgage-backed** funds invest at least two-thirds of their portfolios in pooled mortgage-backed securities.

20. **National municipal bond – general** funds invest predominantly in municipal bonds and have an average maturity of more than five years or no stated average maturity. The funds' bonds are usually exempt from federal income tax but may be taxed under state and local laws.

21. **National municipal bond – short-term** funds invest predominantly in municipal bonds and have an average maturity of one to five years. The funds' bonds are usually exempt from federal income tax but may be taxed under state and local laws.

22. **Other world bond** funds invest at least two-thirds of their portfolios in a combination of foreign government and corporate debt. Some funds in this category invest primarily in debt securities of emerging markets.

23. **State municipal bond – general** funds invest primarily in municipal bonds of a single state and have an average maturity of more than five years or no stated average maturity. The funds' bonds are exempt from federal and state income taxes for residents of that state.

24. **State municipal bond – short-term** funds invest predominantly in municipal bonds of a single state and have an average maturity of one to five years. The funds' bonds are exempt from federal and state income taxes for residents of that state.

25. **Strategic income** funds invest in a combination of domestic fixed-income securities to provide high current income.

HYBRID FUNDS

26. **Asset allocation** funds seek high total return by investing in a mix of equities, fixed-income securities and money market instruments. Unlike Flexible Portfolio funds (defined below), these funds are required to strictly maintain a precise weighting in asset classes.

27. **Balanced** funds invest in a specific mix of equity securities and bonds with the three-part objective of conserving principal, providing income and achieving long-term growth of both principal and income.

28. **Flexible portfolio** funds seek high total return by investing in common stock, bonds and other debt securities, and money market securities. Portfolios may hold up to 100 percent of any one of these types of securities and may easily change, depending on market conditions.

29. **Income mixed** funds seek a high level of current income by investing in a variety of income-producing securities, including equities and fixed-income securities. Capital appreciation is not a primary objective.

MONEY MARKET FUNDS

30. **National tax-exempt money market** funds seek income not taxed by the federal government by investing in municipal securities with relatively short maturities.

31. **State tax-exempt money market** funds invest predominantly in short-term municipal obligations of a single state, which are exempt from federal and state income taxes for residents of that state.

32. **Taxable money market – government** funds invest principally in short-term U.S. Treasury obligations and other short-term financial instruments issued or guaranteed by the U.S. government, its agencies or instrumentalities.

33. **Taxable money market – non-government** funds invest in a variety of money market instruments, including certificates of deposit of large banks, commercial paper and banker's acceptances.

Table 2: Morningstar Fund Categories

U.S. Stock Funds
1. Large-Capitalization Value
2. Large-Capitalization Blend
3. Large-Capitalization Growth
4. Mid-Capitalization Value
5. Mid-Capitalization Blend
6. Mid-Capitalization Growth
7. Small-Capitalization Value
8. Small-Capitalization Blend
9. Small-Capitalization Growth
10. Specialty Communications
11. Specialty Financial
12. Specialty Health
13. Specialty Natural Resources
14. Specialty Precious Metals
15. Specialty Real Estate
16. Specialty Technology
17. Specialty Utilities
18. Specialty Unaligned
19. U.S. Hybrid
20. Convertibles

Taxable Bond
21. Government Long-Term
22. Government Intermediate-Term
23. Government Short-Term
24. General Long-Term
25. General Intermediate-Term
26. General Short-Term
27. General Ultrashort-Term
28. International Bond
29. High-Yield Bond
30. Multisector Bond
31. Emerging Markets Bond

International Stock
32. Europe
33. Latin America
34. Diversified Emerging Markets
35. Pacific/Asia
36. Pacific/Asia (no Japan)
37. Japan
38. Diversified Foreign
39. Diversified World
40. International Hybrid

Municipal (Tax-free) Bond
41. Muni National Long-Term
42. Muni National Intermediate-Term
43. Muni Single State Long-Term
44. Muni Single State Intermediate-Term
45. Muni Bond
46. Muni New York Long-Term
47. Muni New York Intermediate-Term
48. Muni California Long-Term
49. Muni California Intermediate-Term

Source: Morningstar News Release, January 12, 1999.

Table 3: Lipper Open-End Fund Classifications

General Equity Funds
1. Capital Appreciation Funds
2. Equity Income Funds
3. Growth Funds
4. Growth & Income Funds
5. Micro-Cap Funds
6. Mid-Cap Funds
7. Small-Cap Funds
8. S&P 500 Index Objective Funds

Sector Equity Funds
9. Environmental Funds.
10. Financial Services Funds
11. Health/Biotechnology
12. Natural Resources Funds Real Estate Funds
13. Science & Technology
14. Specialty & Miscellaneous
15. Utility Funds
16. Telecommunication Funds

World Equity Funds
17. Canadian Funds
18. China Region Funds
19. Emerging Markets Funds
20. European Region Funds
21. Global Funds
22. Global Small-Cap Funds
23. Gold-Oriented Funds
24. International Funds
25. International Small-Cap Funds
26. Japanese Funds
27. Latin American Funds
28. Pacific ex Japan Funds
29. Pacific Region Funds

Mixed Equity Funds
30. Balanced Funds
31. Balanced Target Maturity Funds
32. Convertible Securities Funds
33. Flexible Portfolio Funds
34. Global Flexible Portfolio Funds
35. Income Funds
36. Ultra Short Obligation Funds

Short/Intermediate-Term U.S. Treasury and Government Funds
37. Intermediate U.S. Treasury Funds
38. Intermediate U.S. Government Funds
39. Short-Intermediate U.S. Government Funds
40. Short U.S. Government Funds
41. Short U.S. Treasury Funds

Short/Intermediate-Term Corporate Fixed-Income Funds
42. Intermediate Investment Grade Debt Funds
43. Short Investment Grade Debt Funds
44. Short-Intermediate Investment Grade Debt Funds

General Domestic Taxable Fixed-Income Funds
45. Adjustable Rate Mortgage Funds
46. Corporate Debt Funds A Rated
47. Corporate Debt Funds BBB Rated
48. Flexible Income Funds
49. General Bond Funds
50. General U.S. Government Funds
51. General U.S. Treasury Funds
52. GNMA Funds
53. High Current Yield Funds
54. Multi-Sector Income Funds
55. Target Maturity Funds
56. U.S. Mortgage Funds

World Taxable Fixed-Income Funds
57. Emerging Markets Debt Funds
58. Global Income Funds
59. International Income Funds
60. Short World Multi-Market Income Funds

Short/Intermediate Municipal Debt Funds
61. Intermediate Municipal Debt Funds
62. Short/Intermediate Municipal Debt Funds
63. Short Municipal Debt Funds

General Municipal Debt Funds
64. General Municipal Debt Funds
65. High Yield Municipal Debt Funds
66. Insured Municipal Debt Funds
67. Other States Intermediate Municipal Debt Funds
68. Other States Short/Intermediate Municipal Debt Funds
69. Single-State Municipal Debt Funds
70. California Short/Intermediate Municipal Debt Funds
71. Florida Intermediate Municipal Debt Funds
72. Florida Insured Municipal Funds
73. Massachusetts Intermediate Municipal Debt Funds
74. New York Intermediate Municipal Debt Funds
75. New York Insured Municipal Debt Funds
76. Pennsylvania Intermediate Municipal Debt Funds
77. Virginia Intermediate Municipal Debt Funds

Money Market Funds (Taxable)
78. Institutional U.S. Government Money Market Funds
79. Institutional U.S. Treasury Money Market Funds
80. Institutional Money Market Funds
81. Money Market Instrument Funds
82. U.S. Government Money Market Funds
83. U.S. Treasury Money Market Funds

Money Market Funds (Municipal)
84. California, Connecticut, Massachusetts, Michigan, New Jersey, New York, Ohio, Pennsylvania, and Other States Tax-Exempt Money Market Funds
85. Institutional Tax-Exempt Money Market Funds
86. Tax-Exempt Money Market Funds

CHAPTER 5

The Investment Management Front Office

*The fundamental reason for the huge success of mutual funds was a
simple promise: performance. ... You could turn your money over to
a [fund manager] confident that his hard work, meticulous research,
and peculiar genius would deliver consistently superior returns.*

— David Whitford (1999)[1]

The Investment Management Cycle

In pursuit of performance, active mutual fund managers (indeed, all active investment managers) carry out a
never-ending cycle of analyzing investment opportunities, making buy and sell decisions, ordering, executing,
and settling trades, maintaining and analyzing portfolio records, reporting the results of their activity, and
launching back into the decision process. (Passive managers do all of this except the analysis and decision
making.) Figure 1 graphically depicts the components of this investment management cycle. The investment
management organization—the fund's *investment adviser*—employs people in several distinct roles. These
people interact with one another as well as with systems that store and maintain data about the portfolio of
securities held by the fund. They also interact with external parties—information providers, brokers, trading
partners, depositories, clearing houses, and custodians—as they carry out the investment management cycle.
Collectively, their activities comprise the process of investment management, and are the focus of the next three
chapters.

Figure 1: The Investment Management Cycle

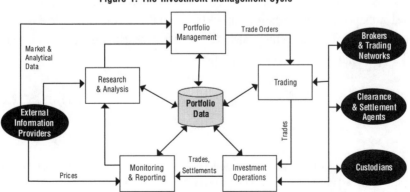

Industry observers commonly divide the steps in the investment management cycle into two main components:

- *Front-office* functions, which involve making investment decisions and implementing them via trading; and
- *Back-office* functions, which comprise the administrative, record keeping, and reporting activities that occur after the trade is made.[*]

Front- and back-office functions differ fundamentally in nature. Within a management company, they are performed by completely different groups of people, and are often performed by completely separate organizations. Some mutual fund management companies do them all. In some cases, the management company performs the front-office functions (portfolio decision making and trading) internally, and contracts out back-office functions to a service provider. In other cases, fund managers contract with separate sub-advisory organizations to perform some or all of the front-office functions.

This chapter focuses on the investment management front-office, and what it does for a mutual fund, while Chapter 6 covers back-office functions. Front-office functions fall into two major groups. First, investment managers must *decide* what to buy and sell. Active managers engage in research and analysis to identify securities that are and aren't attractive, match these to the needs of their portfolio to invest or produce cash, and order trades. Passive managers do no research—the makeup of a passive portfolio of securities is determined by the makeup of the benchmark it mirrors. Both types of managers strive to make their funds' portfolios of securities conform to their investment objectives. Second, once they have decided, investment managers *trade*. Both active and passive managers engage in trade order management—the process of creating orders to buy or sell securities, transmitting them to the appropriate brokers or trading networks, and executing trades with these counterparties.

These front-office activities are the primary determinants of how well a fund performs relative to the market. Active fund managers hope to outperform the market by astute securities selection and efficient trading. An active manager succeeds to the extent that he or she identifies the right securities to buy, or sell, and executes trades to buy, or sell, them at favorable prices. Passive managers aim to match the market performance (as defined by the performance of the benchmark) with as little cost drag as possible. A passive manager succeeds to the extent that he or she efficiently matches the fund to its benchmark, particularly when cash must flow in or out of the portfolio.

---

[*] Some in the industry also identify an investment management "middle office," concerned with reporting and control of trade activity. Since there is not universal agreement as to the definition of the middle office, we do not use it here.

Investment Analysis and Portfolio Management

Investment analysis lies completely within the realm of active management. Industry observers describe the analysis and decision making activities investment managers carry out with a mix of somewhat over-lapping terms. *Research* generally refers to the process of gathering data from various sources that can help identify buy or sell opportunities. *Analysis* refers primarily to processing that data into useful information, although some people use the term broadly to include research. *Portfolio management*, narrowly defined, means making buy and sell decisions based on the results of research and analysis and the current state of the fund's portfolio of securities. This is how we use the term in this chapter. However, some people use the term portfolio management much more broadly, to encompass all the activities that result in portfolio decisions, including research and analysis. All these functions collectively comprise the investment adviser's role.

Different fund managers organize their front-office functions differently. In many firms, especially larger ones, the analysts, portfolio managers, and traders are all separate individuals or teams. In some cases, however, portfolio managers prefer to do their own analysis and research. In other cases, particularly among fixed-income funds, portfolio managers may do their own trading. Some of the variation stems simply from personal preference, some from economics. For example, very small managers can't afford separate individuals for the functions. We will discuss the functions in this chapter as though they are performed by separate individuals, but in reality, this is not always the case.

Sometimes, one fund has one portfolio manager, as when Peter Lynch was *the* manager of the Magellan Fund. Many fund companies assign teams of managers to their funds, and some managers and teams handle multiple funds. The fund's prospectus explains how the fund's portfolio management responsibilities are assigned. However the responsibility is structured, the portfolio manager exercises the investment advisory function for the fund, deciding what to buy or sell and when to do so. Active portfolio managers make their buy and sell decisions for two reasons:

1. to respond to cash flows to or from the fund caused by shareholder purchases and redemptions; and
2. to improve the performance of the fund by taking advantage of opportunities they perceive in the securities markets.

Passive portfolio managers must respond to shareholder cash flows, but make no trades in an attempt to improve performance. Since they do not believe that identifying market opportunities is possible, their funds tightly conform to the benchmarks. However, they do buy or sell securities to bring the fund back in line when the benchmark itself has changed. For example, mutual fund management company T. Rowe Price was added to the S&P 500 on October 12, 1999, replacing Data General.

Equity Analysis and Portfolio Management

In actively managed funds, equity analysts attempt to find market opportunities for the portfolio manager. The analysts search for particular stocks or groups of stocks that are either underpriced (buy opportunities) or overpriced (sell opportunities) by the market. Analysts tend to focus on subsets of the overall market, such as companies within certain industrial sectors, and, in some cases, work a specific list of candidate stocks. Ultimately, the analysts issue investment recommendations about particular stocks, similar to those that analysts working for brokerage firms produce for the firms' clients. They pursue a variety of approaches to making these identifications, ranging from the purely qualitative to the purely quantitative.

At the qualitative end of the scale stands the *fundamental analyst*, who attempts to understand the state of a company so as to make predictions about its future earnings. Fundamental analysts not only study the reports published by and about a company, but also interview its management, and even visit the company to observe operations. They study the industry in which the company operates, reading trade journals, and attending conferences. They evaluate how well the company stacks up against others in its industry, and try to anticipate how the industry itself is likely to perform. For example, a fundamental analyst might recommend a particular software company as a potential buy, because research shows that it has good products, sound management, a compelling business plan, and solid financing, and because it is in a segment of the industry that the analyst believes will experience strong growth. The recommendation is even stronger if the analyst can detect a reason why the market mistakenly undervalues the company. Fundamental analysts usually specialize in specific industries or sectors because of the industry expertise their approach requires. Crabbe Huson, for example, explaining how it selects stocks for its Contrarian Fund, describes its fundamental analysis approach: "We ask questions: Is the company healthy? Is there a catalyst for a business or price change? What events may cause that change? What's the potential for profit or loss? Buying decisions are made only after our questions are answered fully."[2]

Quantitative analysts stand at the opposite end of the spectrum from fundamental analysts. Technical analysts, sometimes called chartists, study patterns in prices and volumes within the stock market itself to try to predict how a company's stock may move in the future. (Before the widespread use of computers, technical analysts spent much time drawing graphic charts of prices.) Other quantitative analysts evaluate stocks using computer models that attempt to predict stock prices, or identify over- or under-priced stocks, by looking for correlation between the stock prices and one or more predictor variables, such as economic indicators, or the issuer's financial measures. For example, the prospectus for Scudder's Micro Cap fund describes its quantitative approach: "The fund uses a proprietary computer model to comb through the financial data of each micro-cap company in order to analyze such factors as earning trends, valuation measures and financial strength, and to rank these companies based on their return potential."[3]

Not surprisingly, many if not most fund groups follow neither purely qualitative nor purely quantitative approaches. Many, for example, use some quantitative techniques to develop a large list of candidate stocks for consideration, and then reduce that to a smaller list of stocks to recommend by conducting more qualitative analyses. The advisers for the Goldman Sachs CORE Large Cap Value Fund do this: to pick stocks, they "use the Goldman Sachs' proprietary multifactor model, a rigorous computerized rating system, to forecast the returns of securities," and supplement this with "qualitative fundamental research from the highly-regarded Goldman

Sachs Global Investment Research Department."[4] In other words, once their model suggests that a stock might be a good buy, they take a hard look at the company's fundamentals to see whether they believe it really is.

The portfolio manager uses the analyst's recommendations as one input in making buy and sell decisions. He or she balances these recommendations against the fund's cash flow needs and current composition of the fund's portfolio of securities. (Allstate may be a great buy, for example, but the manager might have to forego it if the portfolio is already over-weighted with insurance stocks.) Portfolio managers operate under constraints from several sources.

- *Regulations*. The 1940 Act and subsequent regulations set boundaries on what portfolio managers can do. For example, a registered fund cannot own more than 5 percent of the outstanding stock of a company, no matter how attractive a buy that stock appears to be.

- *Prospectus Rules.* The portfolio manager must abide by the guidelines laid out in the fund's prospectus. Some prospectuses are very constraining—for example, the Hennessy Leveraged Dogs Fund* requires that the fund hold only those ten stocks within the Dow Jones Industrial Index that currently have the highest dividend yields. Others funds allow the portfolio manager great leeway to pursue performance—for example, the Massachusetts Investor Trust prospectus says the fund holds mostly equities "under normal conditions," and "generally" invests in large cap stocks, but makes no guarantees.[5] And Legg Mason opened a "go-anywhere" fund in 1999 (Legg Mason Opportunity Trust) that industry observers believed was specifically designed to allow a particular high-performing portfolio manager to buy any sort of securities he saw fit without being accused of "style-drift."[6]

- *Policies*. Different management companies set different levels of constraints as a matter of policy. In some fund families, the portfolio managers can do just about anything they want to do that isn't forbidden by the regulations or prospectus. At the other end of the scale, some management companies subject their portfolio managers to strict investment policies. Take the General Electric Funds for example. In 1999, *The Wall Street Journal* described their "taut guidelines" for stock selection.[7] One fund could only buy stocks with a price/earnings to growth ratio of less than 1. Another fund had to maintain all its sector weightings within two percentage points of the weightings within the S&P 500. These, and other GE rules, are neither regulatory nor prospectus requirements, but rather prescriptions set by GE Funds' management.

Compliance monitoring, described in the next chapter, concerns itself with ensuring that the manager is following all the relevant rules.

---

* Michael B. O'Higgins popularized this "Dogs of the Dow" strategy, which several funds pursue, in his 1990 book *Beating the Dow*. It advances the notion that the ten highest yielding stocks in the Dow 30 are depressed in price and will bounce back.

THE MANY WAYS TO SKIN A CAT

Morningstar divides the world of mutual funds into about 50 categories, based on the funds' investment objectives and approach. Even within a category, however, funds have plenty of room to make investment decisions in their own particular ways. Consider, for example, the funds in Morningstar's Emerging Markets Stock Funds category. Most if not all of them have precisely the same investment objective in their prospectuses: long term capital appreciation derived from investing in stocks in emerging market countries. Most of them define emerging markets based on the World Bank's per capita income definition or a similar measure. Most of them state that they will hold primarily equity securities spread among several countries, but reserve the right to move to fixed-income securities when conditions warrant. After that, they start to diverge. Examination of a few prospectuses reveals quite a bit of variation in how exactly they go about pursuing that investment objective.[‡]

- The *Legg Mason Emerging Markets Trust* starts with a list of 1,000 potential stocks from which to choose. The investment adviser uses a combination of "on the ground" fundamental research and quantitative valuation techniques to choose from among the stocks on the list. In parallel with stock selection, management allocates the portfolio among countries based on a separate analysis that "merges quantitative and fundamental approaches."

- Management of the *Dreyfus Emerging Markets Fund* searches for value stocks—ones with low price to book ratios, price to earnings ratios, or other stated characteristics of undervalued stocks. It employs a bottom up style, "focusing first on stock selection then enhanced by broadly diversified country allocation."

- The *Nations Emerging Markets Fund* follows a step-by-step process to select stocks. First, it starts with a list of "800 companies in the most promising markets." It then "uses fundamental research to select 80 to 100 stocks in 15 or more countries" for further analysis. It visits companies to confirm the results of its analyses, and invests in those that pass all the screens.

- Grantham, Mayo, van Otterloo & Co. even draws the investor a picture of how its managers pick securities for the *GMO Evolving Countries Fund*, describing each step in the process. They analyze countries, industrial sectors, and companies in parallel, and then bring it all together in a portfolio construction model that incorporates risk considerations.

Fund Investment Process

[‡] All the information and quotations are taken from the prospectuses for the funds current as of November 1999.

Fixed-Income Analysis and Portfolio Management

As the ICI, Morningstar, and Lipper categorization schemes in the last chapter illustrate, a fixed-income fund usually concentrates on a particular sector of the debt securities market. A fixed-income sector is typically defined by type of issuer (e.g., U.S. Treasury, federal agency, corporation, municipality) and the average maturity of the holdings (e.g., short-term, intermediate-term, long-term). Fixed-income funds can be either actively or passively managed. Passive fixed-income funds simply mirror an index that represents their sector—for example, the Vanguard Short-Term Bond Index Fund seeks to replicate the performance of the Lehman Brothers 1–5 Year Government/Corporate Bond index. Active fixed-income managers attempt to outperform the market in which they compete by picking bonds and/or sectors that are likely to outperform within the portfolio's investable universe.

There are three common approaches used by fixed-income analysts and managers to pursue this goal. They are duration adjustment, relative value analysis, and issue selection. At the heart of all three approaches is an understanding of the spectrum of U.S. Treasury bond yields that represent the risk-free alternative to all other debt instrument investments. These yields, plotted against time (usually for Treasury securities ranging from three months to thirty years in maturity), combine to form the Treasury yield curve—the basis of the entire U.S. fixed-income market.

- *Duration Adjustment*. Successful duration adjustment strategy depends on the accurate prediction of the future direction of interest rates. If a manager expects the economy's general level of interest rates—and, therefore, the general level of bond yields—to fall (typically as a result of macroeconomic forces such as weak economic growth or a Federal Reserve policy bias toward easier credit conditions), he or she will lengthen the average maturity of bonds held in the portfolio. This also increases the portfolio's average duration, a proxy, expressed in years, for the average length of time that a bond investment is outstanding (and a measure of the bond's sensitivity to interest rate changes). Conversely, if the manager expects yields to rise, longer-maturity bonds will be replaced with shorter-maturity securities, and the portfolio's average duration will be shortened.

  A manager may apply duration adjustments to the entire portfolio, or only within a particular maturity segment (short-, intermediate-, or long-term yields), when yield changes are not expected to occur in parallel fashion along the entire curve. In all cases, however, duration adjustments are made *relative* to the portfolio's performance benchmark. Overall, a portfolio's duration will be positioned short of, neutral to, or long of the duration of the market index by which its performance is measured. The successful application of interest rate forecasting and duration adjustment is extremely difficult but can produce spectacular performance results.

- *Relative Value Analysis.* Fixed-income portfolio managers often employ relative value analysis to choose sectors and/or individual securities to hold in a portfolio. Relative value measures the divergence of yield spreads from average historical relationships. For instance, if a portfolio's investment guidelines permit investing in the U.S. Treasury and corporate bond sectors, a manager will follow the historical relationships of Treasury and corporate bond yields at different maturity points along the yield curve. If the corporate yield spread widens (increases) from its average at, say, the ten-year maturity point, the manager will sell Treasury holdings and buy corporate bonds of similar coupon and maturity. Stated another way, the manager noticing the wider yield spread is also recognizing that corporate bonds have underperformed Treasuries and, are therefore historically cheap to Treasuries. The manager's reaction will be to sell Treasuries and buy corporates, waiting until the relative yield relationship has returned to its historical average (meaning that corporates by then will have outperformed Treasuries) before reversing the trade. This strategy is also known as sector rotation. Active relative-value managers employing sector rotation seek to profit from repeatedly exploiting even tiny aberrations in historical yield relationships.

- *Issue Selection*. A portfolio manager uses issue selection to identify individual bond issues with characteristics, either good or bad, that have not been fully reflected in a bond's yield (or, in relative value parlance, in the spread between the bond's yield and the yield of a corresponding Treasury security). From an optimistic perspective, these characteristics might include the issuer's strengthening corporate cash position or undervalued fixed assets, or a likely upgrade in credit rating as provided by one of the major rating agencies such as Moody's or Standard and Poor's.

  A debt security's yield relative to Treasuries is determined in part by its credit risk. The greater the risk of default, the higher the spread a corporate bond's yield must be versus the alternative risk-free Treasury yield to attract buyers. If a fund buys a bond that subsequently receives a credit upgrade, the fund's performance benefits from the tighter spread of the corporate's yield to the underlying Treasury; that is, the bond's price has changed (up or down) *relatively better* than the Treasury's price. As an example, Neuberger Berman describes how its fixed-income analysts do exactly this. They "look for securities that appear underpriced compared to securities of similar structure and credit quality, and securities that appear likely to have their credit ratings raised. In choosing lower-rated securities, the managers look for bonds from issuers whose financial health appears comparatively strong but that are smaller or less well known to investors."[8]

  Prepayment analysis is another component of issue selection. Many debt securities have provisions for being retired before their stated maturity dates. Corporate bonds may be structured with call provisions that give the issuer the right, at its discretion, to redeem the issue ahead of its stated maturity date. Mortgage-backed securities may be partially or entirely retired early if the holders of the underlying mortgages repay those mortgages early, as homeowners typically do when interest rates fall and refinancing becomes popular. All else equal, debt securities with prepayment risks must offer greater yields to offset these risks. Prepayment analysis attempts to discover issues for which the real prepayment risk is less than the perceived risk on which the yield is based. Analysts for a fund that holds mortgage-backed securities, for example, study the characteristics of the mortgages underlying the securities, attempting to find ones that they believe are held by homeowners less likely to refinance than generally believed. They might ask: what kind of homes are they? what's the state of the economy in that region? what pre-payment assumptions were used when the mortgages were securitized?

Two types of analysts are most commonly encountered in fixed-income investment management organizations.

Credit analysts resemble the fundamental analysts of the equity side, in that they study the fundamental situation of the issuer to determine the risk of default associated with the security. Like the equity analysts, they analyze financial results, management quality, industry trends, economic factors, and anything they think sheds light on the issuer's ability to meet the interest and repayment obligations of the debt security. For example, the adviser for the Seligman High Yield Bond Fund selects bonds issued by "companies that it believes display one or more of … strong operating cash flow and margins, improving financial ratios (i.e., creditworthiness), leadership in market share or other competitive advantage, superior management."[9] In other words, the fundamentals of the issuing company indicate that this bond is a good credit risk.

Quantitative analysts develop and run mathematical models to help them understand the behavior of both individual securities and the fund's portfolio as a whole under different sets of assumptions. Much of what they do is analyze scenarios—what would happen to a specified security or portfolio based on changes in interest rates, prepayment speeds, or other factors. They also look for patterns in historical data, not only data on securities prices, but also macroeconomic and demographic variables. The quantitative analyst attempts to point out opportunities to the portfolio manager, and also to quantify the risk associated with a particular strategy. At Pacific Investment Management, for example, fixed-income analysts continuously run complex programs that examine the interest spreads among large numbers of corporate, Treasury, and mortgage-backed bonds to identify bonds that offer attractive yields.[10] Analysts sometimes run such complex and esoteric models that the industry has come to use the term rocket scientists to label them.

Like the equity manager, the fixed-income portfolio manager balances the analyst's recommendations and findings, the fund's cash flow needs, and the current portfolio structure. When deciding which securities to buy, the portfolio manager considers not only which specific issues offer opportunities for superior performance, but also what their addition would do to the overall risk exposure of the fund. For both analysts and portfolio managers, the fixed-income security decision-making process is one of continually asking "what if?" Answering the "what if" question involves running computer programs that calculate various portfolio measures, such as duration and average weighted maturity, under various scenarios. Fixed-income portfolio managers also have to comply with the same sorts of regulatory, prospectus, and policy constraints as do equity managers.

WHAT DOES IT HOLD?

The only way to really check whether a fund is complying with the investment policies and strategies described in the prospectus and statement of additional information is to see exactly what the fund holds. Indeed, one of the reforms embedded in the 1940 Act was a requirement that fund holdings be disclosed. Legally, however, a fund only has to do this twice a year, listing the portfolio holdings as of the close dates for its semi-annual reports. And most funds stop at that level of disclosure.

Fund managers argue that frequent disclosure is an all-around bad idea. The whole point of a mutual fund, they say, is to let a professional investment manager do something the average individual is not equipped to do. Second-guessing the manager by examining the holdings is inconsistent with this philosophy. Even worse, frequent disclosure might allow other players in the market to anticipate, and therefore counteract, the investment adviser's strategy, a practice termed front-running. "The less awareness the market has of what you do as a portfolio manager, the better," says one industry consultant.[11]

Some funds do respond slightly to the demands of pension plan sponsors whose participants can select the funds as investment options in their 401(k) plans. These institutional asset management clients (and their consultants) are accustomed to getting quarterly reports about their investments, and most fund groups accommodate this schedule. Standard & Poor's Corporation also requires funds to provide quarterly reports of their holdings to it, in confidence, for the fund to be eligible to be on S&P's list of Select Funds. For most individual investors in most funds, however, the norm remains semi-annual reports with data that may be a month old when published.

A few smaller funds have attempted to take advantage of this pattern, and differentiate themselves by frequent disclosure. As far back as 1995, GIT Investment Funds—sold in 1998 to Madison Investment Advisors—began displaying its portfolio holdings on the Internet and updating them daily, an action that drew much attention in the press. A few other small funds have followed suit since then. The Thornburg Funds, for example, put holdings on their web site but take steps to prevent front-running. They only put a new holding on the site when they have completed all the buying they are going to do, and remove it only when they have completely liquidated the position.

Perhaps the most dramatically disclosed fund has been the OpenFund, which, starting on August 31, 1999, posted every trade it made on the Web, with commentary. It even featured a webcam, called TraderCam, that showed the OpenFund trading room to anyone who cared to click to it. And they invited shareholders to e-mail in any suggestions they might care to make about investing strategy. Another small fund, the Baron Asset Fund, put links on its web site that point investors to the web sites of the companies whose stock the fund owns, "to bring our shareholders closer to the companies we invest our money in," according to the marketing director.[12] While the ultimate success of these strategies remains to be seen, they certainly have added a new dimension of meaning to the "mutual" in mutual fund.

Data and Tools

Analysts and portfolio managers have acquired an increasingly sophisticated set of data feeds and tools to support their research and analysis activities. Virtually everyone in the investment management front office has a personal computer desktop, sometimes more than one, loaded with systems that deliver data and functions to support investment analysis. These include:

- current prices for securities, typically from information vendors, who get them from exchanges, OTC markets, and dealers;

- news feeds, both text and video, to keep apprised of the latest happenings in the business world;

- earnings estimates, research reports, and other analyses generated by researchers and analysts working for brokerage firms;

- large, centralized securities databases, containing information about both securities (historical prices, dividends, yields, etc.) and their issuers (financial figures, ratings, ratios, etc.);

- statistical analysis software that enables the analyst to derive financial ratios, variances and standard deviations, and regression equations from the data;

- modeling packages that enable the analyst or portfolio manager to analyze the behavior of a portfolio under certain assumptions, and compare it to model portfolios or benchmarks.

The Tower Group estimated that the U.S. investment management industry as a whole spent about $200 million in 1998 for data and analytical tools.[13] This industry includes not just mutual fund managers, but also bank trust departments, insurance companies, and all the other institutions that manage investment portfolios.

Trade Order Management

The activities of the analysts and portfolio managers culminate in decisions to buy or sell securities. *Trade order management* refers to the set of activities undertaken to carry out these decisions. The portfolio manager generates a trade order—an instruction to buy or sell a specific issue or type of issue. (Some fixed-income trades are specified in terms of attributes—for example, "we want to buy $25 million worth of a AAA grade ten-year corporate bond, at a yield spread of no more than 35 basis points to the ten-year U.S. Treasury issue.") The portfolio manager gives this order to the firm's traders for execution.

In industry parlance, mutual funds make up part of the *buy side*, the institutions that acquire securities to hold in a portfolio that serves a purpose, such as the mutual fund's purpose of providing a pooled investment vehicle for shareholders. Other buy-side participants include pension funds, insurance companies, bank trust departments, and corporate treasury departments. Broker dealers and other intermediaries belong to the *sell side*. Sell-side firms buy and sell securities primarily to make money via the transactions themselves, as when a broker charges a commission for executing a stock trade. Sell-side firms sometimes take positions in securities (that is, buy them for their own account with their own capital), but only because they hope to sell the holding at a profit. Of course, some firms participate on both sides—Merrill Lynch, for example, is an enormous broker, but it also manages large pools of assets in its proprietary mutual funds and unit trusts.

Traders who work for the fund's investment adviser are know as *buy-side traders*. The buy-side trader takes the order from the portfolio manager, and interacts with the sell side to complete it on as favorable terms as possible. Favorable terms include a reasonable commission charge and a good price, that is as low as possible when buying and as high as possible when selling. The success with which the trader carries out this task can have a significant influence on the fund's performance.

Developments in the securities markets in the United States over the past few years have made the buy-side trader's task increasingly complex. Given a trade order, the mutual fund trader must decide how to work it to get *best execution*. Best execution is another term to describe the most favorable combination of price, commission, and other services. The trader must decide where and how to place that trade, and what broker, if any, to use.

Trading Venue

The evolution of the U.S. capital markets over the past few years has given today's institutional buy-side trader a range of options for placing a trade order. On both the equity and fixed-income sides of the market, rapidly advancing technology is dramatically changing the way trading is done in the United States. Since U.S. securities trading is so fluid, the descriptions and examples below cannot be exhaustive or definitive—instead, they serve to illustrate the types of alternatives the fund trader must manage.

Exchanges: Equity products—primarily common and preferred stocks—can be traded in three ways: on an exchange, over the counter, or via a crossing network. Exchanges, such as the New York Stock Exchange (NYSE), the American Stock Exchange (AMEX) and regional exchanges, have traditionally embodied auction markets—central physical locations where people interact face-to-face to execute deals. Each exchange has market makers, or specialists, whose job it is to ensure that there is a market in a particular stock or stocks. The specialist *must* buy the stock when no one else will, thus providing liquidity. Brokers, whose firms must be members of the exchange, take customer orders to the specialist. Figure 2 shows the flow of trade execution processes for a trade in an exchange-listed stock.

A fund trader may send an order to the NYSE by telephone or electronically to a floor broker, or electronically to a specialist. Which method a fund trader chooses depends on the size of the order and the technology in place at the fund's investment adviser. Traditionally, a fund trader telephones his or her order to a sell-side firm that is a member of the exchange and has brokers on the exchange floor. The order request is written on a floor-order ticket and handed to a floor broker who walks over to the booth of the specialist for the particular security.

Figure 2: Equity Trade Executed on an Exchange

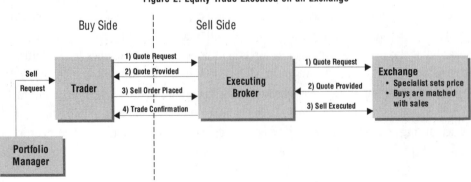

The method is still in wide use, particularly for large orders where the fund trader wants the order to be worked on the floor. The floor broker can observe the dynamics around the specialist's booth, and choose the best time to enter the bidding. All trades completed via a floor broker are captured via a NYSE automated system, but the brokerage firm must call the originating fund trader to tell him or her how the order was filled, e.g., number of trades, quantity of each trade, price.

The fund trader may choose to route the order electronically to the floor broker, or even directly to the specialist. These methods require systems that connect the investment adviser's trade order management system with systems within the sell-side brokerage firm. This electronic ordering can eliminate errors when recording the request on a ticket, and assists the floor broker in managing open orders. However the trade is placed, buy-side firms usually pay for execution of exchange-listed stocks via an explicit commission paid to the sell-side brokerage firm.

Corporate bonds can also trade on an exchange if the issuing company is listed, which implies that the company has met capital and other requirements prescribed by the exchange. Registered mutual funds' use of derivative securities is largely limited to futures and options. These still trade primarily on exchanges via open outcry auctions, although this is changing, particularly in Europe. In 1999, however, these instruments accounted for less than 1 percent of the assets of U.S. mutual funds.[14]

Over the Counter: Until 1971, the OTC market was simply the process of Wall Street dealers trading shares of stocks not listed on an exchange. In 1971, the National Association of Securities Dealers (NASD) created NASDAQ (NASD Automated Quotation), a network of telephone lines and computer systems to support this activity. The system displayed quotes in trading rooms around the country, and dealers called each other via telephone to execute trades based on these quotations.

Unlike exchange markets, the OTC market has no specialist as the single entity through which all buy and sell orders for a given security must pass. Instead, competing market makers stand ready to complete transactions with a firm that enters a trade order. Mutual fund traders typically go directly to one of the market makers for a stock they wish to trade. When a fund does go through a broker on the OTC market, it typically does not pay an explicit commission. The intermediary makes its money through the spread between the bid and offered price for the security. For example, the dealer might match someone willing to sell 10,000 shares of Happy Kids (NASDAQ: HKID) at $10\text{-}1/4$ per share to the fund who would pay $10\text{-}3/8$ per share, with the dealer keeping the $1/8$ per share for compensation.

The trading of fixed-income products has largely evolved in the over-the-counter market, a network of brokers and dealers who act as agent or principal in the purchase or sale of securities. Compared to equity-securities trading, fixed-income trading remains largely manual, with buy-side traders telephoning or e-mailing sell-side firms to strike deals. Figure 3 shows an example of OTC fixed-income trading, in which a fund sells a bond.

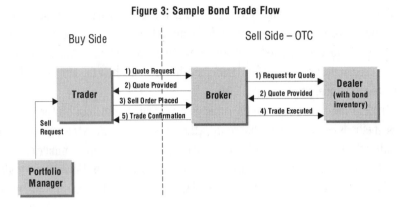

Figure 3: Sample Bond Trade Flow

Electronic Trading Networks: The basic notion of matching buyers and sellers directly via an electronic network has been around at least since 1969, when the network now known as Instinet was created. However, it was only with the adoption of liberalizing SEC rules in early 1997 that these alternative trading systems really took off. On January 20, 1997, the SEC required NASD to give electronic communications networks (ECNs) access to NASDAQ trading and quotation systems. ECNs are computerized trading systems into which subscribers place limit orders—orders to buy a stock subject to a maximum price, or sell it subject to a minimum price. The system attempts to match buyer with seller, and, if it can do so, the trade is executed.

The major attractions of the ECN are the elimination of the middleman cost in the transaction, and the anonymity the system provides. In theory, a fund places its order on the appropriate ECN, where a counterparty finds it and agrees to execute the trade. As of late 1999, however, ECNs handled mostly retail trades, i.e., trades initiated by individual investors, rather than institutional trades, because they lacked sufficient liquidity.[15] (A market is liquid to the extent that buyers can be easily found for all who wish to sell. Market makers on the exchanges and on NASDAQ provide liquidity.) As a result, the electronic systems to date have handled easier trades (smaller lots, heavily traded issues), but have done these at less cost than traditional brokers.[16] At the end of 1999, ECNs accounted for one-third of the order flow on NASDAQ. Instinet, perhaps the largest of the ECNs, handled over 41 billion shares during 1999.[17]

ECNs are also emerging to support the online trading of fixed-income products. The variety of solutions is not as robust as for equity products, but solutions are rapidly emerging. As of November 1998, The Bond Market Association identified twenty-six entities that offer or intend to offer electronic markets in fixed-income securities. In late 1999, several firms, including mutual fund management companies such as Putnam and Alliance Capital Management, began working together to create a network to disseminate bond bid and offer prices electronically.[18] In both equity and fixed-income securities, trading is moving more and more to electronic networks of various types, and the face of securities trading in the United States is likely to change dramatically in the next few years. "You will not recognize these markets in five years," predicts the chairman of NASD.[19]

International Trading: Many funds invest in securities issued outside the United States, and must, therefore, trade in the associated venues. Exchanges outside of the United States have made much greater progress toward shifting to electronic markets than have the U.S. exchanges, but few U.S. buy-side firms are directly connected to the foreign exchanges. Funds handle foreign security trading in several ways. For a fund that does relatively little trading in foreign issues, the adviser may just use U.S. brokers with which it has relationships, and allow them to deal with the foreign brokers or exchanges. If the adviser trades in a particular market frequently enough, it may deal directly with foreign brokers that serve that market (for example, the buy-side trader in New York may simply call a broker in Tokyo, or Hong Kong, or London). Some investment advisers have staff physically present in foreign locations. AMVESCAP, for example, the parent of the AIM and Invesco fund families, has investment management operations in several foreign countries, handling foreign trading for the funds. Finally, a fund may contract with a foreign sub-adviser for international portfolio management and trading, as Vanguard does with Schroder Capital Management for its International Growth Fund. As of 1998, 32 percent of all international stock funds were sub-advised in this way.[20] Which approach a particular fund chooses depends on the size of the fund and the management company, and the management company's experience in dealing with foreign markets.

Broker Selection

A trader may decide to place an order with a sell-side broker for a number of reasons. It may be the only way to get liquidity, i.e., to find a ready buyer or seller. The success of electronic networks depends on matching buyers and sellers being on the network simultaneously, something that may not occur for thinly traded issues. Brokers can seek out counter-parties for a trade, or even use their own firm's capital to help complete the trade. For large orders for a given issue, this use of the brokerage firm's capital may be necessary to complete the trade. When a fund wishes to sell a larger block of a stock than the market can easily assimilate, the brokerage firm may assist by buying the block for its own account.

This is all part of getting best execution. When the fund decides to buy or sell an issue, it bases the decision upon an assumption of a particular buying or selling price. If the trade involves a large amount of the issue relative to normal trading volumes, or if other market participants are watching for the fund manager's decisions, there is a danger that it will generate a market effect, that is, that the trade itself will cause the price to change significantly. For example, if the fund wants to sell 12,000 shares of a stock that normally trades only 15,000 to 20,000 shares per day, other players will lower the level of their bids as soon as they see the large sell order. The mutual fund trader could decide to work the order over several days, but that leaves the fund open to having the price change in an unfavorable direction. Brokers help funds avoid such market effects either by completing the order in smaller parts, or by acting as the counter-party for all or part of the order themselves, known as block trading.

The fund pays the broker for handling a trade either by an explicit commission, or via the spread. Buy-side firms such as mutual funds may also receive research services from the broker in return for some part of the commissions generated by the fund's trading business. Research services include not only information, but

SOFT DOLLARS AND THE COST OF TRADING

May 1, 1975, is known as May Day on Wall Street, for that was the day on which the SEC ended the practice of fixed commission rates for listed stock trades. It triggered an upheaval in the industry—the emergence of discount brokers, massive consolidation among old firms, formidable negotiating power for institutional investors. And commission charges went down steeply. But by the late 1990s, they seemed to be stuck at something like five and one-half to six cents per share for mutual funds and other large institutional customers, and the SEC and others were beginning to question whether something was wrong. Commissions on ECN trades typically ran from one to two cents per share[21]—why were the funds paying so much more for so much of their trading business?

Mutual funds are obligated to seek "best execution" for their portfolio trades, but what exactly does that mean? It does not just mean getting the lowest possible commission for a trade. A much bigger and more important part, most investment managers argue, is avoiding negative market impacts. As most investment professionals will quickly point out, paying two cents less per share in commission doesn't mean much if the poor execution of the trade resulted in an unfavorable price swing of a dollar per share. Funds also have to consider factors such as the broker's reliability, access to specific markets, willingness to extend capital, and the value of the products and services they provide.

The value of products and services provided raises the issue of soft dollars. Soft dollar services stem from the days when commission rates were fixed. These fixed rates often far exceeded brokers' actual costs of executing trades, especially large trades for institutions such as mutual funds. To compete for business from institutions, brokerage firms would provide financial or investment research products to the buy-side institution in addition to executing the trade, in return for the standard commission. This practice was termed a "soft dollar" transaction, since it was paid for by a portion of the standard commission.

In 1975, fixed commissions were set aside, but soft dollar transactions were not forbidden. The 1975 Amendments to the Securities Exchange Act of 1934 specifically allowed investment managers to pay for research services with commission dollars, and in 1986, the SEC clarified its interpretation of the rules.[22] In the 1986 interpretation, the SEC stated that an investment adviser could legitimately pay soft dollars for products and services, as long as the adviser had made a good faith determination that the amount paid was commensurate with the value of the products and services received. By and large, the amount paid was considered to be that amount of the commission or mark-up charged by brokers for trades that exceeded the rates otherwise available for execution of similar securities trades.

In the late 1990s, the issue had bubbled to the surface again. In 1997 and 1998, the SEC conducted a series of examinations of the soft dollar practices of 75 brokers and 280 investment advisers. The SEC found some out-and-out abuses. Renaissance Capital Advisors (not a mutual fund manager), for example, was using soft dollar payments to cover items like parking, meals, travel, lodging, furniture rentals, and telephone bills.[23] Abuses were the exception, however; most organizations could show that they were using the soft dollars to fund legitimate research. The SEC staff was not satisfied with the record keeping and disclosure practices of many firms, and recommended that the SEC formally adopt new, tightened requirements in both areas.

In 1999, however, the SEC turned toward mutual funds and their investment advisers and brokers, posing the question as to why such a large portion of trades were done with brokers (rather than ECNs) at commission rates of 5 to 6 cents per share (rather than much lower rates). At least some observers believe that many funds are not taking advantage of the savings that ECNs have made possible.[24] The SEC completed a year-long review of best execution practices among investment advisers and brokers in mid-2000, and was expected to issue a "best practices guide" by year end.

also computer hardware and software that support research. The term "soft dollars" refers to the cost of the research services provided in such an arrangement. Federal securities laws explicitly allow investment managers, including mutual fund investment advisers, to direct brokerage transactions to particular brokerage firms in return for soft dollar-funded research. The adviser must be able to show that the overall amount paid the broker is reasonable as compared to the overall value of the services the broker provides—trade execution plus research.

A fund trader can contribute significantly to the performance of the fund through the skill with which he or she gets trades executed. Funds often place big orders, orders that could easily induce a market effect. The fund trader must decide how to complete an order to get as close as possible to the market price prevailing at the time the order was placed. This may mean breaking it up into smaller trades that go out anonymously over ECNs, dealing with a brokerage firm for a block trade, or attempting to cross the trade directly with another institution.

The Cost of the Front Office

The single biggest component of expense for most actively managed mutual funds is what they pay their investment adviser for front-office functions. While the investment advisory fee often includes back-office functions as well, the major part of the fee goes toward paying for decision making and trading. In some cases, in which the fund has contracted separately for investment advisory and back-office functions, the fee amount for the front-office functions is stated explicitly. For example, in 1998, the Vanguard International Growth Fund paid Schroder Capital Management International an investment advisory fee of 16 basis points (out of a total management fee for the fund of 49 basis points) for its portfolio management services. FRC reports that the average asset-weighted advisory fee for the industry in 1998 was 48.3 basis points.[25] This fee pays for the compensation for the analysts, portfolio managers, and traders; the information systems and other tools they use; the support infrastructure they need, such as space, secretaries, etc.; and, in most cases, some profit for the firm that employs them.

The first part of the "active versus passive" argument focuses on these advisory fees. A passively managed fund, which does not utilize research, analysis, or much portfolio decision making, pays very little in advisory fees. An actively managed fund usually pays a significant amount for them. If one believes that making effective securities selection decisions is not possible, then paying for all this decision support and decision making is futile. Thus the proponents of passive management argue that shareholders in active funds pay a premium for a service that is worthless.

The second part of the argument turns on trading costs. Most active funds trade more than passive funds, because the active portfolio manager often trades in the attempt to improve fund performance. The passive manager trades only when he or she is forced to as a result of cash flow needs or changes in the benchmark. Thus the actively managed fund incurs greater transaction costs involved in trading—money spent on brokerage commissions or the spreads. As discussed in Chapter 3, portfolio trading costs are not always possible to determine, but they can be significant. American Century, for example, a fund group that has been aggressive in reducing trading expense by using ECNs, paid about $80 million in 1998, about 12 basis points, for broker-age commissions on its portfolio trades.[26]

Active funds are also more likely than passive funds to order trades that result in unfavorable market impacts. A passively managed fund usually buys or sells relatively small amounts of the various securities that make up its benchmark (basket trades), amounts too small to have any impact on prevailing prices. Once an active fund manager has decided that a particular security is unattractive, he or she wants to dispose of it, no matter how large the fund's holding. Sometimes it is impossible to divest a large block of a security without a price effect no matter how carefully it is worked. Those who believe that improving performance is an unattainable goal view both the transaction and the market impact costs incurred due to pursuit of performance as a waste of money.

Clearly, whether or not the cost of portfolio decision making and trading involved in active fund management is excessive depends on whether one believes in active management. Another part of the active-versus-passive argument revolves around shareholder taxes, and that's covered in Chapter 7.

The spectacular amounts earned by a few portfolio managers have made portfolio manager compensation a particularly visible part of what funds pay their investment advisers. However, few portfolio managers make the millions per year attributed to such figures as Jeff Vinik ($5 million per year when he was managing Fidelity's Magellan Fund)[27] or Mario Gabelli ($15.8 million for serving as portfolio manager to several mutual funds).[28] Surveys suggest that the median annual compensation for mutual fund portfolio managers is about $275,000.[29] A 1999 survey conducted by the Association for Investment Management Research (AIMR) found that compensation varied according to factors such as the size of the firm and the type of fund managed. For example, the median for U.S. domestic fixed-income fund managers was $255,000, while for domestic equity fund managers it was $299,000.[30] Much of this total compensation typically represents bonus based on investment performance.[31] Table 1 summarizes the results of the 1999 AIMR compensation survey for various investment positions in mutual fund management companies.

Life in an Investment Management Front Office

A fund company's analysts, portfolio managers, and traders live hectic professional lives, with two activities dominating the daily work cycle: communicating with persons both within and outside their firm, and sifting masses of data. The portfolio managers and analysts who handle Invesco's *Equity Income* and *Balanced* funds, and the equity traders who support them, clearly illustrate this pattern.

Founded as Investors Independent Corporation in 1932, Invesco is one of the oldest mutual fund management companies in the United States. Today a subsidiary of the international asset management firm AMVESCAP, the Invesco Funds Group manages about $40 billion in the Invesco family of funds from its office in Denver's Tech Center. The Equity Income Fund, started in 1960, holds mostly domestic equities and seeks high current

Table 1:
Summary of Results of AIMR/Russell Reynolds Compensation Survey
for Respondents from Mutual Fund Management Companies

Position	n[1]	1999 Median Compensation $				90th Percentile[3]
		Salary	Bonus	Non-cash[2]	Total	
Chief Investment Officer	15	$180,000	$218,620	$139,000	$625,000	$2,783,333
Head of Equities	10	226,500	250,000	100,000	565,750	700,000
Head of Fixed Income	17	228,000	220,000	162,500	555,000	2,696,667
Portfolio Manager - Domestic Equities	136	144,500	130,000	38,750	299,000	1,277,778
Portfolio Manager - Domestic Fixed Income	112	131,125	100,000	25,000	255,625	902,222
Portfolio Manager - Global/International Equities	44	150,000	100,000	50,000	310,000	808,000
Portfolio Manager - Global Fixed Income	20	121,000	80,000	10,500	250,000	733,333
Securities Analyst - Domestic Equities	158	100,000	50,000	10,000	165,006	380,000
Securities Analyst - Domestic Fixed Income	78	96,000	45,000	7,250	141,000	302,000
Securities Analyst - Global/International Equities	39	90,000	50,000	4,000	149,000	410,000
Securities Analyst - Global Fixed Income	15	85,000	45,000	5,000	155,000	212,500
Trader	5	80,000	30,000	11,000	109,000	143,750

Source: *1999 Investment Management Compensation Survey*, Association for Investment Management and Research and Russell Reynolds Associates, 1999.

[1] Number of respondents in this position who work for mutual fund management companies.

[2] Value of non-cash compensation received during the year (usually stock options).

[3] The 90th percentile value for median total compensation, except where there are fewer than 10 respondents, in which case the value given represents the highest value reported.

income with a secondary goal of capital appreciation. The Balanced Fund, started in 1993, holds a mix of common stocks (62 percent in December 1999) and fixed-income securities to provide high total return through both income and growth.

A team of equity analysts, some of whom are also assistant portfolio managers, provide the portfolio managers with expertise on specific sectors and industries. Sean Katof, for example, covers capital goods, transportation, basic materials, and consumer cyclicals. As he puts it, his role "is to *know* the sectors I cover — what's going on in them, what the leading firms are doing, what the challenges and opportunities are, and especially what's going on with the companies we hold." He gathers information from many sources, including sell-side analysts who work for the brokerage firms. "I go to them," he says, "when I want to know what the sell side is thinking about a firm or industry. They're more deeply and narrowly focused than we are—where I cover several sectors, a sell-side analyst might concentrate on just ten companies in one industry."

Sean gets the most valuable information, though, by talking to people who work in the industries he covers. Invesco's analysts visit or conduct a conference call with every firm whose stock they hold at least once per quarter. Sean also talks with others in the industry who have insights that could prove valuable, such as suppliers. "Say Boeing tells us they expect production to be flat next year. Well, what do their suppliers see—are they getting parts and materials orders from Boeing that are consistent with that forecast?" Like other analysts,

Sean attends industry conferences, follows the industry trade journals, and tracks breaking industry news via sources like Bloomberg and CNN. He attends several meetings per day with company management or analysts.

Chris Bedowitz, also an assistant portfolio manager and analyst, covers the health care, technology, and telecommunications sectors. He echoes Sean's description of the overwhelming mass of data that flows toward them each day. Like every analyst, he has dozens of voice mail and e-mail messages, mostly from sell-side analysts and salesmen, queued up by mid-morning each day. He faces a daily stack of mail eight to ten inches high, crammed with trade journals, company press releases, and research reports from sell-side analysts. Weeding through all this to get useful information, Chris maintains, is the analyst's real job. He relates an analogy drawn by a former director of research.

> *"It's like you and every other analyst have had the pieces of a jigsaw puzzle dumped out in front of you. You don't have anything that tells you what picture your puzzle is supposed to represent. You don't have all the pieces to complete your puzzle. You have pieces for other people's puzzles in your stack. People give you more pieces and take pieces away as you work. Your job is not to complete the picture—that would take too long, and would be worthless by the time you're done. Your job is to figure out what the picture is before anyone else does."*

Invesco uses a team of portfolio managers for the funds, and Peter Lovell handles the equity portion of the Balanced Fund, and two other funds. He makes stock selection decisions and allocation decisions, i.e., how much to overweight or underweight the fund's holdings in a sector as compared to the S&P 500. As a matter of policy, the fund holds between fifty and sixty issues, no one of which makes up more than 3 percent of the total portfolio value. Peter lists five criteria a company must meet before he will decide to hold its stock in the fund:

1. it must have earnings greater than the average for its sector;
2. it must have a strong balance sheet;
3. it must have an attractive PE/growth ratio;
4. it must display some area of competitive advantage;
5. it must have strong management.

In addition to these factors, some of which are very qualitative, he also reviews charts of general market trends that help him evaluate the stock's relative valuation. Invesco is a growth shop, Peter says. They look for stocks where both the company fundamentals and the earnings growth indicate that the stock price should rise.

Like the analysts, Peter is inundated by messages—via telephone, e-mail, and mail—from the brokerage firms on the sell side. "They're of limited value to me," he says, "they all have their own agendas to pursue. I get much better information from our internal analysts." Occasionally, he says, the brokerage firms are helpful in getting them access to executives of companies they might otherwise have difficulty reaching. By and large, however, he looks for the Invesco analysts to tell him what's going on in their sectors, what stocks look like promising opportunities, and where the problems are.

Once he's made a decision to buy or sell, he sends the order to the traders via Invesco's trade order management system. The system checks the order for compliance with regulatory and prospectus rules, and if no tests fail, sends it within seconds to the trading desk. Peter says he never gives the traders any instructions to direct an order to a particular broker. Instead, the investment management team—analysts, portfolio managers, and traders—meets quarterly to draw up general guidelines for apportioning order flow to different brokers, based on how helpful the various firms have been with research, trading help, and other services.

Pat Johnston, Invesco vice president, heads the equity trading function. In the trading room, Pat is a whirlwind of multi-channel communication. Her desk features an array of no fewer than six computer screens, and she divides her attention among these, the two or three simultaneous conversations she is having with other traders in the room, and the constantly ringing telephone. "This is a multi-processing job," she says, with considerable understatement.

Pat directs the efforts of six traders, who handle the two hundred or so equity trades the various Invesco funds generate on an average day. She herself has been a trader for over seventeen years; collectively, her team totals over sixty-five years of trading experience. The Invesco portfolio managers take advantage of this experience, generally relying on the traders to find liquidity as they deem best. "Our traders are awesome," says Chris Bedowitz, "I wouldn't dream of telling them where to work a trade."

Pat describes how she might work a trade, using a particular buy order as an example. Several sell-side firms had issued positive reports on this issue the previous day. Before the NYSE opened, she went on to AutEx, which advertises bids and offers to brokers and institutions like Invesco, to see what was out there for this stock. She called a brokerage firm they use a great deal and with whom they have good relations, to discuss the situation. Because of the reports on this company, there was much activity around the specialist's booth on the NYSE floor, and the brokerage firm, which also had a trader on the floor, could tell her what was going on. She weighed her options: she could put the entire Invesco order up before the opening, but that might move the market. On the other hand, the opening price could be the best one of the day. Finally she decided to buy part of the lot Invesco wanted at the opening, and then lay back and "let the market breathe" before adding to the holding. Ultimately, this strategy was successful—Invesco got the shares it wanted via several trades at an average price significantly lower than the closing price for the day.

"The role of the fund's traders is different now than it was ten years ago," Pat says. "Then the trader was more of a clerk, simply transmitting the orders to the brokerage firms' traders. Now we work the trades, and how well we do can make a big difference." She particularly values the electronic markets (they use Instinet and B-Trade) for their low cost, and even more importantly, the anonymity they provide. "If I want to sell a big block and I show that to a broker, I know I'll start seeing bid levels go down almost immediately."

The electronic markets have had a big impact, she maintains. "Trading has changed more in the last year and a half than it did during my entire previous fifteen years on Wall Street." She points out that Invesco currently deals with eighty sell-side brokerage firms and two electronic networks. One of these, Instinet, currently ranks number four in the list of brokers by trade volume, and electronic trading is increasing. She expects the trading landscape to change even more dramatically over the next few years, as the electronic networks rationalize and gain access to greater pools of liquidity.

Pat and the traders know the general guidelines for allocation of order flow to brokers, and they consult these when they can get the same quality of execution from multiple brokers. "We never sacrifice best execution to direct order flow," Pat says, "but when there's a tie, we will look to see if one broker is below its allocation for the quarter, and if so, we will direct the trade that way." Invesco uses soft dollar funding it gets from its order flow to brokers for three things: to pay for some market information feeds, including Bridge and Bloomberg; to obtain research that the sell-side firms provide to the portfolio managers and analysts; and to defray some of the custody fees that the funds would otherwise pay.

In late 1999, both the Equity Income and Balanced funds were very successful—both were rated four stars by Morningstar, both ranked high in their Lipper categories, and both had enjoyed net subscriptions for the year. The investment management front-office team was doing well when compared to their peers in other funds. But they're not infallible, Chris points out. "Sometimes we'll decide to sell something we hold, saying 'the fundamentals have deteriorated.' What that really means is that we made a mistake when we bought it. Fortunately, that doesn't happen too often."

CHAPTER 6

The Investment Management Back Office

A provider of back-office services ... takes care of the nitty-gritty chores that nobody likes to think much about, but that must be done properly—or else.

– Carol E. Curtis (1999)[1]

The front and back-office functions in investment management resemble respectively the motivator and hygiene factors in Herzberg's famous theory of motivation.[2] Front-office activities—analysis, portfolio management, trading—determine the income and growth in value in the fund's portfolio. They contribute visibly to the fund's performance. They resemble the motivation factors of Herzberg's theory, exciting customer attention and giving investors a reason to want to invest in the fund. Back-office functions, on the other hand, are hygiene activities that meet the basic requirements of running a viable fund. They cannot contribute to a fund's return by making the value of the portfolio holdings better (although they can drag it down if they cost too much). They don't excite anyone outside the investment management organization (and few within it). But, like hygiene factors in work, back-office functions *must* be there—unless they are done reliably, correctly, and consistently, there won't be a fund at all.

After the analysts have found stocks and bonds to buy or sell, and the portfolio managers have made their decisions, and the traders have implemented those decisions on the markets, much work remains to be done to turn all that into value for shareholders. The trades must be carried to completion—confirming the various parties' understanding of trade details, moving money, and transferring security ownership. The securities themselves must be held in safekeeping. The effects of the trades must be reflected in the securities inventory records kept by the investment adviser, to support subsequent investment decision making. This inventory must be kept current as the securities in the inventory earn and receive dividends and interest, and issuers split, reorganize, and carry out other corporate actions. The results of the investment adviser's activity must be examined to ensure compliance with regulatory, prospectus, and policy requirements. Reports must be prepared for internal and external parties. Carrying out or overseeing all these activities falls within the responsibility of the investment management back office.

Back Office Players

While the term *back office* refers most specifically to the investment manager's investment operations group, this operations group interacts with several external players to carry out the back-office functions. These external players include clearing agents, depositories, and custodians.

Investment Operations

The central component of an investment manager's back office is the investment operations group that maintains securities records, performs various monitoring and reporting functions, and oversees the trade process to completion. The back office is typically part of the same organization as the investment adviser, although it can be separate. Several firms provide back-office functions on an outsourcing basis for smaller fund groups. Figure 1 shows the major functions of the back office, and one of the many ways it can be organized.

- *Data Management* – In the previous chapter, Figure 1: The Investment Management Cycle showed a data store connecting all the front- and back-office members involved in the process. The data management group within investment operations plays an important role in maintaining this data store—records of the fund's trades and the inventory of its securities holdings. As new issues are acquired, data management must set up the security master records in the system, which for some instrument types (for example, debt securities with individual payment schedules), can be quite complex. Data management also ensures that the system takes various feeds of information each day, typically from external information vendors, via automated computer transmissions. These information feeds include securities prices, and dividend and other corporate action notifications. For securities for which automated pricing is not available, operations must obtain and manually enter the prices. Finally, the group may help maintain automated computer links between the fund and its custodian, so that data regarding holdings and activity can be exchanged and compared.

- *Accounting* – The accounting group ensures that the securities inventory is kept correctly. It posts income transactions, such as dividends, interest payments, and paydowns (the combination principal

Figure 1: Major Functions of an Investment Management Back Office

and interest payments made on mortgage-backed securities). As corporate actions such as stock splits, name changes, and calls occur, accounting ensures that the inventory is adjusted to correctly reflect their effects. Every investment management back office performs this level of securities accounting, since the investment management front office depends on this information about the state of the portfolio to support its analyses and trading decisions. The next chapter will describe the more specialized fund accounting required specifically for registered, open-end mutual funds.

Accounting typically works closely with the custodian, whose role is described below, to make sure the internally-maintained securities inventory matches the records of the custodian. The operations group also tracks the cash balances at the custodian, reconciling their records each day with the reports sent by the custodian. These balances change as dividends and interest are received, and as trades are settled. As necessary, they instruct the custodian to wire or receive funds. For example, when shareholder subscriptions result in a net inflow of cash to the fund, operations must get this cash into the proper bank accounts so that the custodian can settle the securities purchase trades that are made to invest the cash. If the fund is trading on foreign markets, operations may handle the fund's needs for foreign exchange to settle trades. In addition, holding securities gives the fund the right to vote via proxy on shareholder questions, so these must be monitored and voted.

- *Trade Operations* – The major part of the operations group provides trade support—that is, it takes the steps required to complete trades that the front office has executed. These actions are collectively known as the trade settlement process, and are discussed in detail below.
- *Compliance and Risk Monitoring* – Back office staff monitor the trades and holdings of the fund to ensure that the investment adviser is neither breaking the rules, nor subjecting the funds to undue levels of risk. Portfolio compliance monitoring and risk monitoring are discussed in detail below.

Clearing Agents and Depositories

Prior to the 1960s, the standard method of transferring ownership of securities was to physically transfer a certificate representing ownership from the seller to the buyer. By the 1960s, however, the volume of securities trades in the United States grew to the point that issuers, their transfer agents, the exchanges, and the brokerage firms could no longer process the paperwork required by this traditional approach. In response to this paperwork crunch, two independent and parallel approaches were introduced: *securities clearing corporations* and *depositories*.

A clearing corporation approached the problem of handling high trade volumes by acting as a settlement intermediary between all parties involved in a trade. The clearing corporation nets all the securities and cash flows to and from each of its members each day, and creates a net movement of securities and cash for each member. Because of this netting, the clearing corporation guarantees the members that if one side or another to a trade failed to settle, the solvent party could still complete its side of the trade, with the clearing corporation as counterparty.

The National Securities Clearing Corporation (NSCC) clears and settles virtually all retail equity, corporate bond, and municipal bond transactions in the United States today. Originally, corporate securities clearing agents were divisions or subsidiaries of the exchanges. In 1975, amendments to the Securities Exchange Act of 1934 gave the SEC oversight of clearing agencies, and the major markets (NYSE, ASE, and NASD) spun off their subsidiaries into NSCC.

A depository holds securities in its own custody, and records changes in the ownership of those securities by making book entries in its computer systems. The securities themselves might be represented by physical certificates residing in the depository's vault, or they may simply be computer records (uncertificated). Different depositories hold different types of securities. The Depository Trust Company (DTC) provides custody for almost two million issues, including corporate equities and bonds, municipal bonds, mortgage-backed bonds, U.S. Treasury and agency bonds, and various types of money market instruments. The Federal Reserve is the depository for U.S. Treasury bills and notes. The Bank of New York's vault holds bonds that have physical coupons and physical certificates for some issues. The Participatory Trust Company (PTC) was the depository for some mortgage-backed securities, until it merged with DTC in 1998.

Over the years, the clearing and net settlement functions of NSCC and the depository functions of DTC have converged, to the point that the two organizations agreed to merge in 1999. Today the typical portfolio trade executed on behalf of a mutual fund is completed with a netted transfer of money and a book entry change in ownership via the combined DTCC.

The Custodian

The 1940 Act gives mutual funds several options for maintaining custody of their securities, but nearly all U.S. mutual funds today use independent banks as custodians. Table 1 shows the major custodians of mutual fund assets as of mid-1998. While Table 1 shows figures only for open-end mutual fund custody, most custodians also hold assets for other types of clients—pension funds, trusts, and so on. The cumulative market share column suggests how concentrated the industry is, with the top ten players accounting for 87 percent of mutual fund assets. This reflects the fact that the low margins and large investments required for specialized information technology make custody a business that favors significant economies of scale.

The custodian holds the fund's securities in safekeeping and manages the cash movements involved in settling trades and income payments. At one time, many of the fund's securities holdings took the form of physical certificates, and the custodian held these in its vault. Physically issued securities are much less common today, but do still occur. When a fund does hold certificates, these are kept in the custodian's vault. More commonly, the securities exist only as computer records with the custodian, depository, and issuer. Figure 2 depicts the common relationships among issuers of securities, depositories, custodians, and funds.

The custodian maintains both cash and securities accounts at each of the depositories. The securities account contains all the securities held by mutual fund and other clients of that custodian. The cash account is used to move money to and from the depository in the settlement of trades and other transactions, such as

Table 1: Mutual Fund Custody Providers (Registered Open-End Funds)

1998 Rank	Institution/Custody Group Headquarters	Assets in Custody ($millions)	# of Funds *	Cumulative Market Share
1	State Street Corporation / Boston	1,861,993	2,807	25.5%
2	The Chase Manhattan Bank / New York	858,000	1,096	35.4%
3	The Bank of New York / New York	732,000	1,402	48.1%
4	Bankers Trust Company / New York	329,720	321	51.1%
5	Brown Brothers Harriman / Boston	292,180	629	56.8%
6	PFPC Bank / Lester, PA	280,224	900	64.9%
7	First Union National Bank / Philadelphia	180,000	271	67.4%
8	Mellon Trust / Philadelphia	157,200	959	76.1%
9	Investors Bank and Trust / Boston	98,361	878	84.1%
10	UMB Bank / Kansas City	92,966	354	87.3%
11	Firstar Trust Company / Milwaukee	65,000	231	89.4%
12	Norwest Bank / Minneapolis	29,000	292	92.0%
13	Northern Trust Company / Chicago	25,772	226	94.1%
14	Fifth Third Bank / Cincinnati	22,000	136	95.3%
15	Union Bank of California / San Francisco	18,072	93	96.2%
16	Star Bank / Cincinnati	16,752	286	98.8%
17	Citibank N.A. / New York	15,000	48	99.2%
18	Custodial Trust Company / Princeton, NJ	6,222	43	99.6%
19	Bank One Trust Company / Columbus, OH	4,022	29	99.8%
20	The Huntington National Bank / Columbus, OH	2,600	17	100.0%

Source: *The 1998 Custody Service Guide*, Securities Data Publishing, 1998.
All figures are as of June 30, 1998.

* Domestic open-end funds only

dividend and interest payments. When the exchange-listed stock trade settles, the depository moves money from the cash account of the buying custodian (or broker) to the cash account of the selling custodian (or broker), and changes its ownership records by adding to the buying custodian's security account and subtracting from the selling account.

Issuers of securities, or their transfer agents, make income and dividend payments to the depositories, which allocate them to the appropriate custodial accounts. Custodians then allocate the income to their clients for which they are holding the securities. In cases where the holding is in physical form, the issuer or transfer agent sends the income directly to the custodian. The custodian allocates the income it receives from the issuer, either directly or via the depository, to the client accounts it holds. The investment management back office, which is itself keeping a securities inventory and accruing income, compares its expectations with the custodian's actual receipts to ensure that everything is correct.

Some U.S. mutual funds hold securities that are issued and traded outside the United States. This trading in foreign markets requires the fund to use *sub-custodians* who can participate in the local markets, interact with the local clearing agencies, and hold accounts in the local depositories. Rule 17f-5 under the 1940 Act

Figure 2: Relationships among Issuers, Depositories, Custodians, and Funds

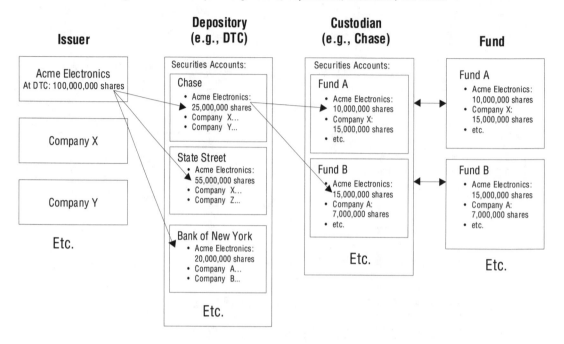

governs the custody of mutual fund assets outside the United States. It allows a fund to use a U.S. bank or a qualified foreign bank, so long as certain safeguards are in place. As a practical matter, mutual funds typically delegate the tasks involved with dealing with sub-custodians to a global custodian. The global custodian is usually a large bank, such as Citibank, Chase, or State Street, that has built a network of sub-custodians with which it interacts on behalf of its clients, including mutual funds. Often the global custodian's contract with the fund will guarantee that the sub-custodians will meet stated performance standards, e.g., collect income on payment date.

Custodians often combine other support functions along with basic custody in their offerings. The list below includes some of the more common offerings.

- *Securities Lending.* Funds may earn extra income by lending the securities in their portfolios, typically for short periods, to counterparties that must deliver securities that they do not own. The custodian arranges the lending transactions, and typically assumes any default risk involved in the transaction.
- *Short-Term Investment Funds.* The custodian sweeps all cash sitting overnight in the fund's custodial accounts into an internal short-term fund that it maintains. This relieves the portfolio manager of having to make overnight cash investments.

- *Credit Lines and Overdrafts.* Funds may occasionally face short-term cash deficits, typically as a result of shareholder redemptions. A manager could hold a large cash reserve to cover this eventuality, but that drags down fund performance. Liquidating portfolio holdings to meet short-term cash needs is even less attractive. Instead, the fund manager may choose to borrow money for short periods from the custodian to cover these situations. The 1940 Act permits this type of borrowing as long as it complies with stringent guidelines.
- *Fund Accounting, Fund Administration, Compliance, and Risk Monitoring.* Custodians offer to perform all of these functions (each of which is discussed in detail later) that are normally viewed as part of the back office.
- *Reporting and Information Delivery.* The custodian holds records of the fund's securities holdings and activity. To add value, the custodian offers reporting and electronic delivery of this information for various purposes. For example, some investment managers get the securities inventory each day from the custodian.

Each of these services carries an additional price tag. As basic custody service becomes an increasingly low-margin business, custodians seek to expand their lines of service to generate additional revenue.

After the Trade is Made—the Settlement Process

Executing a trade means getting agreement between a buyer and a seller to exchange a specific quantity of a specific security at a stated price. The way this is done ranges widely, from informal human interactions—a nod of the head or wiggle of a finger on the floor of an exchange, a few words in a quick telephone call—to totally automatic matching done inside an Electronic Communications Network. However it is done, it triggers a series of interactions among several parties that eventually results in the buyer of the security getting ownership and the seller getting cash. Collectively, this chain of events constitutes the trade settlement process.

Figure 3 summarizes the entities and activities involved in settling one of the most common types of trade, that of an exchange-listed equity, for example, IBM or General Motors common stock. On the day of the trade known as trade date, or T, the exchange starts the settlement process by determining whether the attributes of the trade (quantity, price, etc.) as submitted by the selling broker or specialist are the same as those submitted by the buying broker or specialist. If they are, the exchange considers the trade matched, and sends the record of the trade to the clearing organization, in this case the National Securities Clearing Corporation (NSCC). Simultaneously, the broker sends a notice of execution (NOE) to the investment adviser.

NSCC and other clearing organizations provide central locations to which trades are submitted for clearance processing, which includes trade comparison, netting and money settlement. The clearing corporation interposes itself between the buying and selling parties, guaranteeing the settlement of all successfully matched trades. The clearing corporation generates settlement obligations that initiate the delivery/receipt of securities

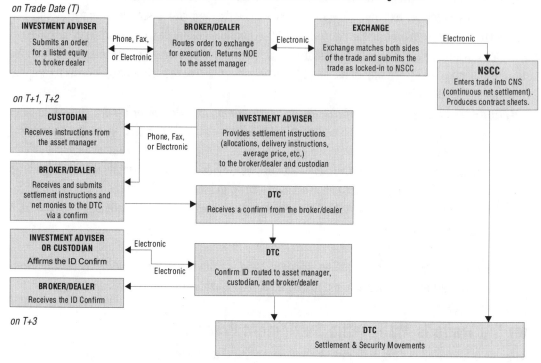

Figure 3: Execution, Clearance, and Settlement of an Exchange Trade

and receipt/delivery of monies. Without the clearing organizations, each party involved in trading would have to set up agreements and facilities to deal directly and individually with every other party, creating a network of monstrous proportions.

As of this writing, listed equities in the United States settle in three days. However, the industry is moving to shorten the cycle to one day, i.e., next day settlement or T+1, perhaps by 2004. On the days between trade and settlement, the various parties exchange information to ensure proper settlement. Currently, the investment adviser has until the morning of T+2 to give the broker delivery details, such as the allocation of the order (i.e., which fund will actually own the shares being bought), the prices of the allocations, and the name of the custodian. The adviser gives matching information to the fund's custodian so that the custodian can move money properly on settlement date.

Upon receipt of the delivery details from the investment adviser, the broker—in the case of our exchange-listed stock example—communicates these to the Depository Trust Corporation (DTC) in the form of a confirmation. As part of the trade settlement process, DTC routes confirmations to the investment adviser, the custodian, and the broker dealer. The confirm says, in effect, "This is what we at DTC believe all of you have agreed upon regarding this trade." If both sides respond affirmatively to this notification (affirm the confirm) within the agreed-upon deadlines, ownership is switched and money changes hands on T+3.

Other types of securities clear and settle through different paths, but all follow the same basic pattern. Once the trade is made the various counterparties exchange information to confirm their understanding of the trade details. These interactions are facilitated by different clearance and settlement agents, depending on the type of security being traded. The time between trade and settlement also varies—in the United States some securities, such as Treasury notes and commercial paper, settle on trade date; outside the United States, some settlement

STP AND T+1 SETTLEMENT

Both money and securities exist today mostly in the form of electronic records. Yet the process of trading and settling securities remains riddled with anachronistic manual interventions that add cost, delay, error, and risk to the process. Automating the trading cycle from end to end is such an important and obvious goal that the industry has long since adopted a universal term for it: straight-through processing (STP).

Moving to straight-through processing—automating all the interactions involved in the investment management cycle—is immediately attractive for several reasons. It reduces cost and risk at a time when both are becoming more important and visible to the market. Undertaken properly, it positions the fund manager to move quickly as new capabilities, such as more liquid electronic markets, come online. And straight-through processing techniques will be sorely needed if the industry is to get to T+1 settlement.

In 1992, a task force studying the securities industry argued that the settlement window for securities trades should be reduced from five days to three, believing that a shortened settlement cycle would reduce credit and market risks incurred by clearing firms. The SEC adopted this recommendation for implementation effective June 1, 1995. This change did in fact produce a more efficient and less risky trade cycle, as evidenced by the fact that the rate of trade failures fell even as overall trade volumes increased. To achieve this, industry participants—asset managers, brokers, clearing agents, custodians—had to streamline their operations, and invest in new support systems.

The enormous increase in trading volume over the past few years has caused the SEC to look at once again shortening the settlement cycle, this time to the day after trade date, or T+1. While the SEC has not established a deadline for doing this, many observers believe that it will happen in 2004. The shortened cycle is expected to reduce risk associated with unsettled trades (since they won't be unsettled for very long), and again force the industry to make its operations more efficient.

Most industry participants will need to improve their operations significantly to handle T+1 settlement. As Jill Considine, president of DTC, points out, the industry simply will not survive with the volume growth that's anticipated unless post-trade processing is changed.[3] Streamlining operations, implementing straight-through processing, and getting to T+1 settlement are all part of the required changes. As Ms. Considine puts it, "One can debate whether STP is a driver or an outcome…but it doesn't matter. STP is an essential part of our move to T+1." A trade process settlement that is mostly manual simply cannot get any significant volume of trades settled in a one day window.

Ultimately, fund shareholders will be among the beneficiaries of this change. Both reduced trade failures and improved operations reduce the cost of securities processing, a cost that shareholders now bear as part of the fund's expense ratio.

cycles remain weeks in length. In all cases, however, the process ends with the transfer of ownership and movement of money.

The trade operations group makes sure trades are processed to completion successfully. They obtain records of trades that have been executed by the front office, and compare them to the notifications that come in from the broker and clearing organization. They confirm the trades with the brokers and affirm the trades through DTC. If one of the parties involved in the settlement sends a non-recognition notice (called a DK, for "don't know"), they research and resolve the problem so that the trade can settle properly. Most often, DKs result from one of the parties—investment manager or broker—not including enough information on the record it creates of a trade, rendering it impossible for the trade to be recognized.

Having a discrepancy cause a trade to fail—that is, to be invalidated and have to be re-done—can cost money for the investment manager. For example, consider the case in which the adviser sells a security, the security's price on the market falls significantly, and then the trade fails. If the adviser has to make the sale again at the new, lower price, someone has lost money. If this happens, the regulations make it clear that the investment adviser, not the fund, is on the hook for the losses. The SEC interprets Section 206 of the 1940 Act, the anti-fraud provisions, to mean that advisers are expected to insulate clients from trading losses.[4] The SEC has made it clear that an adviser cannot use soft dollar arrangements to absorb any loss for which it is responsible—it has to come out of the adviser's pockets. Needless to say, the back office works hard to ensure that trades do not fail. When a trade failure does occur, the trade operations group must determine who is at fault (e.g., adviser, broker, counter-party), and the amount of loss that must be made up to the fund.

Portfolio Compliance and Risk Monitoring

The Investment Company Institute publishes a guide for mutual fund directors to help them understand their obligations, requirements, and restrictions. When it comes to portfolio compliance, the guide is straightforward: "as part of its overall 'watchdog' role, the board of directors must monitor the investment company's compliance with investment policies and restrictions."[5] Failure on the part of the fund to comply with legal and prospectus restrictions can lead to legal liability for the directors themselves. In actuality, a fund's directors engage the manager, the custodian, or another entity to carry out the operational steps involved in compliance monitoring, while they retain ultimate responsibility.

Different fund groups organize the compliance monitoring function differently, and many aspects of compliance are not related to the portfolio composition. These other aspects of compliance—dealing with such issues as distribution and regulatory reporting—are discussed in the next chapter. Portfolio compliance and risk monitoring are sometimes termed investment management middle office functions. Since they focus primarily on the trades and securities holdings of the fund, they resemble back-office functions and are discussed here. Portfolio compliance monitoring falls into two broad categories: pre-trade compliance, and post-trade compliance.

WHEN COMPLIANCE MONITORING FAILS

Portfolio compliance monitoring seeks to prevent rules violations that may be unlikely to occur, but which have serious consequences when they do occur. The case of PaineWebber's *Short Term U. S. Government Income Fund* illustrates just how serious those consequences can be.

In the early 1990s, PaineWebber brokers sold this fund to their clients as an alternative to money-market funds or CDs, an alternative that would provide a higher yield at only a slightly higher risk. (Some brokers started calling it the CD buster.)[6] The fund's prospectus stated that it sought the highest level of income consistent with preservation of capital and low volatility of NAV. Further, an appendix to the prospectus disclosed that the fund would avoid certain types of securities, including specific types of interest only and principal only stripped mortgage-backed securities. This approach to pursuing this objective proved successful—by 1993, the fund had gathered $1.3 billion in assets.

Unfortunately, however, the portfolio manager for the fund started violating these rules in pursuit of better performance. He bought some of the explicitly forbidden securities—"inappropriate IO and PO securities," as the SEC termed them in its enforcement procedure findings.[7] No compliance monitoring detected or flagged these acquisitions. No one suspected any problem at all, as long as interest rates remained low. When interest rates increased sharply in the first half of 1994, however, the response of these securities—a steep drop in price—illustrated precisely why they shouldn't have been in the portfolio in the first place. To compound the problems, the portfolio manager disguised this price drop—he overrode the prices they were getting each day from the custodian with prices he derived himself, prices that averaged about 27 percent higher.[8] No compliance monitoring procedures caught this, either.

Finally, in early May, cash flow needs forced the fund to sell some of these securities, at prices much lower than the manager had been using, and the cat was out of the bag. On May 6, the fund was revalued using the custodian's prices for the securities, and the NAV dropped 4 percent in one day. Brokers and shareholders screamed, senior management began investigating, and the SEC took notice. Over the next few months, the entire story came out. The results were catastrophic.

- PaineWebber ended up paying $283 million to fix the problem—$250 million to buy the questionable securities from the fund, and $33 million to settle shareholder lawsuits.
- The SEC fined PaineWebber $500,000 for failing to adhere to the prospectus in managing the fund.
- People lost their jobs—the portfolio manager, and both the chief investment officer and the president at Mitchell Hutchins, the PaineWebber subsidiary actually managing the fund.
- Shareholders bailed out, reducing the fund's assets from $1.3 billion to $600 million within a year.
- In an attempt to regain credibility, PaineWebber engaged a third-party subadviser, PIMCO, to manage the fund, at a cost to PaineWebber of about $1.5 million per year.
- Both the portfolio manager and the chief investment officer were sanctioned by the SEC.

From the SEC's point of view, it was a clear-cut case of failure to monitor compliance. Said Colleen Mahoney, SEC deputy director: "The case is a reminder to firms to pay attention to what their portfolio managers are doing. This fund was recklessly invested and PaineWebber wasn't monitoring their manager properly. Well, if the fund companies don't, we will." [9]

All fund groups perform post-trade compliance monitoring in one way or another. The compliance group examines records of the fund's portfolio holdings at periodic intervals, usually quarterly or monthly, looking for cases in which a rule has been broken. This monitoring is typically evidenced by checklists that are completed and signed by a compliance officer. For many fund companies, this activity remains manual—compliance officers pore over reports of fund holdings, ticking off their findings on paper checklists. Others have automated at least part of it, having computer programs compare records of fund holdings with the rules, and highlighting exceptions.

Unfortunately, periodic post-trade monitoring leaves open the possibility that a problem trade could go undetected for a considerable time, with the potential risk of significant cost involved in unwinding it. For example, consider the case in which the adviser violates the industry concentration rule by taking a position in a certain security, but doesn't discover the fact until three weeks later, by which time the value of the position has declined by $100,000. From the fund director's point of view, this is simply a condition that the adviser must fix. Regulations make it clear that the adviser, not the fund, is liable for any resulting loss. The adviser must "make the fund whole."

Pre-trade compliance monitoring helps the investment adviser avoid this problem in the first place. Advisers that have had costly compliance violations typically become very interested in implementing pre-trade compliance procedures. Pre-trade compliance checking is implemented via a computerized trade order management system. First, the compliance staff articulates the rules in a way that they can be input to the system. Then, as each trade order is entered, the system checks it against the rules. For example, when the portfolio manager enters an order to buy Intel, the system goes though a hierarchy of checks—Is this a forbidden issue? If not, does it violate the rule on how much of a single stock we can own? If not, does it drive us over the limits for the industry?—the list can go on. If there is an apparent violation the system signals an exception. Investment management staff check to see whether the violation is real, in which case the trade cannot proceed.

Pre-trade compliance checking does not eliminate the need for post-trade or back-end compliance monitoring. Market action may bring a fund's position out of compliance with a regulation even if no trades have been made. For example, a fund that had a prospectus limit of 15 percent for any individual sector could find that rising prices had raised the market value of its holdings in one sector to the point that it violated the 15 percent rule. Periodic monitoring of the fund positions against the rules catches these types of violations.

Even if a fund's investment adviser follows every regulation, prospectus requirement, and management company policy perfectly, that does not eliminate *risk* for the fund. For example, a fund holding a perfectly acceptable (from the compliance standpoint) portfolio of bonds could incur significant losses if interest rates shift significantly in the wrong direction, or a major issuer defaults. Risk management involves analyzing these and other types of bad things that might happen to the fund, and determining what should be done to reduce their potential impact. The function is harder to describe than other investment functions, since the discipline is only a few years old, and no two firms approach it in the same manner. Some observers argue that asset managers such as mutual funds are only just beginning to apply risk management techniques.[10]

COMPLIANCE VERSUS RISK: THE PIPER JAFFRAY AFFAIR

A fund's manager can operate in complete compliance with the regulations and the language in the fund's prospectus, but still subject the fund to unacceptable levels of risk for its shareholders. The incident of the *Piper Jaffray Institutional Government Income Fund* illustrates the difference between compliance and risk monitoring.

This fund was aimed at institutions and high net worth individuals that wanted to earn better than deposit account rates on their excess cash. In the early 1990s, the fund gave them exactly what they sought, and by 1993, had attracted $800 million from investors the likes of the Minnesota Orchestra and the towns of Maple Grove and Mound, Minnesota. Portfolio manager Worth Bruntjen's investing strategy had made the fund the best performing of short-term government funds in 1993, and the money poured in.[11] To accomplish this, however, he had to take some considerable risks.

In early 1993, Bruntjen had nearly 60 percent of the fund's assets invested in three types of mortgage-backed derivative securities:[12]

- Principal-Only Strips – securities that do not bear interest, and entitle the holder to receive only the principal component of the payments made on the underlying mortgages;
- Inverse Interest-Only Strips – securities that pay the investor in inverse proportion to the interest payments being made on underlying securities; and
- Inverse Floaters – securities that pay the holder an interest rate that adjusts periodically in the opposite direction of a specific index.

In all cases, these were issues the market value of which would rise if prevailing interest rates fell, and fall if interest rates rose. Effectively, Bruntjen was making a large bet with the fund's assets that interest rates would continue to fall.

No Piper Jaffray compliance checking procedures caught this for the simple reason that no regulatory or prospectus rules were being violated. The 1940 Act does not ban funds from holding derivatives. The fund's prospectus explicitly stated that it could hold these types of securities. Other mortgage-backed funds bought these same types of derivatives, although in nothing like the proportions Piper did. The problem was not one of compliance but of risk—no one noted that Bruntjen's bet was unhedged—that is, that the fund held nothing that would mitigate the effect of rising interest rates on the derivatives. No one noted the size of Bruntjen's bet and the consequences if it failed.

Unfortunately, fail it did in 1994. Interest rates rose, the market values of the derivatives plummeted, and the fund lost more than 20 percent of its value. Piper fought the consequences for years. Shareholders filed several lawsuits, which Piper eventually paid over $138 million to settle (the Minnesota Orchestra was awarded $6 million, plus interest).[13] Many observers believe that it was the financial drain from this affair that ultimately persuaded Piper to allow itself to be acquired by U.S. Bancorp in 1997, ending 102 years of independent existence.[14] The fallout continued into the new century, with KPMG agreeing in March 2000 to pay $13.9 million to settle a class action suit filed against it for its role in auditing the fund.

The SEC finally weighed in four years after the fact, filing suit in 1998 against Bruntjen, five other individuals, and Piper Capital Management (by then part of U.S. Bancorp). The SEC did not charge, however, that Piper had failed to comply with prospectus restrictions on the types of securities it held. Instead, it alleged that misleading marketing materials had portrayed the fund to investors as conservative even while Bruntjen's management made it highly speculative. It also accused several staff of engaging in NAV manipulation in 1994 to try to disguise the fact that the fund's value was collapsing. In short, the SEC concluded, Bruntjen had employed "devices, schemes, and artifices to defraud investors in the offer and sale of securities." [15]

The great sin of omission Piper committed that allowed all this to happen was its failure to monitor the risk of the portfolio that their manager had built. Had they seriously evaluated in 1993 the extent of the fund's exposure to a rise in interest rates, management could have forced Bruntjen to unwind or hedge his positions, reducing or eliminating the risk.

Risk monitoring can be as simple as measuring certain attributes of the fund's portfolio, for example, duration, credit rating profile, country exposure, and comparing them to targets or benchmarks. Portfolio managers do this sort of monitoring in the normal course of running the fund. In other cases, risk management may involve running computer models that project what would happen under various circumstances such as interest rates change, foreign exchange rates change. Value at risk (VaR) modeling attempts to express the amount of risk inherent in a fund's portfolio of securities at any given time by explicitly calculating how much money the fund could lose under specified circumstances. The model repeatedly simulates the portfolio's behavior as it changes underlying assumptions, and develops a profile of the resulting outcomes. Doing VaR calculations requires specialized computer systems, and staff dedicated to using them.

However a fund's management handles risk monitoring, it remains a combination of art and science, with much of the art lying in human judgements about the validity and applicability of the quantitative results. A VaR model may show that the fund could lose $10 million tomorrow if German interest rates fall, but will those rates fall? And even if we believe that they will, what's the best action to take? The best that directors and shareholders can ask for today is that fund management monitor risk using some systematic technique, and act upon the results it receives.

The Cost of the Back Office

Most often, the cost to the fund for many back-office functions is included in the fund's advisory fee. The ICI and the industry consulting firms Strategic Insight and FRC include both front-office (i.e., investment decision making) and back-office (settlement and record keeping) operations, along with other management company functions, such as contract administration, within a composite figure. Strategic Insight found in 1998 that this "Advisory and Administration" fee averaged about .47 percent, or 47 basis points, on an asset-weighted basis across all funds.[16] The allocation of this amount between back and front office varies from fund to fund, but in most actively managed funds, the back-office share of this amount is much lower than the front-office share.

Custody is usually priced separately, since it is almost always provided by a separate organization. Strategic Insight reports that custody fees averaged only about 2 basis points across all funds in 1998. Over the past ten years, custody fees have been driven down dramatically through competition. In 1992, State Street Bank contributed significantly to industry price competition when it won the custody business of the California Public Employees Retirement System (CalPERS), one of the largest pools of managed money in the country. To win the business, State Street offered fees 50 percent lower than the then prevailing rate for custody.[17] This fierce price competition has fueled industry consolidation, with such competitors as J. P. Morgan and Morgan Stanley selling their custody portfolios and exiting the business.

Compliance and risk monitoring costs are impossible to determine because they are always bundled within a larger package of services. They are usually part of the fund administration services provided by the management company. The actual procedures may be carried out by staff working for the investment manager, the fund administrator, the custodian, or a combination of these.

The Back Office at David L. Babson

David L. Babson, a major contributor to the development of growth stock investing, founded his namesake investment management firm in 1940. He managed the company until he retired in 1978, and in 1995, Massachusetts Mutual Life Insurance Company acquired it. In late 1999, David L. Babson & Company (DLB) managed about $17 billion for mutual funds, institutions, and individual investors. In this respect, it resembled many U.S. investment managers who manage money for a variety of products, some of which are open-end funds. DLB managed money for the David L. Babson fund family, the Babson and Jones family, and a handful of others (for which they were sub-adviser), totaling about $12 billion. The other $5 billion was held in about 200 accounts for institutions such as pension plans and endowments, and for about 500 high net worth individual investors and wrap accounts.

For most of its existence, DLB had no separate back office. Each portfolio manager had an assistant who settled trades, maintained data, managed custodial relationships, and produced reports. In 1997, growing volume prompted DLB to create a centralized back office for greater efficiency. Joanne Yetka, who had worked at fund giants Fidelity and Putnam, came in to manage the new operations group.

Joanne describes how the back office worked in late 1999. "Our operations can best be summarized by considering the computer systems we use to support them. We have three major investment support systems: Merrin for equity trading, Bloomberg for fixed income trading, and PMIS, our portfolio accounting system, to keep the books of record for the portfolios (Figure 4). All the trades are captured into one of the two trading systems on the day they are executed. Each day these systems transmit their trades to PMIS. Bloomberg also sends PMIS security information about any fixed income issues being acquired for the first time."

Brandi Peachey and Rachel Ventresca on the trading desk make sure that the 9,000 or so trades Babson makes in a typical month settle properly. Babson's Merrin system connects to Oasys (a vendor system for communicating trade orders and executions among brokers and institutions), and they use this to transmit allocations—which account gets what share of a trade—to the brokers. Brandi deals with any exceptions or questions that arise in this process. Rachel deals with affirmations to DTC. "DTC routes all the confirmations to us, and Merrin automatically matches and affirms the equity trades," she says. "We print out the confirmations for the fixed income trades, and then manually enter the affirmations for them into DTC's system." Rachel deals with exceptions and problems in this process. "We seldom if ever have a problem settling a trade for one of the funds," she points out. "Usually if there is a DK, it is for one of the individual accounts, where something has changed about the settlement instructions and the broker hasn't picked this up."

Brandi and Rachel notify the custodians of trades via fax. Equity trades go out via auto-fax: a Merrin feature that electronically generates and sends faxes. For fixed income trades, they print a paper trade ticket,

Figure 4: Systems Support for the Back Office at David L. Babson

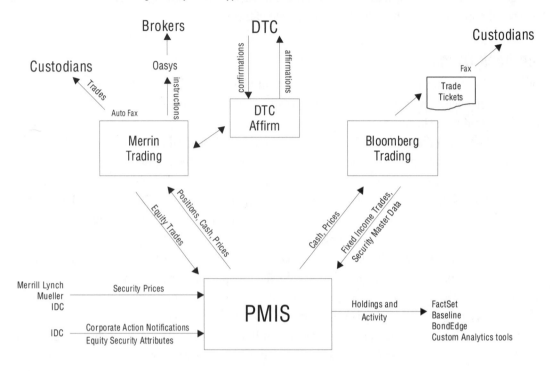

and then manually fax that to the custodian. The nine David L. Babson funds all use Investors Bank & Trust (IBT) as their custodian. The institutional and individual investor accounts, however, use a total of over 100 custodians among them.

Joanne continues to describe the operations. "PMIS keeps the inventory—the books of record. PMIS posts trades as they come from the trading systems. To keep a correct inventory and do our reporting, however, we also have to maintain our security master records, and post securities prices and corporate actions. Some of this activity, such as the pricing feeds from Merrill Lynch, Mueller, and IDC, and the simpler corporate action notifications from IDC, are largely automated. Others require manual intervention." Susan Fowler in Portfolio Administration handles these.

Susan describes her role in security master maintenance. "For new fixed income securities that Bloomberg Trader sends, I just have to add our industry group codes, custom security type, and description information. Everything else gets set up in PMIS automatically. When the equity managers acquire a security we don't already own, we have to enter a new security master record on PMIS manually. I get a copy of the trade ticket, and go onto the Bloomberg information terminal to get all the data about the security. Then I use PMIS screens to create the new security master record." In late 1999, Babson accounts held slightly over 10,000 different securities among them, adding several new ones on a typical day.

Susan described her role in handling pricing and corporate actions as mostly one of dealing with exceptions. "Most of the prices come in on the feeds and post automatically. Sometimes we'll find that we didn't get a price, usually for a thinly traded bond, and we'll have to call a broker, and enter the price manually." She also looks up and enters interest rates for a few floating rate notes and factors for a few mortgage-backed securities that do not come automatically on the electronic feed.

For corporate actions, she manually enters the more complex ones that aren't automatically posted from the IDC feed. The Exxon-Mobil merger on November 30, 1999, for example, required such manual intervention. Exxon holders converted each share of Exxon to one share of Exxon Mobil Corp. Mobil holders exchanged each share they held for 1.32015 shares of the new Exxon Mobil stock. Each day Susan monitors the capital changes notifications faxed out by CCH, Incorporated, and checks to see which are held in Babson accounts and must therefore be processed. PMIS automatically captures and processes straightforward corporate actions—cash and stock dividends and splits—and these she merely verifies.

Joanne describes how the data in PMIS are used. "Merrin needs to be refreshed each night with the current holdings, as well as cash balances and prices. Bloomberg keeps track of the fixed income inventory itself; we just pass cash and prices to it. This information is also downloaded to a number of systems the portfolio managers and analysts use to support their decision making. Many of the equity managers use FactSet and BaseLine for portfolio analytics; the fixed income managers use BondEdge. And, of course, some managers and analysts have their own customized tools, built in Access or Excel, into which they load their data. We have to support all of these."

Greg Volpe handles portfolio administration for the mutual fund accounts. Each day he reconciles the cash balances at the custodian for each fund with the cash balances in PMIS, making whatever adjustments are needed. At the end of each month, he reconciles the security positions between IBT and PMIS. "Any discrepancies we see are almost always related to timing," he says. "The bank's records are settlement-date based— that means they don't post a trade until the day it settles. Our records in PMIS are trade-date based—we post each night the trades executed that day. So at the end of the month, we're off by three days' worth of trades. Once we account for this, the records almost always match, and on the few occasions they haven't, it's always been due to a failed trade."

Portfolio compliance checking at Babson is divided among several entities. Babson's general counsel is also the compliance officer, and he is ultimately responsible to the fund directors for ensuring that compliance monitoring is performed. The portfolio administration group has loaded compliance rules into the two trading systems so that they can perform pre-trade checks. The portfolio managers and traders deal with exceptions that these pre-trade checks uncover. The Babson funds have engaged IBT, the custodian, to perform periodic post-trade compliance evaluations, and to report the results to the compliance officer.

Dan Wright, senior vice president in charge of both investment operations and information technology, describes their task as one that never ends. "We have a pretty good system and organization setup now, but we can't stop here. We need to get to straight-through processing, so we're ready when T+1 hits. Next month, we'll start detailed evaluation of a new, integrated suite of software, which, if it works as advertised, will get us where we want to be. We could build interfaces, and satellite systems, but that's not our philosophy, we don't want to be a software development company. We want to use software just as it comes out of the box. So, we keep looking for something that can come out of the box doing what we need."

CHAPTER 7
Fund Accounting, Audit, Legal, and Other Support Functions

The 1940 Act's main concern is the integrity, accuracy, and security of mutual fund investment portfolios and operations. One aspect of that concern is the Act's attention to the financial and other records of funds and to their outside accountants.

— Mutual Fund Law Handbook (1998)[1]

All asset managers perform the front- and back-office functions described in the previous chapters, regardless of the products they offer—mutual funds, pension investments, trusts. They make investment decisions, order trades, execute and settle the trades, keep records, and monitor their contractual and regulatory compliance and their exposure to risk. This chapter discusses investment management functions specific to mutual funds. These include fund accounting, auditing, legal support, and other compliance and reporting functions often termed "fund administration."

Fund Accounting

Every investment manager, whether or not it manages assets for a mutual fund, must do some form of investment accounting. The back office keeps securities inventory records so that the portfolio manager and others in the front office have accurate, current information on which to base investment management and trading decisions. Registered mutual funds have additional, stringent accounting requirements laid out by the 1940 Act and subsequent regulation. These are so specialized that many investment managers deploy two separate layers of accounting—one to provide data for investment decision making, and one to perform fund accounting in accordance with the regulations. Often they contract with specialized service providers to perform their 1940 Act fund accounting, while maintaining their own internal portfolio accounting system for control and decision-making purposes. For example, David L. Babson, described in the last chapter, maintains the securities inventory for all its accounts internally on PMIS, but contracts with IBT, the custodian for the mutual funds holdings, to perform fund accounting for them. The fund accounting group, be it internal or external, keeps the fund's general ledger and books of record. It produces the information that goes into the semi-annual reports for the shareholders and the regulators. However, one requirement dominates the fund accounting job—the need to establish the net asset value (NAV) per share for the fund every business day between 4:30 and 5:50 P.M., eastern time. One journalist has described this process as "hours of preparation followed by minutes of intense number crunching," and characterized its routine success as "a small miracle."[2]

Rule 22c-1(b) under the 1940 Act requires that an open-end fund compute the NAV per share at least once each business day—Monday through Friday, excluding holidays listed in the prospectus, days the NYSE is closed, and days on which the fund received no orders to purchase or redeem shares. A fund may calculate the NAV more often than once per day, but very few do. Rule 22c-1(d) requires the fund's directors to set the time during the day for calculating the NAV, but for all practical purposes, they all do it between 4:30 P.M. eastern when the NYSE closes and 5:50 P.M.—the deadline for getting prices to NASDAQ.

Figure 1 summarizes this daily activity in the typical fund accounting group. Fund accountants spend most of the day preparing to strike the NAV, posting activity and making sure that the ledger records are correct. They generally start by reconciling the cash and securities records they maintain with those maintained by the custodian and the investment adviser. Events such as trade failures, unexpected corporate actions (e.g., a dividend comes in that no one expected because someone missed the notification), or mistakes (e.g., the custodian posts a receipt to the wrong fund), may cause the records to need correction. Fund accountants compare information they get from the adviser or custodian, or, if they have automated reconciliation systems in place, resolve exceptions these systems reveal. Where needed, they make changes to the inventory of cash and securities maintained in the fund accounting system.

Next, the accountants update those cash and securities records with the effects of the day's activity not related to trading. Bonds make interest payments or reach maturity, equities pay dividends in cash or stock, and asset-backed securities generate paydowns that include both principal and interest. All of these change cash or securities balances. Each fund accountant reconciles the report of activity from the custodian with the fund accounting system's projections for the fund. When they find discrepancies, the accountants investigate and resolve them, and make any needed adjustments to fund records.

Fund accounting may or may not provide the investment adviser with a report on cash availability; in many cases, the adviser manages cash separately from fund accounting. When accounting does this function, it gives the adviser a report of cash on hand, as well as projections of the cash flows expected over the next few days. These flows stem both from portfolio activity (trade settlements, maturities, dividends, and interest) and shareholder activity (share purchase and redemption settlements, dividend payments to shareholders). This helps the adviser to anticipate cash availability and needs, and to plan investment strategy accordingly.

Next the fund accountant updates the fund's records to reflect the previous day's activities. Investors placed orders yesterday to purchase and sell fund shares, and these were processed at yesterday's NAV. This capital stock activity has changed the number of shares outstanding in the fund, and has generated a cash flow.

The fund's records must reflect the proper number of shares to support calculating today's NAV per share. Similarly, the portfolio manager placed buy and sell security trades yesterday. The fund books recognize portfolio trades on T+1, i.e., on the day after the trade was made. Posting the fund trades is a computerized process in many accounting shops—trade records are fed into the fund accounting system from the adviser's trade order or portfolio management systems. In these cases, the accountant reviews control reports, makes sure the process worked correctly, and resolves exceptions.

Figure 1: Summary of Daily Activities of Fund Accounting

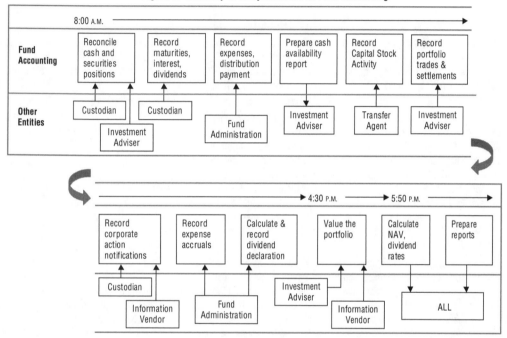

During the day, the accountant posts three more items to the fund's records in the fund accounting system: corporate actions, expenses, and fund dividends. Notifications of upcoming corporate actions for equity securities (dividends, stock splits, etc.) come in from information vendors and from custodians. Some of the simpler actions, such as cash dividends, can be posted automatically to the system from electronic feeds. Others, such as reorganizations, require manual intervention because of their complexity. The fund accountant makes sure that all these corporate actions for securities the fund holds have been identified and properly captured in the system.

The fund's NAV each day must include all the expenses the fund has accrued through that date. Some expenses that accrue regularly day-by-day (such as the fund directors' compensation), or that can be calculated based on a set formula (such as the investment advisory fee) are determined automatically by the fund accounting system. For these the fund accountant must set up the rules initially, then monitor the accounting system's calculations each day. Some expenses are not so regular (such as the cost of getting outside counsel's advice on an SEC letter), and the accountant must enter these when they occur. These expense accruals form liability accounts on the fund books. Many funds today have more than one class of shares, and often fund accounting must accrue expenses for these classes differently, ultimately resulting in a different NAV per share for each class.

SHARE CLASSES

Section 22(d) of the 1940 Act requires that the price each investor pays for a fund share be described in the prospectus and calculated according to a scheme applied uniformly to all shareholders. Up until the 1970s, this requirement presented no particular issue. Investors in no-load funds bought their shares at NAV; investors in load funds paid the offering price—NAV adjusted for a front-end load. Effectively, every shareholder in a fund bought the single class of shares offered by that fund.

Rule 12b-1, promulgated by the SEC in 1980, started to change this. Rule 12b-1 allows management companies to use fund assets to pay for distribution. This opened an avenue for fund companies to create other distribution payment schemes besides pure no-load or front-end load. In the years since 1980, fund companies have created literally dozens of such schemes.[3] Rule 22d-1 of the 1940 Act regulations allows them to do this so long as any such scheme applies uniformly to all shareholders that belong to the class so affected. As a result, many funds today feature multiple share classes, reflecting different distribution strategies, as discussed in detail in Chapter 8.

From the point of view of fund accounting, different share classes mean different expense amounts applied to subsets of the overall investment pool, as shown in the diagram. The first step in determining the NAV per share for a multi-class fund is to determine the asset value for the overall portfolio and allocate it to the classes. The investors in each class participate in the ownership of the fund in proportion to the number of shares that each class owns. The second step is to apply expense accruals for each class. Expenses vary by class—some classes will have 12b-1 fees deducted, others will not. Finally, once the appropriate expense accruals have been netted against the gross asset values, the NAV per share for each class is calculated by dividing the class' net asset value by its number of outstanding shares. These figures are reported separately to NASDAQ, and shown separately in the newspapers.

To qualify for tax pass-through status, funds must pay out to their shareholders essentially all of the dividend and interest income they receive, and the capital gains they realize from security sales. Funds that hold dividend or interest-paying securities pay dividends to their shareholders on a regular basis—monthly, quarterly, semi-annually.

Growth-oriented funds holding equity securities that seldom pay dividends may distribute income and gains as infrequently as once per year, if at all. On those days on which a dividend or capital gain payment is to accrue to the fund's shareholders, fund accounting determines what amount the shareholders should get. This information is passed to the transfer agent, which ultimately calculates the distribution amount for each individual shareholder and makes the payments.

BUYING REALIZED GAINS

To satisfy the requirements for pass-through tax status and avoid paying tax at the fund level on income and realized capital gains, a mutual fund must distribute substantively all income and gains to its shareholders each year. Funds that generate income (dividends and interest) typically distribute this income regularly throughout the year. However, many funds distribute the entire year's realized capital gains, i.e., the net gains they have made in selling portfolio securities, during the last few months of the year. According to the IRS code, if the fund declares the distribution in October, November, or December, it is considered paid in that tax year, even though the payment to the shareholder doesn't occur until after year end. So, many funds simply wait until late in the year when they can calculate the year's gains, and make one distribution of them all.

An investor who purchases shares of a fund into a taxable account shortly before this payment is made purchases a tax liability. (If the shareholder is purchasing shares for a retirement or other non-taxable account, then these tax considerations do not apply.) A specific example best demonstrates this.

American Century Ultra, a midcap growth fund, distributes its capital gains once per year. In 1998, it declared a capital gains distribution of $3.12 per share for shareholders in the fund as of the start of day December 18, payable on December 31. On December 17, the last day one could purchase shares and qualify for the payout, the NAV for the fund was $34.06. The next day, it dropped to $31.37, since someone purchasing shares this day would do so "ex-dividend"—that is, he or she would not get the gains payment. (The net $2.69 per share drop in NAV resulted from the combination of the $3.12 per share gains payout offset by market price movement in the fund's portfolio of securities.)

A shareholder who purchased $10,000 worth of the fund immediately before it went ex-dividend would have received 293.600 shares. He or she would have then accrued a distribution of $916.62, and the value of the shares would have dropped to $9,210.23 (293.600 shares times the December 18 NAV of $31.37). Had the shareholder used the distribution to purchase $916.62 worth of shares at the December 31 reinvestment price of $31.41, he or she would have ended up with a total of 322.782 shares (worth $10,784.16 at year end), but would have the tax liability on the $916.62. A shareholder who waited until December 18 to make the $10,000 purchase would have bought 318.776 shares at 31.37, but would have received no gains distribution and incurred no tax liability. Those shares would have been worth $10,650.30 at year end.

So which is better—$10,784 worth of fund with the tax liability on a $917 distribution, or $10,650 worth of fund and no tax liability? In this scenario, purchasing on December 18 instead of December 17 would have been a better choice for anyone with a marginal tax rate greater than 15 percent. But the figures change for any other purchase date (for example, if the investor had purchased the shares on December 15, when the NAV was $33.46), because the NAV changes each day. For someone looking at purchasing into a fund that will pay its distribution several weeks out, the picture grows cloudy. A distribution looming in the immediate future might justify delaying a purchase, but delaying for distributions too far into the future is a bad idea because the investor cannot predict market action. The investor considering a share purchase near year end should do some homework, analyzing the likely size and timing of a gains distribution, as well as the volatility of the fund's prices. Of course, all of these factors are uncertain, so there will never be one right answer.

The taxes shareholders pay on realized capital gains form another point of contention between the advocates of passive versus active management. An actively managed fund is more likely than an index fund to sell holdings, generate realized capital gains, and have to distribute these to shareholders. The shareholders, therefore, will have to pay taxes sooner (as a result of the fund's portfolio activity), instead of later (when they finally sell their fund shares). Some fund managers have recently launched funds that are managed explicitly to avoid having shareholders have to pay tax on portfolio income or gains. The prospectus for the Vanguard tax managed funds, for example, states that the funds "aim to minimize the impact of taxes on investors' total returns by operating in a tax-efficient manner," i.e., by minimizing portfolio turnover, avoiding income paying issues, and imposing a redemption fee on short-term investors.[4]

In June 2000, Representative Jim Saxton (R-NJ) floated a proposal to change the tax treatment of mutual fund distributions, to eliminate the tax shareholders pay on capital gains that the fund has realized but that they (the shareholders) have not. In other words, Saxton proposed to defer taxes on gains shareholders receive but reinvest in the fund. They would pay taxes on these gains only when they eventually liquidate their holdings. However, as of late 2000, there was no sign that Congress might actually pursue this proposal.

Finally, at 4:30 P.M. eastern time each business day, once the New York Stock Exchange closes, fund accounting launches into the flurry of activity that marks the daily NAV calculation. Step 1 in the process is to determine the price at which to value each of the fund's securities holdings. Rule 2a-4 of the regulations requires that this be the current market value, unless no market quotation for the security is readily available. Most holdings for most funds have a readily available market value: they have been trading during the day that has just ended, or a broker has committed a bid price, or there is a well-defined formula for calculating the price based on the price of other securities. For some securities that have not traded and for which no market price is known, the assets must be priced at fair value, as determined in good faith by the fund's board of directors. For example, in late 1997, a Fidelity representative said that "Fidelity uses fair value to price roughly 1,500 securities every day—mostly bonds and other instruments that don't trade actively on major exchanges."[5] This 1,500 represents a small fraction of the tens of thousands of issues the various Fidelity funds hold.

Once the accountant is satisfied that each security has a good price associated with it, the portfolio can be valued. Valuation means calculating the total value of the fund's assets by extending quantity by price for all securities holdings, summing these, and adding in non-security assets such as cash, accrued interest, and pre-paid expenses. Liabilities, in the form of accrued expenses, net against this gross value to produce the net asset value. The accountant divides the net asset value by the number of outstanding shares to arrive at the net asset value per share. This figure is transmitted to NASDAQ by 5:50 P.M., so NASDAQ can distribute it to all interested parties, including the news services, so it shows up in the next morning's paper. It also goes to the fund's transfer agent, so that the day's shareholder transactions can be priced (more about that in Chapter 11). Most of the time, most of the funds hit this deadline. Occasionally, when the underlying securities markets are exceptionally active, delay in getting securities priced may prevent funds from getting priced. For example, on October 28, 1997, when volumes on the exchanges were more than twice normal, a number of fund groups with hundreds of individual funds were unable to calculate NAVs before the NASDAQ deadline.[6] If pricing or other problems prevent fund accounting from striking the NAV per share in time to make the NASDAQ cutoff, the papers report N/A for the fund's NAV the next day. Funds face no explicit sanction for missing the NASDAQ cutoff, but doing so is embarrassing, and a fund company draws the SEC's attention if it posts N/As too often.

Money market funds present an exception to the way mutual funds are priced. Since they hold short-term fixed-income securities, the price of which should not fluctuate widely while the fund is holding them, the fund's NAV per share remains constant at $1.00. If the fund knows it is going to hold a security to maturity, it may value it using amortized cost rather than the current market price—unless, of course, something bad happens to the security that threatens the fund's ability to get face value at maturity. The income that these securities generate accrues each day to the fund's shareholders. Thus fund accounting for a money market fund concerns itself primarily with calculating this income accrual (and making sure that nothing has threatened the $1.00 NAV).

BREAKING THE BUCK

Money market mutual funds try very hard to maintain a constant $1.00 NAV. Although they are not legally required to maintain this price, "breaking the buck," i.e., letting the NAV fall below a dollar, is tantamount to admitting abject failure. In effect, it says that the investment adviser was so inept that he or she couldn't even pick debt securities that would hold their value for the few days or weeks until they matured. Since breaking the buck means the kiss of death for a fund, a management company will usually subsidize a fund in danger of having this happen, putting in its own capital to maintain the NAV.

When a fund does get into this danger, it usually results from a faulty risk assessment—that is, a debt security that the investment adviser thought was safe has turned out to have some sort of problem. The case of General American Life Insurance Company, which threatened a number of funds with the spectre of breaking the buck, illustrates how this might happen.[7]

General American, a policyholder-owned seller of whole life insurance, fell into a variant of the ancient trap of borrowing short and lending long. To strengthen its financial performance, General American began issuing short-term funding agreements, instruments similar to short-term notes. These agreements had one feature that turned out to be very important—the buyer could demand that General American buy them back at par at any time upon seven days' notice. General American took the money and invested in conservative securities that paid 25 to 30 basis points more than they were paying the buyers of the agreements. In mid-1999, $6.8 billion worth of these funding agreements were outstanding.

Unfortunately, General American had a less responsible partner in the deal, ARM Financial Group, that was using its share of the proceeds to invest in much more speculative securities. When interest rate changes eroded the value of these investments, Moody's downgraded ARM, triggering a chain of events that forced American General to take over ARM's half of the agreements, along with the investments ARM had made with the proceeds. This in turn prompted Moody's to cut General American's rating of debt and financial strength from A3 to A2. And that started a run.

Within a week, General American had received demands to redeem $4.4 billion worth of the funding agreements, and it became clear that the rest of the $6.8 billion would shortly follow. The bond market simply could not absorb all the securities that American General would have to sell to raise the money for these redemptions, meaning that General American could not raise the cash to meet its obligations. General American faced insolvency, just like a depression-era bank with a line of depositors at the door. So in mid-August, the insurer turned to Missouri regulators, seeking protection to enable it to effect an orderly liquidation over a longer period.

Suddenly, some two dozen money market mutual funds found themselves with over $2 billion worth of funding agreements that they could not liquidate immediately. Alliance, Federated, Schwab, and Oppenheimer each held over $300 million of these securities among the funds in their families. Other fund families held lesser amounts. If anything happened to threaten General American's workout—if the bond markets tanked, for example—they would be forced to recognize a significant decline in value of these securities. Some advisers began making plans for bailouts that would keep the funds' NAVs at $1.00 in case the General American workout failed, or shareholder liquidations forced them to sell the agreements at a steep discount. Alliance, for example, got a letter of credit from its parent, Equitable, to give it access to cash with which to protect its NAV.

Fortunately for the funds, a white knight rode in to save the day before things got too ugly. On August 25, 1999, General American agreed to be acquired by MetLife, ending its 66-year life as an independent company. MetLife agreed to pay off the holders of the funding agreements immediately, in full. While Moody's grumbled for a while about possibly downgrading MetLife's ratings, the crisis was over for the fund companies. Within the next few weeks they unloaded all the agreements at face value, and nobody had to break the buck.

Once the prices are out, the fund accountants produce reports, or, more accurately, the fund accounting system produces reports. These go to the investment adviser, fund administration, the management company, anyone who has a stake in the fund's operations. They include information on the fund's status and activity, such as a current inventory of holdings, a summary of the day's trade and other activity, a recap of the pricing activity and results, and, possibly, compliance monitoring reports (described below).

The number of funds one accountant can handle varies with the complexity of the funds. A PricewaterhouseCoopers study found in 1998 that the typical ratio varied from one to four funds per accountant, with the overall average being 2.3.[8] Some fund accounting groups organize parts of their staff functionally, with individuals specializing in corporate actions, expenses, etc. Others take a purely fund-based approach, with individuals performing all the functions required for the fund or funds for which they are responsible. Regardless of the organization, each fund will have an assigned accountant to make sure that all the preparatory steps are taken during the day, and to shepherd the fund through the NAV process.

While some management companies perform fund accounting in-house, many give this function over to third-party service providers. Fund accounting does not provide any potential for competitive advantage—it must be done correctly, but there is no way to make the fund more attractive by doing it better. Therefore, most funds seek the provider that can do it correctly and reliably at least cost. Most very large fund groups can realize the economies of scale to do it internally. Most smaller fund groups outsource it.

Table 1 shows the major third-party fund accounting providers in the United States as of late 1998. A comparison of this list with the list of custodians in the previous chapter shows much overlap. The custodian already has much of the data needed to support fund accounting, and is committed to making the large investment in information technology for securities processing. Fund accounting provides a natural, revenue-generating extension to custody, and many providers pursue it.

The annual cost of fund accounting found among the participants in the 1998 PricewaterhouseCoopers study ranged between .4 and 2.7 basis points. The actual amount depends on such factors as the characteristics of the fund, e.g., the types of securities it holds and how difficult they are to price, the amount of trading it does, and the economics of the contract the fund complex has with the accounting provider, e.g., whether fund accounting is done internally or outsourced, whether fund accounting is bundled with other services, how many funds the fund accountant handles.

A Day in the Life of a Fund Accountant

State Street Bank performs the accounting for more open-end mutual funds than any other organization in the United States. Among these are the funds managed by one of the largest and oldest fund families in the industry—which we will call "L&O" here. Today, several State Street fund accounting teams divide responsibility for L&O, each doing the work for about two dozen funds. These teams occupy a sea of cubicles on the third floor of State Street's facility at Boston's Lafayette Place. Russell Donohoe is a floater in one of these L&O teams. As a floater, his duties vary from day to day. When everyone on the team is in, Russell double-checks the work of

Table 1: Third-Party Fund Accounting Service Providers
(Funds and Assets as of March 31, 1998)

Organization / Headquarters	No. of Funds	Total Assets ($millions)
State Street Bank and Trust / Boston	2,250	917,650
PFPC, Inc. / Wilmington, DE	802	180,632
The Chase Manhattan Bank / New York	428	155,567
SEI Investments / Oaks, PA	382	140,425
First Data Investor Services Group* / Westborough, MA	460	104,121
BISYS Investment Services / Columbus, OH	372	101,598
Investors Bank & Trust / Boston	802	98,769
The Bank of New York / New York	80	68,621
Forum Financial Group / Portland, ME	112	41,796
Brown Brothers Harriman & Co. / Boston	102	26,600
Firstar Trust Company / Milwaukee	133	17,158
Countrywide Fund Services / Cincinnati	71	10,807
Fifth Third Bank / Cincinnati	34	5,395
Sunstone Financial Group / Milwaukee	37	4,057
Mutual Fund Services Company / Dublin, OH	10	980
Totals	**6,075**	**1,874,176**

Source: *The 1998 Fund Accounting Service Guide*, Securities Data Publishing, 1998.

*In 1999, First Data Corporation sold its Investor Services Group, including the third-party fund accounting business, to PNC, parent of PFPC, Inc.

other fund accountants, and helps out wherever there is a problem. When one of the team's fund accountants is out, Russell takes over his or her funds for the day. On this particular day in early December 1999, Russell is covering for a team member out on vacation, and is performing the accounting for seven funds—three fixed income and four equity.

The fund accountant's day at State Street runs from 10:00 A.M. to 6:00 or 7:00 P.M. When Russell arrives in the morning, he starts his work on his assigned funds by verifying activity that others have already processed. "We have some specialized groups," he points out. "Corporate actions are handled for all funds by one centralized group. So are cash settlements and pricing. This allows the fund accountant to handle more funds— usually five or six funds for experienced staff." In addition, State Street is the custodian for the funds he is handling, so he doesn't need to manually reconcile custodial and fund accounting records.

After verifying the corporate actions postings for his funds (there weren't any on this day), Russell turns his attention to securities trades. The previous day was slow for the fixed-income funds—only the emerging markets fund has made a trade, buying a Brazilian bond. He enters this trade into State Street's fund accounting system, Multi-Currency Horizon (MCH). MCH occupies one window on the 20-inch, high-resolution monitor on Russell's desk. NAV Alert occupies a second window. "NAV Alert is an analysis tool for us, but also a backup system," Russell explains. "Anything we enter into MCH is automatically fed to it. We use it to analyze impacts on the fund, and, if anything happens so that MCH is down, we could use it to prepare the fund for pricing as well." During Russell's two-year tenure at State Street, however, they have never had to use this backup.

Next, he turns to currency forward contracts that his international bond funds use to hedge their currency exposure, marking them to market with the day's exchange rates, and checking the effect on the fund. He prints a page showing the results of the activity, marks it to note he has double-checked it, and puts it in a tray on the desk. From time to time other members of the team pick up these sheets and double-check them. Russell rechecks sheets that others have completed. "We like to have everything looked at by at least two pairs of eyes," he explains.

Around 11:00 A.M., something unusual rolls in from the cash area. Several of the L&O bond funds, including one domestic high yield fund Russell is handling, had held a bond that defaulted when the issuer went bankrupt. Now, apparently, the bankruptcy proceedings have resulted in the bond holders getting a cash payment. L&O has long since written off the holding, and no longer shows the bond in any fund's securities inventory. So the payment is simply booked as a long-term capital gain, not associated with any security. "First time I've ever seen something like this," he comments.

Equity trades for the L&O funds feed into MCH via an automated, computer-to-computer link called electronic trade delivery (ETD). For some reason, ETD is late today, so Russell still can't verify the trades for his equity funds. He checks the funds' expense accruals. The L&O funds are set up in MCH with two types of expenses. The system calculates some—the management fee and 12b-1 commissions—based on the value of assets in the fund that day. Others accrue at a fixed rate per day. For example, one fund accrues $15.76 per day for legal, $49.26 per day for director's fees, and so on. Three of the funds have multiple share classes, with some expenses that accrue at the composite level, and others at the class level. Russell verifies that these all have been calculated and posted properly.

As the day goes by, he continues to examine different aspects of the funds' books, verifying entries, occasionally making adjusting entries. Around noon he handles the income accruals for the bonds held by the fixed-income funds. Shortly thereafter, he turns his attention to the changes in the fund's shares that resulted from yesterday's shareholder activity. Then it's the dividends the funds pay or accrue. None of his equity funds are hitting a dividend ex-date today, but the fixed-income funds do calculate accruals. He does these calculations and posts them to the system. As always, he rechecks and documents what he has done, and tosses the file up to the mail tray for someone else to check.

By mid-afternoon he has completed the fixed-income funds. For each of these he does a test pricing run, which calculates the NAV per share based on yesterday's securities prices. Once again he double-checks the effects on the NAV for each component of the fund's books. He examines anything that has a significant effect on the NAV. For the emerging markets debt fund, he finds an NAV impact resulting from a change in the value of the currency forward contracts. He checks this, and determines that it is valid, resulting from a large change in the exchange rate for Turkish Lira. Satisfied that the fixed-income funds are ready, he exports their data to external files so that NAVigator, State Street's pricing system, can pick them up and complete the NAV calculations once the securities prices are available.

At 4:00 P.M., ETD finally delivers the trades for the equity funds. ("I've never seen it this late before," Russell comments.) Russell and the other members of the team work intensely to get the equity funds ready to price, verifying the correct posting of the equity trades. Around 4:45 supervisors start calling out "export, please," as the deadline for fund pricing approaches. Unless a fund's data has been exported, NAVigator will not pick it up and calculate its NAV. Russell finishes exporting all his funds, and turns to organizing and filing the mass of printouts that have accumulated on his desk.

Just before 5:00 P.M., someone calls out "PPs are in," indicating that prices for the privately placed securities, usually the last to arrive, are in the system. The level of activity picks up noticeably. One corner of the floor on which the fund accountants work is devoted to computers for pricing. First, pricing specialists verify every security price that has changed by more than a stated tolerance from the previous day's price, by obtaining a second price quotation from another information vendor, such as Reuters or Bloomberg (primary prices come from Bridge). Once they have done this, and satisfied themselves that the prices are valid, they run "NAVcalc," the process that applies the security prices and calculates the NAV per share. Russell gets the output that shows the results of NAVcalc for his funds shortly after 5:00. Once again he double-checks everything. Does this NAV look reasonable in light of everything we did today? Is the overall change in NAV per share consistent with the impacts we calculated for the individual components? Once he is sure that everything is correct, he designates the fund as "balanced," so the NAV per share can go on the transmission to NASDAQ at 5:50 P.M.

At 5:25 someone finds a bad security price, and the NAVs for some of the funds have to be recalculated. ("This is a ripple effect from getting the equity trades so late," Russell comments. "We didn't have as much time as we usually do to check prices.") There is a flurry of activity as accountants work to complete and verify these funds before the 5:50 P.M. deadline for submitting NAVs to NASDAQ. At 5:48 P.M. the last fund is balanced, and all the funds make the transmission.

By 5:50, the tension and activity levels in the room have dropped noticeably. Russell and the other fund accountants get ten-page printouts summarizing the books for each of their funds. They do one final round of double-checking the figures; make sure every adjustment or reconciliation they made is clearly documented; and complete their filing, so that there are no loose ends left for tomorrow. Finally, as 7:00 P.M. approaches, all the accountants have finished their days, and the floor is deserted. State Street Bank's fund accountants have once more performed their daily small miracle.

Fund Audit

Like all publicly traded companies in the United States, a mutual fund must be audited each year by an independent auditor. It must issue an audited annual report to its shareholders, and include with its annual report to the SEC a letter from its independent auditor on the adequacy of its internal controls. These reports, along with the internal reports issued to management, form the visible output of the rigorous examination process that comprises the fund audit.

Audit of a mutual fund concentrates on whether the information reflected on the required financial reports presents fairly in all material respects the fund's financial position and operating results, in accordance with generally accepted accounting principles (GAAP). Much of the auditor's work is directed to examining the processes with which the fund keeps its records, especially the controls in place to ensure that those processes are performed correctly. In addition, the auditor performs substantive tests of the fund's records in five areas.

1. *Investments*. The 1940 Act itself requires the auditor to confirm all the fund's securities holdings, including unsettled purchases, as of the audit date with the custodian or brokers. The auditor also verifies the valuations the fund has assigned to these securities, by independently obtaining prices (as required by SEC rule) for all securities as of the audit date, and comparing these to the prices used by the fund's accountants for that date. The auditor further reviews and tests the processes with which fund management monitors compliance with regulatory and prospectus restrictions on portfolio holdings.

2. *Investment Income and Realized Gains*. The auditor tests whether all income earned by the fund's holdings has been recorded in the fund's financial records. It examines portfolio sales transactions, and tests the calculation and classification of capital gains. This examination of gains and losses typically includes a review for wash sales—securities dispositions on which capital loss is disallowed for tax purposes due to proximity to acquisitions of identical securities.

3. *Accruals and Expenses*. The auditor examines expense records to determine whether they are in accordance with the provisions of the investment advisory agreement, prospectus, and other relevant contracts. The auditor recalculates the management fee and any other fees that are based on the assets of the fund, and compares them against the fees actually charged. Other expenses are reviewed for proper authorization.

4. *Taxes*. The auditor reviews the fund's compliance with requirements of the tax laws, especially those that allow it pass-through status. Should a fund fail to meet the requirements for pass-through status, the consequences (i.e., having to pay taxes at the fund level) would severely harm the fund and its adviser—through mass shareholder redemptions, bad press, and even litigation.

5. *Shareholders' Equity*. The auditor reviews the internal controls of the fund's transfer agent, usually by considering a report on the results of a control examination issued by independent auditors for the transfer agent, and tests the computations of the net asset value per share that are used in the daily purchase and sale transactions for fund shares.

Finally, the auditor reviews the financial reports the fund issues. Mutual fund financial statements typically include a year-end balance sheet, a statement of operations for the most recent year, and statements of changes in net assets for the two most recent years. In some cases, a statement of cash flows may also be required. Additionally, the statements include a five-year summary of financial highlights, and a schedule of *every* security holding as of the statement date, including name, quantity, value, type, and category (industry or similar grouping).

REPORT OF INDEPENDENT ACCOUNTANTS

To the Shareholders and
Board of Trustees of
Vanguard Wellington Fund

In our opinion, the accompanying statement of net assets and the related statements of operations and of changes in net assets and the financial highlights present fairly, in all material respects, the financial position of Vanguard Wellington Fund (the "Fund") at November 30, 1998, the results of its operations for the year then ended, the changes in its net assets for each of the two years in the period then ended and the financial highlights for each of the five years in the period then ended, in conformity with generally accepted accounting principles. These financial statements and financial highlights (hereafter referred to as "financial statements") are the responsibility of the Fund's management; our responsibility is to express an opinion on these financial statements based on our audits. We conducted our audits of these financial statements in accordance with generally accepted auditing standards which require that we plan and perform the audit to obtain reasonable assurance about whether the financial statements are free of material misstatement. An audit includes examining, on a test basis, evidence supporting the amounts and disclosures in the financial statements, assessing the accounting principles used and significant estimates made by management, and evaluating the overall financial statement presentation. We believe that our audits, which included confirmation of securities at November 30, 1998 by correspondence with the custodian, provide a reasonable basis for the opinion expressed above.

PricewaterhouseCoopers LLP

Thirty South Seventeenth Street   **25**
Philadelphia, Pennsylvania 19103

January 6, 1999

The auditor's report for the Vanguard Wellington Fund, shown here, is typical of those found in mutual fund annual reports. A mutual fund audit rarely results in a qualified opinion—that is, one in which the auditor notes any divergence from GAAP. The SEC would not permit financial statements with an opinion qualified for such a divergence (or for a limitation on the scope of the audit) to be included in a registration statement, thus effectively suspending further sales of the fund's shares. Therefore, as a practical matter, fund management must correct any shortcoming that the fund's auditor believes represents a material departure from GAAP. Rarely, however, do fund management and the auditors find themselves in an adversarial position over an accounting issue at year end. In the vast majority of cases, the auditors work with fund management throughout the year to identify troublesome practices and suggest corrections before they become audit issues.

Overall, the industry paid $200 million, or an average of just under $30,000 per fund, for auditing services in 1998.[9] The cost of auditing for an individual fund varies widely, from under $10,000 to over $50,000, depending on a number of factors. The least expensive funds to audit hold a relatively small number of easily priced securities, require only basic attestation services, and have their records kept by a complex whose internal processes the audit firm knows have been examined and found to be well-controlled. More expensive audits are required for funds that hold large numbers of securities, or especially complex or hard-to-price securities (for example, certain derivatives, private placements, or emerging-market securities), require extra services such as the preparation of financial reports, or require that the auditor spend more time and effort examining internal procedures of the fund's record keeper. Large fund complexes that have many individual funds audited by one audit firm are often able to obtain lower audit fees, as the auditors are able to rely on common control systems and perform large numbers of audits simultaneously, allowing them to spread certain fixed audit costs over a larger number of funds.

Fund Legal Support

A number of fund activities require the support of attorneys, either employees of the management company, outside counsel, or, in many cases, both. The matters with which fund management typically needs legal work fall into several major groups.

- *Organization and registration of funds*. When a new fund is to be set up, attorneys work with the management company to ensure that all of the decisions concerning fund design and operations have been made in compliance with the regulations, and that these are properly documented in Form N1-A, the registration statement. Attorneys work with the management company not only on the original filing, but also on the post-effective amendments to the registration statement that the funds must file. Funds file post-effective amendments on Form 485APOS when there has been a material change, such as a revision of fundamental investment policies, or when a new fund in a series is being introduced. Funds file Form 485BPOS for non-material changes, including updated financial information. Typically, each fund files a 485BPOS once per year, since the prospectus cannot be used if the financial information it contains is more than sixteen months old. All of these filings require legal review.

- *Drafting and review of contracts*. Since funds have no employees, but instead contract with outside parties for all their services, every fund must have a series of contracts drawn up and periodically reviewed and changed. The most common contracts include those for investment advisory, distribution, fund administration, transfer agent, and custody services. The fund's Board of Directors or Trustees is charged with overseeing these contracts, ensuring that the agents with which the fund has contracted are discharging their duties properly. For example, Section 15(c) of the 1940 Act requires that the fund's independent directors evaluate the terms of the investment advisory agreement on an annual basis, and requires their majority vote to approve or renew it. The management company uses legal assistance in preparing these contracts, and the directors use legal assistance to help ensure that they properly execute their responsibilities in overseeing them.

- *Ensuring compliance*. Attorneys work with management company staff to develop operating procedures that comply with the federal and state regulations. They also develop compliance monitoring and reporting processes that help the management company and fund directors verify that the fund is complying with regulations as it operates. For example, the directors of a money market fund are required by the regulations to adopt procedures through which they can ensure that the fund holds suitable securities, and that it maintains a stable net asset value.[10] Attorneys contribute to and/or review a number of documents that funds produce—such as advertising and sales literature, proxy statements, and shareholder letters—for compliance with the relevant regulations.
- *Interpretation of regulatory pronouncements*. The SEC issues dozens of rules, proposed rules, no-action letters, interpretive releases, and other pronouncements that affect mutual fund companies each year. Since these often have legal implications for the management company or fund, attorneys review them and evaluate their impact and advise management on how to respond.
- *Preparation for SEC examinations*. The SEC conducts examinations of fund groups from time to time, usually concentrating on some topic in which the SEC staff is particularly interested at the moment. (For example, the SEC conducted a number of examinations focusing on directed brokerage and soft dollar arrangements in 1999.) Typically, the SEC sends the fund company a letter ahead of time, identifying what records the SEC staff will want to see when they arrive. Attorneys review this letter to help the fund group respond to these requests, including identifying what is and is not applicable. In addition, attorneys may be called on to prepare further communications during the course of the examination to clarify issues that arise.
- *Representation in SEC or other legal proceedings*. Mutual fund management companies may become embroiled in legal proceedings just like other corporations or individuals. The SEC may institute enforcement proceedings, as it did in the cases of Piper Jaffray and PaineWebber discussed in Chapter 6, if the staff believe that someone has acted illegally. Occasionally shareholders and others file suits against a fund's directors, management company, or investment adviser. In all such cases, the organizations or individuals involved must be advised and represented by counsel.

Overall, the industry paid about $200 million in 1998 for these legal services, or an average of just under $30,000 per fund.[11] Legal expense varies considerably from fund to fund according to several factors. A fund will use more legal service when it is being set up, or is making significant changes in its organization, when it is under regulatory scrutiny (such as an SEC examination), or when some external event, such as a merger or lawsuit, calls for unusual levels of legal work. Over 200 law firms provide legal services to open-end mutual funds, with no single firm controlling more than about 7 percent of the market, according to Strategic Insight data as of the end of 1999.

Other Fund Administration Functions

People in the mutual fund industry use the term *fund administration* to mean different things. In its most expansive usage, fund administration refers to everything about running a fund that is not investment advisory or distribution. In its narrowest usage it means administering a fund's contracts with its service providers, and taking care of certain compliance and reporting functions. We use the term here in this latter, more restricted sense, distinguishing the major support functions such as fund accounting and shareholder servicing from fund administration.

Chapter 6 discussed portfolio compliance monitoring—the process of ensuring that the securities holdings of the fund remain in compliance with regulations and prospectus rules. Fund administration monitors and ensures fund compliance in a broader context as well. In addition to following the rules regarding portfolio composition, funds must comply with operating requirements of federal and state regulatory agencies. (For example, they must monitor the personal securities trades made by all individuals deemed to be "access persons" for the fund.) They must follow the tax guidelines of the IRS and the individual state governments (as to when a municipal issue qualifies for state tax exemption, for example). They must file the required financial reports with the regulatory agencies, such as the semi-annual reports to the SEC. Responsibility for these compliance and reporting functions falls to the fund administration group.

Most often, this group is housed within the management company. Some service providers offer fund administration outsourcing, typically in conjunction with other services, such as custody, fund accounting, and shareholder processing. The amount and type of these administrative functions performed by the service providers account for some of the variation in fees funds pay for investment advisory, fund accounting, custody, and legal service.

One may be able to determine how a particular fund's administration is handled by accessing the fund's registration form in the EDGAR database, available via the SEC's web site. The SEC requires mutual funds to electronically file many of their submissions, including Form N-1A, the registration statement. Item 15—Investment Advisory and Other Services—in the Statement of Additional Information describes the fund's agreements with the investment adviser, principal underwriter, and other significant service providers. Item 29—Management Services—in the Other Information section provides a summary of any substantive provisions of management-related service contracts that have not been discussed in earlier sections.

For example, the *Pioneer America Income Trust* filed a post-effective amendment (number 14) to its registration on February 19, 1999, and this is available from EDGAR. As exhibits to this filing, the fund has attached not only the text of the administration agreement it has executed with Pioneering Management Corporation, but also a detailed list of services to be provided. These lists, which are organized into two broad categories—fund accounting, administration, and custody services; and legal services—are reproduced in Figure 2. The information in this registration reveals that Pioneering Management performs almost all fund administration for its funds internally, only using outside counsel for some legal functions. Other funds may take quite different approaches to obtain these services. For example, perusal of the November 30, 1999, post-effective amendment filed by the *Eaton Vance Income Fund* reveals that it contracts with its custodian, Investors Bank and Trust, for fund accounting as well as the preparation of shareholder reports.

Figure 2: Excerpt from Pioneer America Income Trust Form N1-A

EXHIBIT 2: PIONEERING MANAGEMENT CORP.
Fund Accounting, Administration, and Custody Services (FAACS)

LIST OF SERVICES PROVIDED TO PIONEER MUTUAL FUNDS SERVICES LISTED BY FAACS TEAM, OR FUNCTIONAL AREA.

FAACS Administration
- Provide direction, supervision, and administrative support to all FAACS teams
- Prepare or review and submit all tax reports for Funds
- Oversee fund distributions for regulatory compliance
- Assist in planning for new product introductions

Fund Accounting
- Maintain all accounting records for Funds
- Calculate and report daily net asset values per share and yields
- Recommend income and capital gains distribution rates
- Prepare funds' financial statements and assist in fund audits
- Maintain accounting records for institutional portfolios
- Perform periodic tests to verify each Fund's compliance with its prospectus and applicable regulations

Global Custody and Settlements Division
- Enter portfolio trades into Fund Accounting records
- Support corporate actions analyses
- Validate trade data and communicate them to Custodian Banks
- Act as liaison with Custodian Banks for trade settlements, security position reconciliations, and relaying global market updates to Investment Adviser
- Provide daily cash reporting to portfolio managers
- Resolve trade disputes with counter-parties

Pricing and Corporate Actions
- Ensure accuracy and timeliness of prices supplied by external sources to provide daily valuations of all security positions held by every Fund
- Validate and communicate corporate/class action information to Fund Accounting
- Present monthly valuation report to Funds' Board of Trustees
- Provide valuation and corporate actions services for securities held by institutional portfolios, but not by Funds
- Provide systems support to users of fund accounting and portfolio pricing software, and manage relationships with applicable software and hardware vendors

- Develop and maintain custom applications and systems interfaces for FAACS teams
- Manage Year 2000 project
- Provide user support and vendor liaison for trading, compliance, and analysis systems
- Implement and manage systems interfaces with Investment Adviser, Custodian Banks, and other service providers

Shareholder Reporting and Audit Liaison
- Review and complete Funds' financial statements
- Manage the Fund Audit process to ensure timely completion of shareholder reports
- Prepare reports related to contract renewals and soft dollar payments for Board of Trustees' review
- Provide financial information to Legal Department for prospectus updates and other regulatory filings
- Prepare regulatory reports such as N-SAR, Form S, and EDGAR filings
- Provide financial information to Pioneer management and industry trade groups
- Provide liquidity, commission, and soft dollar reporting to Pioneer management

Funds Controller
- Manage fund expense payment cycles (e.g., timeliness and accuracy of payments, allocation of costs among portfolios)
- Coordinate and standardize fund expense accruals and forecasting
- Provide expense reporting to Fund Accounting, FAACS management and auditors
- Compile daily reports of shareholder transactions from all sources (e.g., PSC, PMIL, BFDS, variable annuity agents, 401(k) administrators, third party record keepers) for entry into fund records
- Provide daily reconciliation of receivable, payable, and share accounts between fund records and entities listed above
- Manage the daily estimating process to minimize "as of" gains and losses to Funds
- Communicate daily fund prices and yields to PSC, PMIL, etc.
- Provide fund-related analyses to Pioneer management

EXHIBIT 3: THE PIONEER GROUP, INC. –LEGAL DEPARTMENT

REIMBURSABLE SERVICES:

Filings under Investment Company Act of 1940 and Securities Act of 1933

- Prepare and File (via EDGAR) Rule 24f-2 Notices (coordination with Pioneer Fund Accounting and Hale and Dorr LLP as necessary)
- SEC Electronic Filing (EDGAR) Responsibilities
    - Prepare Fund Registration Statements and Related Filings for filing on EDGAR and complete filings
    - Maintain and develop enhancements to Pioneer's EDGAR systems and procedures, including contingency planning
    - Maintain EDGAR related databases and document archives
    - Liaison with third party EDGAR agents when necessary
    - Prepare proxy statements and related materials for filing on EDGAR and complete filings

Blue Sky Administration (State Registration)

- Principal liaison with Blue Sky vendor (Bluesky MLS, Inc.)
- Coordinate SEC filing schedule and fund documentation with Blue Sky vendor
- Monitor status of state filings with Blue Sky vendor
- Transfer Agent coordination
- Review vendor statements and invoices
- Conduct vendor due diligence, as appropriate
    - Hiring oversight
    - In-person meetings
    - Arthur Andersen audit

Miscellaneous Services

- Assist Pioneer Fund Accounting in the preparation of Fund Form N-SARs
- Managing internal participation in prospectus simplification project. Charge Funds only for portion that relates to Funds–this excludes work on behalf of distribution or management companies, including coordination internally.

NON-REIMBURSABLE SERVICES:

Filings under Investment Company Act of 1940 and Securities Act of 1933

- Maintain Pioneer Mutual Funds SEC Filing Calendar
- Interact as necessary with the staff of the investment adviser, distribution company, and transfer agent to ensure awareness of Fund disclosure requirements
- Coordinate internal review of Prospectuses and SAIs
- Coordinate Hale and Dorr LLP review and internal review of Hale and Dorr LLP material
- Identify business and other situations that trigger requirement to supplement Prospectuses and SAIs

Proxy Statements

- Assist Hale and Dorr LLP in the preparation of proxy statements
- Coordinate internal review of proxy statements and related documents
- Review proxy related materials prepared by the distribution company to ensure compliance with regulatory requirements
- Review the transfer agent's proxy solicitation efforts to ensure compliance with regulatory requirements
- Act as liaison between Hale and Dorr LLP and transfer agency staff with respect to the proxy solicitation process

Miscellaneous Services
- Monitor the preparation of shareholder reports by the distribution company
- Prepare and File (via EDGAR) Section 16 filings (re: Pioneer Interest Shares)
- Maintain Officer and Trustee Securities Holdings (Fund and non-Fund related)
- Code of Ethics Administration (as it relates to Disinterested Trustees)

Regulatory Oversight
- Monitor proposed changes in applicable regulation and inform appropriate Pioneer personnel of the proposals and impact on Funds
- Act as liaison with Hale and Dorr LLP in the implementation of changes

Special Projects
- Coordinate implementation of Document Directions software system (for prospectus production) purchased by Pioneer in late 1997
- Provide advice with respect to Year 2000 issues
- Prospectus simplification efforts on behalf of distribution or management companies, including internal coordination

CHAPTER 8

Fund Distribution: the Broker Channels

*Mutual fund companies have three choices. They can use brokers to sell
the fund. They can pull in buyers through advertising. Or they can starve.*

— *The San Francisco Chronicle (1986)*[1]

For over forty years—from the passage of the Investment Company Act in 1940 until after the adoption of Rule 12b-1 in 1980—this description of how mutual funds were sold held true. During that period, the industry divided neatly into two camps: load funds sold through brokers who earned a commission on each sale and no-load funds directly marketed to investors with no commission involved. Over the past twenty years, however, the industry has evolved a much more complex and fragmented pattern of channels through which funds are sold.

Today, investors can buy funds via a wide variety of intermediaries, as well as directly from the fund companies. They may or may not pay sales commissions, and if they do, they may pay them when they buy the fund shares, when they sell them, and/or periodically as they hold the fund. This chapter and the following two chapters explore these and other topics in *mutual fund distribution*: how it evolved, how funds are sold to investors, the organizations and individuals who do this selling, how they are organized and compensated, and the attendant issues and controversies.

Overview of Fund Distribution

In the mutual fund industry, distribution means the process of selling a fund's shares to investors. The 1940 Act requires that an open-end fund stand ready to redeem any shares offered by shareholders on any business day. It does not require that funds sell shares every day, but most funds seek to do so, for at least three reasons. First, the funds use the proceeds of sales to generate cash to meet demands caused by shareholder redemptions. Without cash generated by fund sales, a fund would have to liquidate portfolio holdings to satisfy redemptions, thus impeding the manager's pursuit of the fund's investment objective. Second, management companies generally want their funds to keep growing, since investment advisory and many other management fees grow along with the value of the fund's assets. Finally, although this is the subject of some controversy, funds may achieve economies of scale through growth, so that a larger overall asset pool provides a lower expense ratio for all shareholders. The argument about whether or not this really happens is reviewed in Chapter 16.

Occasionally, a fund will grow so large that its size interferes with its adviser's ability to pursue the investment objective, and the manager *closes* the fund, stopping sales to new investors. For example, Pilgrim Securities closed its *SmallCap Opportunities Fund* in early 2000, saying that this was needed to ensure that the adviser could "continue to invest in companies and at valuation levels consistent with the fund's investment style."[2] In other words, Pilgrim believed that the inventory of small cap stocks was so limited that a continued inflow of cash to the fund might force the investment adviser to purchase illiquid or otherwise undesirable securities. While a few funds are closed like this each year, the vast majority of open-end funds engage in constant distribution of their shares.

The Evolution of Mutual Fund Distribution

Until the 1970s, mutual funds held mostly equity securities, and served primarily to offer the small investor a way to participate in the stock market. They were sold much the same way stocks were sold—by brokers who received a commission for executing the transaction. Most often, the shareholder paid a front-end load—a commission on the purchase transaction, similar to the commission paid on a stock purchase. These commissions amounted to as much as 8.5 percent of the purchase amount on a small transaction, with the commission rate decreasing as the size of the purchase increased. A small percentage of fund families, the no-load funds, sold their shares directly to the investors without any intermediary or sales commission, but in 1970, these funds accounted for less than 6 percent of the industry's total assets under management.

The first major change in this pattern occurred in the 1970s, when no-load funds began to grow in popularity. Figure 1 shows the portion of total assets under management held by the no-load segment of the industry between 1970 and 1999. As Figure 1 shows, much of the growth in popularity of no-load funds closely correlated with the growth of the money market fund segment. In the late 1970s and early 1980s, money market funds exploded from nowhere to become almost 80 percent of the industry, driven largely by the artificial cap Regulation Q placed on banks' ability to pay interest to depositors. Money market funds are, for all practical purposes, no-load funds. They compete against other short-term savings vehicles that carry no commissions, and investors move their money into and out of them quickly. The prospect of paying a substantial commission on a short-term investment would make load money market funds extremely difficult to market. They remain rare even to this day—money market funds that impose any type of load hold less than 2 percent of all money market fund assets.[3]

As investors moved their money to equity and long-term fixed-income funds in the mid-1980s, the proportion of the industry represented by money market funds declined. The proportion of industry assets that no-load funds had attained likewise began to decline. However, it did not return to its previous low level. Some large fund groups converted at least some of their equity offerings from load to no-load, and new no-load equity and fixed-income funds had been launched. Figure 1 shows that no-load funds have continued to account for somewhat over one-half total industry assets. Figure 2 shows the breakdown for long-term funds, i.e., all except

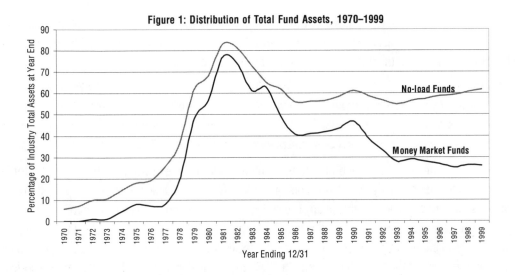

Figure 1: Distribution of Total Fund Assets, 1970–1999

money market funds, for the past fifteen years. As Figure 2 shows, the relative industry shares of load and no-load long-term funds have gradually approached a fifty-fifty split.

During the 1980s, however, the nature of distribution changed dramatically. Before 1980, load was virtually synonymous with broker sold, and no-load meant directly marketed. Shareholders directly shouldered the distribution costs for load funds in the form of commissions; no-load fund sponsors paid for distribution out of their management and advisory fees. All this began to change with the adoption of Rule 12b-1 in 1980.

Representatives of the mutual fund industry had argued to the SEC during the 1970s that increased size in a fund was a benefit to existing shareholders because it brought economies of scale to fund operations. This

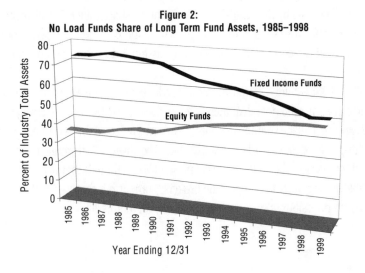

Figure 2:
No Load Funds Share of Long Term Fund Assets, 1985–1998

justified using fund assets—i.e., the assets of those existing shareholders—to pay for distribution, since the fund gained from the resulting purchases. In 1980, the SEC responded to this argument, adopting Rule 12b-1, which permitted and set out the rules for an investment company to engage

> *directly or indirectly in financing any activity which is primarily intended to result in the sale of shares issued by such company, including, but not necessarily limited to, advertising, compensation of underwriters, dealers, and sales personnel, the printing and mailing of prospectuses to other than current shareholders, and the printing and mailing of sales literature.[4]*

Rule 12b-1 required that any such plan to use fund assets to finance distribution be written, that it be approved and renewed annually by the directors or trustees (or, if it is added to an existing fund, by the shareholders), and that it be terminable at any time upon a vote of either the directors or shareholders.

John Bogle had won a specific ruling allowing The Vanguard Group to use fund assets to finance advertising and other marketing activities shortly before the SEC issued Rule 12b-1 to allow all fund groups to do the same.[5] Many observers at the time believed that the SEC's intent in adopting Rule 12b-1 was to give no-load fund groups like Vanguard more flexibility in arranging for distribution.[6] Instead, the major effects of the rule were to blur the lines between load and no-load funds, and to enable load fund sponsors to devise a variety of commission arrangements to fit both investor preferences and new distribution channel requirements.

During the 1980s, many funds, both load and no-load, added 12b-1 fees amounting to an annual charge of .25 percent of fund assets (25 basis points) to pay for advertising and other marketing expenses. Most load funds also added 12b-1 fees, often as high as 125 basis points annually, to compensate brokers in new ways. By passing on some or all of this fee in the form of a *trail commission,* paid out periodically to the brokers who controlled a shareholder account, a distributor could encourage the broker to keep the assets in the fund. Management companies also used 12b-1 fees to create *contingent deferred sales charge* (CDSC) funds, as an alternative to funds with front-end loads. In a CDSC arrangement, the broker earns a commission on the purchase transaction, but it is paid by the fund's distributor, not the shareholder. The distributor then recovers the money paid out to the broker over some number of years from the 12b-1 fee. If the shareholder redeems the shares before the commission is recovered, a back-end commission is deducted from the liquidation proceeds to reimburse the distributor.

By the late 1980s, the SEC had received many angry letters from investors and industry critics who complained that fund companies did not adequately disclose these 12b-1 fees they assessed, making it difficult to determine the real expense load the shareholder bore.[7] The press reflected this sentiment in articles claiming that mutual funds "disguise expense burdens"[8] and "cheat the investor"[9] through their creation of a "fee jungle."[10] Some fund companies labeled their funds "no-load" even though they deducted substantial 12b-1 fees from the shareholders' accounts to compensate brokers. Some funds featured both front-end loads and perpetual, large 12b-1 commissions. Between 1988 and 1993, regulators took several steps to address these issues.

In 1988, the SEC strengthened the disclosure rules, forcing funds to explicitly describe all fees and loads, including 12b-1 charges, in tables at the front of the prospectus. In 1993, the SEC prohibited any fund from terming itself "no-load" if it assessed a 12b-1 fee of greater than 25 basis points. (Fund groups that had no 12b-1 fees at all, such as Vanguard and Scudder, took to calling themselves "pure" no-load funds, to distinguish themselves from the 25 basis point 12b-1 no-load funds.) Also in 1993, the NASD adopted rules that placed limits on what funds could charge in commissions.

Another significant regulatory change came in 1995, when the SEC adopted Rule 18f-3, allowing companies to offer multiple classes of shares in the same fund. The industry had found that different load structures in the same fund could be used to accommodate different target markets. For example, brokers could sell shares with a front-end load, financial planners might be induced to sell the same fund if all it had was an ongoing 12b-1 fee, and institutions such as pension plans might also buy it, but the 12b-1 fee had to be lower. One shareholder might prefer to pay a commission at the time of purchase, while another might prefer an ongoing 12b-1 fee to a front-end load. Fund companies responded by providing different options within a fund, but to do so they had to get around some regulatory obstacles.

Section 22(d) of the 1940 Act requires an open-end fund to sell its shares at a single, defined price—the current offering price described in the prospectus, which is the NAV adjusted for any commission. Rule 22d-1, however, does allow a fund to have multiple commission schemes and, therefore, multiple offering prices, as long as each applies to a defined category of investor. One way to define categories is to divide the fund into multiple classes of shares, each with a different commission scheme. During the 1980s and early 1990s, many funds obtained exemptive orders from the SEC that allowed them to do this. Since 1995, when Rule 18f-3 allowed all funds to establish multiple classes of shares, most load funds and many no-load funds have become multi-class. (This accounts for some of the differences one sees in tallies of the total number of funds available today—if one counted each class as a separate fund, then there were almost 14,000 funds in 2000; if one counted all the classes in a fund as a single fund, then the total was closer to 8,000.)[11]

Some funds use another method—a master/feeder or hub and spoke arrangement—to achieve economy of scale in investment management. In this arrangement, the master or hub, which is usually a partnership rather than a registered fund, actually owns a portfolio of securities in accordance with the investment objective. The registered mutual funds sold to investors, the feeders or spokes, all own only one security, the shares of the master fund. Each feeder fund can have its own load structure, and be distributed in a different channel from other feeders or spokes. In fact, the spokes don't have to be registered mutual funds at all—they could be bank trust funds or offshore funds, for example. At the end of 1999, there were just under 700 U.S. registered funds, or fund classes, that were actually feeders or spokes.

The many different share classes or feeder funds today address the various channels through which funds are distributed. Figure 3 shows the breakdown of the industry's assets by major distribution channel, as of late 1999. The seven channels shown are those defined by Strategic Insight, a consulting firm that gathers and

Figure 3: Distribution of the Fund Assets by Distribution Channel as of December 31, 1999

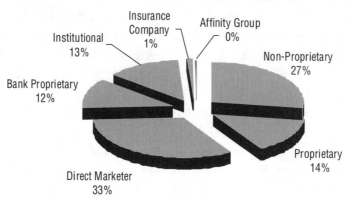

Source: Strategic Insight

publishes industry data (the ICI uses a slightly different breakdown of distribution channels). Strategic Insight provides the following brief definitions of each channel.

- *Non-Proprietary* funds are sold primarily or exclusively through brokers not affiliated with the fund's manager.
- *Proprietary* funds are sold primarily or exclusively through the captive sales force of the fund's management company.
- *Direct* indicates that the fund is directly marketed to the public without an intermediary broker.
- *Bank* funds are advised and/or sold primarily by a specific bank.
- *Institutional* indicates that the fund is sold primarily or exclusively to institutional investors or high net worth individuals.
- *Insurance* funds are sold primarily through the captive sales force of management companies whose primary business is insurance.
- *Affinity* indicates that the fund is marketed exclusively to a defined group of investors, who often but not always have an affiliation with the fund's management company.

The first of these channels—proprietary and non-proprietary brokers—are discussed below in this chapter. The next chapter takes up the remaining channels. Finally, Chapter 10 covers two major topics that cross distribution channels—advertising and retirement investing—and steps back to take an overall look at marketing in the fund industry.

ALPHABET (AND NUMBER AND WORD) SOUP: FUND SHARE CLASS IDENTIFIERS

Even before Rule 18f-3 was adopted in 1995, fund groups had created many multi-class funds by requesting exemptions, but when the SEC permitted the practice to everyone, classes exploded. Unfortunately, no one was able to establish a standard system of labels for these share classes. In 1994, the ICI proposed a standard class identification scheme that included six categories. The industry largely ignored it. Some confusion has inevitably resulted—John Bogle, for example, termed the multiple classes with their varying load schemes "a perplexing miasma."[12]

To the extent that any commonality in share class designators exists, it is limited to classes A, B, and C, which *most* fund groups use in a similar fashion.

- Most funds use class A to designate shares that carry a front-end load. Almost 90 percent of the funds labeled class A at the end of 1999 were front-end load funds, and most of those carried a maximum load above 4 percent.* But not every fund used A to mean front-end load—over 300 no-load funds also designated their shares as class A.

- Class B typically signals a contingent deferred sales charge (CDSC)—92 percent of the time, as of late 1999. Again, the major exceptions were 170 or so no-load funds that called their shares class B.

- Class C most often indicates a level-load fund—89 percent of funds labeled C were also labeled level load, with about 150 no-load funds also using this label. Level load generally means a perpetual 12b-1 fee, with perhaps a small front-end load of 1 percent.

After that, the patterns break down completely. The Simfund database contains over 200 values for share class designators, ranging from letters (D, E, F, G, H, I, ...Y, Z), through numbers (1, 2, 3) to words (e.g., Institutional, Traditional). Different funds use these designators to mean completely different things. For example, within the 335 funds that call themselves class D, one can find the full spectrum of sales commission arrangements. Here are just a few:

- the *Merrill Lynch Americas Income Fund* class D features a front-end load that tops out at 4 percent, and a 25 basis point annual 12b-1 fee;

- the *Sentinel Balanced Fund* class D carries a CDSC that starts at 6 percent and an annual 12b-1 fee of 75 basis points to pay off the distributor-fronted commission;

- the *PaineWebber Blue Chip Fund* class D is a level-load fund, with no front-end load or CDSC, but a 100 basis point annual 12b-1 fee;

- the *PIMCO Capital Appreciation Fund* uses class D for no-load shares that carry a 25 basis point 12b-1 fee; and

- the *Morgan Stanley Dean Witter Capital Appreciation Fund* class D shares are pure no-load.

The **only** reliable way to determine exactly what the fund means by its class label is to read the prospectus.

---

* All figures are derived from data in the Strategic Insight Simfund database as of the end of 1999.

Underwriters, Distributors, Wholesalers

Most funds—and all funds that charge shareholders sales commissions, or loads—contract with a "principal underwriter" defined by the 1940 Act as an entity that can sell the fund's shares to others either as a principal (that purchases and resells the shares) or as an agent (that arranges the sale of the shares). In practice, it makes little difference beyond legal niceties whether the underwriter is a principal or an agent—in either case the underwriter has the exclusive right to distribute the fund's shares. In the industry today, the term "distributor" is used more often than the legal term "principal underwriter" to describe the organization playing this role.

A fund's distributor must be registered as a broker dealer under the Securities Act of 1934. Most often the distributor is affiliated with the fund's manager as part of the fund complex—the Fidelity funds are distributed by Fidelity Distributors Corporation, Inc., the AIM funds are distributed by AIM Distributors, Inc., and so on. A number of independent distributors serve fund groups, usually smaller groups, that do not have in-house distribution. For example, SEI and Bisys both provide distribution services for hundreds of funds, the sponsors of which have chosen not to use an affiliated distributor.

Each fund executes a distribution agreement to govern the relationship with its principal underwriter. The distribution agreement, in addition to formally appointing the principal underwriter, typically covers a set of substantive issues.

1. *Procedures and conditions for selling fund shares*. The distribution agreement identifies the responsibilities that the distributor assumes regarding the solicitation and execution of sales to inter-mediaries or investors. It specifies share pricing and sales charge arrangements, usually by reference to the fund's current prospectus or SAI, and describes the distributor's obligations to settle with the fund for all sale transactions.

2. *Procedures and conditions for purchasing fund shares*. The distributor has to agree that it will repurchase fund shares upon the request of the intermediary or investor, and agree to insulate the fund from the effects of any errors or omissions made by it or the counter-parties with which it inter-acts. For example, if a dealer firm fails to settle a trade, that's the distributor's problem, not the fund's.

3. *Registration requirements*. The fund affirms that it is registered under the 1933 and 1940 Acts, and that it will use its best efforts to maintain its registration.

4. *State blue sky qualification*. The fund agrees to do whatever is needed to qualify shares for sale in the states, territories, possessions, etc., in which the distributor wishes to sell the fund, so long as this is not disadvantageous to the fund. (Chapter 11 covers blue sky regulations.)

5. *Other duties of the distributor*. The agreement may specify other requirements, such as the distributor's obligation to maintain certain records, comply with all prospectus requirements, and avoid making any representations inconsistent with the prospectus, such as misrepresenting the risk of a fund.

6. *Allocation of costs.* The agreement spells out what costs the fund bears, e.g., that of producing copies of the prospectus and SAI, versus what costs the distributor bears, typically all those costs related to selling activities.
7. *Duration.* The agreement has a stated termination date, along with the conditions under which the agreement can be extended, e.g., approval of the directors or shareholders, and approval of the non-affiliated directors.
8. *Termination.* The agreement may be terminated by either side, and the agreement specifies the notice each side must give to end the agreement.

The distributor may distribute fund shares through its own representatives, or through other agents, such as brokers or financial planners. These different means by which fund distributors get shares into the hands of investors define the industry's distribution channels. In the non-proprietary broker channel, the fund's principal underwriter or distributor acts primarily as a *wholesaler*—selling to the separate brokerage firms that sell to the investors. The wholesaler establishes selling agreements with each brokerage firm that will sell the fund's shares, as depicted in Figure 4. This distribution or selling agreement details the requirements and responsibilities of each party.

1. *Procedures for placing orders, making payments, and registering shareholders.* The selling agreement identifies the dealer's responsibilities in selling the fund's shares to investors. For example, the dealer is held responsible for determining that investing in the fund is suitable for the investor. The agreement typically requires payment for share purchases in accordance with Rule 15c6-1 of the 1934 Act, which governs the settlement cycle for securities. It may describe what responsibilities the

Figure 4: Relationships Among Funds, Distributors, and Brokers in the Non-Proprietary Channel

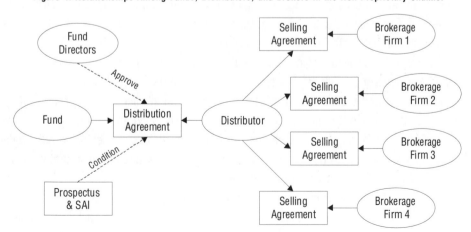

dealer has for providing information about the shareholder under various circumstances, such as defining when the dealer has tax reporting responsibility for the investor's account in the fund.

2. *Suitability and multiple classes of shares.* For funds that have multiple share classes, the dealer firm agrees to be held responsible for determining which class of share is best for the investor's requirements.

3. *Procedures and responsibilities for sales, redemptions, and exchanges.* The agreement spells out the dealer's responsibilities for executing transactions in the fund's shares. This section contains such items as the circumstances under which dealers will be allowed to submit late trades.

4. *Compensation.* This section qualifies and extends the language in the fund's prospectus describing how the dealer firm will be compensated for selling the fund. For example, it may spell out when trail commissions are paid, and the minimum amounts for which the fund will actually make a payment.

5. *Warranties and Indemnifications.* The distributor makes certain warranties to the dealer, including, for example, that the fund will comply with the prospectus language, and that the prospectus and sales literature the fund and distributor issue will not be misleading. The dealer must indemnify and hold harmless the fund and its agents from any damage arising from errors the dealer makes. For example, if the dealer tells the fund to redeem shares that it later turns out the investor really didn't own, the indemnification makes this the dealer's problem to remedy.

6. *Applicable Laws and Regulations.* The dealer is required to confirm that it qualifies to sell securities under the applicable laws of all applicable jurisdictions, as a member in good standing of NASD, or as a bank or bank holding company as defined under the banking laws.

7. *Termination.* The agreement terminates immediately if the dealer ceases to be qualified to sell securities, or either side may terminate the agreement upon specified notice.

A distributor usually employs individuals labeled internal and external wholesalers. External wholesalers call on brokers, financial planners, insurance agents, or anyone else who actually sells securities to investors, pitching the funds they represent to these intermediaries. An external wholesaler typically covers a geographic region, and travels throughout the region calling on clients. Pui-Wing Tam's 1999 *Wall Street Journal* article, reprinted at the end of this chapter, vividly describes the hectic life of a typical fund wholesaler.

As the article points out, a successful external wholesaler receives most of his or her compensation in the form of commissions on the sales of funds within the territory. An average wholesaler for a mid-sized fund group in the late 1990s made around $200,000 annually, but the compensation for top producers went much higher.[13] In a roundtable discussion of distribution, the managing director of sales for the New England Funds said that the wholesalers "are by far the most expensive part of what we do in the distribution model. I mean, these are very highly compensated, competitive individuals."[14]

Internal wholesalers work directly for the distributor, and play various roles. In the most common arrangement, internal or junior wholesalers support the external staff. They perform such functions as scheduling appointments for the external wholesalers, sending information to brokers, organizing seminars, and helping keep the field force up-to-date on fund developments—the "lick, stick, and staple business," as it has been termed.[15] At other firms, the internal wholesalers do more direct marketing to brokers themselves, particularly via telemarketing.

Load Fund Distribution via Brokers

As of early 2000, funds distributed primarily by brokers held approximately 41 percent of the industry's total assets. The broker distributed channel splits into two parts—proprietary and non-proprietary. When an organization (or complex of legally related organizations) both manages the funds and employs the brokers that sell them, this forms a proprietary channel. The American Express Funds, for example, are sold primarily by the financial planners that work for American Express Financial Advisors. When the fund group uses brokers that belong to independent organizations, the funds are distributed through the non-proprietary channel. Putnam and AIM, for example, depend on the brokers working for such completely separate firms as Merrill Lynch and A. G. Edwards to sell their shares to investors.

Figure 5 breaks down the assets held in funds distributed by these two channels, showing the percentage of assets in each category of sales commission, or load. As might be expected, the non-proprietary brokers sell primarily load funds, either front or back end. The no-load assets sold through this channel mostly reside in money market funds. At first glance, it might seem surprising that 57 percent of the assets among funds distributed by proprietary brokers are held in no-load funds, but again the answer lies in the nature of the funds. The vast majority—92 percent—of these assets are in money market funds, most of which are being used as a companion to a brokerage account, for handling short-term investment of cash. The majority of the long-term funds, both equity and fixed income, sold in this channel bear some type of load.

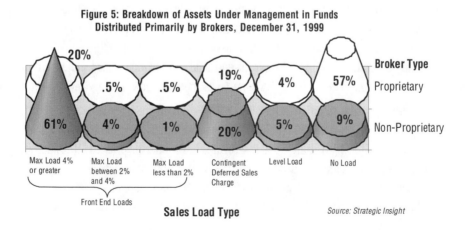

Figure 5: Breakdown of Assets Under Management in Funds
Distributed Primarily by Brokers, December 31, 1999

Source: Strategic Insight

As of late 1999, the ten largest fund groups, measured by assets under management, in the non-proprietary broker-distributed channel were American Funds, Putnam, Franklin Templeton, AIM Management, Oppenheimer Funds, MFS, Alliance, Fidelity, Van Kampen, and Kemper Funds. Collectively, these ten fund groups managed 75 percent of the $1.6 billion in assets attributed to this channel. The concentration among funds distributed by proprietary brokers is more pronounced. The top ten managers—Merrill Lynch, Dean Witter, Smith Barney, American Express, Schwab, Prudential, Evergreen, PaineWebber, Waddell & Reed, and Legg Mason—accounted in late 1999 for 92 percent of the $825 billion in assets among funds in this channel.

Whether they are selling their own proprietary funds or someone else's non-proprietary funds, the brokers' role is the same—to induce the individual investor to purchase shares in the fund. Typically, the sales process involves the broker providing investment advice or other services, for which the broker is compensated in the form of a commission.

Load Schemes and Broker Compensation

Mutual fund distributors have devised dozens of specific commissions schemes, but they all fall into one of three major categories: front-end loads, back-end (CDSC) loads, or level loads. Many funds employ all three approaches in their different share classes. The *Colonial U.S. Government Fund* series, a group of typical load funds sold through the non-proprietary broker channel, illustrates these approaches and how they work.

As this excerpt from the funds' prospectus shows, funds in the *Colonial Intermediate U.S. Government Fund* offer three classes of shares: A (front-end load), B (CDSC), and C (level load). The prospectus also spells out exactly how the commission scheme works for each class.

Front-End Load

Front-end loads are commissions paid directly by the investor when the purchase transaction is made. The commission amount is typically expressed as a percentage of the fund's *offering price*, which is the NAV adjusted for the commission. The *load table* associated with the fund determines this adjustment amount. As the load table for the *Colonial Intermediate U.S. Government* and *Federal Securities* funds illustrates, a front-end load fund often provides for reductions in the commission rate for larger purchases.

To illustrate how a share purchase in a front-end load fund works, consider the example of a $10,000 investment in the *Colonial Federal Securities Fund*, which, at the time, has an NAV per share of $10.00.

- The offering price is calculated as the NAV divided by one minus the commission rate ($10.00/(1-.0475)), or $10.50. Prices are always rounded to the nearest penny.
- The investor gets 952.381 shares ($10,000 divided by the offering price of $10.50 per share). Open-end fund share amounts are rounded to the nearest thousandth of a share.
- The fund gets $9,523.81 (952.381 shares times the NAV per share of $10.00).
- The brokerage firm gets $425 ($10,000 times the dealer concession rate of 4.25 percent).

- Finally, the distributor gets the remainder, $51.19 in this case. The load table shows a difference between what the investor pays (4.75 percent) and what the dealer firm gets (4.25 percent), and this accrues to the fund's distributor. The distributor also "eats the breakage"—that is, absorbs the effect of any rounding errors that occur in the calculations. In this case, there was a $1.19 breakage (.5 percent of $10,000 is $50, not $51.19). This breakage results from rounding the offering price (from $10.49868766404 to $10.50) and the number of shares purchased (from 952.380952381 to 952.381).

Shareholder Fees(*) (paid directly from your investment)			
	Class A	**Class B**	**Class C**
Maximum sales charge (load) on purchases (%) (as a percentage of the offering price)	4.75	0.00	0.00
Maximum deferred sales charge (load) on redemptions (%) (as a percentage of the lesser of purchase price or redemption price)	1.00(†)	5.00	1.00
Redemption fee (%) (as a percentage of amount redeemed, if applicable)	(‡)	(‡)	(‡)

(*) A $10 annual fee is deducted from accounts of less than $1,000 and paid to the transfer agent.

(†) This charge applies only to certain Class A shares bought without an initial sales charge that are sold within eighteen months of purchase.

(‡) There is a $7.50 charge for wiring sale proceeds to your bank.

As the load table shows, the investor could reduce the commission paid by increasing the size of the purchase. Front-end load funds typically also give these volume discounts if:

1. the investor executes a *letter of intent* (LOI) to invest a larger amount within a specified period, often thirteen months; or

2. the purchase plus the total amount already invested in the investor's account, or a group of accounts related to the investor, reaches the levels that qualify for a reduced load. This practice of considering the current amount invested in existing accounts to determine load level on a purchase is termed *rights of accumulation* (ROA).

The fund's prospectus must describe how an investor can reduce the amount of commission he or she might pay through an LOI or ROA.

Colonial Intermediate U.S. Government Fund and Colonial Federal Securities Fund			
Amount of purchase	As a % of the public offering price	As a % of your investment	% of offering price retained by financial advisor firm
Less than $50,000	4.75	4.99	4.25
$50,000 to less than $100,000	4.50	4.71	4.00
$100,000 to less than $250,000	3.50	3.63	3.00
$250,000 to less than $500,000	2.50	2.56	2.00
$500,000 to less than $1,000,000	2.00	2.04	1.75
$1,000,000 or more*	0.00	0.00	0.00

* Class A shares bought without an initial sales charge in accounts aggregating $1 million to $5 million at the time of purchase are subject to a 1% CDSC if the shares are sold within eighteen months of the time of purchase. Subsequent Class A share purchases that bring your account value about $1 million are subject to a 1% CDSC if redeemed within eighteen months of their purchase date. The eighteen-month period begins on the first day of the month following each purchase.

Contingent Deferred Sales Charge

CDSC funds were introduced in the 1980s once Rule 12b-1 gave fund groups a convenient method of recovering money distributors advanced to cover broker commissions. They appeal to brokers because they provide an immediate commission at time of purchase, similar to front-end load funds. They appeal to investors, because all the investor's money is used to purchase shares in the fund at the current NAV per share. To make this possible, the fund's distributor pays the commission to the broker, and then recovers the money from the shareholder over a period of years, by taking an annual deduction from the shareholder's account.

This creates a contingent liability for the shareholder, which is deferred, and eventually paid off from 12b-1 fees, if the shareholder keeps the money in the fund. If he or she redeems the shares before this money has been recovered, however, the distributor must deduct the remaining amount owed from the redemption proceeds. This liability declines over time, as the periodic deductions add up. The table excerpted from the Colonial prospectus shows a typical pattern of the decline in liability as the shares age. A shareholder who redeems in the first year after purchasing the class B shares will pay a 5 percent CDSC fee. This rate declines year by year, until after six years when there is no longer any liability. After eight years, the class B shares convert to class A shares, which carry a lower 12b-1 rate.

The distributor of a successful CDSC fund faces the need to arrange financing of these advanced commissions. For example, during 1998, the *Eaton Vance Tax Managed Growth Fund* Class B, with a distributor-fronted commission rate of 4 percent, had net purchases of almost $2 billion. This meant that Eaton Vance Distributors, Inc. had to pay out something on the order of $75 million in 1998 to dealers who sold these shares, money that it would recover only over a period of years. Essentially, the distributor makes a loan to the brokerage firm, and gets repaid by the shareholders. If the distributor cannot finance this payment

Colonial Intermediate U.S. Government Fund and Colonial Federal Securities Funds	
Holding period after purchase	**% deducted when shares are sold**
Through first year	5.00
Through second year	4.00
Through third year	3.00
Through fourth year	3.00
Through fifth year	2.00
Through sixth year	1.00
Longer than six years	0.00

Commission to financial advisors is 4.00%.
Automatic conversion to Class A shares is eight years after purchase.

from its own or its parent's cash flow, then it must borrow the funds. Some borrow the money from banks or other institutional lenders. In recent years, some distributors have begun securitizing these flows. They package up the rights to expected 12b-1 flows from a fund or group of funds into a sort of bond—much like a mortgage-backed security—and sell these to investors.[16]

Level Loads

Level-load share classes carry a perpetual 12b-1 fee, usually 100 basis points per year, no front-end load paid by the investor, and at most a 1 percent distributor-fronted payment. Colonial's level-load arrangement for its class C shares is typical, with a CDSC for only one year, so that the distributor can recover the 100 basis points paid to the selling brokerage firm in case the shareholder redeems early.

Level loads have generated more controversy than any other share class, since they have misled some investors into believing that they are no-load funds. In 1994, *Newsday* termed them a "marketing illusion," in an article in which the SEC's chief mutual fund regulator expressed concern over how they were perceived.[17] Nor had they been a tremendous hit among investors and brokers. Although the number of funds with level loads grew from under 100 in 1992 to almost 1,800 at the end of 1999, the total assets attributable to this type of fund was only $111 billion, or about 2 percent of the industry total assets. In mid-2000, however, level-load shares had captured almost 50 percent of new load fund sales for the previous twelve months, indicating an upturn in investor and broker interest.

Fund companies that offer level-load classes cite one or more of several reasons for doing so. They believe that some brokers prefer the continuing annual revenue stream from the 100 basis point 12b-1 charge—but admit that this appeals more to established brokers, who have a reliable income stream, than it does to new brokers, to whom the immediate gratification of a transaction commission is more attractive. They believe that investors like the level-load scheme because the brokers get paid more if the value of the fund goes up but less if it goes down. Or they believe that level-load funds appeal to commission-based financial advisers by giving them a product that essentially mimics the fee-based structure (i.e., an annual asset-based charge). As stated by one mutual fund marketer, "it puts brokers and clients on the same side of the table."[18]

The load structures in a fund's prospectus describe what the distributor actually pays the firm with which it has a selling agreement. Those firms subsequently divide up the commission they receive from the fund among the individual representative who has the investor account, his or her management hierarchy, and the firm itself. A registered representative who executes an investor's $10,000 purchase into a fund with a 5 percent front-end load will certainly receive something less than the full $500 of commission the purchase generates.

The major difference between the proprietary and non-proprietary channels is the universe of intermediaries through which they sell. In the proprietary channel, the brokers or planners do more or less the same things as do the brokers in the non-proprietary channels, but they do them for the same company as manages the funds. This has both advantages and disadvantages for the funds.

> **Class C Shares** Similar to Class B shares, your purchases of Class C shares are at the Fund's NAV. Although Class C shares have no front-end sales charge, they carry a CDSC of 1.00% that is applied to shares sold within the first year after they are purchased. After holding shares for one year, you may sell them at any time without paying a CDSC. The distributor pays the financial adviser firm an up-front commission of 1.00% on sales of Class C shares.

For funds selling through the non-proprietary channel, the great challenge is that of "getting shelf space" within the brokerage community. An A. G. Edwards broker, for example, has literally thousands of funds to sell from dozens, if not hundreds, of fund families—why should he or she expend efforts on any one of these over any other? Fund distributors look for ways to provide valuable services to brokers—software, data about investors, seminars—to get their attention and motivate them to recommend the funds of their particular group. They schmooze them. In this channel, the personal relationships wholesalers build with dealers play a large role in getting funds sold.

The funds that use proprietary distribution don't have the shelf space problem with their own captive sales force, but their universe of intermediaries is limited to that relatively small group. For this reason, net sales through the proprietary channel has always badly trailed sales through the non-proprietary channel, as Figure 6 shows. During the late 1990s, many of the players in this channel have concluded that they must expand beyond their captive sales force and distribute via independent brokers and planners if they are to grow at a satisfactory rate. By the late 1990s, such large firms as Merrill Lynch, Prudential, and American Express had all begun distributing their proprietary funds through third parties.

This practice continues to erode the distinction between the proprietary and non-proprietary channels. At one time, the sales forces of institutions with proprietary funds sold only their own firms' funds. As the 1990s progressed, most of these organizations found this to be an untenable position—investors demanded a wider choice—so they had to let their salespeople sell competing products. This erosion is reflected in the response one Prudential broker made to the announcement that Prudential would use third-party distribution for its funds: "The average broker here doesn't sell much in-house funds, so if someone else wants to sell them, more power to them."[19] And industry guru Lou Harvey thinks the proprietary channel will eventually disappear. "Every manufacturer in this business will sell through every distribution channel. If I'm a manufacturer and want to grow assets, why would I tie my hands behind my back? It's just nuts."[20]

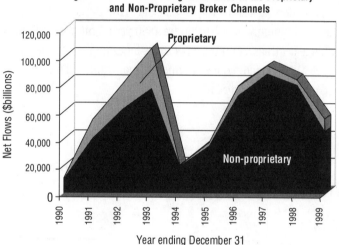

Figure 6: Net Sales of Long Term Funds in the Proprietary and Non-Proprietary Broker Channels

Connecting Brokers and Funds: NSCC's Fund/SERV

NSCC, whose role in clearing and settling a fund's portfolio trades was discussed in Chapter 6, also plays an important role in completing the trades of the shares of the fund itself, especially for those funds sold in the non-proprietary broker channel. NSCC introduced Fund/SERV in 1986 to connect brokerage firms with the fund complexes whose products they sold. Brokers could submit orders and registrations to the fund companies via Fund/SERV, and the funds could respond with confirmations in the same way. Over the past fourteen years, Fund/SERV and complementary NSCC mutual fund systems have added other functions, such as these.

- Mutual fund networking allows brokers and funds to coordinate their respective responsibilities toward the shareholders. Brokers can send shareholder account information changes to the funds, receive status information about those accounts from the funds, and agree with the funds what functions will be done by which party, e.g., who produces the tax forms for the investor.

- Funds can pay their commissions due to brokers via NSCC.
- When an investor switches from one brokerage firm to another, NSCC can notify the funds to make the appropriate changes to their records.
- NSCC can broadcast fund information, such as NAVs and dividend rates and dates to the brokerage community.

Fund/SERV offers both funds and brokers two great benefits. First, it allows hundreds of brokerage firms to deal with hundreds of fund complexes via a single, standardized computer interface. Without Fund/SERV, the brokers and fund complexes would have to define and operate their own computer systems for communicating trades and other information back and forth, as some did in the 1980s. Of course, Fund/SERV isn't free. Funds and brokers pay a small monthly membership fee ($50 per month for basic Fund/SERV membership, for example), and a charge per transaction ($.25 per trade, for example). On the other hand, developing proprietary, one-off computer links would require enormously more time and money on the part of both funds and brokers than does connecting to Fund/SERV.

Figure 7: NSCC Fund/SERV Participants and Functions

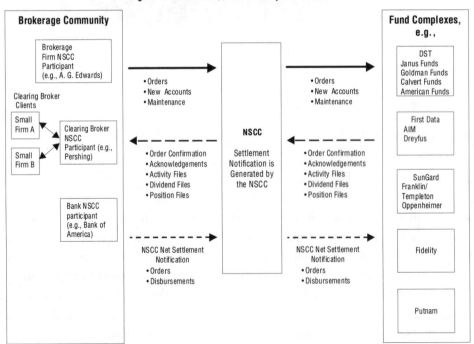

Fund/SERV also provides for net settlement among funds and brokers. Each day, NSCC totals all the positive and negative cash flows accruing to each Fund/SERV participant and creates a single cash flow between itself and the participant. Thus Putnam doesn't have to settle individually with Merrill Lynch, A. G. Edwards, and fifty other brokerage firms, nor does Edward D. Jones have to settle individually with Pioneer, Colonial, and twenty other fund families. Each does just one net settlement with NSCC. These facilities—a standard interface and net settlement—have proven so generally useful that some no-load fund complexes have joined Fund/SERV to connect to bank trust departments and other intermediaries that sell their funds as part of asset management programs.

Issues in Broker Distribution

Over the years, two questions concerning broker distribution of mutual funds have continued to stir controversy—whether investors understand the ramifications of the increasingly complex commission schemes the funds have developed, and whether some distribution features cause conflicts of interest for brokers.

Investor confusion with commission schemes has drawn fire from the regulators and the press from the time Rule 12b-1 was adopted to the present. Every SEC chairman and Investment Management Division head has commented on this question. The press has examined it repeatedly in critical articles. Twice the SEC has taken steps to try to resolve it. In 1993, the SEC amended the disclosure rules and directed funds to prominently display in the prospectus detailed charts of the effects of fees and commissions on a hypothetical investment in each share class. For example, here are the charts Colonial has in the prospectus for its *Federal Securities Fund*.

This table, like all such static tables, holds only for the assumptions made—the amount invested, the fund's rate of return, how long the shares are held, and so on. And of course the tables in a fund's prospectus show only that fund. To help investors compare fund expenses using the assumptions the investors want to use, the SEC put a mutual fund cost calculator on its web site (http://www.sec.gov) in 1999. The cost calculator

Example Expenses help you compare the cost of investing in the Fund to the cost of investing in other mutual funds. The table does not take into account any expense reduction arrangements discussed in the footnotes to the Annual Fund Operating Expenses table. It uses the following hypothetical conditions:
- $10,000 initial investment
- 5% total return for each year
- Fund operating expenses remain the same
- Assumes reinvestment of all dividends and distributions

Example Expenses (your actual costs may be higher or lower)				
Class	**1 Year**	**3 Years**	**5 Years**	**10 Years**
Class A	$586	$822	$1,076	$1,803
Class B: did not sell your shares	$193	$596	$1,025	$2,024
sold all your shares at the end of the period	$693	$896	$1,225	$2,024
Class C: did not sell your shares	$193	$596	$1,025	$2,219
sold all your shares at the end of the period	$293	$596	$1,025	$2,219

prompts the user to enter all the relevant data—amount of investment, fee and commission rates, holding period, expected fund return. It calculates and displays total cost (both fees paid and earnings foregone due to those fees), as well as the value of the investment at the end of the holding period. By running this calculator for different funds and share classes using the assumptions he or she finds relevant, an investor can make valid comparisons among funds.

As long as brokers have sold securities, investors have been concerned about conflicts of interest—temptations for brokers to make recommendations because they are in the broker's best interests, not the client's. Two potential conflicts of interest result from specific mutual fund characteristics. First, if funds distributed by proprietary brokers pay those brokers higher commission rates than do other fund families, this gives the broker an incentive to steer clients toward those proprietary funds. For example, an XYZ broker selling the XYZ U.S. Large Cap fund might receive a 3 percent (out of the total 5 percent) front-end commission, whereas he or she only gets a 2 percent commission selling a Putnam or Pioneer equivalent. If the Putnam or Pioneer fund is really better for the client, and the broker still pushes the XYZ fund, then the broker has succumbed to a conflict of interest. In early 2000, this appeared to be a declining practice—Morgan Stanley remained the last wirehouse, i.e., large national broker dealer, that paid its representatives more to sell its proprietary funds.[21]

Second, different share classes are appropriate for different investors based on the time the investor expects to hold the fund. A front-end load with little or no ongoing 12b-1 is better for the investor who expects to hold the fund for a long time; no front-end load and a larger 12b-1 is better for the short-term investor. The total commission earned by the broker is higher if he or she steers each investor in the other direction. For example, if a shareholder is likely to redeem in two or three years, the broker gets more if the shareholder buys class A shares with a front-end load than if he buys class C with only an annual 12b-1 fee.

These opportunities for conflict have been analyzed by academics,[22] decried in the press,[23] and examined by the SEC and NASD.[24] Both remain controversial issues. The SEC has repeatedly strengthened disclosure rules to help investors understand the implications of different load structures. In 1999, NASD proposed to prohibit brokerage firms from paying their registered representatives more for selling their proprietary funds than for selling outside funds. Both the ICI and the Securities Industry Association have fought the proposal, saying that the rule was ambiguous, and that it was not justified by any demonstrated record of abuses. At this writing, it remains uncertain whether any rule will be adopted.

MONTHLY MUTUAL FUNDS REVIEW—WHOLESALE CHANGES: HAVE FUND, WILL TRAVEL
Small-Town Pitch Can Make For Some Big-Time Profit If It's Taken to the People

By Pui-Wing Tam

December 6, 1999
The Wall Street Journal

WENATCHEE, Wash.—The trip that salesman Tom Schinabeck has planned is complicated and circuitous.

Arriving by plane in the small town of Pasco, Wash., from Seattle, he will head first to Richland, a rural town in the eastern part of the state, to meet five long-time clients. Then he'll drive one hour to the Oregon town of Pendleton. And then it's two more hours in the car, through flatlands to Sunnyside, Wash., for sessions with a few more clients, and several more hours to yet two more little towns. By the end of the day, Mr. Schinabeck will have logged one hour of plane travel, six hours of driving and three fast-food meals (two at Burger King, one at Taco Time).

All this just to sell mutual funds. That's right, mutual funds.

Mr. Schinabeck's willingness to travel to small towns across the Pacific Northwest illuminates how the world has changed for wholesalers, the people who pitch mutual funds to the securities brokers who then pitch them to you. While the business has always been competitive, wholesalers in the past could count on a growing pot of investor money brought on by the long bull market to whet brokers' interest in the funds they peddle. And they could mostly confine themselves to the bigger cities, selling funds to the urban monied masses.

But now, the pace of money flowing into stock funds is off the record levels it hit in 1997. Even as investors continue to pump money into funds, it is disproportionately going into a narrow slice of funds with the very hottest performance, and a large number of funds are suffering net redemptions. Across the board, withdrawals are up more than 36% this year, according to Financial Research Corp., a mutual fund research firm in Boston, as investors spend some of the bounty and turn to more exciting investment pursuits, like online stock trading. Meanwhile, regulators have cracked down on the financial lures that asset managers may dangle before brokers, forcing the fund firms to be more creative about how they can push their funds to the forefront.

So the last thing Mr. Schinabeck needs right now is a late plane, which is what he faces on a recent damp Tuesday. Mr. Schinabeck, who sells funds exclusively for Federated Investors of Pittsburgh, wants to board a 6:30 a.m. flight at Seattle-Tacoma International Airport, but he finds out fog might delay the journey.

"Shoot," says the 31-year-old wholesaler, who has been selling Federated mutual funds to brokers since he got out of college a decade ago. A delay could really mess up his day.

When he started his route across Washington state, in late 1994, he plumbed the larger cities. Since then, however, he has added routes through villages in Alaska and the far-flung reaches of Oregon. This year, Mr. Schinabeck will visit 300 broker offices in small towns across the Pacific Northwest—most of them several times—up from 170 a few years ago. His pioneer lifestyle has earned him the company moniker of Daniel Boone.

The good news in all this is that the traveling appears to be paying off, at least for now. In 1994, Mr. Schinabeck started with $6 million in new sales in the greater Seattle area. Since then, he has focused on selling to brokers associated with Edward Jones, a St. Louis firm that has opened one-person broker offices in towns all across the country. The concentration is working: By 1998, Mr. Schinabeck's sales had jumped to $128 million in new cash. This year, he expects to pull in $160 million. For Mr. Schinabeck himself, this means a nice bump-up in pay. In addition to a regular salary, he gets four bonuses a year based on his quarterly sales figures.

As for Federated, the firm has had flat net flows year-to-date through September, according to Financial Research, even though many of its funds have posted strong returns for the year.

"There are so many mutual funds out there that I try to work with people who can support my business—and that includes Tom Schinabeck," says John Lunt, a retired U.S. Air Force colonel who is now an Edward Jones broker in Wenatchee, a town dubbed the Apple Capital of the World.

But Mr. Schinabeck's efforts are clearly bone-wearying. On the road at least three days a week, the wholesaler is an expert at flying in prop planes and gassing up his rental car before heading into a remote area. He often wears a bow tie to prevent fast-food sauces from staining a real tie, since he usually chows down while driving. On the road, Mr. Schinabeck has been stuck in blizzards. More than once, he has inadvertently crashed into deer and badgers that have darted onto the road while he was driving to small towns at night.

Mr. Schinabeck's wife is no fan of his lifestyle, either. The couple recently bought a new two-acre waterfront home on the outskirts of Seattle, and they're trying now to have children. "She'd like me to be around more often," Mr. Schinabeck says.

On top of all these physical hardships, the plain fact is that "mutual funds aren't that sexy to sell anymore," Mr. Schinabeck says, noting that individual stocks seem to interest a growing number of would-be fund customers.

But on this recent foggy Tuesday, luck seems to be going his way. The mist around Seattle airport clears. Soon, a whirring 40-person plane launches the wholesaler high above Seattle and east over the mountains. An hour later, Mr. Schinabeck lands in Pasco, an apple- and grape-growing community.

Quickly sliding into his rental car, Mr. Schinabeck zooms off to the Edward Jones office of Robert Shillingstad, a local broker kingpin with one of the largest clienteles and assets under management in the area. The two men greet each other like old friends, and Mr. Schinabeck says hello to the four other brokers who have driven in from neighboring towns for the meeting in the nondescript two-story office building off a main road. Pulling out a sheaf of papers, the wholesaler begins his pitch.

"All our Federated funds will distribute capital gains in the next two weeks," an event that will create a tax bill for many investors, Mr. Schinabeck says. But with capital gains out of the way, "we can keep on selling the funds," he adds. Investors are generally advised not to buy funds right before distributions are made because they can get saddled with a tax bill without the benefit of the gains.

Over the next hour, Mr. Schinabeck runs through some of his favorite Federated funds. In particular, he pushes Federated Aggressive Growth Fund, a $93 million portfolio that has produced spectacular returns so far this year based on a huge exposure to smaller technology stocks. "This fund is great for dollar-cost averaging," he says. To add spice to the pitch, he says, "This fund will show up in a lot of the newspapers soon." The fund is clearly one of Federated's best, up 78.6% year-to-date through Nov. 30.

Later, Mr. Schinabeck pulls out his trump card. "One of the things I'd like to do next year is to bring a few fund managers out here," he says, leaning forward over the big oak-brown conference table. "We'd rent a big seminar room at a local hotel, and all you'd have to do is bring your best clients. Maybe we could even get some local media."

Mr. Shillingstad nods in agreement. "That'd be great," the broker concurs.

With the meeting over, Mr. Schinabeck hops back into his car and heads to Pendleton, Ore., a town of about 40,000. Moving along at 65 miles an hour, Mr. Schinabeck gets to the rodeo town half an hour earlier than planned. He stops at a local Red Lion Inn to catch up on voice mail and make calls from the hotel pay phone. "The thing about this job," he says, "you spend a lot of time talking on pay phones."

Soon he is in the Edward Jones office of local broker Steven Bjerke, who also sits on Pendleton's city council. Mr. Schinabeck pulls out the same sheaf of papers and runs through a similar pitch. Before long, the two men have concluded the formal part of their conversation. Mr. Schinabeck asks Mr. Bjerke about his Christmas plans and invites him over to his house the next time the broker is in Seattle.

And so it goes for Mr. Schinabeck. By the end of the day, he will have also driven two hours past apple orchards and fields of hop to Sunnyside, Wash., where broker Brian Bliesner works. And to wrap up the day, he will see broker Gailon Gentry in Yakima, Wash., a larger town 45 minutes from Sunnyside. One office is located in a modest strip shopping center, the other, a squat plain office building. Inside each, Mr. Schinabeck's pitch is enthusiastic—and all but identical: Federated funds have paid out capital gains and are performing well. Think about buying Federated Aggressive Growth Fund. Call anytime, for anything.

Does all the selling and pitching get tiring? "Yes and no," says Mr. Schinabeck, as he slides back into the car for the final two-hour drive of the night, to Wenatchee, Wash., where he has four broker meetings set up for the next day. "You have to tweak the pitch every place you go. And after a while, you get to know the brokers, so you end up pitching less and just shooting the breeze more."

CHAPTER 9
The Direct, Bank, and Institutional Channels

Over the next three to five years, the leading investment managers will use more diverse distribution networks. The traditional reliance on internal captive sales forces, direct sales, bank and insurance distribution channels, and third-party broker/dealers will be supplanted by a heavier use of independent financial advisers, alliances, fund supermarkets, regional brokerages, and electronic trading.

— The Economist Intelligence Unit (1999) [1]

Throughout the 1990s, the division of the net flow of new money into U.S. open-end funds was fairly stable across the major distribution channels, as Figure 1 illustrates. Behavior within the channels themselves evolved, however, in response to competitive developments and changes in regulations. The last chapter discussed this evolution for the broker channels. This chapter covers the other major channels, and how they comprise a complex pattern of overlapping paths that lead investors and their money to mutual fund managers.

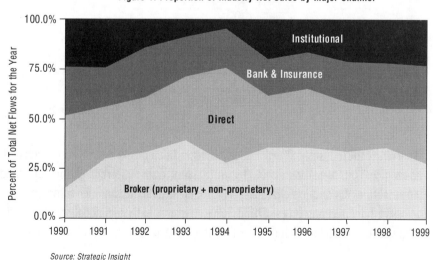

Figure 1: Proportion of Industry Net Sales by Major Channel

Source: Strategic Insight

The Direct Channel

At one time, sales in the direct channel functioned very simply—do-it-yourself investors took responsibility for analyzing and choosing no-load funds, and dealt solely with the fund companies to purchase shares in those funds. No intermediary provided advice or service, or earned a commission on the transactions. A trivial graphic could depict the relationship—it would show two boxes, one for investors and one for funds, connected by a single line, representing a point-to-point exchange of cash and information.

The pure direct channel continues to operate this way. But several factors have combined to build other paths from investors to no-load, directly marketed funds. Figure 2 illustrates this more complex flow. Some investors purchase shares through fund supermarkets to get services they cannot get conveniently from a single fund family, such as consolidated statements and inter-fund family exchanges. Some invest in these funds through fee-based financial advisers or wrap programs, paying for the advice they get on the basis of their total asset base rather than on the transactions or holdings with a particular fund. Finally, many acquire mutual funds via the defined contribution plans their employers offer them as pension vehicles. (The defined contribution path crosses distribution channels, funneling money into funds of all sorts.)

Figure 2: Major Sales Paths Through the Direct Channel

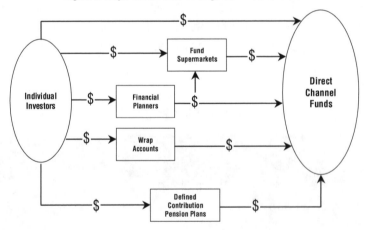

Different observers of the industry define the direct channel differently, depending on which of these paths they include and exclude. Thus one article discussing mutual fund distribution can claim that "direct marketing dominates mutual fund distribution channels"[2] without contradicting another commentator writing at the same time to assert that direct purchases of funds have given way to those made through intermediaries.[3] The first defines the direct channel to include sales through financial planners and supermarkets, while the other does not.

Here we will define the direct channel broadly to include all the paths shown in Figure 2. At the end of 1999, the over 1,800 funds distributed through this broadly defined direct channel held assets valued at $2 trillion, approximately one-third of the industry's total. Figure 3 shows that this channel contained mostly no-load funds. Funds with front-end loads accounted for only 11 percent of the total, and all but a smattering of that 11 percent came from a handful of Fidelity funds, including Magellan, the industry's largest single fund at the time. The majority—74 percent—of the no-load funds were pure no-load, with no 12b-1 charges at all.

Figure 3: Breakdown of Assets in Direct Channel Funds, by Sales Load, as of December 31, 1999

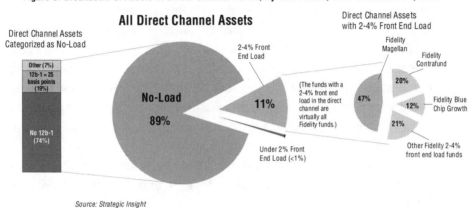

Source: Strategic Insight

From 1985 to 1999, the portion of total industry assets held by funds distributed in the direct channel climbed slowly and fairly steadily, from around 25 percent in 1985 to about 33 percent at the end of 1999. Not all fund families in the direct channel have shared evenly in this wealth, however. At the end of 1999, the ten largest fund complexes in the channel—Fidelity, Vanguard, Janus, T. Rowe Price, American Century, Dreyfus, Scudder, Strong, INVESCO, and USAA—accounted for 82 percent of its assets. Throughout the 1990s, the ten top fund groups' share of the net annual inflow of cash in this channel was between 75 and 90 percent. In 1999, for example, just three fund groups—Vanguard, Janus, and Fidelity—garnered total net sales of $100 billion, over 75 percent of the channel total. During that same year, 40 percent of directly marketed fund families had net outflows—that is, redemptions exceeded purchases.

Pure Direct Marketing

In the pure direct channel, fund companies sell directly to investors who make their own decisions without the aid of a broker, financial planner, or other intermediary. Once, this pattern described the entire direct channel; by 2000 it accounted for just under one-half of sales in the direct channel, or 15 percent of overall industry sales.[4] Funds attract pure direct investors via advertising, exposure through articles in the news media, mentions by mutual fund research firms, and word-of-mouth. The typical sequence of events in the pure direct channel goes something like this.

- An individual with money to invest selects a fund because he or she has seen its advertising, read a newspaper article about it, gathered information via Morningstar or some other research provider, heard about it from friends, visited its web site, or in some other way learned enough about it to decide that it is a good fit with his or her investment objectives.
- The investor obtains a prospectus by sending a letter, calling the fund's toll-free number, downloading it from the fund's web site, or, in a few increasingly rare cases, visiting the fund family's office. Along with the prospectus, the investor gets a new account application.
- The investor completes the application, and mails it and a check to the fund group's transfer agent. The transfer agent, whose functions are covered in Chapter 11, establishes an account for the investor, purchases shares in the fund, and mails the shareholder a confirmation of the purchase. An investor in a hurry to make a big purchase into an existing account with a fund might use the Federal Funds Wire system to get the money to the transfer agent. Investors may also set up programs in which monies are automatically transferred from their bank accounts to make regular fund purchases. (Some fund groups are adding account setup capability to their web sites as well.)
- The fund's transfer agent interacts directly with the investor for all subsequent activity, such as providing account statements and tax forms, and notifying the investor of dividend and capital gains distributions.
- If and when the investor decides to redeem shares in the fund, he or she communicates the order to redeem directly to the fund's transfer agent via mail, telephone, or Internet. The transfer agent executes the redemption trade, and delivers the proceeds to the investor or designated payee via check or electronic transfer.

The fund groups in the direct market are working to automate almost all of these interactions via the Internet. Most fund groups already make prospectuses and marketing materials available via their web sites. During 1999, a few fund groups started letting investors open accounts online, and make their initial purchases via electronic funds transfer. Some funds began to use e-mail to deliver account statements and other communications. Chapter 14 covers these and other mutual fund e-business activities in more detail.

The pure direct channel is the realm of the big no-load fund families—Fidelity, Vanguard, Janus, American Century, and the like—firms whose advertisements are fixtures in the financial sections of newspapers. However, none of these fund families get all of their sales from this pure direct channel anymore. Each of these, as well as the hundreds of other directly marketed fund families, depends to a greater or lesser extent upon fund supermarkets, financial planners and advisers, brokerage wrap programs, and defined contribution pension plans to provide some of their sales flow.

Supermarkets

Charles Schwab originated the concept of the mutual fund supermarket in the early 1990s. Discount brokerage firms, which execute investor trades without providing advice, had long handled no-load mutual fund sales, charging the investor a transaction fee for placing a buy or sell order. Volume remained low, however, since investors could purchase shares directly from the fund groups and avoid the transaction fees. Even so, some customers found that the convenience of having all their investment positions recorded in one place and reflected on a single brokerage statement was worth the cost of these fees.

Schwab's stroke of genius was to forge a way to provide this one-stop shopping convenience without forcing the investor to pay transaction fees. Starting in 1992, Schwab executives began to form agreements with no-load fund families that provided for the funds to compensate Schwab on the basis of the assets under management in Schwab-related accounts. The fund manager would pay Schwab an annual fee of 25 to 35 basis points on the assets that Schwab brokerage customers held in the fund. The fund could treat this as a distribution expense, and fund it via a 12b-1 charge, or the manager could pay it as a record keeping fee, since Schwab would do all the detailed record keeping and reporting for these clients. This approach proved popular enough that the assets in the OneSource program, as Schwab called it, grew from around $15 billion in 1992 to over $100 billion in 1999, and its success spawned numerous competitors.

By one count, brokerage firms such as Schwab, Waterhouse, and Jack White, and the discount brokerage arms of fund companies such as Fidelity, Vanguard, and Dreyfus, operated twenty-two fund supermarkets in late 1999.[5] The total assets attributable to fund supermarkets cannot be precisely determined because of measurement difficulties. Nevertheless, many industry observers believe that the fund supermarkets have been particularly beneficial for the smaller no-load fund families, which otherwise would have faced intractable distribution problems. Funds depending on pure direct marketing have to spend heavily on advertising just to make investors aware they exist. With giants like Fidelity spending tens of millions of dollars per year on advertising, a small firm, say with $10 billion in assets generating less than $100 million in fee revenue, has a hard time spending enough to make itself noticed. If a fund belongs to one or more supermarkets, however, and if its performance is good—e.g., has a Morningstar rating of four or five stars—it can gather assets without much advertising. As Standard & Poor's Investment Industry Survey puts it, "the supermarket format actually levels the playing field by giving a small fund as much public visibility as a large one," perhaps mitigating factors that would otherwise cause industry consolidation.[6]

Financial Advisers and Brokerage Wrap Programs

According to industry research firm FRC, pure direct channel sales involving no intermediary peaked in 1995, and have since actually declined. One FRC analyst attributes this to investors seeking advice to help them deal with increasing amounts of assets: "When you make an investment decision with $5,000, you might be able to do that on your own. But when your nest egg reaches the $250,000 mark, you start to get nervous."[7] Some investors turn to brokers for this advice and purchase funds in the broker channels. But the no-load, direct channel funds have not been excluded from a share of the advice-seekers' assets. Fee-based financial planners and brokerage wrap programs funnel money into no-load funds, and in doing so constitute an important part of today's direct channel.

A fee-based planner—called a financial planner, financial adviser, registered investment adviser, or some similar label—offers investment advice in return for compensation that is based on the amount of assets under management rather than on transaction charges. For example, an investor with $250,000 may pay $2,500 per year (100 basis points) to an adviser who analyzes the investor's situation, formulates an asset allocation strategy, and recommends particular investments, including mutual funds. Since the planner gets paid the $2,500 no matter what—regardless of how many or how few trades the investor executes, what types of assets the investor holds, or which mutual funds are included—the potential for conflict of interest is greatly reduced. The planner and the investor share in the rewards as the investor's assets appreciate in value.

Planners interact with the mutual fund companies in several different ways. Some merely advise the investor, who then opens an account and orders trades with the fund. In this case, the shareholder looks just like any other direct investor to the fund company. In other cases, the adviser orders the trades with the funds in the investor's name. Some advisers go through the discount brokers and their fund supermarkets—for example, over 5,000 independent advisers use Schwab as their back office, placing their clients' mutual fund trades through OneSource. Because the financial planners operate in these different ways, the exact amount of sales and assets they influence remains unclear, although some industry consultants believe they may be involved in as much as one-half of the flow in the direct channel.[8]

Mutual fund wrap programs were rolled out in the early 1990s as a way to offer affluent investors a fee-based package of advice and mutual funds. In the typical wrap program, the investor turns over his or her money to the wrap provider, most often a brokerage firm, that engages a manager to allocate it across a portfolio of mutual funds according to the manager's analysis of the investor's situation. The program may periodically rebalance the portfolio when needed due to market action or a change in the investor's needs. At first, most wrap programs offered only no-load funds, but in recent years some load funds have joined wrap programs as these programs have grown in popularity. In late 1999, mutual fund wrap programs held about $100 billion is assets.[9]

Strategic Insight has noted that the 100 basis points annual asset-based fee has become a *de facto* standard for advice in the mutual fund industry. In late 1999, they asserted that as many as 80 percent of investors being assisted by financial advisers pay no up-front load charges, but rather pay annual fees of about 100 basis points. Further, they pointed out that even for investors paying front-end loads, pro-rating the sales commission over the holding period would result in an effective annual charge of 1 percent or less in most cases.[10]

Affinity Groups

Affinity group funds, which sell primarily to the members of specific standing groups, form a small channel best viewed as a direct sub-channel. In late 1999, the $18 billion of assets in this channel was almost all held by three no-load fund families: General Electric, AMR (American Airlines), and Caterpillar. Each of these was the offspring of an industrial corporation's decision to create registered funds, and investments in each of these still primarily come from employees and affiliates. In 1992, a group called USAffinity formed a family of funds designed specifically to be marketed to affinity groups, but was unable to gather enough assets to be viable. In 1995, it sold the funds to U.S. Trust, which merged them into its own fund family.[11]

Defined Contribution Pension Plans

Tax-advantaged retirement investments have contributed tremendously to both the growth and the stability of the mutual fund industry throughout the 1990s. Figure 4 shows how defined contribution plans in particular have contributed to the industry's assets during the 1990s. By the end of 1999, defined contribution plan holdings in mutual funds amounted about $1 trillion, or almost one-sixth of the industry total. From the point of view of the fund companies, these plan assets have been particularly attractive because they tend to be "sticky"— investors are less likely to redeem them than they are non-retirement holdings.

Figure 4: Mutual Fund Assets Held by DC Pension Funds

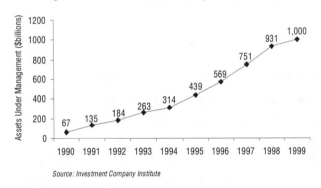

Source: Investment Company Institute

Figure 5 shows the ten leading mutual fund managers of defined contribution plan programs as of the end of 1998, and the defined contribution assets they held at that time. While direct channel funds, particularly Fidelity and Vanguard, lead the pack in attracting defined contribution assets, these flows and assets clearly cross distribution channels. Retirement savings have affected the industry significantly enough to merit special attention, and the mechanics and effects of retirement investing will be covered in the next chapter.

Figure 5: Leading Mutual Fund Managers of Defined Contribution Plan Programs as of December 1998

Manager	DC Assets in Family's Managed Funds ($ billions)*	DC % of Family's Total Assets	Primary Distribution Channel
Fidelity	213.5	33%	Direct
Vanguard	98.8	23%	Direct
American Funds	59.1	22%	Non-proprietary brokerage
Putnam	31.4	17%	Non-proprietary brokerage
American Century	28.2	36%	Direct
T. Rowe Price	27.4	29%	Direct
Merrill Lynch	18.4	9%	Proprietary brokerage
Franklin Templeton	14.2	9%	Non-proprietary brokerage
Janus	13.8	17%	Direct
American Express	10.1	12%	Proprietary brokerage

Source: Strategic Insight, August 1999.

* Strategic Insight explains the derivation of these figures as follows:
"Our survey focused only on mutual funds advised by a particular manager, and does not include 'outside' funds that a manager or distributor may administer... Also note that our tally of fund results covered only 1940 Act structured funds." Thus, these figures may appear to be smaller than other published figures that show the total defined contribution plan administration business of these fund companies, including outside funds and non-fund assets.

Distribution at American Century Investments

With more than $110 billion under management in early 2000, American Century Investments contended with T. Rowe Price and Janus for third position among directly marketed no-load fund companies, behind industry giants Fidelity and Vanguard. American Century had reached this position through both organic growth and mergers. The company had started as Twentieth Century Investments in 1958, when founder James Stowers, Jr., established two funds to provide his insurance and brokerage clients with investments that could outpace inflation. To this end, Twentieth Century specialized in aggressive growth investing. The company grew slowly for two decades, took off with the general expansion of the industry in the 1980s, and by 1995 was managing $26 billion in twenty-seven funds. In that year, Twentieth Century merged with The Benham Group, a fixed-income fund specialist, in a move designed to create a fund family that covered the full spectrum of investment objectives. In 1998, having changed its name to American Century, the company struck a business partnership with J.P. Morgan (through which Morgan acquired a 45 percent economic interest in American Century) to help both firms pursue market opportunities, particularly in defined contribution retirement services.

American Century in 2000 illustrated the complex set of channels in which the modern no-load fund family operated. For several years, the pure direct channel had been diminishing as a relative proportion of new sales. In 1998, American Century President and Chief Operating Officer Bill Lyons stated in an interview that while the traditional direct business was still "tremendously important," and accounted for two-thirds of profitability, it was clear that they could not reach all potential customers through this channel.[12] By 2000, American Century had deployed an organization that reflected this need to address multiple channels, dividing marketing responsibilities among three major groups: direct, retirement plans, and third party.

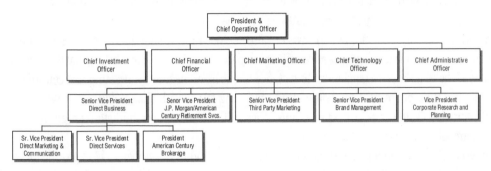

American Century Investments, Organization in Early 2000 (partial)

Marketing in the Direct Channel

Joseph Greene, senior vice president of Direct Marketing and Communications, headed a group of about fifty people in early 2000 to address the traditional, pure direct channel. Approximately thirty of these focused on direct marketing, and the remainder handled communications—producing educational and informational materials for shareholders. The direct marketers were responsible for developing and delivering marketing programs addressed to investors who buy and hold American Century funds without using intermediaries. He described the challenge of this job: "We have to make the right fund product and service offers to the right audience, at the right time, with the right message, and deliver them via the right medium. It's a lot to get right."[13] But getting it right was important, since the direct channel still accounted for over one-half of the fund family's assets in 2000.

To help with this task, American Century had developed a sophisticated customer data mart that its marketers and analysts could mine to help them understand the shareholder base and the needs of its various customer segments. This data mart merged transactional data from the transfer agent system with demographic and behavioral data purchased from external sources. It provided retrieval and analysis tools with which American Century users could study patterns within the customer set, and group customers into meaningful segments for service delivery and marketing. Targeting marketing campaigns to specific segments enabled American Century to make them more effective, increasing direct mail response rate, for example. The company also used this segmentation to help investor relations representatives better handle shareholder interactions—for example, to evaluate suitability when an investor wanted to switch funds. "Our end goal," according to Greene, "is to better serve those investors who come to American Century looking to achieve their investment goals."

In addition to distributing through intermediary channels, American Century was moving to address the increasing investor need for advice within the direct channel itself. In early 2000, the firm delivered an online advice program to its investors via its web site. This program was unique among advice engines offered by the directly marketed funds in that it would recommend funds from families other than American Century when circumstances warranted. Greene commented that while this might produce some short-term erosion, over the long term it would serve to increase shareholder loyalty, since it delivered what the investors were asking for (advice) via a medium they increasingly wanted to use (the Internet).

American Century's direct channel division also included direct shareholder services and brokerage. Company management viewed good service delivery as so integral to effective marketing that they believed that these should be in a single organization. In fact, two members of the direct marketing and communications group devoted their entire time to coordinating marketing efforts with shareholder service—for example, making sure that customer service representatives had full information on marketing programs that might spawn shareholder questions.

American Century launched its discount brokerage operation in November 1997 to provide for investors who wanted to trade in individual equity and fixed-income securities, as well as in funds from other families. "We'd love it if everyone would just invest in our funds, but let's face it, some people are going to want to hold different securities and funds, and they want to do it in one place," Greene said. "While fund supermarkets are major distributors of our funds to investors, we'd like to see our mutual fund customers looking for brokerage services or other funds to remain with American Century and use our brokerage service for as many of their investment needs as possible."

The Intermediated Channels

While the direct channel remained the foundation of the asset base, the patterns within American Century's net sales during the twenty-four months ending in February 2000 (seen in Figure 6) showed clearly why the intermediated channels were also appealing. During that period, sales in the direct channel varied widely, sometimes strongly positive, other times strongly negative. Sales through the broadly defined intermediated channels—retirement plans, broker wrap programs, banks, and other fee-based intermediaries—showed much less variability, and remained generally positive and growing. These channels, especially retirement plan services, brought "sticky" money to the funds.

Retirement Plans – In early 2000 retirement plans accounted for around 13 percent of the assets invested in American Century funds. American Century provided record keeping services for some of these plans; for others, it provided only the investments. Attacking this market had been one of the primary motivators of American Century's partnership with J.P. Morgan, since the two firms approached it in different but complementary fashion. American Century could do the full bundle of services, but reached mostly the smaller plan market. J.P. Morgan had large plan sponsors as clients, but provided investments only. Together they could offer a wide range of options to the full spectrum of clients. As a result, institutional sales through

J.P. Morgan/American Century Retirement Plan Services experienced rapid growth beginning in 1999 and continuing into 2000.

Third-Party Marketing – Third-party retail channels accounted for the remainder—approximately one-third—of the assets under management in American Century funds in early 2000. The Third Party Marketing Department contained three discrete groups that targeted these channels.

- *Insurance*. A number of insurance companies, such as Nationwide, Aetna, and American Skandia, used American Century funds within the variable annuity and defined contribution plan products they offered. For example, American United Life Insurance Company, a pension record keeper specializing in small plans, included several American Century funds (along with funds from other families) as investment options in the bundled 401(k) and 403(b) products it sold. American Century's insurance channel group focused on these clients. Each major insurance company that used American Century funds had a team assigned to call on the company and provide it with marketing materials and support.

- *Bank*. American Century formed a group in 1997 to focus specifically on the bank channel, and by 2000 it was selling to the brokerage units and trust departments of over one hundred midsize, and smaller banks. This group deployed wholesalers who called on and worked with the banks' sales forces, much as traditional load fund wholesalers do. In discussing this effort in 1999, David Larrabee,

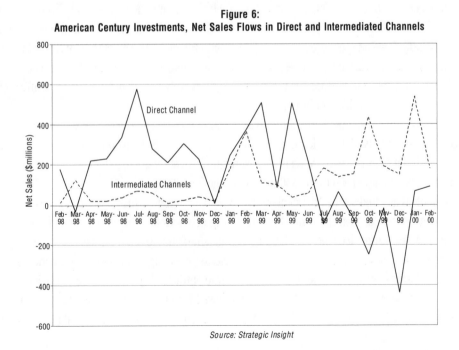

Figure 6:
American Century Investments, Net Sales Flows in Direct and Intermediated Channels

Source: Strategic Insight

former head of the bank sales unit, described marketing in this channel as coming down to "knocking on doors and providing good service."[14] American Century's success in penetrating this market had led to rapidly growing bank sales, and in 1999, banks accounted for around 20 percent of total net sales.

- *Investment Advisers*. The IA group handled both brokerage firms and independent financial Advisers who sold funds to retail investors, usually as part of a fee-based service. Brokerage firms sold American Century funds mostly as part of funds supermarkets or wrap programs. American Century had joined Schwab's OneSource in the second year of its operations, and in 2000 had over $5 billion in assets from this source. Full-service brokers, such as Merrill Lynch or Prudential, used American Century funds in the wrap programs they offered their clients.

Recognizing the growing tendency of retail investors to seek advice, the company planned in 2000 to double the size of its team of wholesalers who focused on wirehouses and regional broker dealers. Like many no-load fund groups, American Century had added share classes with 12b-1 fees (its Adviser class, with a 50 basis point fee), to attack the broker and financial planner market. Whether this would be sufficient remained to be seen—American Century was considering in 2000 whether to add class C shares with larger 12b-1 fees to increase its funds' appeal to the broker dealer community.

Advertising

Supporting all these channel marketing efforts were corporate groups for advertising, brand management, and product management. In early 2000, American Century had just launched a national advertising campaign aimed at enhancing its brand recognition. The campaign targeted both investors and intermediaries with cable and network television spots and print ads. The general theme of the advertisements linked the American Century name with American iconic scenes, such as a seaside house under construction or a college graduation. [15] These ads helped viewers answer the question "Who are you?" about American Century, explained Michael Barr, senior vice president of brand management.

In previous campaigns, American Century had advertised specific products, and superior investment performance. Television spots planned for later in the year might again focus on specific products. American Century stated that it planned an increase in its advertising budget for 2000, a budget that Competitive Media Reporting estimated to have been in the $30 million range for 1999.

The 12b-1 fees assessed on the Adviser class shares paid brokerage firms that distributed those shares, but for the most part American Century funded its marketing activities out of management company revenues. These came from the unitary fee American Century charged the funds for all management company activities, including investment advisory, administration, and investor servicing. Thus marketing contended with the other functional areas within American Century for a share of the finite pool of funding provided by this fee.

The company's structure as a private company allowed it to make these trade-offs as its management judged best. "Being private allows you to think longer term and plan longer term without having to respond to the relentless drumbeat of quarterly earnings," said Bill Lyons.[16] By all evidence American Century was doing this successfully. While the company did not disclose its financial results, assets under management continued to grow, and J.P. Morgan mentioned in its 1999 annual report that its equity investment in American Century had increased in value, suggesting that profits did as well.

The Bank Channel

If the dramatic growth of the mutual fund industry in the 1980s and 1990s came at anyone's expense, it was that of the banking industry. Regulation Q drove money out of bank deposit accounts into money market mutual funds in the late 1970s to kick off the industry's explosive growth spurt. Their money market fund experience taught many Americans the advantages of mutual funds, so that they used them to invest in stocks and bonds as these became attractive in the 1980s. As the mutual fund industry's share of American savings and investments went steadily up, the banking industry's share went down. When a Federal Reserve Bank senior economist studied the industry's historical growth and analyzed the question "where did all this money for mutual fund investments come from?" he concluded that it mostly came from diversion of assets from other savings and investment vehicles, notably bank deposits.[17]

The banking industry has not given up without a fight, however. Banks earn revenue from mutual funds by selling them as part of their retail investment product programs, thereby earning commissions and transaction fees. And some banks manage their own mutual fund families, through which they earn management fees. Figure 7 shows the breakdown of mutual fund assets attributable to sales activity by banks as of 1995, the most recent time the ICI published such figures. At the end of 1999, the total assets held in bank proprietary funds (the bank category currently tracked by Strategic Insight) had grown to over $700 billion. If the non-proprietary funds sold in banks have grown at the same rate, then these assets would have totaled around $400 billion at the same point. (These sales of non-bank funds by banks show up in Strategic Insight's data for other channels, mostly non-proprietary brokerage.)

Figure 7: Mutual Fund Assets Attributable to Bank Sales, 1995

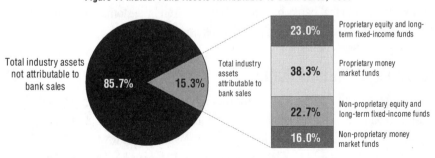

Source: Investment Company Institute, 1996

The ten leading managers in this channel—Bank of America, BancOne, Wells Fargo Bank, BlackRock/ PNC, Chase Manhattan, Northern Trust, U.S. Bancorp, J.P. Morgan, Bankers Trust, Fleet Financial—held 62 percent of the channel's assets as of the end of 1999. No-load funds make up the majority of these bank-managed funds—as of the end of 1999, 93 percent of assets under management were no loads.

Selling investment products has become important to banks. A 1999 survey found that ninety-four of the top one hundred banks (in terms of capitalization) offer securities, including mutual funds.[18] Mutual funds accounted for 43 percent of the revenue banks earned from these consumer investment sales in 1998.[19] Banks sell investment products, including mutual funds, in a number of different ways. Some banks use broker dealers, either bank employees or employees of separate firms that specialize in marketing investments in banks. An increasing number of banks license members of the staff to sell investments as part, but not all, of their duties with the bank. Some banks run hybrid programs—a combination of traditional full-time brokers and licensed bank staff—with relatively low-cost licensed staff making sales wherever appropriate, and more expensive brokers handling those sales situations requiring "high touch."[20]

Regulations have hobbled banks over the years as they have tried to participate in the mutual fund industry. It was not until 1971 that federal law permitted a bank to act as an investment adviser to a fund. The Glass-Steagall Act of 1933 and the Bank Holding Company Act of 1956 prohibited banks from selling securities, and prohibited bank holding companies from owning firms that sell securities. Mutual fund distribution fell under the definition of selling securities, so banks or subsidiaries of bank holding companies could not directly serve as mutual fund underwriters or distributors. Instead, they contracted with outside firms to act as distributors. Thus, for example, when Mellon Bank bought Dreyfus in 1994, it had to move distribution from Dreyfus' internal distributor to an external third party.

The Gramm-Leach-Bliley Act of 1999—also termed the Financial Modernization Act—removed this constraint by creating a new category of "financial holding company" that could contain both banking and securities firms, as well as insurance companies. Among other things, this allowed bank-owned fund companies to do their own distribution; and in early 2000, Mellon Bank became the first to do so, bringing distribution for the Dreyfus Funds back in-house. The ultimate effect on bank mutual funds of this Act remains to be seen, however. While some believe that it could prompt banks to acquire mutual fund companies—or, in a few cases, vice-versa—others hold that banks have already been driven by customer needs and competitive pressures to fully include mutual funds within their product offerings.[21]

Insurance Sales of Mutual Funds

Insurance company proprietary funds—that is, mutual funds that are both managed and distributed by a particular insurance company—form a small channel dominated by a handful of firms. At the end of 1999, assets in this channel totaled only $56 billion, less than 1 percent of the industry total. The top ten firms in the channel—MainStay, Smith Barney, AAL Advisors, Nationwide, Lutheran Brotherhood, State Farm, Princor,

Sentinel, MIMLIC, and Northwestern Mutual—controlled 98 percent of the assets. These are mostly load funds—only 8 percent of the assets as of the end of 1999 were held in long-term funds categorized as no-load.

The insurance channel operates much as the proprietary brokerage channel does. A captive sales force comprising the insurance company's agents, sells mutual fund shares along with insurance policies. However, not every insurance company that manages mutual funds distributes them through this channel. Prudential's funds, for example, fall into the proprietary brokerage channel, since The Pru operates a full-service broker dealer that sells, among other things, these funds. The USAA family of funds, on the other hand, falls into the direct channel, since USAA operates as a direct marketer for all its products.

The Institutional Channel

Institutional funds seek organizations, not individuals, as shareholders. They typically require very high minimum investment amounts, often $2 million or more. In return, they offer the institutional investor the opportunity for a higher return than could be achieved by an equivalent fund offered to retail investors. Several characteristics of institutional funds—the higher minimum investment, more stable flow of funds institutions provide, and generally focused requirements of institutional investors—allow institutional funds to keep their expenses significantly lower than their retail counterparts, as Figure 8 clearly illustrates.

Who are these institutions that invest in mutual funds? According to the Investment Company Institute, they fall into several categories.

- *Fiduciaries*. These are primarily bank trust departments that are managing wealth in individual trust accounts, but also include entities such as legal and accounting firms acting as trustees. Bank trust departments often use mutual funds as investment vehicles for their clients because of the liquidity and easy redeemability of funds. Many banks converted their common trust funds (unregistered investment pools managed strictly for their trust clients) to registered mutual funds in the 1990s, in part to serve their trust client needs.

Figure 8: Comparison of Expenses Between Institutional & Retail Funds

Fund Type	Asset Weighted Average Expense (basis points)*	
	Institutional Funds	Retail Funds
Equity	67	98
Taxable Long-term Fixed Income	50	92
Tax-free Long-term Fixed Income	62	69
Taxable Money Market	30	56
Tax Free Money Market	41	54

Source: Strategic Insight Simfund Database

*Using fund total assets as of December 31, 1999, as the weighting factor.

- *Corporations*. Many corporations, particularly smaller ones, find it less expensive to use institutional money market funds to manage their operating capital than to use in-house managers. Some insurance companies also find it less expensive to use institutional equity funds instead of in-house equity managers. (Insurance company asset managers are strongly slanted toward fixed-income investments because of their need to match the company's underwriting liabilities.)

- *Non-profit organizations and foundations.* This category embraces a wide range of organizations, including credit unions, hospitals, sanitariums, orphanages, schools, colleges, cemeteries, municipalities, townships, and cities. Many non-profits find it easier, less costly, and more effective to use institutional funds to manage their assets than to use internal asset managers. For example, credit unions, even large ones, often put their non-loan assets into institutional mutual funds.
- *Retirement plans.* Retirement plans often hold institutional funds, or the institutional share classes of retail funds, to benefit from the lower cost structure.

Institutional fund assets totaled almost $800 billion at the end of 1999, or 12 percent of the industry total. The ten top fund groups in this channel—Federated, Goldman Sachs, Vanguard, PIMCO Funds, SEI, AIM Management, Dreyfus, Merrill Lynch, and Evergreen Investment—held 63 percent of institutional fund assets. Some of the names in this list have appeared in the lists of top fund groups for other channels as well. While some fund groups such as SEI focus primarily on the institutional channel, most fund groups that offer institutional funds also sell funds to individual investors in other channels.

Institutional funds are, by and large, no-load funds, which represent over 98 percent of the assets in this channel. The handful of funds classified as load-bearing have either a 1 percent front-end load, or a trail commission greater than 25 basis points.

The Distribution Big Picture

Precise delineation of exactly what monies flow through which distribution channels remains difficult. Nevertheless, Strategic Insight has made an attempt to estimate these flows for all channels for all purchases made into long-term mutual funds in 1998. Long term includes stock, bond, and hybrid funds, and excludes money market funds. Figure 9 shows SI's estimated breakdown.

Figure 9 paints a picture of a rich and diverse distribution landscape, in which monies flow from investors to funds through multiple channels, no one dominating. Over time, the industry's emphasis on channels has changed—for a while in the mid-1990s, load fund companies were launching no-load funds to exploit what appeared to be a growing taste for directly marketed funds. In 1999 and 2000, the pendulum had swung so that no-load fund families were launching load funds to exploit investors' growing dependence on intermediaries. Interestingly, evidence suggests that investors themselves remain stable—that only about one in ten mutual fund shareholders makes purchases in more than one distribution channel.[22] This suggests that the big pattern—a majority of intermediary sales, and a minority of direct, do-it-yourself sales—is unlikely to change in the near future.

Figure 9:
Strategic Insight Estimates of 1998 Cash Flows into
Stock and Bond Mutual Funds, by Method of Purchase

	$Billions	% Share
To "Do It Yourself" Buyers:	$26	10%
Direct to Investor	$15	6%
Direct – as Funds	14	5%
Direct – as Variable Annuities	1	0%
Through No-load Supermarkets to Individual Investors	11	4%
Direct, No-load funds	10	4%
Load company Funds at NAV	1	0%
Financial Intermediaries to Individual Investors:	156	60%
Through Registered Investment Advisers	11	4%
Broker Dealer Distributed	72	28%
Brokerage Companies with Commissions	47	18%
Mutual Fund Wraps	23	9%
Broker Companies' Funds	18	7%
Direct and Institutional Companies Funds	5	2%
Bank Distributed	41	16%
Bank Proprietary Funds	26	10%
Third-party Fund Selling in Banks	15	6%
Variable Annuities (excluding DC plans)	32	12%
Defined Contribution Plans	55	21%
Institutional	21	8%
Total	258	100%

Source: Strategic Insight

CHAPTER 10

Cross-Channel Issues: Advertising and Retirement Investing

You'd think a dog chasing his tail in a television commercial is going crazy for the latest flavor of Alpo dog food, right? How about a surfer gliding along a big blue cresting wave—a California vacation?

Wrong. The dog and the surfer are selling mutual funds.

—Andrew Fraser (1998)[1]

This chapter wraps up the discussion of mutual fund marketing and distribution, focusing on three topics that cut across the distribution channel structure covered in the previous two chapters. The first is advertising. Virtually all fund companies, whatever their primary distribution method, engage in some form of advertising, ranging from serious, even dull, declamations of fund characteristics to typical creative mainstream television commercials such as the ones mentioned above. The first part of the chapter focuses on mutual fund advertising—the regulations that govern what can and cannot be done, the ways different management companies approach it, what they achieve with it, and the issues that advertising raises.

Second, the enormous resources Americans have devoted to retirement savings over the past eighteen years have swelled the flow of money into funds in all the distribution channels. The second part of this chapter focuses on the two types of retirement savings vehicles that have contributed most significantly to this effect—individual retirement accounts and defined contribution pension plans. It describes how these work, how they interact with mutual fund investing, and how the fund industry has been affected by them. Finally, the chapter concludes with a discussion of the role and effects of marketing and distribution activities in the mutual fund industry.

Mutual Fund Advertising

Like most business organizations, mutual fund companies advertise to stimulate sales. They use ads to raise investors' awareness of their products, to bolster the image of the management companies, to promote the advantages of mutual funds over other savings and investment vehicles, and to point out the superior characteristics of their particular funds. They place their advertisements in all the usual channels—print, television, radio, billboards, the Internet. Mutual fund management companies and distributors, however, must adhere to stricter regulations controlling what they can say and how they can say it than firms in many other industries. Understanding mutual fund advertising must start with a review of the regulations that apply to it.

The Regulations Governing Fund Advertising

The Securities Act of 1933 regulated the offering and sale of securities to the public, including open-end mutual funds. The 1933 Act required that securities be sold only by means of a prospectus that met stringent requirements for full disclosure of all pertinent information. The Act defined the term prospectus very broadly, to include any advertisement or other communication "written or by radio or television, which offers any security for sale or confirms the sale of any security."[2] A fund could deliver advertising materials that did not meet the standards required for a prospectus, but *only* if that material was accompanied by or preceded by a full current prospectus.

This placed a severe limitation on a fund's ability to advertise effectively, since providing a full prospectus is neither an attractive nor cost-effective means of reaching a wide audience. As the SEC's Division of Investment Management has pointed out, Congress almost certainly did not have open-end funds, with their continuous distribution pattern, in mind when it drafted the 1933 Act.[3] For a typical corporation, which makes public offerings of its securities only at infrequent intervals, the prospectus rule imposed no great burden. For an open-end fund, which attempted to reach new investors every day, it was a severe handicap to have to send a prospectus as the only way to advertise. Mutual fund executive William A. Parker complained in 1936 that the 1933 Act "made advertising in the ordinary form impossible."[4] Nevertheless, the industry operated under this constraint for 22 years.

The first relief came in 1955, when the SEC adopted Rule 134, "Communications Not Deemed a Prospectus."[5] Rule 134 allows notices, circulars, advertisements, letters, or other communications, so long as they (1) appear after the fund's registration statement has been filed, and (2) contain only the specific information permitted by the regulation. Such Rule 134 advertisements still bear the label "tombstone ads," because the original SEC requirements—long since relaxed—restricted the ad to austere, just-the-facts prose enclosed in a box resembling a tombstone. Today, mutual funds actually can exercise a great deal of latitude in designing Rule 134 advertisements.

- They *may* include the name and other descriptive information about a fund, including its investment objective, general attributes, methods of operation, and services offered; the fund's net asset value; the names of the investment adviser (and how long it has been in existence) and distributor; a logo or other graphic design; and an attention-getting headline (as long as the headline does not allude to performance figures).
- They *must* include information about how to obtain a fund prospectus.
- They *must not* include any performance figures, illustrations that represent performance, or allusions to fund performance.

A Rule 134 tombstone advertisement today can be recognized by the fact that it (1) talks about a specific fund, but (2) does not mention the fund's investment performance in any way. Figure 1 shows an example of a tombstone ad.

The SEC gave the industry a second way to advertise when it adopted Rule 135A, "Generic Advertising," in 1972. Rule 135A allows investment company advertising that does not offer a particular security for sale, i.e., a fund, and therefore does not trigger the need to deliver a prospectus. Such advertisements promote a fund

Figure 1: An Example of a Rule 134 "Tombstone" Advertisement

company as a whole rather than a particular fund. A Rule 135A advertisement must comply with the following requirements.

- It may include information explaining mutual funds generally, or different types of funds, such as balanced, growth, no-load, etc., and it may invite inquiries for further information.
- It must include the name and address of the fund group, broker, distributor, or other entity sponsoring the ad.
- If it describes any type of security, product, or service (such as a fund), then the ad sponsor must actually offer such a security, product, or service.
- If the ad invites inquiries in response to which a fund prospectus will be sent, the sponsor must disclose if it is the principal underwriter or investment adviser for the fund.

Figure 2: An Example of a Rule 135A "Generic" Advertisement

Today's mutual fund industry does a great deal of Rule 135A advertising, particularly as part of efforts to develop a brand image for a fund family. For example, John Nuveen & Company ran a controversial Rule 135A television advertisement during the 2000 Super Bowl, that showed, via computer graphics, paralyzed actor Christopher Reeve appearing to walk. In describing the ad, a Nuveen spokesman said that its "purpose was to raise awareness about the impact money can have on the future."[6] Presumably this would then make the viewer more inclined to consider Nuveen as a company with which to invest. Figure 2 shows another, more conventional, example of a generic ad allowed under Rule 135A.

Neither Rules 134 nor 135A allow funds to mention their performance in advertisements, and representatives of the industry complained to the SEC that this severely hampered their ability to reach potential investors. In 1979, the SEC adopted Rule 434d (now Rule 482), which permitted funds to use "omitting prospectuses" as advertisements. This rule allowed a fund to create an advertisement that included any "information the substance of which is included in the section 10(a) prospectus," but which didn't have to include *all* of the prospectus. In other words, the fund could select or summarize any prospectus information to put into an advertisement, and omit the rest. This opened the door to advertising based on fund investment performance.

Rule 482 actually allows fund advertising to contain performance numbers that do not explicitly appear in the prospectus. As the SEC explains it,

> *To make the rule workable, investment companies have not been required to put actual performance figures in the statutory prospectuses, which would have resulted in investment companies constantly having to "sticker" their section 10(a) prospectuses. Rather, advertisements are deemed to meet the "substance of" standard of rule 482 as long as the section 10(a) prospectus describes the methodology used to calculate the performance figures.*[7]

So when a Rule 482 advertisement appears, such as the one in Figure 3, the numbers it shows don't appear anywhere in the current prospectus. Instead, Item 21—calculation of performance data—in the SAI lays out in detail the formulas with which the numbers were derived.

Mutual fund advertisements that cite performance figures have generated much controversy. In the years immediately after the rule was adopted, fund companies enthusiastically advertised their top performing funds, but the lack of standards for presenting performance led to problems. Funds were free to compute and present their performance any way they wished, so naturally they chose the method and interval that showed them to best advantage. For example, fixed-income funds might display their yields over a one-year period when interest rates were dropping, but switch to a one-week figure when rates were rising. In 1985, the head of the SEC's investment management division criticized this aspect of fund advertising practices, saying "If you read the ads, you get the impression there are 50 funds out there that are No. 1. We want investors to have a better basis for comparison."[8]

The SEC acted to correct this problem in 1988, by adopting stricter guidelines for performance advertising. Under the new rules, a fixed-income fund that chose to mention yield had to show a thirty-day yield figure based on an industry-standard formula, and it also had to disclose the fund's total return (income plus changes

Figure 3: An Example of a Rule 482 "Omitting Prospectus" Advertisement

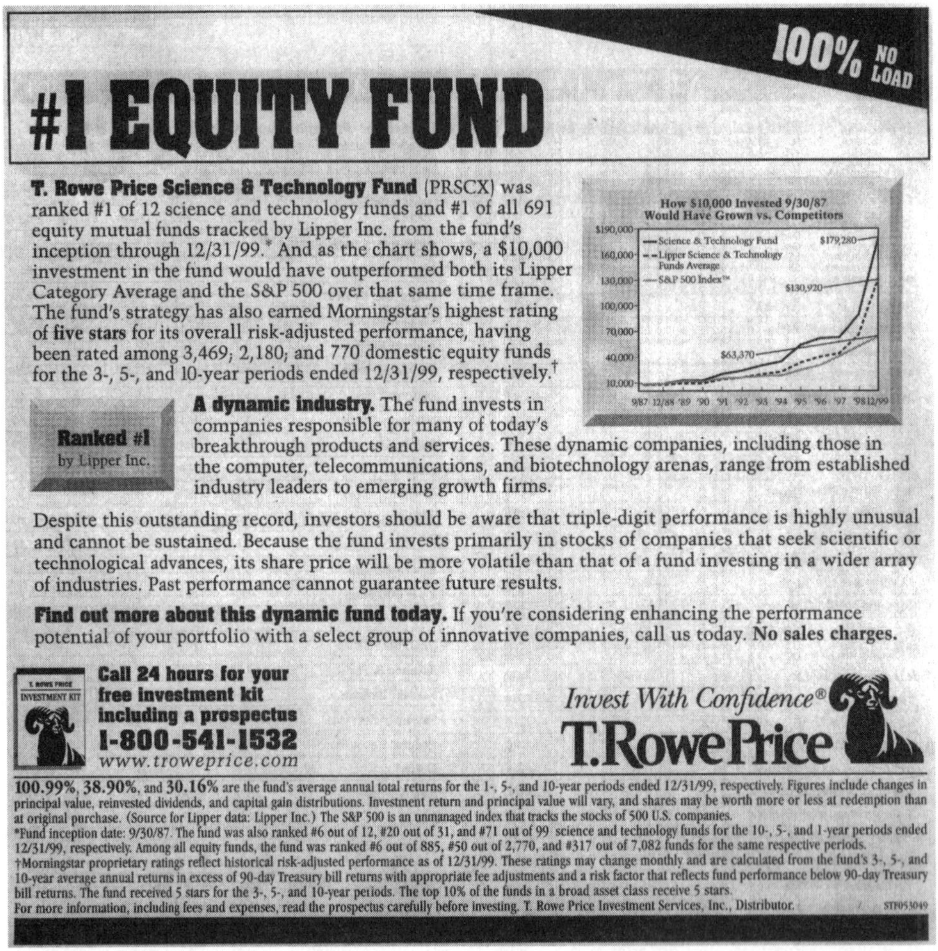

#1 EQUITY FUND

100% NO LOAD

T. Rowe Price Science & Technology Fund (PRSCX) was ranked #1 of 12 science and technology funds and #1 of all 691 equity mutual funds tracked by Lipper Inc. from the fund's inception through 12/31/99.* And as the chart shows, a $10,000 investment in the fund would have outperformed both its Lipper Category Average and the S&P 500 over that same time frame. The fund's strategy has also earned Morningstar's highest rating of **five stars** for its overall risk-adjusted performance, having been rated among 3,469; 2,180; and 770 domestic equity funds for the 3-, 5-, and 10-year periods ended 12/31/99, respectively.†

How $10,000 Invested 9/30/87 Would Have Grown vs. Competitors

- Science & Technology Fund $179,280
- Lipper Science & Technology Funds Average
- S&P 500 Index℠

$190,000 / 160,000 / 130,000 / 100,000 / 70,000 / 40,000 / 10,000

$130,920
$63,370

'9/87 12/88 '89 '90 '91 '92 '93 '94 '95 '96 '97 '98 12/99

Ranked #1 by Lipper Inc.

A dynamic industry. The fund invests in companies responsible for many of today's breakthrough products and services. These dynamic companies, including those in the computer, telecommunications, and biotechnology arenas, range from established industry leaders to emerging growth firms.

Despite this outstanding record, investors should be aware that triple-digit performance is highly unusual and cannot be sustained. Because the fund invests primarily in stocks of companies that seek scientific or technological advances, its share price will be more volatile than that of a fund investing in a wider array of industries. Past performance cannot guarantee future results.

Find out more about this dynamic fund today. If you're considering enhancing the performance potential of your portfolio with a select group of innovative companies, call us today. **No sales charges.**

T. ROWE PRICE INVESTMENT KIT

Call 24 hours for your free investment kit including a prospectus
1-800-541-1532
www.troweprice.com

Invest With Confidence®
T. Rowe Price

100.99%, **38.90%**, and **30.16%** are the fund's average annual total returns for the 1-, 5-, and 10-year periods ended 12/31/99, respectively. Figures include changes in principal value, reinvested dividends, and capital gain distributions. Investment return and principal value will vary, and shares may be worth more or less at redemption than at original purchase. (Source for Lipper data: Lipper Inc.) The S&P 500 is an unmanaged index that tracks the stocks of 500 U.S. companies.
*Fund inception date: 9/30/87. The fund was also ranked #6 out of 12, #20 out of 31, and #71 out of 99 science and technology funds for the 10-, 5-, and 1-year periods ended 12/31/99, respectively. Among all equity funds, the fund was ranked #6 out of 885, #50 out of 2,770, and #317 out of 7,082 funds for the same respective periods.
†Morningstar proprietary ratings reflect historical risk-adjusted performance as of 12/31/99. These ratings may change monthly and are calculated from the fund's 3-, 5-, and 10-year average annual returns in excess of 90-day Treasury bill returns with appropriate fee adjustments and a risk factor that reflects fund performance below 90-day Treasury bill returns. The fund received 5 stars for the 3-, 5-, and 10-year periods. The top 10% of the funds in a broad asset class receive 5 stars.
For more information, including fees and expenses, read the prospectus carefully before investing. T. Rowe Price Investment Services, Inc., Distributor.   STF053049

in NAV per share) for one, three, five, and ten year periods. Equity funds that wanted to mention performance likewise had to disclose returns for all these periods (unless the fund was too young for a period to apply). At the same time, the SEC strengthened the rules requiring fee disclosure, especially 12b-1 fees, in fund advertisements.

The SEC and NASD have continued to tune the regulations regarding the advertisement of fund performance. In 1994, they reacted to fund companies' increasing reference to fund rankings published by agencies such as Lipper and Morningstar. Both organizations adopted new rules standardizing the use of these ratings in fund advertising, rules designed to prevent funds from cherry-picking among the rankings to present only those most favorable to the fund. In 1997, with the SEC's approval, NASD revised its guidelines for the prescribed time periods that funds must include when advertising their rankings.

In 2000, this issue bubbled to the surface again in conjunction with the phenomenal returns some funds achieved in 1999. For example, 177 funds achieved total returns exceeding 100 percent in 1999, the first time that more than six funds had managed this feat in a calendar year.[9] Hundreds more funds had return figures in the high double digits for the year. If fund companies were to use these exceptional figures in their advertising without explicitly pointing out that such performance is unlikely to be repeated, they risked violating the adequate disclosure rules. In 1999, the SEC fined one fund group for failing to disclose in advertising that its exceptional performance was the result of unique IPO activity. Seeing this action, many fund firms added explicit language to their ads in early 2000, warning that the conditions that resulted in such robust performance in 1999 probably would not continue in the future.

For example, in its Rule 482 ad shown in Figure 3, T. Rowe Price has been very careful not to imply that the fund will continue to perform as it has in the recent past. The ad puts the *caveat* in the main body of the text, while relegating the spectacular performance numbers to the fine print. Nevertheless, the widespread display of spectacular 1999 returns in fund advertising has drawn renewed criticism, such as one columnist's assertion that Mark Twain's famous saying should be amended to "lies, damned lies, statistics, and fund ads."[10]

This controversy around performance advertising will never die, since it, like so many industry disputes, reflects the deep philosophical disagreement over the value of active management. An advertisement that calls attention to a fund's superior performance over some period in the past implies that (1) the superior performance results from the actions of the portfolio manager, and (2) the portfolio manager can continue to outperform. A believer in passive management rejects both of those assumptions. Even some active management proponents have problems with the second assumption, that the fund's past performance is a valid predictor of its future performance. In fact, Rule 482 ads must state that "past performance is no guarantee of future results." This doesn't satisfy the critics, who liken this caveat's effectiveness to that of the warnings on cigarette packages—the confirmed performance chaser, like the confirmed smoker, simply ignores the warning.

In addition to stand-alone advertising pieces, fund companies can and do make considerable use of supplemental sales literature, i.e., items that accompany or follow a prospectus. For example, fund companies may insert supplemental sales items into a prospectus, or mail them to existing shareholders in a fund along with statements and confirmations. Since the investor is deemed to have received a full prospectus, these supplemental materials do not constitute advertising that falls under the limitations of Rules 134 or 482, but they are subject to the general anti-fraud provisions of the federal securities laws. They are also subject to the provisions of Rule 34b-1 ("Sales literature deemed to be misleading") of the 1940 Act. As a result, supplemental sales literature that includes performance information must adhere to the performance reporting standards imposed on Rule 482 advertisements.

All of a fund's advertising materials must be submitted for review by the SEC or NASD. Section 24(b) of the 1940 Act requires that any mutual fund ad be filed with the SEC within 10 days after its first use. However, any mutual fund manager or distributor that is a member of NASD must file all its advertisements with that body. SEC Rule 24b-3 (1940 Act) states that this filing with NASD effectively counts as filing with the SEC. For all practical purposes, therefore, NASD is the body that reviews mutual fund advertising, except for that small—about 3 percent—part of the industry that does not belong to NASD.

Fund Advertising in 2000

Mutual fund companies collectively raised their level of expenditures on advertising through most of the 1990s. In 1990, financial services firms spent around $140 million on consumer investment advertising, some of which represented fund companies advertising funds.[11] In 1996, the fund companies themselves were spending almost that much just on television advertising.[12] By 1998, fund management companies alone were buying advertising at an annual rate of over $469 million,[13] and total annual mutual fund advertising spending by fund companies, brokerage firms, banks, and insurers was pushing $900 million.[14] In the great pool of American advertising, however, mutual funds remain small fish—one big consumer products firm (such as Procter & Gamble at $3.5 billion worldwide) spends more in a year on advertising than the entire mutual fund industry does.

The nature and placement of mutual fund advertising has also evolved. Once mainly appearing in print in the financial sections of newspapers and in business magazines, mutual fund advertisements now show up on radio and television, both network and cable; in a wide spectrum of periodicals, from *Fortune* to *Vanity Fair*; on the sides of buses and on billboards in airports, railway terminals, and baseball stadiums; and as banners on web pages. In recent years, television in particular has consumed an increasing portion of the industry's ad budget, as much as 58 percent in early 1999.[15] Mutual fund marketers view television as particularly effective for advertising aimed at building a fund company's brand image. As many firms start to worry about maintaining positive flows in an industry they believe is maturing, they turn to advertising to help them establish the sort of brand identity and customer loyalty that firms such as Disney, Harley-Davidson, and Starbucks command.

Pension Investments in Mutual Funds

At the end of 1998, retirement assets held in mutual funds totaled about $1.9 trillion or 38 percent of total mutual fund assets. These divided almost evenly into two major categories: individual retirement accounts (IRAs) and employer-sponsored defined contribution plans. Both types of retirement savings vehicles have made major contributions to the economics of the mutual fund industry during the 1980s and 1990s.

Individual Retirement Accounts

The Employee Retirement Income Security Act of 1974 (ERISA) first gave individuals a way to make tax-deferred contributions to retirement savings, via what is now termed the traditional individual retirement account (IRA). The traditional IRA allows an annual tax-deferred contribution—currently a maximum of $2,000 for an individual and twice that for a married couple, subject to various limitations—and allows the account owner to defer taxes on all earnings from the account's investments. When the owner or beneficiary withdraws from the account, he or she pays ordinary income taxes on those distributions (and penalties on early withdrawals). Since 1974, legislation has created other flavors of IRA.

- **SEP IRA.** The simplified employee pension IRA was created by the Revenue Act of 1978. Employers set up SEP IRAs for their employees, and can generally contribute up to 15 percent of an employee's annual compensation to the account each year. As the name implies, Congress intended this to be a simple vehicle for small employers to provide pension benefits.
- **SIMPLE IRA.** The SIMPLE IRA also provides small employers (no more than 100 employees) with a simplified approach to pension benefits. Employees can make annual contributions of up to $6,000 per year, and the employer must match this, subject to certain limits. The Small Business Job Protection Act of 1996 created the SIMPLE IRA.
- **Roth IRA.** The Taxpayer Relief Act of 1997 established the Roth IRA, which allows individuals to make annual contributions of up to $2,000, subject to limitations based on income and contributions to a traditional IRA. These Roth IRA contributions are not tax deductible, but all earnings in a Roth IRA are tax deferred.

By far and away, the largest pool of assets is found in traditional IRAs—$853 billion at the end of 1998. During the 1990s, investors increasingly turned to mutual funds as an attractive vehicle for their IRAs. In 1990, 22 percent of IRA assets were held in open-end funds. This climbed steadily until at the end of 1998, 44 percent of IRA assets were in mutual funds. After mutual funds, IRA investors were most likely to hold individual securities through brokerage accounts (34 percent of assets in 1998). The remaining IRA assets resided mostly in unregistered investment funds managed by banks or insurance companies.

IRA investing crosses the mutual fund distribution channels. Directly marketed funds, funds sold through both proprietary and non-proprietary brokers, bank funds, and insurance funds all offer IRA accounts. An IRA account holder must have a trustee to take charge of the assets and ensure that the activities of the account conform to the regulations. Trustees for IRA accounts may be, and often are, directly connected with the financial institution (bank, broker, mutual fund company) through which the IRA is offered. Most mutual fund companies offer an IRA account package that includes trustee services, in return for which they charge a small annual fee.

Defined Contribution Plans

The first corporate pension plans in the United States appeared in the 1870s, but it was not until the passage of ERISA in 1974 that the U.S. government became involved in corporate pensions in any major way. ERISA established an elaborate system of regulations covering virtually all pension plans offered by employers engaged in interstate commerce. In passing ERISA, Congress pursued three primary goals: to ensure that corporations funded their pension plans adequately; to create a guaranty corporation to protect employees when their pensions weren't adequately funded; and to increase benefits that employees actually received by encouraging greater participation and faster vesting.

ERISA was a complicated, far-reaching statute, and almost every year since its enactment Congress has passed some piece of benefits legislation to fine tune or enhance its provisions. As it did so in 1978, Congress added paragraph (k) to Section 401 of the tax code, allowing employees to put certain money in an investment trust, and defer paying income tax on that money until they made withdrawals during their retirements. In 1980, when this change took effect, a benefits consultant named Ted Benna realized that the provisions of paragraph 401(k) could have much wider application than Congress originally intended.

Barron's describes what happened:

> *Toiling at a benefits consulting firm in Bucks County, Pennsylvania, in 1980, Benna had one of those Eureka! moments. He noticed an obscure change in a section of the tax code known as 401(k): as he interpreted it, money could be withdrawn on a pre-tax basis from paychecks and invested tax-deferred for employees until retirement. In 1982, persuaded by a pilot program run by Benna and his partners for their own staff, the IRS gave the green light for widespread use of 401(k)s.[16]*

U.S. corporations were quick to adopt the idea Benna had pioneered. Defined benefit plans, the common type of pension plan U.S. employers had offered to that point, make the employer fully responsible for providing the level of benefits to which the retired employee is entitled. The employer must bear the actuarial and investment risks involved in making sure that the plan has adequate funds to provide the pension benefits at these defined levels. Defined contribution (DC) plans, on the other hand, shift these risks to the employee. The employer's only responsibilities are to provide the plan vehicle, contributions (at a defined level), an adequate set of investment choices to the plan participants, and administration services. The participant's pension benefit is simply the account balance that results from the accumulation of contributions and investment growth.

As the president of the Employee Benefit Research Institute put it, this combination—ERISA tightening the pension rules and 401(k) opening the door for tax-deferred contributions—"had the unintended consequence of freezing the defined benefit pension system and encouraging the massive growth of the defined contribution system."[17] The number of defined benefit plans in the United States peaked in 1983, when there were 175,000 plans. By the end of 1998, this had declined to 42,000 defined benefit plans covering about 42 million participants, as compared to 700,000 defined contribution plans covering about 50 million participants.

While 401(k) plans account for the major share of defined contribution plan assets, there are other types of DC plans. Non-profit organizations such as colleges, hospitals, and churches set up plans in accordance with section 403(b) of the IRS code, and use that section's label as their own. Similarly, state and local governments may set up 457 plans. Finally, some DC plans do not meet the rules that 401(k), 403(b), and 457 plans must meet to qualify for tax deferred status, and are termed non-qualified plans. Figure 4 shows the mutual fund assets held in each type of plan since 1990.

Figure 4: Defined Contribution Plan Assets Held in Mutual Funds, by Type of Plan, 1990–1999

Year	401(k)	403(b)	457	Other	Total
1990	35	n/a	2	15	52
1991	46	68	2	20	136
1992	82	74	3	25	184
1993	140	86	4	33	263
1994	184	90	6	35	315
1995	266	119	8	46	439
1996	350	148	11	60	569
1997	474	189	14	73	750
1998	593	231	20	87	931
1999	777	281	30	116	1,204

Source: Investment Company Institute

Defined contribution plan regulations, features, and operations could form the subject of a book in and of themselves. This chapter will merely cover the high points to illustrate how defined contribution plans and participants interact with mutual funds. Figure 5, on the next page, shows a simplified overview of the major players involved with a defined contribution plan, and the relationships among them.

- *Plan Sponsor.* The employer, or plan sponsor, establishes a defined contribution plan as a benefit to its employees. The plan sponsor decides on the particular rules the plan will follow—e.g., when an employee is eligible to participate, when vesting occurs, whether a participant can take loans from the plan, what investment choices the participants will have—and executes a plan definition document that embodies all these decisions. The plan sponsor typically provides at least some of the money contributed into the plan on behalf of the participants. (For example, many employers match employee contributions up to a specified limit, and some plans are funded exclusively via profit sharing.)

The plan sponsor also arranges for the administration of the plan. Some plan sponsors do this internally, as part of their human resources and finance functions. For example, Procter & Gamble, which has one of the nation's oldest profit sharing defined contribution plans, does all administration internally. More commonly, plan sponsors contract with external organizations to handle plan administration because of the specialized operations and systems involved. Often, plan sponsors, especially smaller companies and non-profit organizations, will buy a package deal which includes a plan definition that meets all the regulations, an array of investment vehicles into which the participants can put their money, and a complete set of administration services.

- *Participant.* Employees who meet plan eligibility requirements—typically tenure in the employ of the sponsor and a threshold for number of hours worked per year—may choose to participate in a plan. In most defined contribution plans, the employees may elect to have some of their compensation deducted and used to contribute to the plan. If the plan qualifies under tax code rules, that is, if it is a 401(k), 403(b), or 457 plan, then at least some of these contributions may represent pre-tax money— that is, the participant can deduct them from his or her taxable income. Some plans allow participants to contribute after-tax money as well.

In a defined contribution plan, the participant usually controls how these contributions are invested, constrained only by the rules of the plan. Typically, a participant specifies a set of investment option elections that tell the administrator how to invest each contribution. (For example, a participant may

Figure 5:
Major Players and Relationships in Defined Contribution Pensions

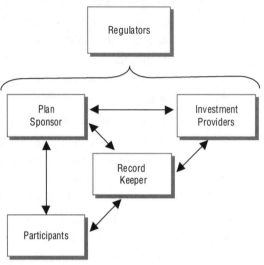

elect to invest 50 percent of each contribution into the large cap growth fund, 30 percent into the balanced fund, and 20 percent into the short-term bond fund.) Participants usually have the right to move their money from one investment vehicle to another, through an operation known as a transfer. Many plans allow a participant to take a loan against the plan balance, subject to limits on both the absolute size of the loan, and its proportion of the total balance in the participant's account.

* *Record Keeper.* A defined contribution plan requires specialized processing and record keeping to maintain a complete and accurate account of each participant's share of the plan assets. The record keeper sets up an account for each participant in a plan, recording descriptive data about the participant, e.g., name, address, and date of birth, as well as the participant's investment elections. As the plan sponsor sends contributions for the participants, the record keeper determines how these are to be invested, and makes and records each investment acquisition (for example, buying shares in a particular mutual fund). As the investments earn income (for example, as mutual funds pay dividends), the record keeper updates the participant's account accordingly. The record keeper also processes transactions the participant orders, such as transfers among investment choices, loans, and withdrawals.

Defined contribution participant record keeping is rendered especially complex by the need to track separately the assets derived from different sources of money. Sources of money include employee pre-tax contributions, employee after-tax contributions, employer contributions, and many more. The source of money from which a participant's plan assets were derived may affect vesting, loan eligibility, tax liability, and withdrawal procedures. Record keepers employ complex computer systems to process plan, participant, and investment activities and maintain the records of defined contribution plans.

- *Investment Provider*. While many record keepers are also investment providers, the two functions can and often do come from separate organizations. Collectively, defined contribution plans invest in a wide range of different types of assets: 1940 Act registered mutual funds, the stock of the plan sponsor's company, non-registered investment pools (separate accounts), guaranteed investment contracts, and individual securities selected by the participant (self-directed brokerage). At the end of 1998, 42 percent, or $931 billion of the assets held by defined contribution plans were in registered mutual funds. At that time, the ten management companies with the most fund assets held by defined contribution plans— Fidelity, Vanguard, American Funds, Putnam, American Century, T. Rowe Price, Merrill Lynch, Franklin Templeton, Janus, and American Express—accounted for 55 percent of this $931 billion.[18]

- *Regulators*. A number of different federal agencies have regulatory responsibilities related to defined contribution plans. The primary regulator for the pension plans themselves is the U.S. Department of Labor, which is charged with overseeing the provisions of ERISA and subsequent regulation. Each plan must submit a series of reports to the DOL each year demonstrating its compliance with the regulations. A number of these report the results of tests that aim at ensuring the plan is not discriminatory in favor of officers, owners, or highly paid employees of the plan sponsor. The Internal Revenue Service has responsibility for the provisions of the tax code that allow qualified plans to have tax advantages. Mutual funds and other securities that provide investment vehicles are subject to the securities regulations of the SEC. When plan assets are invested in bank trust funds, the Federal Reserve is the overseeing agency.

During the 1990s, defined contribution pension plans accounted for about $400 billion of new cash flow into open-end mutual funds. To attract this flow, fund companies have had to sell on two levels—the plan sponsor and the individual participant—and Goldman Sachs has popularized the term "instivitual" to refer to this two-level market. To have any chance of attracting investments, the fund must first become part of the investment options for the plan. If the fund company is selling a bundled service, i.e., record keeping plus funds as investment choices, it must win the plan sponsor's business, usually in competition with other record keepers and investment providers. If the fund company is offering investments only, with someone else doing the record keeping, then it must get record keepers to include its funds among their offerings. Many plan sponsors engage specialized benefits consultants to help them select plan options, investment vehicles, and service providers, and funds competing in this market must sell themselves to these consultants as well.

Once a fund is on the menu of investment choices for a plan, the next task is to get participants to select it. At one time, the large mutual fund companies offering bundled service could insist that only their mutual funds be included in the plan's investment choices. Until 1995, for example, Vanguard allowed plans for which it performed record keeping to choose mutual funds only from the Vanguard family. Competition in recent years has forced record keepers to accommodate a wider range of investment choices by plans, including funds from multiple complexes. For example, in 2000, the Delaware Group performed record keeping for the PricewaterhouseCoopers 401(k) plan, but the plan's investment options included funds managed by American

Express, Neuberger Berman, Lazard, Northern Trust, and Brinson, in addition to Delaware. Each of these companies succeeds in gaining assets only to the extent that they convince participants in the plan to choose their funds over the alternatives.

Fund companies also try to market to individuals who leave their plans, which they often do, since the average American worker can expect to change employers ten times over his or her career. In fact, Congress originally enacted ERISA to address, among other things, the need for faster pension vesting for an increasingly mobile U.S. workforce. Many individuals take their defined contribution plan assets along with them when they leave an employer. The regulations allow an individual to roll his or her assets from the plan into another qualified plan, or into an IRA without incurring tax penalties. Participants may also choose to roll their account balances over to individual accounts when they retire. In recent years, many mutual fund companies have instituted programs to try to induce participants leaving a plan for which they do the record keeping to roll the assets over into IRAs invested in their funds. Even so, the most successful providers still captured less than 50 percent of rollovers in 1999, and the average capture rate was no more than 25 percent.[19]

Administering a defined contribution plan, particularly performing participant record keeping, costs a great deal, often more than can be recovered in administration fees. Mutual fund companies that perform defined contribution record keeping—Fidelity, Vanguard, Putnam, etc.—do so primarily to gather assets into the funds, not to make money on record keeping. A senior executive for one such fund company stated it succinctly: "Our job is not to make money ourselves, but to bring assets to the funds. We succeed if we lose no more than twelve basis points annually on record keeping."[20] It is widely believed within the industry that this reflects a common situation, and that few record keepers break even on the record keeping fees they charge plans and participants.

The industry does a great deal of revenue sharing, a process through which investment managers cross-subsidize pension administrators in return for the assets they gather. For example, a fund manager trying to induce a third-party administrator (a firm that specializes in performing pension administration) to include its funds on the menu for plan sponsors might agree to pay 15 to 30 basis points per year on plan assets in the funds. The exact amount of this revenue sharing is difficult to determine—as FRC points out, most firms treat it as "a closely guarded secret!"[21] For the fund companies, this revenue sharing is effectively a marketing expense—money spent to attract assets to the funds that otherwise would not be there.

Throughout the 1990s, mutual funds attracted an increasing share of defined contribution plan assets as both plan sponsors and participants sought name-brand investment management expertise, and the high level of customer service fund companies provide. Toward the end of the 1990s, some plan sponsors began to move away from retail mutual funds towards less expensive investment vehicles—institutional mutual funds, or separately managed accounts. This movement so far has been slight, and some informed industry observers argued that it would remain small in scale for two reasons. First, many participants prefer retail funds. Strategic Insight summarizes this outlook: "For most DC investors, the investment comfort generated by owning a brand name fund from Fidelity, Vanguard, or Merrill Lynch much outweighs the benefits of an unknown pooled account." Second, the need to cross-subsidize record keeping from investment management profits may limit the use of lower expense—and less profitable—separate accounts. It remains to be seen, however, whether plan sponsor and participant desires to lower the costs of their plans will have a significant impact on the level of defined contribution investing in mutual funds.

Retirement savings have had both direct and secondary effects on the mutual fund industry. They have channeled enormous amounts of money directly into thousands of mutual funds as individuals and plan participants selected those funds to be the investment vehicles for their IRAs or defined contribution plan accounts. Between 1990 and 1998, IRA and defined contribution plan investments accounted for just under 30 percent of the flow of new money into open-end funds. The over $2 trillion of retirement account assets held in mutual funds at the end of 1999 represents this direct effect.

Retirement investing, especially in defined contribution plans, has also helped introduce segments of the American population to mutual funds. As these investors learned about mutual funds through their retirement plans, many of them turned to this same vehicle for other investing needs. As Strategic Insight puts it, many investors whose retirement plans introduce them to mutual funds "broaden their use of mutual funds for retirement purposes within taxable accounts, respond to recent regulatory and tax changes by starting new investments for retirement, or open complementary accounts outside their retirement funding programs."[22] This secondary effect defies precise measurement, but some percentage of the money currently invested in mutual funds is there only because investors learned about funds through their retirement plans.

Conclusions: The Role and Impact of Sales and Marketing Activities

In 1999, FRC and PricewaterhouseCoopers undertook a study of marketing activities in the mutual fund industry. They gathered survey data on marketing costs from twenty-four fund companies that collectively managed about 20 percent of the industry's 1998 assets. During that year, the firms included in the survey spent a total of just over $1 billion on sales and marketing activity, or, on an asset weighted basis, about 10.2 basis points on average assets for the year. Figure 6 shows how this expenditure breaks down into specific categories. Extrapolating these rates to the industry as a whole would suggest that the industry's expenditures on sales and marketing activities in 1998 totaled just over $5 billion.

Such an extrapolation must be viewed only as a crude indicator of the magnitude of industry-wide expenditures. The firms in the survey were not selected on the basis of any random sampling technique. These firms self-reported their marketing expenditures, and nothing guarantees that the different firms adhered to a common standard of measurement. Thus, as FRC clearly points out in its report of the study, any insights developed from the data "should be regarded as an indication of where the industry is and not as statistically proven."[23]

Despite the imprecision of its data, the survey nevertheless strongly suggests that the mutual fund industry spends a significant sum—on the order of several billion dollars per year—on sales and marketing. (Counting

Figure 6: Estimates of Mutual Fund Industry Spending in 1998 on Sales and Marketing Activity

Expense Category	Asset-weighted average cost to average assets under management (basis points)	Extrapolation to overall industry expenditures based on average assets in 1998 (billions)*
Salaries	2.3	$1.15
Incentives	0.9	$0.43
Commissions	1.5	$0.76
Other Staff-related Costs	0.9	$0.46
Advertising & Media Placement	1.2	$0.61
Collateral Materials & Fulfillment	1.0	$0.51
Public Relations	0.1	$0.06
Other Sales & Marketing Expense[†]	2.3	$1.17
TOTAL	**10.2**	**$5.15**

Source: *FRC/PricewaterhouseCoopers 1999 Study of Mutual Fund Distribution Costs and Strategy*

*Based on average industry assets of $5 trillion in 1998.

[†]Other sales and marketing expenses include miscellaneous expenses such as licensing fees, printing and promotion, postage, miscellaneous wholesaler costs, information services, communications research, occupancy, external consulting, and miscellaneous marketing expenses.

the revenue used to cross-subsidize defined contribution record keepers would add to this number.) Most of this represents money paid out of the fee revenues earned by the fund management companies and distributors. It does not include the commissions paid directly from investor assets to brokers and other intermediaries for the role they play in selling funds. Two questions about these marketing expenditures form the focus for continuing discussion and debate in the industry.

Is this expenditure warranted?

Belief about the appropriateness of mutual fund marketing follows from a philosophical view of the true nature of the industry. Goldman, Sachs & Company, in its influential 1995 report on the mutual fund industry, identified the opposing positions when it asserted that "Managing money is not the true business of the money management industry. Rather, it is gathering and retaining assets."[24] Most of the operatives in the industry share this latter view, at least implicitly. They believe that firms manage mutual funds to make a profit. Making a profit requires generating revenue, and assets under management form the source of all revenues. To gather and retain assets to manage, fund companies engage in marketing activities. In this respect, they argue, mutual fund management companies resemble all other for-profit enterprises that sell products to consumers.

It is this notion of mutual funds as consumer products that troubles subscribers to the opposing school of thought, who believe that the true business of the industry is to provide a professional service—to manage money as a fiduciary. Professor Tamar Frankel, author of a treatise on mutual fund law, typifies this view:

"Selling funds as products fosters a 'buyer beware' mentality more suitable for tangible products whose performance is immediately apparent than it is for an ongoing relationship of trust between a money manager and an investor."[25] Aggressive marketing, especially advertising, is as inappropriate to this relationship as it is to the physician-patient relationship.

John Bogle, not surprisingly, is a leading spokesman for this point of view. In one of his books, he clearly articulates the problems that members of this school of thought see in mutual fund marketing.

> First, it costs mutual fund shareholders a great deal of money—billions of dollars of extra fund expenses—which reduces the returns received by shareholders. Second, these large expenditures not only offer no countervailing benefit in terms of shareholder returns, but, to the extent they succeed in bringing additional assets into the funds, have a powerful tendency to *further reduce* fund returns. Third, mutual funds are too often hyped and hawked, and trusting investors may be imperiled by the risks assumed by, and deluded about the potential returns of, the funds. Lastly, and perhaps most significantly of all, the distribution drive alters the relationship between investors and funds... the mutual fund is no longer primarily an *investment account* under the stewardship of a professional *manager*, but an investment *product* under the control of a professional *marketer*.[26]

Bogle has made this philosophy concrete in the form of The Vanguard Group, Inc., a fund-owned management company designed to *not* make a profit. This approach remains distinctly in the minority, however. Most mutual funds are managed by profit-seeking enterprises that consider it perfectly appropriate to engage in marketing activities to increase revenue and profit. For these firms, the real questions about the propriety of marketing activities revolve not around whether they should be undertaken, but around the details of marketing practices—advertising content, commission levels, sales tactics, and so on.

Is this expenditure effective?

Assuming that marketing efforts are appropriate, the question remains as to what they actually achieve. Flows of new money into mutual funds closely correlate to fund performance, especially risk-adjusted performance as measured by Morningstar or similar ratings. Anecdotal evidence on what explicit marketing achieves is mixed. In 1999, for example, a market research firm surveyed the impact of twenty-two mutual fund ad campaigns on 1,000 respondents. They found that only 13 percent even remembered the ads, and those who did were not impressed. The president of FRC, commenting on this study, termed most mutual fund advertising "stilted" and a "waste of money."[27] On the other hand, when Alliance Capital Management achieved strong sales flow in 1999, firm officials attributed at least part of their success to marketing, including a television advertising campaign.[28] And when Scudder, Stevens & Clark sought a suitor to buy it out in 1997, after years of eroding market share, its problems were attributed to "marketing and management missteps."[29] Examples and counter examples of the effectiveness or lack thereof of fund marketing abound. As is the case in most contexts, anecdotal evidence supports both sides of the question.

The FRC/PricewaterhouseCoopers study of mutual fund sales and marketing attempted to address this question more systematically. Analyzing data for 1998, the researchers found that the total expenditures on sales and marketing explained 32 percent of the variability in gross sales for the firms in the study. (Of course, this analysis also labored under the imprecision of the respondents' self-reported data on marketing expenditures.) They concluded from this that marketing can and does have an impact: "Although performance is still the key factor in gross sales, a firm's commitment to sales and marketing can make a difference in a highly competitive industry."[30]

Correlation does not prove causality, however. The data could reflect fund companies spending more on sales and marketing *in response to* increased sales that gave them more discretionary funds. FRC has noted in the past that fund groups move advertising expenditures up or down based on what sales were the year before, cutting ad budgets when sales go down, and increasing the budget when sales go up.[31] The question of marketing effectiveness, especially the magnitude of the effect, remains open.

Discussions of mutual fund marketing often cite industry maturity as a driver for greater emphasis on sales and marketing activities. As the industry matures, many say, a large number of competitors fight over an increasingly saturated market. Achieving competitive advantage through product differentiation becomes more and more difficult, as multiple funds occupy every niche. Certainly performance sells, but depending on superior performance is a two-edged sword—money that flows to a fund when it is hot is likely to flow right back out as soon as the fund's performance cools. Fund companies seek ways to attract assets and retain them across performance peaks and valleys.

Active marketing may not be all that urgent in an industry that is rapidly expanding, where a rising tide lifts all the individual boats. Today, the argument goes, that rising tide is near high slack water. Fund companies had better learn how to market their wares just like the cereal and dog food companies do because the industry's run of easy money is nearing an end. But is it? Chapter 16 picks this topic up again, and specifically examines the question of industry maturity—what it means, and what the data tell us about the state of the mutual fund industry in early 2000.

CHAPTER 11

The Transfer Agent, Part 1— Shareholder Record Keeping

Most investors don't know what a transfer agent is; listed way back in the semi-annual report, they remain anonymous so long as they do their jobs well...they are necessary to operations but too dull to worry about.

– Charles A. Jaffe (1996)[1]

Every security requires a transfer agent—an organization to keep track of who owns the stock, to pay the owners dividends or interest when appropriate, to send required materials such as annual reports to the shareholders, and to transfer ownership when the security is bought and sold. Organizations that perform these functions for typical companies—Sears, Microsoft, Coca-Cola—are called stock transfer agents. Some big companies do their own transfer agent work, but most farm this function out to third parties, often banks. Some companies also use their transfer agents to implement dividend reinvestment and stock purchase programs (DRIPS and DRSPPS), through which shareholders can buy more shares without paying a commission. That about sums it up, however, for stock transfer agent functions.

Mutual funds also use transfer agents to perform these basic functions for their shareholders. But mutual fund transfer agents do much, much more. Over the past twenty-five years, competition in the industry has spurred mutual fund companies to evolve a rich set of options to offer shareholders, options that go far beyond simply tracking ownership and sending dividends and reports. Shareholders can purchase shares in a wide variety of ways; they can set up automatic programs to liquidate shares or exchange them into other funds; they can accrue income daily, and get it paid out in multiple forms and via multiple delivery methods; they can have reports of their holdings and activities presented in various formats via various media, to themselves and to interested parties. Funds also have evolved a complex set of methods for compensating their distribution agents— front-end loads, contingent deferred sales charges, finder's fees, trail commissions, service fees. All of these functions, and more, are implemented by the transfer agent.

Who the Transfer Agents Are

The Securities Exchange Act of 1934 gave the SEC the authority to register and regulate transfer agents as part of its mandate to ensure the prompt and accurate clearance and settlement of securities transactions. In early 1999, about 1,600 transfer agents, mostly stock transfer agents, had registered with the SEC (or, if they were banks, with the Federal Reserve Board). A subset of these focused on mutual funds. In the early days of the mutual fund industry, banks that had developed stock transfer capabilities merely broadened them slightly to accommodate the new mutual funds. As mutual fund processing became more complex, a handful of these organizations evolved along with the industry to specialize in the unique needs of open-end funds.

As of early 1999, the fourteen companies shown in Table 1 competed in the full-service third-party transfer agent business in the United States—that is, they provided the complete range of transfer agent functions for mutual fund companies.[2] These firms processed about 34 million shareholder accounts, or about 17 percent of the total accounts open at the time. Transfer agents internal to the mutual fund management companies handled the remaining 170 million accounts. This service industry had been consolidating for some time, and the consolidation continued in 1999, when PFPC acquired First Data's mutual fund processing business to challenge the DST complex for first place in number of accounts processed.

Table 1:
Full Service Transfer Agent Service Providers as of March 1999

Provider	Number of Fund Groups Serviced	Number of Shareholder Accounts Serviced
DST/BFDS/NFDS	179	14,500,000
First Data Investors Services Group	41	9,007,000
PFPC	100	5,087,000
Chase Global	90	1,716,000
Federated Investors	90	1,441,000
FIRSTAR	68	1,400,000
BISYS	44	410,000
Sunstone	11	191,000
Countrywide	34	57,000
IBT	30	36,000
United Fund Services	18	28,000
Forum Financial	13	18,000
MFS Company	6	18,000
Totals	**724**	**33,909,000**

Source: Strategic Insight, *Mutual Fund Industry Fee and Expense Benchmarks Updated for 1998*, April 1999

A TOUGH BUSINESS TO BREAK INTO: THE SAGA OF AT&T AMERICAN TRANSTECH

In 1988, AT&T thought it saw an opportunity to share in the explosive growth of the mutual fund industry by exploiting its established proficiency as a stock transfer agent to become a mutual fund transfer agent. In 1983, AT&T had spun off its internal stock transfer agent to form a subsidiary, American Transtech. By 1988, American Transtech managed the largest shareowner account base in the stock transfer industry, employing a staff of 2,500 in its Jacksonville, Florida facility. Mutual fund transfer agent service looked like a natural next step, and the Bank of New York (BoNY) seemed to be offering a perfect opportunity to break into that market.

BoNY, then the second-largest third-party transfer agent service provider in the United States, had looked hard in 1987 at what they would have to spend on a new system to stay competitive, and had decided it was too much. Transtech, on the other hand, thought it had already found the transfer agent system of the future—the Multiple Asset System (MAS), which it got when it bought a small development company called AIS. Transtech's CEO thought it all fit perfectly—"the acquisition of AIS, a leader in mutual funds transfer technology, allows us to expand our already formidable line of financial information services. It is a perfect complement to our existing strengths."[3] So, in May 1989, Transtech bought BoNY's transfer agent processing business.

But Transtech couldn't actually buy the customers. The success of the deal for Transtech hinged on their ability to convince BoNY's mutual fund customers to sign up with them as BoNY's designated successor, rather than switching to another provider altogether. Doing this was not a foregone conclusion. Since the funds had to undergo a system conversion (always a nasty prospect) even if they went with Transtech, they might look around for a better deal while they were about it.

Unfortunately, Transtech found that MAS couldn't be made ready to handle a big fund group until late 1990, and this opened the door for competitors who could move more quickly. In November 1989, BoNY's largest client by far, The Dreyfus Funds, announced that they would switch their transfer agent business to The Shareholder Services Group (TSSG). TSSG, an established mutual fund transfer agent, could get Dreyfus up and running six months earlier than Transtech.

Transtech ended up getting a handful of small funds with fewer than 30,000 accounts from the BoNY book of business, far too few to be economical. In 1991, having lost any hope of success in the highly competitive mutual fund transfer agent service market, Transtech quietly sold both MAS and its mutual fund book of business to Kemper Service Corporation of Kansas City, and exited the industry.

During the 1980s and 1990s, a number of the larger mutual fund companies moved their transfer agent functions from third-party providers to internal organizations to reduce costs and improve customer service. Today, smaller fund companies tend to use outside service providers, and larger companies tend to do all or most of their transfer agent processing internally. In many cases, the funds split transfer agent and shareholder servicing functions, using external agents to perform the back-office processing while handling telephone, mail, and e-mail interactions with their clients themselves.

What Transfer Agent Service Costs

Transfer agent service is typically the largest component of a fund's expense after investment management. The ICI has commissioned studies of transfer agent fees, and Table 2 shows a summary of per-account charges and trends through the 1990s. These surveys have found that transfer agent costs have remained essentially flat, despite increasing pressure on fund groups to expand the services the transfer agent provides.

Table 2:
Average Per-Account Charges for Transfer Agent Service

Account Base	1993	1995	1997	1999
Open Only	$25.92	$25.09	$24.87	$26.10
All Accounts	$22.77	$20.93	$20.50	$21.86

Source: ICI, *Mutual Fund Transfer Agent Fee Survey,1999, Preliminary Survey Results.*

In 1998, Strategic Insight found that annual transfer agent expenses ranged from below $20 per shareholder account to over $100 per account.[4] Table 3 shows the median per account annual expense for transfer agent services for a selection of fund types and distribution channels. As this shows, the major source of variation is the distribution channel, since transfer agents perform different functions according to the fund's distribution method. (Brokers often perform much of the shareholder reporting functions for funds they distribute, for example.) Other sources of variation include such factors as the nature of the fund (e.g., how often does it pay dividends), the options and services offered to the shareholders (e.g., what automated exchange programs do they get), and the economies of scale inherent in the size of the shareholder base. By way of comparison, the

Table 3:
Median transfer agent expense (in $ per shareholder account per year)
for selected fund categories and selected channels, for 1998

Type of Fund	Type of Distribution Channel			
	Direct	Broker Dealer Non-proprietary	Broker Dealer Proprietary	Institutional
Equity – Capital Appreciation	$31.89	$25.52	$14.78	$24.71
Equity – International/Global	$32.79	$23.03	$14.71	$25.49
Fixed Income – Government Backed	$33.99	$33.57	$18.91	$29.44
Fixed Income – Corporate High Yield	$37.68	$29.34	$17.20	$26.66
Money Market – General	$38.19	$26.93	$16.23	$71.13

Source: Strategic Insight, *Mutual Fund Industry Fee and Expense Benchmarks Updated for 1998*, April 1999.

typical shareholder account valued at $20,000 might incur between $40 and $200 per year in fees to pay the investment adviser, depending on the type of fund.

What Transfer Agents Do

What do the shareholders get for the $20 to $40 per year most of them pay for the transfer agent? In a nutshell, the transfer agent handles all aspects of their interactions with the funds. The transfer agent maintains their account records; processes their trades into and out of the fund; pays them their dividends and capital gains distributions; sends them various documents, such as confirmations, statements, and tax forms; and pays the intermediaries they use, such as brokers. All of these activities comprise the transfer agent back-office functions.

When a shareholder purchases into a fund via an intermediary such as a supermarket or broker, he or she may see the intermediary performing some or even all of the functions described in this chapter as transfer agent functions. In these cases, the transfer agent interacts with the intermediary who acts on behalf of the shareholder.

Setting Up and Maintaining Shareholder Accounts

To purchase shares in a fund, an investor must establish an account with the fund's transfer agent. The investor does this by filling out an account application, such as the Invesco Funds example shown at the end of this chapter. Typically, the investor sends this application along with the money for the initial purchase into the fund, either directly to the transfer agent, or via an intermediary. The application captures several important types of information that the transfer agent uses to set up the account record for the investor.

- *Information about the Owner.* The *account registration* is the legal description of the ownership of the account. The registration can be simple (e.g., "John Smith") or complex (e.g., "John A. and Jane B. Smith, custodians for Susan C. Smith under the Massachusetts Uniform Transfer to Minors Act"), depending on the type of account. Along with the registration, the investor specifies the address of registration and the owner's tax status and identification (typically social security number).
- *Account Type.* Common types include individual/joint (an individual investor or investors, non-retirement), custodial (usually parents for their children), trust (most often for Individual Retirement Accounts, or IRAs), and various types of institutional accounts (corporations, foundations and endowments, retirement plans). The account type affects the tax status of the account and what options it may exercise.
- *Related Party Information.* The investor may specify the name and address of various parties that play a role in the account. Examples include recipients for duplicate statements (such as a financial adviser or accountant), recipients of cash (from dividend or systematic withdrawal payments), and beneficiaries (on retirement accounts).

OMNIBUS ACCOUNTS

When an investor purchases a mutual fund through Schwab's mutual fund marketplace, the fund's transfer agent never knows who that investor is. Schwab, like many intermediaries, sets up only a single account, an *omnibus* account, at the mutual fund's transfer agent to handle the holdings of all the investors who hold that fund through Schwab. Each day Schwab rolls up all the trades individual investors make buying and selling shares in the fund, and places a few aggregate trades with the fund's transfer agent.

Of course, this means that Schwab must handle many investor servicing functions that the fund's transfer agent would otherwise perform, such as calculating and paying dividends and capital gains, keeping track of the tax cost basis of the investor's holdings, issuing tax forms, and answering shareholder questions. This processing costs money, and part of the fee that Schwab assesses the funds for selling their shares through its mutual fund marketplace goes to cover this sub-accounting that Schwab does. Brokers find omnibus accounts attractive in part because they allow the broker to maintain control over the shareholder account—a shareholder cannot contact the fund directly to redeem shares, for example, because the transfer agent has no record of the individual shareholder.

In addition to brokers, defined contribution plan (e.g., 401(k)) record keepers also often keep omnibus accounts at the fund's transfer agent. These accounts represent the total holdings in the fund for all the participants in a particular pension plan, or even for all the participants in all the plans the record keeper handles.

- *Option Choices.* Every shareholder must choose how he or she wants to receive dividends and capital gains distributions—in cash or as reinvestments in the fund. (Two-thirds of American shareholders reinvest all such distributions.) Most funds offer many more service choices as well, including such things as:
  - automatic investment plans
  - systematic withdrawal plans
  - check writing privileges
  - asset allocation programs
  - consolidation of accounts for statements and other reporting
  - Internet access to account information
  - automatic use of dividends or gains from one fund to purchase into another fund.
- *Commission Reduction Information.* Many load funds give investors discounts on the commissions they pay when their investments reach certain threshold values, called breakpoints. For example, a fund may charge 4 percent on purchases up to $50,000; 3.5 percent on purchases from $50,000 to $100,000, and so on. Investors may be able to link accounts in other funds in the family to qualify for the discount, a practice called rights of accumulation (ROA). They may also make a declaration that they will put enough money into the fund within a specified period—typically thirteen months—to earn a discount. This is termed a letter of intent (LOI).

    The transfer agent sets up the shareholder's records in its computer system when it receives the completed application, and makes changes to those records when the shareholder, or authorized intermediary, requests. These records control how transactions for the account are subsequently processed and reported. The typical transfer agent has a department that specializes in account set up and maintenance. Some trust and custodial accounts can be quite complex, as can the interactions between account types and account options.

Transaction Processing

Every fund's prospectus contains language similar to this statement from American Century: "We will price your purchase, exchange or redemption at the NAV next determined after we receive your transaction request in good order."[5] (For load funds, the price is based on the NAV adjusted for a commission.) In other words, open-end mutual funds all employ *forward pricing*. In order to ensure that existing and remaining shareholders in the fund are protected, shareholders entering and leaving do so at a price struck *after* they have committed their trade order. This ensures that the shareholders entering, the shareholders leaving, and the shareholders remaining in the fund all receive or hold shares of equal value.

Without forward pricing, the fund and its shareholders would be vulnerable to dilution of value through arbitrage. For example, assume that an investor could buy into the fund at the price struck yesterday. In a rising market for the fund's underlying securities, the investor, or arbitrageur, could note that these rising security

---

THE REGULATIONS ON PRICING MUTUAL FUND TRANSACTIONS

Section 22 of the Investment Company Act of 1940 dealt with pricing mutual fund shares for either purchase or redemption. The section stated that shares can only be sold "at a current public offering price described in the prospectus." It further stated that the price had to be related to the current net asset value, and that the price might include a commission amount, as long as it was not "excessive." The Act did not, however, prescribe exactly how and when the NAV would be calculated.

In 1968, the SEC found that the 1940 Act's specification for pricing had left a loophole that needed to be closed. A number of funds at that time were pricing their shares based on the last NAV that had been determined—backward pricing, in other words. As SEC official Barry Barbash described it,

"In the rising markets of the 1960s, backward pricing was often cited by aggressive brokers in seeking to convince potential investors that, by acting quickly, they could purchase fund shares at bargain basement prices that soon would disappear. Backward pricing also led some investors in the 1960s to become speculators in fund shares. A strategy used by some investors at the time was to arbitrage fund shares by purchasing a large block of shares during a rising market, and then quickly selling the shares after the fund's assets were revalued to reflect the market rise. This speculative practice, in addition to causing dilution of a fund's existing shareholders, often interfered with the ability of the fund's adviser to manage the fund effectively."[6]

As a result, in 1968 the SEC adopted Rule 22c-1 under the 1940 Act to preclude this abuse. Rule 22c-1 requires funds to base all purchase and sale transaction prices on "the current net asset value...which is next computed *after* receipt of a tender..." Ever since, all U.S. mutual funds have had to use forward pricing.

prices had driven the fund's current value higher than its current price. If he or she could buy these undervalued shares, he or she would be effectively taking some of the appreciation in value away from existing shareholders. Forward pricing precludes this abuse.

Transfer agents collect unpriced transactions all day, and process them to completion each night after the day's NAV has been determined. These transactions flow in via mail, telephone, the Internet, and numerous electronic transmissions from intermediaries of various sorts. An investor must commit his or her transaction by a stated cut-off time—typically 4:00 P.M. in New York, when the New York Stock Exchange closes—to get the price for that day.

- *Purchase and Sale transactions.* Purchase trades, sometimes called subscriptions, occur when an investor decides to put his or her money into the fund. Sales, also called redemptions or liquidations, occur when the shareholder decides to convert his or her holdings back to cash. In either case, the transfer agent determines the appropriate price for the trade, calculates the number of shares purchased or sold, and records the transaction in the shareholder's records. The price for a purchase depends on the NAV applicable to the trade, and, for load funds, the sales commission the investor incurs. Redemption transactions are always priced at NAV, but in some cases, a commission or fee may be deducted from the shareholder's proceeds.

  Purchase and sale orders can come to the transfer agent via many methods. Some of the commonly encountered ones include:
  - *Mail.* Purchase trades may come to the transfer agent via the mail—the shareholder sends a check along with an application for a new account or an indication that he or she wants to add money to an existing account. Shareholders can also order redemptions by mail.
  - *Telephone.* Shareholders usually can telephone their requests for liquidation transactions. A few funds do not take telephone requests, usually to discourage short-term investors who might try to move in and out of the fund as part of a market timing strategy.
  - *Electronic transmission.* Transfer agents for broker distributed funds receive the bulk of their purchase and redemption trades via electronic transmission from the brokers who have taken the orders from their clients. Other intermediaries such as bank trust departments or fund supermarkets may transmit purchase and sale orders to no-load fund transfer agents as well.
  - *Pre-authorized draft.* Funds may have catchy names for these programs, such as "Fundamatic" or "Investamatic," but whatever the name, they all allow the investor to set up standing orders for the transfer agent to debit their bank accounts on a periodic basis, say monthly, to purchase mutual fund shares. Typically the transfer agent uses the Automated Clearing House (ACH) network to get the investor's money. For example, an investor might supplement her retirement savings program by having $500 automatically taken from her checking account each month and used to purchase shares in a fund.

- *Systematic Withdrawal Plan*. Most fund groups allow investors to set up standing orders to redeem shares on a periodic basis. The transfer agent generates redemption trades based on these instructions, which specify the amount to sell (typically a dollar amount, a share amount, or a percentage of the account balance), and the recipient(s) of the proceeds. For example, an investor might set up a SWP that has $1,000 worth of shares redeemed each month, with $500 of the proceeds being sent via ACH to his son in college, and the other half via check to his daughter in the Peace Corps.
- *Internet*. Many fund groups allow investors to order redemption and exchange trades over the Internet. They sometimes allow purchases, if the investor can authorize a flow of funds from a bank account.
- *Voice Response Unit*. All fund groups provide VRU—sometimes referred to as IVR, or interactive voice response—access to their shareholders. Among the many functions most VRUs offer is the capability to order redemptions.

TRANSFER AGENT PROFILE: DST

DST is the largest of the third-party transfer agent service providers, and, by mutual fund industry standards, an old-timer as well. It started in the early 1960s as an internal department of Kansas City Southern Industries, a railroad that had acquired mutual funds as part of its diversification program. In 1968, KCSI incorporated DST, aiming to use the system and capabilities it had developed internally to generate revenue by servicing other mutual funds. In 1974, DST joined with State Street Bank to form Boston Financial Data Services (BFDS) to do full-service transfer agent processing in the Boston area. When the industry took off in the early eighties, DST was perfectly positioned to attract fund complexes looking for transfer agent service. By 1986, it had become the largest mutual fund transfer agent in the United States, a position it retained through 2000. As one industry research group noted in 1997, DST had a remarkably stable customer base, having lost only two major clients in the previous ten years, one to an internalization, and one in the wake of an acquisition.[7]

As of early 1999, DST provided some aspect of the transfer agent service for over fifty million mutual fund shareholder accounts. For fourteen million of these, DST or one of its subsidiaries, such as BFDS, performed transfer agent processing. For the remainder, DST provided its transfer agent system, TA2000, for use by the transfer agent who handled the accounts.

In recent years, DST has extended its reach to foreign mutual fund shareholder processing, establishing its presence in Canada with CFDS and Europe with EFDS. DST also owns subsidiaries that provide related functions, such as Output Technologies Incorporated (OTI), a print-mail company that serves many of DST's mutual fund clients.

When DST takes prospective clients on a tour of its facilities, it offers one item that is unique in the industry. DST houses its data center in a limestone cave, originally developed by the military, located a few miles from the center of Kansas City. It also keeps two enormous generators mounted on shock absorbers in the cave, so that the computers can keep running without missing a beat even if all the external power fails. In an industry in which reliability is so important, the image of this massive data center securely nestled in the protection of the cave has served DST well as a marketing point.

– *Check Writing*. Almost all money market and some other fixed-income funds feature check writing provisions. The shareholder is given a checkbook, and writing a check effectively orders a dollar-denominated redemption transaction. The clearing bank sends the transfer agent a file each day with the information about these checks, and the transfer agent generates redemption transactions accordingly.

– *Automated Teller Machine*. Funds associated with banks often give shareholders access to their accounts via the bank's ATM network. The investor can move money from his or her checking or savings account to a fund for a purchase, or vice-versa for a redemption.

This list cannot be exhaustive. Between the time this is written and the time it is read, some innovative transfer agents will have devised new methods for investors to move their money in and out of their funds.

- **Exchanges**. An exchange pairs one or more redemption transactions with one or more purchase transactions to move a shareholder's money from fund to fund. Many shareholders find it desirable at some point to make adjustments in the way their money is invested. For example, a person approaching retirement may move some capital from equity fund holdings to fixed-income funds, as controlling risk becomes more important. Other shareholders move money from fund to fund in hopes of increasing their returns by timing the market. (Many funds charge fees to discourage excessive use of exchanges for market timing.) Whatever the reason, the exchange is the transaction through which a shareholder moves money from one fund in a family to another.

  Since exchanges involve no flow of cash to or from the shareholder, investors can order them through many different mechanisms: mail, telephone, VRU, Internet, ATM, anything that can be used to communicate with the transfer agent.

  When the transfer agent processes the transaction, however, money actually flows from fund to fund, and the redemption side of the exchange creates a taxable event for the shareholder.

- **Transfers**. Transfers change ownership of holdings within a fund. Shareholders use transfers most often to effect changes in the registration for holdings. For example, a parent may wish to make a gift by transferring shares to a child's account. Transfers are also used when a shareholder wants to change his or her account registration so significantly that the transfer agent must set up a new account (as, for example, when the trustee on the account changes). The transfer agent then uses a transfer transaction to move the holdings from the old account to the new one. Transfers involve no flow of money and do not affect the fund's balance at all—they merely change the ownership of some of the fund's shares from one shareholder account to another.

- **Other Transactions**. Funds sometimes assess *fees* against their shareholders that they collect via share redemption transactions. For example, some fund groups charge Individual Retirement Account (IRA) shareholders a small annual fee for serving as trustee for the account. If the shareholder does

CROSS-FUND FAMILY EXCHANGES

To complete an exchange transaction, the transfer agent must first determine the net proceeds resulting from the redemption side of the transaction. If the redemption side is share-denominated, the transfer agent must apply the NAV for the fund to calculate dollars. The transfer agent then divides these dollars by the NAV of the fund into which the exchange is going. This gives the number of shares to be purchased in that fund. When the transfer agent system is processing the nightly cycle for a fund family, and the exchange is between two funds in that family, doing all this is straightforward. The system has the NAVs of both funds as it does its calculations.

But what if the two funds come from different fund families, and are processed by different transfer agents? Mutual fund supermarkets allow their investors to switch their holdings among funds in the supermarket, even if the funds come from different families. The supermarkets want to make these switches look just like exchanges: both the redemption and the purchase transaction should get the same day's NAV. After all, one of the big selling points of the fund supermarket is the ability to move easily from fund to fund, just as though they were all in one big family.

This is easier said than done. The supermarket would like to just roll up all the dollar-denominated trades for each fund, and all the share-denominated trades, and send two omnibus trades to the transfer agent. But if the investor denominates the redemption side of an exchange in shares (e.g., "move *all* of my shares out of that crummy fund"), then the quantity on the purchase side can be determined only after the redemption side has been processed. The purchase trade can't be rolled in with other trades to be sent to the transfer agent, because it doesn't have a quantity yet. In the early days of the fund supermarkets, a switch between funds of different families was a two-day event. The redemption was priced on night one, and then, when the dollars available to purchase had been determined, the purchase was priced on night two. The investor was effectively out of the market for a day.

Recently, the supermarkets have become more sophisticated in how they approach this issue. They get the NAVs from the fund groups and run a special program to price the redemption side of switches to determine the dollar amount of the purchase transactions. If need be, they arrange with the funds' transfer agents to take their trades later in the night, to give them time to do this pre-processing. Then they can include both sides of the switch in night one's transmissions to the transfer agents, and the investor's money moves seamlessly from one fund to the other without the day's delay.

not pay this fee in another way, the transfer agent generates a fee transaction that redeems enough shares to cover the fee amount.

Most shareholders today hold their shares in book form—that is, the shares exist only in the form of records on the transfer agent's computer system. A small percentage of mutual fund shares are still represented by physical certificates, however. Transfer agents must process *deposit* transactions to convert a certificate's shares to book form, typically so they can be redeemed or exchanged. Conversely, when the (now relatively rare) occasion calls for creation of a certificate, the transfer agent must be able to process a transaction to *issue* one. Issue and deposit transactions have no effect on the value or amount of a shareholder's holdings.

Transfer agents use *adjustment* transactions to make changes in a shareholder's account balances, typically to correct mistakes. For example, if the transfer agent processed a purchase trade to the wrong fund (perhaps because the shareholder's letter was ambiguous), and corrected the mistake by entering the trade to the correct fund five days later, the shareholder might have missed a dividend on the purchased shares. In this case, the transfer agent could make the shareholder whole by processing an adjustment transaction. The adjustment would give the shareholder the amount of shares that would have come from the reinvested dividend had the trade been processed correctly from the first. Every transfer agent seeks to reduce the need for adjustments as much as possible.

Finally, the transfer agent must be able to *reverse* any transaction it processes to correct mistakes. In the case mentioned above, when the transfer agent learned of the mistake—probably when the shareholder or broker called—it would enter a reversal transaction that undid everything the first and erroneous purchase transaction had done. The transfer agent would then enter the correct transaction, making it effective as of the date it should have been processed in the first place.

Trades like this, which force the use of some prior date's price, are called *as-of trades*. As-of trades can cause losses. Assume, for example, that a $9,000 purchase should have occurred on April 1 when the price was $9.00/share, but wasn't processed until April 5, by which date the price had risen to $10.00/share. The shareholder should get 1,000 shares for the $9,000, but by April 5 those 1,000 shares are worth $10,000 to the fund. Who pays this extra $1,000 to make both the shareholder and the fund whole? As-of processing often requires determining whose fault the mistake was—transfer agent, investor, broker—so that the guilty party can be assessed accordingly.

Transfer agents usually have one or more departments that specialize in processing transactions. A common organizational pattern has one group specializing in purchases, one in redemptions, exchanges, and transfers, and a third group of highly trained and experienced individuals handling reversals, adjustments, and very complex transactions.

The Daily Processing Cycle

Over the course of each day, the transfer agent receives mail, telephone calls, faxes, email, and electronic transmissions from a variety of internal and external sources, all bearing transactions to be processed. Early in the evening, the fund accountant for the funds determines the day's NAV per share and transmits this to the transfer agent. Once the NAV is available and all the day's trades have been entered, the transfer agent system can process the trades. This processing includes pricing the trades, calculating commissions (for load funds), accruing and paying dividends and capital gains, ordering money movements, and reporting to various parties.

Pricing and Commission Calculation

Investors may denominate their financial transactions in dollars, e.g., purchase $10,000 worth of shares in Fund X, or in shares, e.g., redeem 500 shares from Fund Y or exchange half the shares in Fund X to Fund Y. To process these transactions, the system first determines the per-share price at which to convert dollars to shares

Figure 1: The Daily Processing Cycle

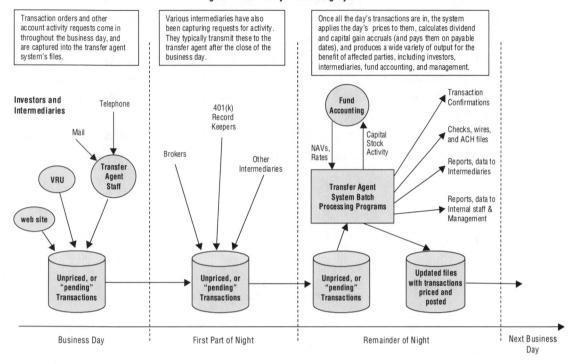

or shares to dollars. For all redemptions, and for purchases into no load funds, the system prices the trade at the applicable NAV.

When an investor purchases shares in a fund with a front-end load, the transaction is priced at a public offering price that reflects the effect of the commission. For example, an investor buying into a fund with an NAV of $10.00 and a front-end load of 4 percent would actually pay $10.42 per share. The fund would get $10 per share, and the intermediaries involved (typically a broker and the fund's principal distributor) would get the remainder as commission. The transfer agent system determines the appropriate commission level and price, considering the fund's load table, the amount of the transaction, and any volume discount to which the investor is entitled. (Fund load structures were discussed in Chapter 8.)

Redemption transactions from load funds may involve a back-end charge—sometimes a redemption fee (which goes to the fund to compensate it for the expense caused by the redemption), sometimes a commission, such as a contingent deferred sales charge. In such a case, the transaction is priced at NAV, and the appropriate amount is deducted from the proceeds. (Although not normally part of the daily cycle, the transfer agent also calculates and pays asset-based commissions and fees, such as 12b-1 commissions to brokers, or service fees to supermarkets like Schwab. The transfer agent periodically determines the shareholder assets that qualify for this fee or commission, extends them by the appropriate rate, and pays the intermediaries the sum derived from the shareholder assets they control. For example, funds that are part of a supermarket pay the brokerage firm 25 to 35 basis points annually on the average value of their accounts.)

As part of the pricing process, the transfer agent system updates records for the fund, the shareholder, and, if appropriate, the intermediaries. It creates entries in the system's database or files that will trigger confirmations and money movements, and which will be included in reports to various interested parties. Figure 2 shows an example of one of the most important reports from this process, the share and cash activity summary that goes to fund accounting, sometimes called the supersheet. This tells fund accounting the net effect on the fund of the day's activity by investors, so the fund accountants can properly figure it into the next day's NAV calculations.

Figure 2:
The Supersheet, Part 1—The Share Activity Summary

Report: SHRPROOF							Summary of Share Activity for 03/15/98
			Fund: 222 U.S. Growth and Income				
Category	Posted to Shareholders	Unpaid Purchases	Paid & Waiting	Unsettled Liquidations	Net Outstanding	Accumulated Liquidations	Total Shares Outstanding
Beginning Balance	99,164,535.993	53,443.516	6,340.086	-208,420.403	99,015,896.192	257,819,660.699	356,835,556.891
Direct Purchase	11,758.049				11,758.049		11,758.049
Wire Order Purchase Placement		18,960.132			18,960.132		18,960.132
Wire Order Purchase Settlement		-19,879.422	19,879.422				
W/O transfer to Shareholder	8,116.482		-8,116.482				
Wire Order Liquidation Placement				-42,726.845	-42,726.845	42,726.845	
Wire Order Liquidation Settlement	-38,331.139			38,331.139			
Direct Liquidation	-12,829.034				-12,829.034	12,829.034	
SWP Liquidation							
Exchange In	16,635.869				16,635.869		16,635.869
Exchange Out	-25,937.277				-25,937.277	25,937.277	
Distribution Reinvest	1.894				1.894		1.894
Adjustments							
Fee Liquidations	-1.511				-1.511	1.511	
Daily Total	-40,586.667	-919.290	11,762.940	-4,395.706	-34,138.723	81,494.667	47,355.944
Ending Balance	99,123,949.326	52,524.226	18,103.026	-212,819.109	98,981,757.469	257,901,155.366	356,882,912.835

The Supersheet, Part 2—The Cash Activity Summary

Report: CASHPROOF   Summary of Cash Activity for 04/22/98

Fund: 123 Corporate High Yield

Category	Receipt $	Dealer Commission	Distributor Commission	CDSC	Tax Withholding	Fees	To/From Fund
Purchases							
Paid by Check	29,485.64	-1,007.80	-139.62				28,338.22
Paid by Wire	0.00	0.00	0.00				
W/O Paid	0.00	0.00	0.00				
NSCC Settled	63,013.01	0.00	-274.85				62,738.16
Exchanges In	2,000.00	0.00	0.00				2,000.00
Div - Batch	0.00						
Div - Online	-85.49						-85.49
Gain – Batch	0.00						
Gain – Online	0.00						
Cash Fee	0.00					0.00	
Total	94,413.16	-1,007.80	-414.47			0.00	92,990.89
Deposit to RPO	0.00						
Liquidations							
Direct	-217,832.16			0.00	-3,923.59	-7.50	-221,763.25
Shrs for Fees	0.00			0.00		-90.00	-90.00
SWP	-13,185.58			0.00	-380.37	0.00	-13,565.95
W/O Settle	0.00			0.00	0.00	0.00	0.00
NSCC Settled	-245,806.01			0.00	0.00	0.00	-245,806.01
Cash Adjustmt	0.00						0.00
Exchanges Out	-32,084.17			0.00	0.00	0.00	-32,084.17
Div Reclaim	0.00						0.00
Total	-508,907.92			0.00	-4,303.96	-97.50	-513,309.38
Cash Distributions							
Dividend	-320.99					0.00	-320.99
Gain	0.00					0.00	0.00
Net Cash	-414,494.76	-1,007.80	-414.47	0.00	-4,303.96	-97.50	-420,318.49

The Supersheet, Part 3—Notes

The supersheet provides a capsule summary of a day in the life of a fund. The share activity summary, or share proof, summarizes all the ins and outs of fund shares resulting from the day's shareholder activity, and its effect on the fund. In the example here, the fund started the day having issued 356,835,556.891 shares since its inception. Of these, 99,015,896.192 were currently outstanding (i.e., owned by shareholders), while shareholders had bought and previously redeemed another 257,819,660.699 shares.

The U.S. Growth and Income Fund did not have a good day on March 15, 1998. Shareholders purchased roughly 30,000 additional shares, but redeemed roughly 41,000 shares, for a net redemption of about 10,000 shares. Both purchases and redemptions came directly from shareholders (direct purchases and direct liquidations), and through brokers (wire order purchase and liquidation placements). In addition, shareholders exchanged about 10,000 more shares out of the fund than they exchanged into it. Other activity was minimal. (Settlements of wire order trades do not affect the number of outstanding shares, but merely shift them from one category to another.) So, the fund ended the day with about 20,000 fewer outstanding shares.

The cash activity summary, or cash proof, depicts the cash effects of the shareholder activity for the day. The Corporate High Yield Fund also had a rough day on April 22. Cash flowing in, mostly from direct purchase transactions, or settlement of wire order trades, totaled $94,413.16, of which a thousand or so went to pay commissions. Cash flowing out—to pay direct and SWP liquidations, to settle wire order liquidations, and to settle exchanges out—totaled $508,907.92. There was little dividend or capital gain activity that day. So, the fund had a net cash outflow of $420,318.49 for the day.

Dividend and Capital Gains Processing

After the day's transactions have been priced and posted, the transfer agent system processing typically turns next to shareholder dividend and capital gains accruals and payments. On any given night, there may or may not be accruals and/or payments, depending on the fund. The pattern of dividends and capital gains the fund pays its shareholders reflects the nature of the underlying securities in which the fund itself invests.

Shareholders in fixed-income funds typically accrue dividends each day, as the fund accrues interest in the bonds it holds. The stocks that equity funds hold typically declare dividends on a periodic basis, so equity funds do the same. An investor who holds shares in an equity fund on the fund's declared record date is eligible to participate in the dividend. Funds of all types distribute their capital gains—the profit resulting from the fund selling securities—periodically to shareholders who hold shares as of the record date. (Funds holding mostly mortgage-backed securities distribute both dividends and capital gains each period, as mortgage holders make principal and interest payments on the mortgages underlying the securities.)

Different transfer agent systems handle accruals differently—some determine each shareholder's accrual each day, and some wait until payment date to calculate the accrual for the entire period. When the payment date for a dividend or capital gain distribution arrives, however, the system performs several steps for each shareholder as part of the batch cycle:

- It makes a final determination of the dollar value the shareholder gets as part of this dividend or gain.
- It determines from the shareholder's records in the system how he or she wants to receive the payment, and whether any tax withholding must be taken.
- It generates one or more transactions to effect the dividend or gain payment:
  - a purchase of additional shares for the investor who wants to reinvest;
  - a money movement order for cash payment for the investor who wants to receive cash—usually a check or ACH transaction (or inclusion in a group payment to an intermediary); or
  - an internal money movement transaction with a matching purchase transaction for the shareholder who wishes to use the dividend or gain to purchase shares of another fund in the family.
- It accumulates totals for fund accounting and management reporting.

Most dividend and capital gain processing occurs on the nights of payment dates for regular distributions. In fact, getting the nightly processing cycle finished in time on nights on which there are large funds paying their dividend challenges many transfer agents. Most fund groups also pay out the accrued dividend when a shareholder completely redeems his or her holdings in a fund. Most transfer agents, therefore, do some dividend and capital gain processing every business night.

Ordering Money Movement

All of the activity the transfer agent processes each day involves the movement of money among investors, intermediaries, funds, and transfer agent accounts. Figure 3 summarizes the major flows. As Figure 3 suggests, the transfer agent sits in the middle of the money flow between the fund on one hand and the investors and intermediaries on the other. Every transfer agent has a department that concerns itself with the monitoring and control of these cash movements.

Transfer agents exchange money with many brokerage firms on a net settlement basis. They don't attempt to create a check or wire for every transaction, but rather add up all the flows to and from the broker for the day, and receive, or pay, the net amount due. NSCC Fund/SERV, discussed in Chapter 8, takes this a step further. It creates one net settlement cash transaction for each fund, each day, representing the net total of the fund's cash exchanges with all brokers with which the fund is interacting through Fund/SERV. (It does the same thing for the brokers.) For a transfer agent handling a load fund complex, this can reduce the number of checks or wires needed for settling with brokerage firms from dozens or even hundreds to just one per fund.

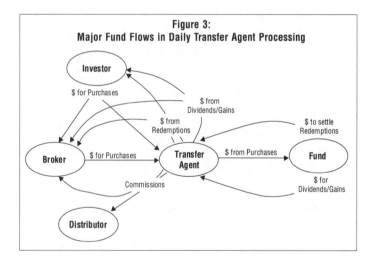

Figure 3:
Major Fund Flows in Daily Transfer Agent Processing

Reporting

The transfer agent produces many reports as part of its daily processing, and on other cycles—weekly, monthly, quarterly, on demand—as well. Some of these go outside the fund complex to investors, brokers, and other intermediaries, and various third parties, reporting the shareholder's activity or account status. Transfer agents also produce a number of tax-related forms that go both to the shareholder and the government. Finally, the transfer agent produces much internal reporting that is needed to help control the operations of the fund complex.

- *To Shareholders, Intermediaries, and Interested Parties.* The transfer agent must confirm transaction activity as soon as it is processed. The trade confirmation, an example of which is shown at the end of the chapter, may go to the shareholder, the intermediary, or both, and copies may be sent to interested parties, such as the investor's accountant. Transfer agents also send confirmations when a change is made in some attribute of the shareholder account. When the address of registration on an account changes, the transfer agent sends confirmations to the account holder at both the old and new addresses to help prevent fraud. The transfer agent system typically produces all these types of confirmations automatically as part of normal processing. While most confirmations continue to go to the shareholder via mail, some transfer agents are beginning to offer electronic delivery via e-mail.

  Shareholders must receive periodic statements that show the balance, value, and activity summary for their accounts. Most commonly, funds send these statements once a quarter, at calendar-quarter end. Since fund company management recognizes that these statements often provide their most visible point of contact with the shareholder, they go to great lengths to make them attractive, informative documents. The sample T. Rowe Price monthly statement shown at the end of the chapter illustrates some of the common features of shareholder statements. It reports two different funds that the investor holds, summarizes the beginning and ending positions within each fund, the dividends and gains that were distributed, and the trade activity for each fund. Some statements also feature a graphical summary of how the shareholder's fund holdings are allocated among different asset classes. As with confirmations, investors may direct the transfer agent to send copies of their statements to interested parties.

  Most transfer agents today also provide annual statements to their shareholders showing the tax cost basis of redemption transactions—assuming the transfer agent has sufficient information to determine this cost. The investor uses this information when completing Schedule D on his or her tax return.

  In those cases where the investor buys shares in a fund through an intermediary such as a broker or a fund supermarket, this intermediary may produce some or even all of the shareholder's confirmations, statements, tax forms, and other reports. When transfer agent staff set up these shareholder accounts, they enter code values that instruct the transfer agent system which, if any, reports to produce for the account.

- *Tax Reporting.* Mutual fund transfer agents commonly produce five types of tax forms for their shareholders, except where an intermediary has taken over this responsibility.

  - *1099DIV* – Dividends and Distributions. The transfer agent produces these early in the calendar year to summarize for income tax reporting purposes all the dividend and capital gain distributions the shareholder has received from the fund during the previous year.

  - *1099B* – Proceeds from Broker and Barter Exchange. This form contains all the disposition transactions—redemptions and exchanges out of the fund—the shareholder executed during the tax year. The shareholder must account for these trades on his or her Form 1040, Schedule D.

- *1099R* – Distributions From Pensions, Annuities, Retirement or Profit-Sharing Plans, IRAs, Insurance Contracts, etc. The transfer agent produces this form for each retirement account to report all the distributions (meaning redemption of shares in this case) to the shareholder during the year.

- *5498* – Individual Retirement Arrangement Information. For each IRA account the transfer agent processes, it produces this form, summarizing the contributions (meaning share purchases) for the account during the year, and stating the account value at year end.

- *1042S* – Foreign Person's U.S. Source Income Subject to Withholding. The transfer agent produces this form for foreign holders of U.S. mutual funds to report all items of income received from the fund, and any tax withheld on that income.

- *Management Reporting.* Finally, the transfer agent produces dozens or even hundreds of reports—daily, weekly, monthly, quarterly, on demand—to help manage the funds and their relationships with their counterparties, and to ensure regulatory compliance. These reports capture various aspects of the fund complex's activity over a period, or the current status of key indicators of the fund's health.

  - *Status and Activity Reporting* – Many reports simply describe what has been going on in the fund, at varying levels of detail. Every day the transfer agent produces reports that detail all the day's activity, and balance the records—ensuring that the starting positions plus the day's activity equal the ending positions. Transfer agents for load funds produce reports that show commission amounts by broker, so that they can settle with their brokers for the day's activity. Transfer agent management uses reports of activity processed to monitor the performance of the staff. Executives of the management company get reports of the overall activity so they can see how the funds are doing. The number of internal reports produced by any transfer agent runs into the hundreds.

  - *Sales Reporting* – Sales reporting provides detailed and summary information about money flows—purchases and redemptions—broken down by the attributes that are important to the fund group as it manages its sales effort. These attributes differ according to the distribution methods the funds use. Load fund groups track sales by agents—wholesalers, brokerage firms, individual representatives, banks, bank branches—to help determine who is effectively selling the fund. No-load funds track sales by channel (direct mail, financial planner, supermarket, etc.) and by characteristics of the investors (account type, location, etc.), to see where their sales are coming from, and to help determine what marketing efforts are succeeding.

  - *Blue Sky Compliance Monitoring* – State regulations, known as blue sky laws, cover the offering and sale of securities, including mutual fund shares, within state lines, and these typically require registration of the securities themselves. (The term blue sky law reportedly originated with a judge, who was trying to protect investors from unwittingly buying a particular stock offering that he claimed had as much value as "a patch of blue sky.") Fund administration must monitor the

---

TRANSFER AGENT PROFILE: LIBERTY INVESTOR SERVICES COMPANY

The evolution of Liberty's transfer agent illustrates the forces that have led so many fund groups to internalize this function. In 1986, The Colonial Group, at the time one of the leading broker-distributed fund families, decided to internalize the transfer agent in two steps. First, it would start performing all the functions with internal staff, while continuing to use the Bank of Boston's Eagle transfer agent system. Second, it would develop its own system and switch from Eagle to this new system. Colonial had found that depending on a third party constrained them from innovating as quickly as they wanted. As Herb Emilson, Colonial's president, put it, "every time you asked them to add or change any little thing, they would say 'that will be six months and $200,000.' We needed to get control of our own destiny."[8]

Colonial internalized the transfer agent staffing in 1986, and by 1989 was up and running on CTRAN, its brand-new, tailor-made system. The transfer agent, now a separate subsidiary called Citadel Services Corporation, performed back-office functions in Boston and telephone service from a new facility in a suburb of Denver. Seeking to exploit its new capabilities and system, Citadel entered the third-party transfer agent business and attracted several clients, including the Met Life/State Street Funds and the Founders Funds.

In 1992, the opportunity to provide service to a fund family even larger than Colonial itself prompted senior management to rethink the company's priorities. After careful consideration, they decided that the third-party service business actually distracted them from their real strength, managing money. As a result, they declined to take on the new fund group, and started to shut down the third-party business they already had. By 1994, Citadel had disappeared, and once again Colonial's internal transfer agent was handling only the Colonial funds.

In 1995, The Liberty Financial Companies, which managed its own small family of funds, and owned the Stein Roe Funds in Chicago, acquired the Colonial Group. Over the next few years, Liberty continued to acquire funds, all of which it converted to the old Colonial transfer agent, which was renamed Liberty Investor Services Company. By 1999, LISCO performed all transfer agent functions for the approximately 1.5 million shareholders of the Colonial, Stein Roe, Crabbe Huson, and Newport families of funds.

---

number of shares sold state by state, and register additional shares in a state as necessary. The transfer agent provides reports and data feeds with daily activity by state so the blue sky compliance monitoring group can ensure that the fund complies with state registration requirements.

–   *Escheatment* – The transfer agent must report on all accounts for which the holder can no longer be located. Unclaimed property laws, or escheat laws as they are often termed, enable states to take possession of unclaimed bank accounts, insurance policies, and mutual funds. When a transfer agent sends mail to a shareholder, and the Post Office returns it as undeliverable, the account becomes an RPO (returned by post office) account, and the escheatment clock starts ticking. If the transfer agent is unable to locate the shareholder within a specified period—usually three to five years—the state claims the holdings.

Most accounts become lost because the shareholder moves, fails to notify the transfer agent of the change of address, and is unaware that the account has been placed on the RPO list. Investors who die, leaving the heirs without sufficient information about their holdings, also contribute to the problem. One account of mutual fund escheatment estimated that about two percent of the U.S. shareholder base falls into the lost, RPO status.[9] This has spawned a small niche business within the industry for firms that specialize in finding owners of these dormant accounts in return for a share of the account value.

– *Proxy Processing* – The 1940 Act and subsequent regulations give mutual fund shareholders the right to vote on a number of specific questions concerning their fund, such as approving the contract with the investment adviser. Funds effect this voting by sending proxies to the shareholders, giving each a number of votes equal to the number of shares he or she holds as of the record date. The transfer agent starts this process by determining each shareholder's eligibility, i.e., number of votes, and creating a data file with this information along with the shareholder's name and address.

Many internal transfer agents turn this file over to a third-party proxy processor to handle all the subsequent steps, which include printing and mailing ballots to send to the shareholders, and tabulating the results as shareholders send in their votes. The major third-party transfer agent service vendors include proxy processing in their array of services.

Transfer Agent Back-Office Technology

The transfer agent system represents the single biggest component of information technology required to support shareholder administration back-office functions. These systems comprise hundreds of batch and online programs that embody literally millions of lines of business logic. The replacement cost of a transfer agent system such as those run by DST or PFPC is easily many tens of millions of dollars. The Bank of New York decided in 1988 to leave the third-party transfer agent business, in large part because it anticipated having to spend $30 million or more to replace its transfer agent system.

Transfer agent system processing reads, writes, and updates data in an extensive database of information representing the world of shareholder activity. This database may contain dozens of tables or record types that store information about four basic entities.

- *Fund*. The system stores all the standing rules of the fund that control shareholder account setup (e.g., this fund allows SWPs but not check writing) and processing (e.g., load tables and dividend schedules), as well as the rates and NAVs needed to price transactions and calculate dividends and capital gains.
- *Investor*. To process the shareholder's account properly and produce and deliver the appropriate reports, the system must have data on the investor and his or her accounts with the funds. This includes information about the investor contained on the account application, as well as balance and summary information developed as the investor interacts with the fund.

- *Intermediary or other interested party.* The system requires data on intermediaries to handle commission and fee calculations and payments properly. In addition, the system must have the needed data on all the various interested parties who will receive duplicate reports, make trade orders, receive payments, or otherwise participate in the account.
- *Transaction.* The major volume of data in any transfer agent system's database lies in the records of the transactions the transfer agent has carried out for the shareholders—trades, distributions, adjustments, commission payments, option changes. For a large fund family such as Vanguard or Putnam, the transaction records in the transfer agent system occupy hundreds of gigabytes of computer disk storage.

Most legacy transfer agent systems are mainframe-based, but most today use the mainframe primarily as a data server and batch processor. Transfer agent staff interact with intelligent workstations that present the transfer agent system's functions via a graphical user interface. Wrapping the legacy system this way allows transfer agents to preserve their investment in the legacy systems, while providing their staff with the productivity gains associated with the latest graphical interfaces. In addition to interfaces provided by its online screens and windows, the transfer agent system sends data to and receives data from other computers via dozens of file exchanges and transmissions.

Most transfer agents today also use document imaging systems to facilitate processing. They categorize and scan incoming mail, and workflow control software then routes the images of the documents for subsequent processing. Transfer agent staff setting up new accounts and entering trades have images of documents on their workstations next to the windows with transfer agent system functions. Imaging and workflow systems enhance management control by positively tracking the status of all items as they make their way through the transfer agent, reporting any problems or delays. As we will see in the next chapter, these images, once captured and processed, serve to support client service as well.

TRANSFER AGENT PROFILE:
FIRST DATA INVESTOR SERVICES GROUP

First Data Investor Services Group, once the second largest third-party transfer agent service provider in the United States, has been termed "a recovered patient of reconstructive surgery."[10] This label reflected its evolution as an assembly of once independent parts, at least one which had been split and later brought back together. The trail of acquisitions that resulted in the FDISG of the late 1990s is evidenced by its use of not one, or even two, but three separate transfer agent systems.

One root of the FDISG family tree lies within one of the early mutual fund transfer agents, Bradford National Corporation, which encountered financial difficulties in 1984 that forced it to sell off all its assets to pay creditors. Among these was Bradford's transfer agent business, then named Fidata Systems, which it sold, along with its new transfer agent system PAR (Personal Asset Recordkeeping), to Pittsburgh-based Mellon Bank in 1985. A second main root arose in Shearson Lehman Hutton's subsidiary The Boston Company (TBC), which got into the mutual fund service business in the early 1980s. In 1989, American Express, the parent of Shearson, decided to move TBC's transfer agent business (now named The Shareholder Services Group) to its newly formed Information Services unit. Along with TSSG came its transfer agent system, FSR (Full Service Retail). (TBC's other mutual fund service functions, notably fund accounting, stayed at TBC.)

These two branches came together in 1990, when Mellon decided that the transfer agent business wasn't so attractive after all, and sold its business and system to TSSG. For a while in the early 1990s, TSSG ran several clones of FSR to service different clients, but in a major effort, managed to scale back to the two basic systems. PAR supported remote clients (i.e., fund groups doing their own transfer agent work) while FSR continued to support those clients for which TSSG performed the transfer agent functions.

Ironically, the old TBC operations, which had been split when Mellon bought the transfer agent business, came together again in 1996 due to who else but Mellon. Mellon had bought all of TBC in 1994, but then decided that they did not want to be in the third-party fund accounting business, so sold that part of the acquisition to First Data. Thus the reconstructive surgery.

With First Data's acquisition of the fund accounting business (as well as pension record keeping units), TSSG was renamed FDISG. In 1997, FDISG acquired a third transfer agent system—SuRPAS, along with its vendor, Funds Associates Limited. FDISG stated that SuRPAS would enhance its ability to support asset allocation and wrap programs, as well as mutual fund supermarket programs.

In 1999, First Data Corporation decided against continuing in the mutual fund servicing business and sold FDISG to PFPC for $1.1 billion. This acquisition vaulted PFPC into contention with DST for the position of industry leader in shareholder processing, but also gave it the task of deciding how to rationalize not three but four separate transfer agent systems.

This is your application.

$1,000 minimum investment per fund except as noted. No initial minimum is required for EasiVest (Section 8). Please do not use this application for an INVESCO prototype retirement plan (IRA, 403(b) or other qualified plan).

1. Your Account Registration

TAX ID

Social Security or Taxpayer Identification Number. For UGMA, use minor's SSN

Social Security Number of Joint Owner, if applicable

INVESTMENT IN: ☐ New account
☐ For new fund under existing
INVESCO Account #_____
☐ Change of registration: Account #_____

Please check only one box below for type of registration.

INDIVIDUAL ☐

Owner's first name   Middle initial   Last name

JOINT ☐

First owner's name

Second owner's name

TRANSFER ON DEATH FOR INDIVIDUAL AND JOINT ACCOUNTS; BENEFICIARY MAY NOT BE A MINOR, JOINT OWNER, TRUST OR ESTATE

Transfer on Death– Beneficiary's name (not a current owner)

Beneficiary's Social Security Number and Date of Birth

* Transfer on Death is only available for Single Name and Joint Tenants with Right of Survivorship registrations. Upon death of owner, fund shares pass automatically to Beneficiary without necessity of probate.

TRUST ACCOUNT ☐

Name of trustee

Name of trust

Date of trust

GIFTS/TRANSFERS TO MINORS ACCOUNT (UGMA/UTMA) ☐

Custodian (one name only)

As Custodian for (one minor only)

Minor's date of birth

under the_____Uniform Gifts (Transfers) to Minors Act.
(Custodian's primary state of residence)

Successor in case of death of Custodian (one name only)

ORGANIZATION OR OTHER ACCOUNT ☐

Name of corporation, partnership, estate, etc. Corporations should also complete and return a Corporate Resolution.

2. Mailing Address

Street

City   State   Zip code

(   )   (   )
Daytime telephone   Evening telephone

E-mail address

OWNER'S CITIZENSHIP ☐ U.S.A.
☐ Resident alien_____
Country
☐ Non-resident alien_____
Country
Residence for tax purposes_____
Country
Non-resident aliens with a U.S. address must also submit IRS Form W-8.

3. Your Fund Selection(s)

If you do not choose a fund, your investment will be made in Cash Reserves.

MONEY MARKET

☐ 44	$_____	U.S. Government Money Fund
☐ 25	$_____	Cash Reserves
☐ 40	$_____	Tax-Free Money Fund
☐ 96	$_____	Money Market Reserves (minimum $100,000)
☐ 95	$_____	Tax-Exempt Reserves (minimum $100,000)

BOND

☐ 32	$_____	U.S. Government Securities
☐ 30	$_____	Select Income
☐ 31	$_____	High Yield
☐ 35	$_____	Tax-Free Bond

COMBINATION STOCK & BOND

☐ 15	$_____	Equity Income
☐ 71	$_____	Balanced
☐ 48	$_____	Total Return

STOCK

☐ 21	$_____	Growth & Income
☐ 10	$_____	Blue Chip Growth
☐ 20	$_____	Dynamics
☐ 60	$_____	Small Company Growth
☐ 61	$_____	INVESCO Endeavor
☐ 46	$_____	Value Equity
☐ 23	$_____	S&P 500 Index Fund – Class II (minimum $5,000)

SECTOR

☐ 50	$_____	Energy
☐ 57	$_____	Financial Services
☐ 51	$_____	Gold
☐ 52	$_____	Health Sciences
☐ 53	$_____	Leisure
☐ 42	$_____	Realty
☐ 55	$_____	Technology – Class II
☐ 39	$_____	Telecommunications
☐ 58	$_____	Utilities

INTERNATIONAL

☐ 09	$_____	International Blue Chip
☐ 56	$_____	European
☐ 34	$_____	Latin American Growth
☐ 54	$_____	Pacific Basin
	$_____	Other:_____

TOTAL $_____

(over)

4. Investment Method

☐ **By Check:** Please make payable to INVESCO Funds Group, Inc.
☐ **By Automated Transfer from your bank** (complete Section 7)
☐ **EasiVest Program:** Be sure to complete Sections 7 and 8.

5. Making Transactions

Please choose the ways you wish to make transactions. If no box is checked, you will automatically have telephone privileges for both exchanges and redemptions.

☐ I wish to make **purchases** by requesting INVESCO to move money automatically from my fund account to my bank via the Automated Clearing House (ACH). (Please complete Section 7 below. $50 minimum per transaction.)

☐ I wish to make **redemptions** by requesting INVESCO to move money automatically from my fund account to my bank via the Automated Clearing House (ACH). (Please complete Section 7 below. $250 minimum per transaction.)

I wish to make exchanges:	I wish to make redemption requests:
☐ by telephone and in writing.	☐ by telephone and in writing.
☐ only in writing.	☐ only in writing.

6. Distribution Options

All distributions will be reinvested in additional fund shares unless you indicate otherwise below. Cash payments may be made to a designated bank account (please complete Section 7) or to your address of record.

Dividends	Capital Gains
☐ Pay to bank account	☐ Pay to bank account
☐ Pay by check ($10 minimum)	☐ Pay by check ($10 minimum)

7. Bank Information

For Telephone Transactions, Distributions, and EasiVest (See Sections 5, 6 and 8)

Name of bank

Address of bank

City, State, Zip

ABA number (available from your bank)

Bank account number   _Bank phone number_

This is a: ☐ Checking account   ☐ Savings account

Please enclose a voided, unsigned check or savings deposit slip.

8. EasiVest

You may invest regularly by automatic deduction from your bank/credit union checking or savings account. Shares will be purchased for you on the specific date(s) you choose, or the next business day when that date falls on a weekend or holiday. Each purchase must be for $50 or more. Unless you indicate a specific start date below, purchases may start immediately after we receive your application.

$_____ Fund _____
Day(s) of month:_____ Start Date:_____

$_____ Fund _____
Day(s) of month:_____ Start Date:_____

9. Direct Payroll Purchase

☐ Check here to receive information on purchasing shares through automatic payroll deduction.

Questions? Please call
1-800-525-8085

OAP 1901 12/99

10. Employment Information

Rules of the National Association of Securities Dealers (NASD) require that we ask for the information below. All information will be kept confidential.
Are you employed by, or associated with, an NASD member firm?
☐ Yes   ☐ No
If yes, please name the member firm: _____
Employer's address _____
Your occupation _____

11. Signature

Each person whose signature appears on this application agrees to the following statements:

◆ I have received and read a current prospectus of the fund(s) designated for investment and agree to be bound by its terms. INVESCO Funds Group, Inc. (INVESCO) is hereby authorized to answer, without liability, requests for information concerning the account established by this application.

◆ I understand that exchanges can be made only between identically registered accounts; that I have the exchange privilege which will, on the basis of this application, authorize the funds' Transfer Agent to open accounts in the same form as this account for all funds into which I may desire to exchange my investment; and that all information provided in the above items will apply to any fund(s) into which I may exchange. The responsibility to read the prospectus(es) of any fund(s) into which exchanges are made is hereby accepted.

◆ Any instruction given on this account and any account into which exchanges are made are hereby ratified and neither the fund(s) nor the funds' Transfer Agent will be liable for any loss, cost or expense for acting upon such instructions (by writing, telephone or other means) reasonably believed to be genuine and in accordance with the procedures described in the prospectus. As a result of this policy, I may bear the risk of any loss due to unauthorized or fraudulent telephone instructions; provided, however, that if the fund(s) fail to employ the procedures described in the prospectus, the fund(s) may be liable. Subject to the preceding sentence, I release the funds, INVESCO and their affiliates from any and all liability for acts or omissions done in good faith under the authorizations and privileges contained in this application.

◆ I agree that INVESCO may send a single updated prospectus or financial report to my household for accounts within the same series of INVESCO funds that have the same address as I do, in order to provide greater mailing efficiencies and cost-savings for the funds. I understand that I may receive my own copies of prospectuses and financial reports at any time by calling or writing INVESCO.

☐ Do not household my accounts for prospectuses and financial reports.

◆ I certify, under penalties of perjury, that the Social Security or Tax Identification Number given above is correct, and (unless the box below is checked) I am not currently subject to IRS backup withholding as a result of my failure to report all dividend and interest income on my tax return.

☐ The Internal Revenue Service has informed me that I am subject to backup withholding.

All owners must sign. For UGMA/UTMAs, custodian should sign.

First owner's signature   _Date_

Second owner's signature   _Date_

Additional owner's signature   _Date_

Additional owner's signature   _Date_

Unless INVESCO Funds Group, Inc., notifies you that it is rejecting this application to purchase shares, upon proper completion and receipt of this application, INVESCO Funds Group, Inc., agrees to accept this application.

By _____   _Senior Vice President_

Mail completed application to:
Post Office Box 173706, Denver, Colorado 80217-3706

ACCOUNT CONFIRMATION

SCUDDER

ACCOUNT NUMBER   **9963537359-5**

This statement confirms activity on 05/15/98

Page 1 of 1

Scudder Preferred Investor Services
Priority access to our most experienced investor
representatives

Fund Information ● Transactions ● Account Updates

Please call a *Preferred Investor Services Associate* at:
1-800-553-6360

Scudder Investor Services, Inc., Distributor, confirms any purchases as agent.

DAILY TRANSACTION SUMMARY

DATE	TRANSACTION	DOLLAR AMOUNT	SHARE PRICE	NUMBER OF SHARES	TOTAL SHARES OWNED
GROWTH AND INCOME FUND					
05/15/98	AUTOMATIC PURCHASE -ACH	$150.00	$30.22	4.964	31.431
	VALUE AS OF 05/15/98	$949.84			

Account Statement – May 1998

Invest With Confidence
T.Rowe Price

T. Rowe Price
P.O. Box 89000
Baltimore, MD
21289-0220

Tele*Access
1 (800) 638-2587

Customer Service
1 (800) 225-5132

Investor number

1002637   AT   **AUTO   T2 0 0550 02056-

The Spectrum Income Fund....One investment. Nine funds. A powerful strategy for reducing volatility and increasing income potential through diversification. Request a prospectus and read it carefully before investing.

Total Market Value
$ 16,368.20

Dividend and Capital Gain Summary

	This Month	*Year-to-Date*
Taxable	$ 0.00	$ 0.00
Tax – free	1.54	5.84
Tax – deferred	0.00	0.00
Total	**$ 1.54**	**$ 5.84**

Portfolio Summary

Regular	*Type of Account*	*Type of Fund*	*Beginning Balance*	*Ending Balance*	*% of Assets*	*Share Price*
Mid – Cap Growth	Indiv	Equity	$ 16,382.29	$ 15,805.16	96.6%	$ 31.77
Tax – Exempt Money	Indiv	Money	511.50	563.04	3.4	1.00
Total regular			**$ 16,893.79**	**$ 16,368.20**	100.0%	
Total market value			**$ 16,893.79**	**$ 16,368.20**		

Account Statement – May 1998

Invest With Confidence
T.RowePrice

Account type
Individual

Mid-Cap Growth

Account number
670057422-5

Tele*Access code
47

Date	Description	Amount	Shares	Shares Owned	Share Price
5/1	Beginning Balance	$ 16,382.29		494.485	$ 33.13
5/1	Periodic Purchase – ACH	100.00	+ 3.002	497.487	33.31
5/31	Ending Balance	$ 15,805.16		497.487	$ 31.77

Year-to-Date Activity

Purchases	$ 500.00

Account type
Individual

Tax-Exempt Money

Account number
521112312-4

Tele*Access code
15

Date	Description	Amount	Shares	Shares Owned
5/1	Beginning Balance	$ 511.50		511.500
5/1	Periodic Purchase – ACH	50.00	+ 50.000	561.500
5/29	Dividend Reinvest	1.54	+ 1.540	563.040
5/31	Ending Balance	$ 563.04		563.040

Yield: 3.29% *for 30 days ended 5/31/98 vs.* 3.33% *on 4/30/98* .

This dividend is for 31 days vs. 30 last month.

All transactions are valued at $1.00 per share.

Year-to-Date Activity

Tax – free dividends	$ 5.84
Purchases	$ 250.00

CHAPTER 12

The Transfer Agent, Part 2—
Customer Service

Service quality ... is a critical component of customer retention that has bottom line implications. All other things being equal, mutual fund companies that invest in improving customer service should experience an increase in shareholder referrals and investments.
— Investment Company Institute (1994)[1]

The transfer agent back office, described in the preceding chapter, remains largely invisible to most investors, except for the checks, confirmations, and statements they might receive from it. But shareholders typically get more for their service fees than just these back-office record keeping activities. Every fund complex gives its clients access to service representatives to ask questions, get information about their accounts, register complaints, and request transactions. The transfer agent fee buys service as well as record keeping for shareholders and their agents.

Every fund complex has a group that specializes in customer service. For some fund companies, this group is contained within the transfer agent. Other fund companies separate the groups that provide customer service from the back-office record keepers. The definition of customer varies across fund groups as well. The customer service groups for directly marketed funds deal mostly with the shareholders; those for broker distributed funds provide service for the brokers as well as the shareholders. For both types of fund groups, other agents, such as pension administrators and bank trust departments, play an ever larger role and require special service. Figure 1 summarizes the relationships among investors, their intermediaries and agents, and the fund company's customer service group.

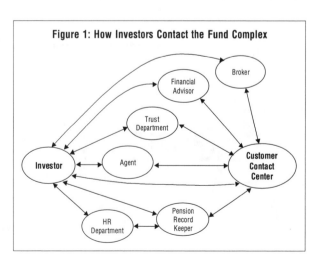

Figure 1: How Investors Contact the Fund Complex

Many investors simply contact the fund directly via mail, the toll-free telephone number, the Internet, or, in a few cases, by visiting an investor center. Investors who have purchased their shares directly from a no-load fund company with no intermediary assistance have no alternative to contacting the fund directly for service. Investors who go through intermediaries—e.g., brokers, bank trust departments, financial advisers, insurance agents—to buy shares sometimes contact the fund company directly for service, but often go instead to these intermediaries. The broker, trust officer, financial adviser, or agent then calls or writes to the fund's service center.

When the investor is part of an omnibus account, the intermediary provides all of the customer service. Defined contribution plan participants who invest in mutual funds contact either their company's human resources department or the plan's record keeper, not the fund's service group, for information or assistance. Fund supermarket clients do the same. In these cases, the fund's transfer agent doesn't know anything about them individually, so the fund's customer service group cannot help them with anything but general questions about fund characteristics or rules. The fund's service group deals with the pension record keeper or the firm running the fund supermarket.

How Mutual Fund Investors Receive Service

The National Investment Company Service Association (NICSA) conducts a survey each year of shareholders of a sample group of mutual funds to explore shareholder service trends and cost patterns.[2] Figure 2 shows the means of communications the shareholders who participated in 1999 preferred for contacting their fund companies. As Figure 2 shows, they strongly preferred speaking with a person on the telephone, followed by sending mail, interacting with a voice response unit, and sending e-mail messages and faxes. Many industry observers believe this preference for the telephone will eventually give way to increasing use of the Internet, but, as of 1999, this had not yet happened.

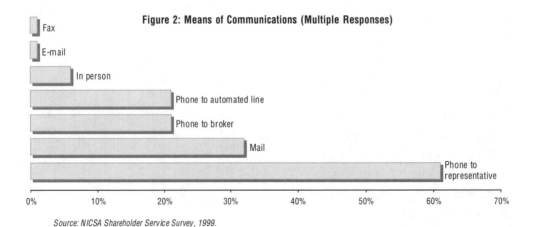

Figure 2: Means of Communications (Multiple Responses)

Source: NICSA Shareholder Service Survey, 1999.

Telephone to a Customer Service Representative

As Jack Brennan, CEO of The Vanguard Group, once put it, "Firms like Vanguard in the United States were virtually created by the 800 number."[3] Behind the 800 numbers, however, stands an army of customer service representatives (CSRs) to answer the questions, take the transaction requests, and resolve the problems. While the ratio of service representatives to shareholders varies widely by distribution channel, directly marketed funds often find that they need a CSR for every 7,000–10,000 shareholders. Large fund groups such as Fidelity, Vanguard, and T. Rowe Price have literally hundreds of CSRs. The special management issues involved in assembling and retaining this work force are discussed in the section below on staffing the customer contact center.

Telephone to a Voice Response Unit

As ubiquitous as voice response units (VRUs) have become these days, it is easy to forget that mutual fund service providers were among their first and heaviest users. A VRU (or, as it is sometimes termed, an Interactive Voice Response unit, or IVR) combines a telephone interface on one side and computer interface on the other. The telephone interface side speaks to the caller offering a set of menus with service options. The caller selects options either by keying on the telephone touch-tone keypad or speaking to a speech recognition processor. The computer side of the VRU acts on these selections by retrieving and speaking data (such as fund NAV or account balance), or offering further options.

The excerpt from the MFS VRU menu, at the end of the chapter, shows a typical set of functions that fund groups offer their shareholders. VRUs serve primarily to handle inquiries, such as requests for fund prices and yields, and account balances and values. Most fund groups allow callers to order literature, e.g., prospectuses, and duplicate statements via the VRU. Most directly marketed fund groups allow shareholders to place redemption and exchange orders through the VRU, although few get large volumes of transactions this way. Some funds sold through brokers do not allow shareholders to order transactions through the VRU.

The cost of handling a call via VRU is a small fraction of the cost of providing the same service via a human operator—a call that costs five dollars for a human representative to handle typically costs only fifty cents when handled by the VRU.[4] Many fund groups—indeed, many organizations across different industries—use the VRU as the front end through which every caller must go. Even if human interaction is eventually required, the VRU can get the caller's identification and determine the nature of the caller's request to reduce the time required for a CSR to service the call.

Correspondence

Shareholders still send a great deal of mail to their fund companies, and the customer service units still send many letters to the shareholders. The correspondence unit may be part of the customer service group, or it may be part of the transfer agent back office. In its normal processing cycle, the transfer agent back office handles incoming mail that orders a standard transaction, such as a redemption or exchange. Mail that poses a question or complaint, or is not correct or complete, goes to staff that specialize in customer correspondence.

Much correspondence deals with NIGO (not in good order) transaction requests received from investors and agents. If a shareholder or broker sends a request that the transfer agent cannot act upon because of some flaw, such as a missing signature guarantee, an incomplete application, or incompatible account option choices, the correspondence unit will send a letter explaining the problem and requesting clarification. Each correspondence unit maintains a battery of letter templates tailored for common NIGO situations. They plug in the particulars such as name and address, and the word processing software generates the letter.

Fund companies find preparing and sending correspondence to be one of their more expensive service functions. PricewaterhouseCoopers' studies of mutual fund transfer agent expenses have found that sending a canned letter using a template costs an average of $5.00 per letter, while preparing and sending a completely customized letter averages over $35.00. Fortunately, only a small fraction of shareholder interactions require correspondence, and over 90 percent of that correspondence can be handled with canned letters.

Broker or Other Agent

A shareholder serviced by an agent—broker, trust officer, financial adviser, record keeper—may contact the agent instead of the fund company. Often the agent can handle the request without contacting the fund. Many brokerage firms have direct access into the funds' transfer agent systems, so that they can check shareholder records directly. In addition, brokers, fund supermarkets, and pension record keepers often do much of the detailed shareholder accounting on their own systems, so that the investor must deal with them for many account-related matters.

Of course, the agent must sometimes turn to the fund's service center to respond to an investor's request. Fund groups that sell through agents typically devote portions of their service unit to agent requests. Load funds typically have a broker desk in the customer contact center. Fund groups in general often segregate their service functions according to the groups they handle—financial advisers, pension record keepers, bank trust departments, and so on.

Walk-In Centers

Some fund complexes maintain storefront offices, or walk-in centers, at which investors can interact directly with a representative. Fidelity, for example, maintains a nationwide network of branches, but these house Fidelity's brokerage business as well as the funds. Mutual fund companies that do not also offer brokerage services seldom have more than one walk-in center, and this typically co-resides with a major operational site, such as the firm's headquarters.

As Figure 2 suggests, relatively few investors choose this route to conduct business with their funds. The move toward electronic business threatens to make the walk-in centers even less important. In June 1999, for example, the Scudder group of no-load funds announced that it would shut down its five walk-in offices, and focus instead on electronic service via the Internet. As one Scudder executive explained it, "Direct physical distribution of mutual funds no longer has much of a future. Instead, there's a magical new world around e-commerce."[5] (How the Internet and electronic commerce affect the mutual fund industry is the topic of Chapter 14.)

E-mail

In the late 1970s, a group of computing pioneers created the ARPAnet, the earliest forerunner of the Internet, to allow users across the United States to share the scarce resources that defense and research computing centers then represented. As soon as the ARPAnet became operational, however, its users discovered what they *really* wanted to do with it—send and receive electronic mail (e-mail). Throughout the history of computer networking, e-mail has been an enduringly popular application, and it represents one of the most commonly used functions on the Internet today.[6]

Most fund groups provided a means for their investors to send them e-mail as one of the earliest features on their web sites. Currently, e-mail still accounts for a relatively small fraction of customer contacts for fund companies, although history suggests that this will grow as e-business via the Internet becomes more widespread. As early as 1998, Fidelity and Vanguard were receiving several thousand e-mail messages per week, and had special staff devoted to responding to them.[7]

Recently, several fund groups have begun to offer customer statements via e-mail. The high cost of printing and mailing statements makes them an attractive candidate for electronic distribution. However, securities laws make it more difficult than it would appear at first glance to use the Internet to deliver statements. A fund group using this approach must be able to ensure that the information is protected and that it is actually received by the shareholder, and must make it available for online access for a reasonable period. For example, Fidelity, which announced its online statement program in mid-1999, said that it would maintain up to sixteen months of historical statements online.[8]

The Mutual Fund Customer Contact Center

Until recently, everyone used the term *call center* to refer to the organization that deployed customer service representatives to take telephone calls from investors and their agents. Perhaps this phrase should be retired in favor of the more general term *customer contact center*. "Call" implies the use of a telephone, but investors and agents today may interact with their fund's support functions via fax, e-mail, or other Internet communications. The most advanced contact centers create an integrated queue of requests—telephone calls, e-mails, web requests for callback—that customer service representatives handle according to their priorities.

Each fund group either maintains a customer contact center of its own, or contracts with a third party to provide the function. In many cases, fund groups that outsource their transfer agent back-office functions perform investor service from their own, internal contact centers. This reflects the widespread belief that the quality of this visible service has competitive implications. The back-office functions, on the other hand, must be performed correctly, but they offer little opportunity for the fund to differentiate itself from the competition.

Among the 483 funds included in the 1997 ICI study of transfer agent costs, 22 percent used hybrid transfer agents, with some functions outsourced (usually back office) and some performed internally (usually customer contact).[9] Only 13 percent were completely external—that is, they had third-party providers handle customer service as well as transfer agent back-office functions. For the remainder, the management company performed all transfer agent and customer service functions internally. The fact that 87 percent of the funds in this survey had the management company perform the customer service functions internally reflects the importance fund groups attach to this function. In its 1998 study of customer retention, Strategic Insight maintained that shareholders who own a fund for two years bond to the fund during that time, and become less likely to sell the fund even when performance declines.[10] One might debate the role that good customer service plays in establishing the bond, but certainly poor service will drive customers away, making the bonding impossible.

Contact Center Functions

Figure 3 shows how one industry consulting group believes mutual fund contact centers spend their time. Specifically, Figure 3 shows the percentage of resources the centers use, on the average, to deal with requests in each category. This differs from a breakdown of the purpose of the calls themselves, since investors often make one call to accomplish several things, e.g., change my account options, and do this exchange, and mail me a duplicate statement. Nevertheless, this breakdown represents a cross-section of what customer contact centers do.

Fund Level Inquiries

Many investors call, write, or e-mail to find out something about the funds—the NAV, the dividend rate and schedule, rules for investing, options offered, the investment style, the historical performance, and an endless list of other things. These requests often come from investors who are not already shareholders.

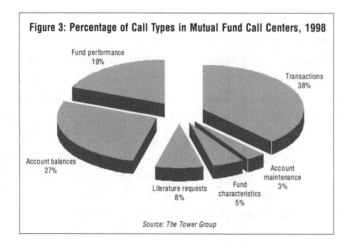

Figure 3: Percentage of Call Types in Mutual Fund Call Centers, 1998

Fund performance 19%

Transactions 38%

Account balances 27%

Literature requests 8%

Fund characteristics 5%

Account maintenance 3%

Source: The Tower Group

Most fund groups put fund-level information on their web sites as one of their first offerings. The SEC ruled in 1996 that the prospectus delivery required before an investor could purchase shares in a fund could be done via download, as long as the prospectus was materially the same as the printed version. Today, almost all fund literature is available on the fund groups' web sites. Nevertheless, CSRs continue to spend much of their time answering fund-level questions posed by curious or bewildered investors.

OFF THE WALL: THE THINGS CSRs HAVE TO HANDLE

In 1993, *The New York Times* ran a Sunday-edition article[11] about T. Rowe Price's call center, describing how the firm's 300 young phone representatives strove to give the fund group a "friendly, trustworthy voice." In the article, it listed some of the challenging situations the phone reps had to handle, along with the recommended responses.

Situation: Dozens of callers dial zero when they should have dialed O, and get T. Rowe Price when what they were really trying to do was order a kit advertised on television to help them market their bizarre inventions.
Recommended Response: Make nice with them; they might be current, or potential, customers.

Situation: A caller asks for a prospectus for every single one of T. Rowe Price's 45 funds.
Recommended Response: Offer to send summaries, or a sample, anything but the whole truckload.

Situation: An investor insists that a couple of weeks ago he absolutely did not move his money into a fund that has since plunged.
Recommended Response: Politely offer to play back a tape of the call.

Situation: Lloyd Bentsen (then a Texas Senator, and later U.S. Treasury Secretary) can't locate a substantial account.
Recommended Response: See if it's registered under the name of his bank. It is.

Situation: One caller wants to carry his complaint to the top, and demands to speak to Mr. Price himself.
Recommended Response: Say "Sorry, sir. He's dead. Would you like to speak with a supervisor?"

Literature Requests

Every fund group produces many pieces of literature, sometimes called collateral material. Both investors and agents contact the fund service centers to order these materials: prospectuses, statements of additional information, account applications, fund reports, guides to investing, and so on. These requests come in via the CSRs, the VRU, the web site, e-mail messages, and letters, and the fund company mails the appropriate materials in response, typically within one or two days. Literature fulfillment—the process of capturing and servicing these requests—is complex and expensive enough to have spawned a niche service business of its own, described in Chapter 13.

Account Level Inquiries

Often the shareholders or their agents call to find out something specific about an existing account, such as the current balance or value, what price a trade was processed at, or whether a requested action has been completed. Providing this personal financial information requires the CSR (or VRU or web site) to have access to the transfer agent system's data. It also requires security—a fund cannot divulge personal financial information to anyone other than the shareholder or authorized agent. CSRs ask callers for their account numbers, and then for things like their social security numbers and addresses to verify identity. For VRU or web site access, funds typically require a requestor to provide an identifier—often called a personal identification number, or PIN—along with a password to verify that the individual has authority to get the requested information.

Transaction Requests

Investors and their agents may request financial transactions, typically redemption or exchange trades. They may also request non-financial transactions, such as changes to account characteristics or options. Transaction entry requires the same or even more stringent levels of security as personal financial information inquiry. In most cases, for example, fund groups will only remit the proceeds of large redemption transactions ordered via telephone, VRU, or electronic means to an address established before the transaction was ordered, such as the address of registration.

Figure 4 shows a breakdown of the costs that fund groups incur in deploying their contact centers. Staffing stands out clearly as the most costly component. This reflects shareholders' preferences for talking with a person whenever they have anything other than the most straightforward inquiry. It also highlights a powerful motivation fund groups have for diverting service functions to the Internet. If customers serve themselves on the Internet, the fund company can reduce the number of staff otherwise needed to answer the phones, and, in turn, reduce the overall cost of providing service.

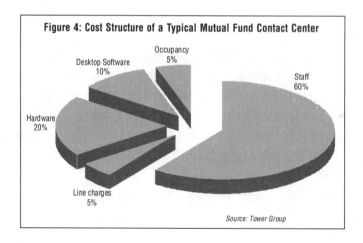

Figure 4: Cost Structure of a Typical Mutual Fund Contact Center

Occupancy 5%
Desktop Software 10%
Hardware 20%
Line charges 5%
Staff 60%

Source: Tower Group

Staffing the Contact Center

To most shareholders, the voice that speaks for their fund is that of a college graduate in his or her early twenties, holding down an entry-level job as a customer service representative. In early 1999, for example, T. Rowe Price's CSRs at its Tampa facility averaged 25 years of age.[12] Few individuals remain in this demanding job for more than three years. CSRs typically field from 75 to 100 calls per day, all of which are recorded for possible later review, and many of which involve less-than-friendly shareholders or brokers. Most CSRs view it as a great place to break into the business, but not one they'd want to stay in for very long.

Keeping an adequate supply of qualified staff poses an ongoing challenge for most fund companies. Over the past ten years, the job has clearly grown more difficult. Fund groups have successfully diverted an increasingly large portion of investors' simple requests to voice response units and web sites, leaving the complex requests for the CSRs to handle. In the late 1990s, the tight labor market in the United States compounded the problem. Thus finding, hiring, and training CSRs is a never-ending battle for most mutual fund service organizations.

Many have turned to sites in the South, the West, and the Southwest to find new pools of CSR candidates. Fund companies have established customer contact centers in Tampa, Scottsdale, San Antonio, Albuquerque, Colorado Springs, Charlotte, and other cities not normally considered to be mutual fund centers. In these cities they have found pools of college graduates they can hire at a reasonable cost. They also find that they are more likely to hang onto the CSR they hire in Albuquerque or San Antonio than the one they hire in Boston, where the presence of a half dozen large fund centers makes employees very mobile.[13]

Training and Licensing

All CSRs undergo extensive training, sometimes as many as twelve weeks, before they go onto the telephones with customers. Many of them are licensed as well. Selling mutual funds requires an NASD Series 6 (Investment Company/Variable Contracts Representative) license. While some groups, particularly those distributed by brokers, argue that accepting a purchase order over the phone from an investor does not represent selling, some firms take a conservative approach and use Series 6-licensed CSRs. Others compromise and use unlicensed CSRs to handle calls that clearly do not involve share purchases, but require them to transfer the caller to a licensed CSR who handles any purchase-related matters. In addition, a contact center that uses Series 6-licensed CSRs needs at least some supervisors who hold the NASD Series 26 (Investment Company/Variable Contracts Principal) license to oversee them.

Licensing the CSRs and supervisors is costly. Both the training needed to pass the NASD exam and the annual registration fee add to the costs of running the center. In addition, staff members who have obtained their licenses generally command higher salaries than unregistered staff members—10 to 15 percent higher is typical.

THE (SWISS) ARMY AT VALLEY FORGE

Answering shareholder calls during significant market events has always posed a challenge for mutual fund service centers. In the spring of 1987, a crash in the bond market prompted a deluge of calls to the fund companies, as investors sought to redeem or exchange their bond fund holdings, or simply to get information. Many fund companies found themselves overwhelmed by this flood of calls, and service levels plummeted as calls went unanswered.

The Vanguard Group, located a few miles from Valley Forge, Pennsylvania, where Washington and the Continental Army spent the harsh winter of 1777, was among the fund groups overwhelmed by the spike in call volume. Unacceptable, said Vanguard management. "Not getting an answer from a mutual fund company is the equivalent of a line of people waiting outside a bank to retrieve their money and not being able to get it,"[14] said Jack Brennan, then second in command at Vanguard. So Vanguard's CEO John Bogle took immediate steps to make sure it wouldn't happen again—he established a contingency backup force called the Swiss Army.

The Swiss Army program at Vanguard required everyone, from Bogle and Brennan on down, to be trained for telephone service, to put in at least four hours per year on the phones, and to drop everything to staff the phones in time of crisis. Bogle explained the genesis of the name in a speech in June 1987. "Since 1515, Switzerland has been content to let the great powers of Europe fight their own wars and pay the terrible price involved. It has maintained its neutrality not by *having* an army, but by *being* an army."[15] Like Switzerland, all of Vanguard would be an army of reserves, available to take to the front lines when an emergency arose.

The bond market problems of the spring of 1987 paled by comparison to the stock market crash that occurred a few months later in October of that year. On Black Monday, October 27, the Dow plunged 554 points, the largest single-day decline in history. Mutual fund shareholders rushed to the telephones. Many fund groups were again overwhelmed, but not Vanguard. On Monday as the market plunged, Vanguard raised the red-and-white Swiss flag at its headquarters, signaling the Swiss Army to mobilize for the next day's calls. Hundreds of managers, including Bogle himself, went to the telephones, and kept the average wait time for callers to within Vanguard's target of fifteen seconds, despite receiving 75,000 calls on Tuesday, October 28.[16]

Vanguard continues to rely on the Swiss Army as a low-cost way to handle peaks in call volumes or cope with incidents like ice storms that keep many of the regular telephone associates from getting to work. Consultants and others who work with Vanguard know there is always a chance that a meeting scheduled with a Vanguard manager might have to be rescheduled because of the preemptive call of the Swiss Army.

Dealing with Volume Fluctuations

Mutual fund customer contact centers can't just staff for a normal volume level, either. The frequency with which shareholders contact their funds varies enormously due to both seasonal and cyclical effects.

- *Seasonal Effects*. Tax considerations drive much shareholder activity. As a result, funds experience much higher volumes of calls, letters, and transaction requests from December through the end of tax season in April than during the rest of the year. The days approaching April 15, the deadline for making contributions to IRA accounts, are particularly hectic as shareholders rush to get their transactions in under the wire.

- *Cyclical Variations*. Visible and upsetting events in the capital markets, such as dramatic stock market declines, the Mexican economic crisis, or the Orange County default, drive call volumes up.

Most industry observers believe that mutual fund shareholders, by and large, do not overreact to such events by inappropriately rushing to sell their holdings. Nevertheless, many shareholders do contact their funds when such events occur, often seeking nothing more than information and reassurance.

Because mutual fund contact centers experience such highly variable volumes, staffing for optimal coverage is difficult. Fund companies use several different approaches to cope with this problem.

- Fund contact centers often use temporary employees during the peak seasonal periods. Strong Capital Management, for example, has been a leader in using part-time investor service specialists to handle volume fluctuations in its Milwaukee center, offering on-site day care and other amenities to attract and retain experienced staff.
- They may time their hiring to acquire new employees just as the busy season starts. First Data Investor Services Group, a third-party service provider, has used this strategy, trusting to business growth and normal attrition to prevent an overstaffed situation once tax season is over.
- Some fund companies partially outsource contact handling to a third-party provider for peak cyclical periods. For example, BFDS, a third-party transfer agent, handles overflow calls for the Scudder Funds, i.e., calls that Scudder's internal contact center can't get to in time. This partial outsourcing solution can also provide around-the-clock coverage. The fund company's center fields the calls that come in during normal business hours, and the overflow site handles the calls that come in during the remaining hours.
- Finally, many companies adjust internally, borrowing staff from other areas, and working CSRs longer hours during crunch times. Vanguard has formalized this practice with its Swiss Army program that can divert staff from other functions at a moment's notice to handle temporary overloads in the contact center.

Customer Contact Center Technology

As Figure 4 illustrates, technology represents the other large component of customer contact center costs—hardware and software make up 30 percent. Mutual fund transfer agents have long deployed sophisticated telephone call center technology backed by an array of computer application systems. Figure 5 depicts the architecture of the computer and telephone technology supporting a modern mutual fund customer contact center.

Every fund company offers its shareholders toll-free numbers they can call to request information or order transactions. Funds allocate different numbers for different groups and purposes: for example, shareholders with large holdings might get a special number, and the number to call to request literature may be different from that for account inquiries. Shareholders, agents, and prospects call these numbers using the standard public switched telephone network. Since 97 percent of U.S. households have a telephone, the toll-free numbers provide virtually universal access.

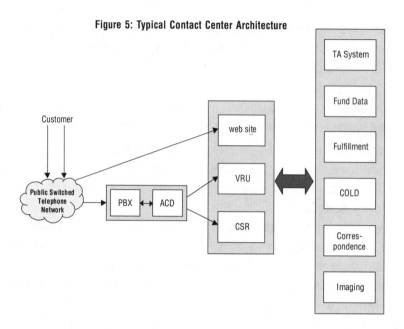

Figure 5: Typical Contact Center Architecture

These calls come into a private branch exchange (PBX) at the service center and typically to an automated call distributor (ACD). The ACD routes the calls to the VRU or to a CSR according to several criteria: the number that was called, the workload among representatives or even call centers, or the area code from which the call was made. ACDs can route calls among representatives that are in different physical locations, to help level the work load. They also capture and report data on call volumes, wait times, queue lengths, and abandoned call rates to help management ensure that the contact center meets service level criteria.

When the call does go to the CSR, the telephony is often integrated with the computer systems the CSR uses, so that the call comes to the CSR along with a computer screen of basic information. For example, if the caller is an existing shareholder, and the VRU has captured the shareholder ID, then the CSR may get the basic account inquiry screen already pre-filled with the appropriate information. This process is termed a "screen pop." In especially advanced configurations of computer telephony integration (CTI), the system may be able to identify the customer from the telephone number from which he or she is calling. In such cases, a caller may be startled to hear him or herself being greeted by name without having entered any sort of identifying information.

Fund service centers today recognize that shareholders compare them not only to other fund groups, but across industries to other service organizations as well. If L.L. Bean can handle telephone requests swiftly and unerringly, then why can't the ABC Fund Company? If FedEx can track a shipment minute-by-minute as it wends its way across the United States, then why can't the transfer agent know the exact status of a request-in-process? Every contact center works toward meeting a set of stated service levels. Commonly measured service level criteria include:

- average wait time for a caller (typically targeted at under ten seconds);
- wait time distribution (e.g., 80 percent of all calls to a CSR answered within twenty seconds); and
- abandoned call rate; that is, the percentage of callers who hang up before their call is answered (typically targeted at no greater than 1 to 4 percent).

Modern ACDs measure and report these and other service level characteristics.

Mutual fund service centers record the calls made to their CSRs. They must record calls concerning trades, account inquiries and complaints to create a record of the transaction as required under the Securities Exchange Act of 1934, Rule 17-Ad. Since no one can tell if an incoming call will lead to a trade order, inquiry, or complaint, as a practical matter they record all calls. This practice also allows them to monitor CSR performance and research complaints later. State laws require the fund complex to inform the caller that the call is being recorded. Thus, many CSRs answer the phone with something like "Hello, ABC Funds, this is John Smith speaking on a recorded line, how may I help you?"

In general, the CSR strives to handle all customer requests with no handoffs and no callbacks. Everyone—the customer, the CSR, the fund group's management—wants the caller's issue to be resolved then and there during the course of the call, by the CSR that first takes the call. This has both competitive service and cost implications. If the CSR can satisfy the caller immediately, not only does this make the caller happy, but it eliminates the time and effort required to create a follow-up item, research it, track it, and call the client back.

To hit these service level targets, the mutual fund CSR today accesses an integrated array of computer systems designed to address any conceivable shareholder request. The list below briefly describes the modules of system function that might be found on the CSR's computer desktop. Different companies combine these functions within physical systems in different ways. For example, correspondence functions may reside in a separate system, or they may be combined into a customer service workstation, along with contact management, literature order entry, and a graphical interface to the transfer agent system.

- *Transfer agent system.* CSRs, VRUs, and web sites all need the information maintained in the fund group's transfer agent system to respond to shareholder and agent requests. The current share balance, the transaction history, the account options in effect—all these and more reside in the transfer agent system's files or databases. CSRs usually access the transfer agent system via special customer service front-end programs, designed to facilitate the functions they perform. For example, the front end usually features inquiry windows containing data to answer the most common questions, as well as easy transaction entry windows for telephone redemptions and exchanges.
- *Imaging and work flow system.* During the 1990s, many mutual fund transfer agents installed document imaging systems. In addition to supporting back-office operations, imaging systems greatly

enhance customer service. When a shareholder calls about an application or letter he or she sent in, the CSR can retrieve the image of the document within seconds and answer the caller's question. Typically the images are linked to the records in the transfer agent system for the transaction(s) the letter generated, so the CSR can retrieve one easily from the other. Without imaging, the CSR can only promise to call the shareholder back at some later time, after the documentation has been retrieved from paper or microfilm archives.

- *Case management.* Case management systems create and maintain records of contacts, or cases, that shareholders and their agents make with the customer contact center. They capture information about the caller, the issue of the call, the time and date, and any subsequent activity, such as a call back. Using the case management system, a CSR can determine what contact a caller has already had with the organization. The CSR also uses the case management functions to create an item that requires follow-up action, such as a customized piece of correspondence. Some fund groups use the workflow functions of the imaging system to handle case management.

- *COLD.* The periodic account statements shareholders and their agents receive typically prompt many calls to the contact center—the shareholder sees something on the statement that he or she doesn't understand or doesn't like. To respond most effectively to a question concerning a statement that the shareholder is viewing, the CSR needs to view exactly the same document. That way, when the shareholder says: "This adjustment transaction on the bottom of page 3 makes no sense to me," the CSR can look on the bottom of page 3 also, see what the shareholder sees, and respond appropriately.

   Computer output to laser disk (COLD) makes this possible. The same print file that goes to the laser printer to create the printed statements (or confirmations, or any other document) goes to the COLD unit and is written onto high capacity optical disk storage. The COLD retrieval and display system the CSR uses can retrieve this data and display it on the CSR's computer screen exactly as it appears on the printed sheets the shareholder received. As with imaging, this helps the CSR meet the "no handoffs, no callbacks" target.

- *Fulfillment.* Fulfillment systems capture orders for literature and transmit them to the physical distribution center where the items are picked and shipped. Often fund groups combine the order entry part of fulfillment with information about the shareholder or agent to guide the CSR as he or she takes the order. (For example, the limit on how many pieces of an item a broker can order might be keyed to the volume of business the broker does with the fund complex.)
   Many fund companies set up special groups to service fulfillment and other requests made by prospects, as opposed to current shareholders. They assign different toll-free numbers in advertising and documents that are likely to generate fulfillment requests. Nevertheless, all CSRs must have some means of entering a request for literature, since this may come up in any call.

- *Correspondence.* Correspondence systems help service representatives generate letters, typically by providing templates with text that addresses the commonly encountered situations. They also provide a means for storing the letters that are sent (often in the imaging system), so that CSRs can refer to them when needed to answer caller questions. Most of today's correspondence systems are based upon a general-purpose word processing utility package, such as Microsoft Word. The most sophisticated ones link tightly to the CSR's other systems, so that they capture the name and address from the transfer agent system, for example, and create a record of the interaction in the case management system.

- *Fund Data.* Many questions that come to the CSRs pertain to a fund—what are its objectives? what has its performance been? who is the manager? what options does it offer? and so on. No CSR can memorize this information for a fund family that has dozens or even hundreds of funds. Rather than have CSRs dig through prospectuses or printed cheat sheets to get the answers, many centers provide this information in online databases. These fund databases give the CSR quicker access to fund information than he or she could get flipping through paper, and the fund company can keep the CSR's information up-to-date much more easily in a database than it could if the material were printed.

Life in a Mutual Fund Service Center

Pioneer and MFS represent two of the grand old names in the mutual fund industry. The Pioneer Fund and MFS' Massachusetts Investors Trust (MIT) are among the longest lived funds in existence (see "Present at the Beginning" in Chapter 2). Today both complexes offer a full range of funds, distributed primarily via broker dealers. And both operate sophisticated service centers. Looking at these two centers as they stood in mid-1999 provides a thumbnail sketch of what goes on in mutual fund service centers generally.

Pioneer serves its 1.5 million shareholders and the thousands of brokers who distribute its funds from centers in Boston and Omaha, each of which houses about 40 CSRs. Its various 800 numbers come to an ACD that places each call into one of two queues: one for general shareholder and broker calls, and one for calls concerning retirement accounts. The ACD also balances the load between Boston and Omaha. Call Center Vice President Mary Mosher explained the scheme: "From 8:00 to 9:30 in the morning (eastern time), Boston gets all the calls. Omaha gets them all from 7:30 to 9:00 P.M. (eastern). During the day we split them, usually evenly, but we can easily change that, as, for example, when we want all the calls to go to Omaha because we are having a staff meeting in Boston."

MFS likewise has its teleservice functions split between two locations, Boston and Kansas City. In mid-1999, Boston housed about 135 CSRs, while Kansas City, a relatively new facility, added another 75. MFS' ACD put most calls into one of four queues: regular teleservice, for most shareowner calls; broker calls; retirement, for calls about IRA and qualified plans; and Inner Circle, for calls from selected brokers. (MFS operated a completely separate group of CSRs to serve the 401(k) plans it administered.) Since Kansas City had less experienced CSRs at the time, MFS generally programmed its ACD to send regular shareowner teleservice calls there, and retirement, broker, and Inner Circle calls to Boston. Like Pioneer, MFS adjusted the ACD's routing as needed to balance the workload.

MFS and Pioneer have proceeded down separate but parallel paths in support technology. MFS uses DST's transfer agent, imaging, and customer service workstation technology, and was a codeveloper with DST of AWD (imaging) and IWS/CSW (intelligent workstation/customer service workstation). Pioneer followed a similar path with First Data Investor Services Group (FDISG). They use FDISG's PAR transfer agent system, and were the beta site for IMPRESS, FDISG's document imaging and work flow system. These systems provide the backbone of the CSR's support tools.

It's July 13, 1999, and Bob Mandile is one of Pioneer's most senior CSRs, having been in the job—his first after finishing college—for almost two years. Because of his seniority, Bob is taking mostly retirement queue calls, which tend to be more complex. On his computer desktop he has arranged the icons for his support tools: PAR, IMPRESS, Textual Help (a database of legal rules and "how to" help), a retirement plan billing and cash entry system, and Internet access to Pioneer's web site. Working on a slow weekday afternoon, he mostly takes calls that the ACD pushes to him, but keeps an eye on the electronic scoreboard on the wall, showing the status of all the queues. Bob notices that a call in the other queue has been waiting over thirty seconds, and, since he has no call from his own queue at the moment, he switches and takes the waiting call.

"Most commonly people call just to inquire about account balances or values," he explains between calls. "They could get these from the VRU, but for lots of people it's easier to ask a phone rep, or they like to talk to a person rather than a machine. A lot of the brokers have the 800 number on their speed dialer." He goes on to say that transaction requests (redemptions and exchanges) are the next most frequent type of calls. When one of these comes through he records the request on a pre-printed form and goes back later during his processing time to enter it into PAR. "The worst calls come when there has been a problem, and the broker is complaining. They're not fun, but fortunately there aren't that many of them."

A few blocks away at Boston's Lafayette Place, Phil Meltzer, twelve months out of Boston College, is on the phone for MFS. Phil takes a variety of overflow calls from other areas, since he is one of the most experienced MFS Teleservice Representatives. He keeps four windows open on the large, high-resolution monitor on his desk. He uses the Identify Caller window of the Customer Service Workstation application to log and categorize calls and the Lookup Notebook window to get basic information about shareowner accounts. For transaction entry or more in-depth historical data, he turns to a window that gives him access to the mainframe functions of TA2000, the transfer agent system. Finally, an AWD application provides access to the imaging and work flow system. In this window he views images of letters and applications shareowners have sent in and creates and retrieves work flow items. When one caller requests a full exchange from one fund to another, for example, he creates work requests to stop the systematic withdrawal on the old account, and establish it on the new one.

Both Pioneer and MFS had faced the challenge of heavy call volume during the 1999 tax season, from year end 1998 through April 15. Pioneer's volumes peaked at about 5,000 calls per day during the first two weeks of April, dropping to half that number afterwards. MFS' larger base of just over four million shareowners and almost 200,000 intermediaries made an average of 16,000 calls per day during the height of the busy season, dropping back to an average of 9,000 per day after April 15. Pioneer borrowed staff from other areas to help meet the peak load; MFS took calls on Saturday. And both firms worked their CSRs long and hard during the period, postponing training and staff meetings until volumes abated.

Phil Meltzer recalled tax time: "We did nothing but take calls back-to-back from early morning to late evening. I took 180 calls one day in early April. It was brutal."

MFS and Pioneer both cope with a turnover rate in their service centers that approaches 100 percent annually. And in both companies, most CSRs leave for other jobs within the complex. "All in all, about 80 percent of those leaving the CSR role stay within MFS," says Jan Clifford, president of MFS Service Center, Inc. She goes on to explain that one path for CSRs at MFS is into a sales support role, sometimes leading to a position as a wholesaler. "After a year on the telephone with shareholders and brokers, a good CSR knows what interests people and can communicate effectively. It's a natural fit for sales."

Neither Pioneer nor MFS has a rigid requirement that CSRs have college degrees, but in both companies, most CSRs currently do. Nor do they require that their CSRs hold Series 6 licenses. Pioneer allows CSRs to become licensed as a perk based on their seniority, believing that this helps them attract staff. MFS declines to license its CSRs except in a few specialized positions, believing that the oversight requirements this would entail are too burdensome. Managers at both complexes point out that it is the brokers, not the CSRs, who sell the funds to the investors, so no licensing is required for the CSRs.

While they don't require licenses for their CSRs, both firms do require the CSRs to be trained. Pioneer's basic training program lasts four weeks, followed by on-the-job training during the new CSRs' first weeks on the phones. MFS puts new CSRs through eight weeks of training, plus another three weeks for those slated to answer retirement plan calls. Jan Clifford muses about the situation: "We train them for two or three months, then they're coming up to speed for a couple of months, and then they're gone after another six months. It's a big investment for a short payback, but it has to be done to maintain our quality of service."

Neither firm sees the phone centers going away anytime soon. Jan Clifford believes that MFS' experience has been representative: during the 12 month period beginning in August 1999, MFS saw its VRU and web site usage increase dramatically, by almost 800 percent in the case of web site usage. Live call volume, however, remained about the same. Many shareowners and brokers still want to talk with a person. For the foreseeable future, several hundred young people in Boston, Omaha, and Kansas City are likely to find their way into the mutual fund industry through the service centers run by Pioneer and MFS.

How to Use MFS-TALK
A quick and easy way to get 'round-the-clock information about your MFS funds

To get information fast, call 1-800-MFS-TALK (that's 1-800-637-8255)

Call Us Anytime
MFS TALK provides 'round-the-clock telephone access to your MFS account. You can call toll free any hour of the day. All you need is a touch-tone phone.

MFS TALK cannot be used with a rotary or non-touch-tone phone.

If you have a rotary phone, call 1-800-225-2606 any business day between 8 A.M. and 8 P.M. eastern time.

The first time you call
Enter your account number or your Social Security number

- If you use your SSN, the first time you'll be asked to choose a personal identification number (PIN). Follow the step-by-step instructions and choose a PIN you can easily remember. Once you have selected your PIN, you will only need your SSN and PIN to access your account. This option is available to certain retirement plans.

- If you use your fund and account numbers, you'll need to enter your pre-assigned PIN. This PIN is the last four digits of your SSN unless you have changed it. If you will sometimes be using your SSN to get information, you may want to change this PIN to match the one you selected. To access your account in the future, you'll need your fund and account numbers and your PIN.

MFS TALK is designed to allow you to obtain information a number of different ways. By listening to the prompts, you'll be able to guide yourself through the system and find the way that's easiest for you.

Basic Options	Number
Price and Performance	1
Funds you own	2
Watch List	3
Literature, fund objectives, market outlook	4
MFS mailing and Internet address	5
MFS TALK features	6

System Shortcuts	Number
Return to main or previous menu (star)	*
Speak to service representative (during business hours)	0
Rewind	7
Forward	9
Skip to end of list or message (pound)	#

A wide variety of features

The following are direct numbers for some of the more popular options, but expermient with the system to find what works best for you. Once you're familiar with the system and you no longer need to hear the instructions, you can press the appropriate key at any time during the message.

Shortcuts from the main menu

General Fund Information	Number
Current NAV	1 1 1
High/low prices	1 1 2
Price on a specific date	1 1 3
Yield	1 1 4
Total Return	1 1 5
Div/cap gain rate	1 1 6

Accounts You Own	Number
Balance and value (all accounts—SSN access only)	2 1 1
Balance and value (one account)	2 1 2
Year-end value	2 1 3
Last five transactions	2 1 4
Last div/cap gain transaction	2 1 5
Prior Year, year-to-date div/cap gain	2 1 6
Price/performance (one fund)	2 2 1
Price/performance (all funds—SSN access only)	2 2 2
Purchase shares	2 3 1
Exchange between funds	2 3 2
Duplicate statement*	2 4 1
Duplicate tax form*	2 4 3
Change PIN	2 5

*Duplicates will be mailed to the address shown on your statement.

CHAPTER 13
Other Service Providers

Great fleas have little fleas upon their backs to bite 'em,
And little fleas have lesser fleas, and so ad infinitum.
— Augustus De Morgan (1872) [1]

Like De Morgan's hierarchy of biters, most industries have hierarchies of greater and lesser firms that support and draw support from one another, and the mutual fund industry is no exception. Funds support investment advisers, administrators, transfer agents, custodians, brokers. These in turn buy services from and support other more specialized firms, such as information providers, banks, law firms, software vendors, and consultants. Previous chapters have discussed many of these support service organizations directly or indirectly as they examined investment management, distribution, and client service. There are a few more yet to discuss.

We saw in Chapter 3 that the National Investment Company Service Association (NICSA) enrolls mutual fund industry service providers in its membership. In mid-1999, NICSA included 350 firms. About half of these were management companies that provided services internally. The other half, the third-party providers, form a good representative sample of the types of firms that serve the industry. Table 1 below shows a breakdown of these organizations by the type of service they provide.

This final chapter on industry functions and the organizations that perform them covers five common industry functions that are often outsourced, functions that have not yet been discussed in detail: specialized printing, literature fulfillment, proxy solicitation and processing, unclaimed property, and lockbox. Finally, it mentions a few of the other unique niches occupied by specialist firms.

Table: 1

Type of Organization	Count
Internal service providers (i.e., affiliated with management companies)	154
Third-party transfer agent and fund accounting service providers	40
Software vendors and specialized IT consultants	33
Accounting and management consulting firms	29
Printing and mailing service providers	22
Banks providing custody, lockbox, and other services	20
Information vendors	12
Training, recruiting, and human resource management services	10
Proxy solicitors and processors	8
Legal firms	6
Literature fulfillment service providers	5
Unclaimed property specialists	3
Other	8
Total	350

Printing Services

Day in and day out, every transfer agent prints a steady stream of internal and external documents—confirmations, checks, letters, and management reports of all sorts. Periodically, however, when shareholder statements must be produced, this stream swells to a massive torrent. When statement time arrives, usually at the end of each calendar quarter, the transfer agent must produce a multi-page, complexly formatted document for almost every shareholder it serves, and deliver it, usually via mail, within a few days of quarter-end. (While a few transfer agents were beginning to offer electronic statements via the Internet in early 2000, the vast majority of shareholder statements continued to be printed and mailed.) The challenges this requirement poses support a thriving market for third-party printing and mailing service providers.

Some transfer agents, particularly the very large ones such as those of Fidelity and Vanguard, do almost all of their printing internally. However, many outsource the more difficult jobs to specialists. Shareholder statements form the staple of this outsourcing for two reasons.

1. *Special Equipment Needs.* Shareholder statements grow ever fancier and more complex. They may be printed in multiple colors and contain pie charts and other graphics. They may be of varying lengths and formats, depending on the number of accounts a shareholder has and the options he or she chooses. Once printed, statements must be sorted in various ways to facilitate stuffing and mailing: by number of pages and by zip code ranges, for example. They may be mailed with insertions, such as special announcements or product brochures, selected for each statement according to characteristics of the shareholder. These features all require special printing and handling equipment not otherwise needed to satisfy everyday printing requirements.

2. *The Volume Spike.* Statements impose extraordinary requirements to print and mail large volumes of documents under a tight deadline. A transfer agent that acquired printing capacity to handle this peak would have many times the capacity needed for daily operations. For example, a transfer agent handling one million shareholders might print 25,000 confirmations, 10,000 checks, and 100,000 pages of internal reports on a typical night. That same transfer agent would have to print from 3 to 6 *million* pages at quarter-end to complete the statements (in addition to all the normal day's printing, plus some month-end reports). And they have to get all these statements in the mail no later than five days after quarter-end.

Many transfer agents find that it is not economical to maintain the capacity and specialized capabilities needed for statement printing, and instead, give this work to third parties: the printing and mailing service providers.

Printers serving the mutual fund industry come in two flavors, as shown in Table 2. Some financial printers handle prospectuses, annual reports, and marketing materials—traditional print shop work. Some firms, however, take on the transaction-based printing, such as statements. To handle this work, these firms share several characteristics.

1. They make a heavy investment in state of the art printing equipment. For example, large, computerized presses can cost as much as $10 million each.

2. They maintain expertise in graphic design in general, in shareholder statement design in particular, and in the production processes involved in generating statements.

3. They employ skilled information technology staff to develop the data manipulation programming needed to transform raw data into finished statements.

Typically the printer receives one or more data feeds from the fund's transfer agent to start the statement process. The printer's computers sort, organize, and format this data, and use it to drive the printers, inserters, and sorters. Transfer agent staff review samples of the statement run for quality assurance, often using special accounts set up specifically to test various aspects of statement production. Finally, the statements are stuffed into envelopes and mailed.

Table 2: Mutual Fund Shareholder Statement Printing Service Providers as of 1998

Firm	Statements?	Prospectuses?	Annual Reports?	# of Mutual Fund Clients
Cadmus Financial Communications	N	Y	Y	18
Daniels Printing LP	N	Y	Y	30+
Dataware Technologies	N	Y	Y	5
Financial Graphic Service, Inc.	N	Y	Y	n/a
Financial Graphics Services, Inc.	N	Y	Y	6
Global Compliance	N	Y	Y	95
Hanson Printing Company, Inc.	N	N	Y	10
Merrill Corporation	N	Y	Y	150
PACKARD Press	N	Y	Y	n/a
Winthrop Printing	N	Y	Y	17
Bowne & Company, Inc.	Y	Y	Y	n/a
Command Financial Press	Y	Y	Y	45
Communications Concepts, Inc.	Y	Y	Y	n/a
First Data Investor Services Group	Y	N	N	103
Infographix	Y	N	N	70
Moore	Y	N	N	50+
Output Technologies, Inc.	Y	Y	Y	n/a
R.R. Donnelly & Sons	Y	Y	Y	300
Scott Printing	Y	Y	Y	7

Source: *The 1998 Shareholder Communications Guide*, Securities Data Publishing, 1998.

All of this is expensive, whether a transfer agent produces the statements itself or contracts with a printing service provider. Activity cost studies in mutual fund companies have indicated that statement preparation and mailing can easily account for 30 percent of the entire cost of providing transfer agent service for the account.[2] For many shareholders, however, the account statement is the one important type of communication they get from their fund between the day they make their initial investments and the day they redeem their shares. Thus, fund companies, and their printers, continually refine their shareholder statements to make them better than the competition's.

Many of the firms that offer printing and mailing services also offer literature fulfillment, since that function also involves printing and mailing steps.

Literature Fulfillment

Both investors and agents contact the funds continuously to order prospectuses, statements of additional information, account applications, fund reports, guides to investing, and many other pieces of literature. The process of capturing and servicing these requests is termed literature fulfillment. Many fund groups contract with external specialist organizations to perform at least some of the functions involved in fulfillment.

Typically the transfer agent retains some or all of the telephone contact through which literature orders are placed, while giving the inventory control and shipping part of the operation to a third party.

The complete cycle of literature fulfillment involves several discrete functions.

- *Receiving and Storing Inventory.* The operator must maintain an inventory of the materials being ordered. Traditionally, this has meant receiving boxes of brochures and forms from printers, and storing them in a warehouse for easy retrieval. In recent years, advancing print technology has enabled fulfillment operators to print some—but not all—items on demand. The operator must record these receipts in its inventory control system, just as any distributor of groceries or video games does.

- *Receiving Orders.* Orders come to the transfer agent's telephone representatives, telemarketing staff, VRUs, web sites, and in some cases, to the fulfillment operator's own telephone reps. The fulfillment operator must get all of these orders into the system it uses to keep inventory records and to issue picking slips and shipping instructions. Typically, fund groups want to mail responses to fulfillment requests no later than the next day after the request is received, so these orders must be captured and processed immediately.

- *Picking and Shipping.* The fulfillment system issues instructions to staff in the warehouse to pick and assemble the items to make up a shipment. It orders any print-on-demand items to be printed. It issues shipping instructions—bills of lading, mailing labels, FedEx forms, etc. Staff walk through the warehouse, collect the inventory, stage it, package it, prepare it for shipping or mailing, and send it out.

- *Inventory Control.* As material is ordered and shipped, the supply shrinks, and items must be replenished. The fulfillment system must post removals, as well as receipts, and issue reports of items to be ordered. The more sophisticated systems can weigh such factors as the order lead time, expected usage, required safety stock, and current outstanding orders in determining when an item should be ordered.

UPPING THE ANTE AGAIN: PERSONAL PERFORMANCE ON STATEMENTS

Once upon a time, shareholder statements were nothing but columns of numbers showing the bare facts: You started with so many shares, you bought and sold this many, and here's where you ended. Over the years, however, intensifying competition in the industry has combined with advancing computer and printing technology to make statements ever fancier. Laser printers allowed great variation in type styles and sizes. Printer programming allowed formats to be changed on the fly, tailoring each shareholder's statement to the information at hand. Graphics were added, especially to depict asset allocation and fund returns over time. Industry observers started to rate fund groups according to how "good" their statements were, and the funds, in turn, began touting these ratings in their marketing literature.

The American Century statement, the first page of which is reproduced on the following page, features one of the latest improvements: personalized performance. This lets the shareholder see how his or her investment actually did, not just how the fund did under a set of standardized assumptions. Investment professionals point out that most shareholders do not, in fact, earn the published investment returns. These benchmarks assume no purchases or redemptions during the year, and reinvestment of all dividends and capital gains.[3] Any given shareholder's performance might differ from that of the fund as a whole.

Actually determining this individual performance is not as straightforward as it seems. There are both conceptual difficulties (experts argue over what exactly is the correct way to calculate it) and practical considerations (some approaches are computationally intensive—i.e., they use a lot of computer power). For example, an internal rate of return calculation, one way to calculate performance, requires the computer to repeatedly solve a discounted present value problem, trying different discount rates until it finds one that results in a zero net present value.

The industry has been discussing the notion for years. In a speech at a Securities Industry Association conference in 1998, SEC Chairman Levitt said that all fund companies should personalize the statements they send customers by providing tailored returns. "Very, very few have provided this information...that strikes me as shortsighted" he said.[4] As of mid-1999, only a few fund groups had joined American Century in actually doing it.

- *Reporting and Data Feeds.* The fulfillment operator must report back to the transfer agent in more or less detail. At the least, it must report the volumes of activity on which it assesses its fee. Many fund complexes want and receive much more extensive information, which may include such things as:
  - detailed and summarized reports of who received what;
  - status information about the operation, e.g., what was processed, what's pending, what's backordered, etc.;
  - data feeds that allow the transfer agent to merge records of fulfillment orders with other information about the shareholders in its data files;
  - status data about the inventory, e.g., what's low or out-of-stock;
  - cost allocation information, e.g., shipping costs by recipient type.

AMERICAN CENTURY

Investor Relations
1-800-345-2021
www.americancentury.com

Quarterly Statement
Period Ending June 30, 1999

Page 1 of 6

James Century and
Jane Century
JTWROS
4500 Main Street
Kansas City MO 64111-6200

Investment Portfolio Summary

Portfolio value on 06-30-1999 $59,747.13

Your portfolio value on 03-31-1999................................$58,944.74
Change this quarter ....+802.39

Your portfolio value on 12-31-1998................................$56,903.84
Year-to-date change ....+2,843.29

Personal Portfolio Performance

Portfolio Value

This graph compares the total value of your portfolio to the net amount you've invested. **Your portfolio is all of your American Century accounts included on this statement.** *Net investment* is the total amount you put in minus the total amount you withdrew (including any dividends and capital gains paid to you as cash).

Portfolio Return

Your year-to-date total portfolio return since 12-31-1998 .... 6.75%
Your 12-month total portfolio return since 06-30-1998 .... 15.90%
Your average annual return since 07-13-1992 .... 16.63%

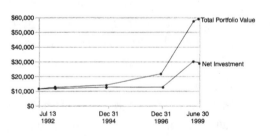

Asset Allocation

Entire Portfolio

Domestic Equity	98%
Select	67%
Income & Growth	31%
Money Market	2%
Capital Preservation	

International	0%
Domestic Equity	98%
Asset Allocation/Balanced	0%
Specialty	0%
Bond	0%
Tax-Free Bond	0%
Money Market	2%
Tax-Free Money Market	0%

Courtesy of American Century Investments.

All in all, this doesn't sound very much like mutual funds and investing, but rather like catalog mail-order merchandising similar to L. L. Bean or Land's End. Many transfer agents feel exactly this way and are quite happy to farm it out to somebody who is good at handling warehouses, physical inventories, and picking and shipping. The ones who don't are generally large fund complexes that believe they have the size and volume to achieve economies of scale, and/or can do it better themselves by making fewer mistakes.

Proxy Solicitation and Processing

Mutual funds must submit a number of questions to the vote of their shareholders. In concept, this is straight-forward enough. The fund determines how many votes each shareholder gets, distributes ballots to the shareholders, collects the ballots the shareholders return, and counts the votes. In practice, the complexities involved in completing all this successfully within a short time cause many fund groups to turn to outside agents who provide specialized proxy services.

The fund's transfer agent starts the process by determining the shareholders' eligibility. This step resembles that of determining eligibility for a capital gain distribution—programming in the transfer agent system determines how many shares each account is eligible to vote on the designated record date. The transfer agent creates a data file with the name, address, and votes for each shareholder. The proxy processor takes over from there. Using the data the transfer agent has provided, the proxy service prepares and mails the solicitations containing the literature describing the questions and a ballot with which to vote.

Traditionally, shareholders voted their proxies by filling out a paper card and mailing it back. Today, proxy processors use telephone and Internet voting with increasing frequency. For security purposes, each share-holder gets a unique control number with the initial mailing that he or she must provide when attempting to vote on the telephone or web site. For example, Liberty Funds Distributors has established a proxy voting capability on their web site for certain Colonial, Stein Roe, and Newport Funds (but they still use a proxy processor for tabulation and reporting). Liberty stated that a web site vote costs about $.05 instead of the $.32 needed to return a paper ballot. [5]

Next, the processor must count the votes as they come in and inform fund administration of the results. Shareholders often ignore proxy mailings, and response rates can be quite low. However, some questions, such as fund merger propositions, require the vote of a certain percentage of the outstanding shares to pass. This means that sometimes fund management has to hire a proxy solicitor, which might be the proxy processor, to get out the vote. This is done via subsequent mailings, and even telephone calls if needed. Finally, the proxy processor presents the fund administration with the final tabulations to document the shareholder vote.

WHAT PRICE PROXIES?

Even a normal, everyday, uncontroversial proxy solicitation costs the fund some amount of money. After all, the ballots have to be printed, mailed, collected, counted, and reported. For generating really big expenditures, however, nothing beats a proxy fight.

In September 1998, Donald A. Yacktman, head of Yacktman Asset Management, filed an unusual proxy with the SEC. Yacktman wanted the shareholders of the Yacktman Fund, then around $500 million in assets, and the $50 million Yacktman Focused Fund, to dismiss the four independent directors on the funds' six-member board. Over the preceding year, Yacktman and the independent board members had developed increasingly antagonistic relations. Yacktman accused the board members of criticizing and interfering with portfolio management to the point of making it difficult to retain staff. Board members responded that Yacktman regularly ignored prospectus constraints as he went about making investment choices.

So each side tried to fire the other. The board voted to remove Yacktman as president of the funds. Yacktman filed the proxy and hired D.F. King, one of the largest proxy solicitation firms, to persuade shareholders to vote his way. The directors set their own proxy solicitor, Shareholder Communications Corporation, into motion. In a filing with the SEC, the directors estimated that they would spend $500,000 on their proxy campaign, money that came straight out of the funds. Although he did not disclose the figure, Yacktman likely spent a similar amount of his management company's funds on his campaign.

Two months and $1 million later, the shareholders voted 51 percent to 49 percent to support Yacktman and oust the independent directors. That was not the end of the story, however. Yacktman had sued the directors over their use of fund assets to mount their proxy solicitation effort. The SEC weighed in on the side of the directors, maintaining that the directors' use of the assets was proper. The directors went on to pay about half of the $465,000 the funds owed Shareholder Communications, but were ousted before they could pay the second half. When Shareholder Communications sued for the money they were still owed, the funds, now controlled by Yacktman, counter-sued to regain what they had already paid.

The SEC did not miss the implications for independent directors in this ugly, expensive little squabble. It finally ruled that directors have access to independent counsel, where independent meant that the legal firm has not represented the adviser or its affiliates for the previous two years. In addition, the Yacktman case prompted several insurance companies to modify their standard Directors and Officers policies to make it easier for directors to insure themselves against suits by an investment adviser. Prior to this, fund directors always shared a policy with the investment adviser. As the Yacktman affair demonstrated, however, if directors are to be truly independent, they must be prepared to fight the investment adviser if necessary.

Unclaimed Property

Chapter 12 described escheatment, the process by which the states claim property that has been classified as lost. In 1997, the SEC, concerned about the growing incidence of securities holdings (including mutual funds) being escheated, issued rules requiring transfer agents to search for lost shareholders. Specifically, transfer agents must initiate a search no later than twelve months after the first mail is returned, using an automated database service, at no cost to the security holder. Only after it had conducted this search could it turn the account over to the state.

Unclaimed property trackers help transfer agents exercise due diligence in making the searches and in reporting lost accounts to the states. State unclaimed property regulations remain uncoordinated and confusing. Different states have different dormancy periods (how long before the lost property is considered abandoned). They require reports of lost property at different intervals, with different information, in various formats. Some states accept only electronic reports, some only paper, some both. And all states have become increasingly aggressive in enforcing unclaimed property laws as they search for additional sources of funds. Not surprisingly, many transfer agents choose not to try to master this wealth of arcana, but contract instead with a specialist to handle it for them.

ESCHEATMENT OF THE RICH AND FAMOUS

One would think that in Boston, of all places, they would recognize the name Fiedler, as in Arthur Fiedler, legendary conductor of the Boston Pops. After all, a ten foot high bust of Fiedler greets anyone who walks along Boston's Esplanade, or passes on Storrow Drive, one of the city's busiest thoroughfares. But the prominence of the name was not enough to deter the Commonwealth of Massachusetts' escheatment process.

In 1996, Maureen Goggin of *The Boston Globe* told the story.

"In 1968, when her husband Arthur was maestro of the Boston Pops, Ellen Fiedler put $53,000 in a mutual fund.

"Twelve years later, by then a widow, she moved from Brookline to Cambridge, and Massachusetts Financial Services lost track of her. When she died in 1984, Mrs. Fiedler's three children were unaware of her mutual fund holdings, which were not included in her $2.5 million estate.

"In 1992, the company forwarded Fiedler's securities to state Treasurer Joe Malone's abandoned property division...no one from the state contacted Fiedler's heirs. Her holdings—now worth $132,000—went into the general fund. Her children didn't locate or recover the money until The Globe contacted them last month." [6]

But the Fiedlers shouldn't feel singled out in all this. Cary Grant and Lucille Ball (yes, the real ones) and other celebrities have also turned up on states' unclaimed property lists. Since the states have little motivation to find the owners and give up this property they otherwise keep, the average rate of return of unclaimed property to owners in 1996 was under 25 percent. Massachusetts, which at the time of the Fiedler incident was busily reducing the staff that searched for unclaimed property owners, didn't even hit 17 percent. State officials claimed that the job of locating lost property owners was best done by private enterprise—in other words, firms that charged the owners a fee for revealing the location of the property. While these "heir-finders," as they are called, are not supposed to charge more than 10 percent of the asset value of the lost property, many charge much more since enforcement is spotty at best. [7]

Thus the SEC's action. While the SEC couldn't do much about state practices, it could and did do something about those of the transfer agents. In 1997, the SEC required, among other things, that transfer agents make the initial searches for owners of lost property without turning to third parties that charge the shareholder for returning something he or she already owned.

Lockbox

Some fund groups, especially those that are directly marketed, receive many checks via the mail. To complete the processing of these checks, the transfer agent must deposit each check in the correct bank account and capture the transaction—usually a share purchase—for which the check is paying. Many banks, as part of their suite of cash management products, offer a method of streamlining these functions, known as a lockbox operation. Companies of all sorts—utilities, department stores, cable TV operators—use these to receive payments for bills. Mutual fund transfer agents use them for purchase transaction payments, especially subsequent purchases into existing shareholder accounts. A transfer agent using a lockbox typically sends its shareholders envelopes that are pre-addressed to this lockbox location, as well as purchase stubs that have the account number printed in optical character recognition (OCR) type or some other machine-readable form. These often accompany account statements and transaction confirmations.

In a typical lockbox operation, processing goes through four major steps, as shown in Figure 1. The mail goes to a post office address from which the bank collects it. Lockbox staff open the mail and separate out those items that require special handling. For example, shareholders persist in sending address changes, complaints, questions, and other items using those pre-addressed envelopes that are supposed to be used only for purchases. If the shareholder has sent in the pre-printed purchase stub along with the check, then the payment is ready to process. If not, the operator has to create a form with the account number in machine-readable form. The lockbox operators group the payments to be processed into batches to help ensure accuracy.

Figure 1: Lockbox Processing Workflow

Process mail and create batch	Capture data from turnaround document and check	Reconcile and deposit checks	Send remittance data plus transactions to transfer agent
• Automated machines open mail	• Operator encodes checks	• System reconciles payments received	• Operator transmits remittance data and transactions to the transfer agent
• Operator sorts out exception items	• Turnaround documents and checks processed on transports	• Operator sends encoded checks to check processing	
• Operator creates purchase stubs where needed	• System reads checks (MICR) and turnaround document (MICR, OCR, bar code) and creates images and transactions	• Bank creates a deposit in the transfer agent's account	
• Operator creates batches by control number for processing			

Source: The Tower Group, 1998.

Second, the operator encodes the checks, that is, keys the check amount into a machine that writes it in magnetic ink characters on the bottom so it can be read by the processing machines. The encoded checks and the purchase stubs go into high speed readers that capture the account number from the purchase stub and the amount paid on the accompanying check. Often the process includes taking an image of the payment coupon and the check to be transmitted to the transfer agent. When the operator finishes a batch, he or she reconciles it by comparing the total amount processed with a manually-derived total of the check amounts. Once this matches, the encoded checks are sent to check processing in the bank for clearing and collection and deposit into the transfer agent's account.

Finally, the lockbox operation sends the transactions it has created—typically including the shareholder account number and purchase amount—to the transfer agent. It also sends items that couldn't be handled in the normal stream, items that the transfer agent will have to process as exceptions. The transfer agent feeds the data into its system to produce purchase transactions that are priced and posted along with the transactions coming from other sources.

Mutual fund transfer agents pay for lockbox service in the form of a charge of a few cents per check processed. For some transfer agents, this costs less than it would if they captured the transactions themselves. Other transfer agents choose to handle this function internally, acquiring and operating the equipment to read the magnetic ink and other types of characters on checks and purchase stubs. Over time, electronic business is likely to reduce the role of lockbox processing, as physical checks in the mail give way to electronic payments.

Others

In addition to the organizations described above, a number of organizations in the NICSA member list provide very specialized services. The firms and services that fall into this other category include:

- At least one company specializes in providing financing for deferred commission schemes, such as contingent deferred sales charge plans. This company loans the principal distributor the money to be fronted to the selling brokers in return for an income stream generated as 12b-1 fees are assessed.
- One firm provides NASD licensed teleservicing staff, on an as-needed basis, to transfer agents whose call volume is exceeding its internal capacity to handle.
- A handful of funds print checkbooks for use by shareholders holding accounts with check writing privileges.
- Several firms expedite international mail and express delivery.
- One firm specializes in helping fund companies prepare their filings to EDGAR, the SEC's electronic document repository.

CHAPTER 14

Mutual Funds and the E-Business Revolution

If I had to put it on a scale, at the low end of the scale I think the Internet will impact business as much as the telephone did. And at the high end of the scale, it could have the same impact as the industrial revolution.
— Harvey Golub (1999) [1]

E-business exploded into a major issue, if not *the* major issue, with which business organizations both within and outside of the mutual fund industry wrestled at the end of the twentieth century. Prophecies appeared on a daily basis, foretelling the total transformation of business and society as we know it. For the mutual fund industry in particular, observers argued about both the magnitude and direction of this effect. As Bernstein Research put it in their discussion of the future of the industry in early 2000, "it is not clear whether the Internet will prove to be a friend or foe to the mutual fund industry." [2] It posed destabilizing challenges and at the same time, offered enticing new opportunities.

Any assessment of the current state of e-business in the mutual fund or any other industry is doomed to become obsolete almost as soon as it is written. At the accelerated pace of Internet time, generations of developments can occur in the period between the date a chapter like this is written and the date it actually appears in print. Thus writing about the current state of affairs—who is currently doing what exciting things with the Web and e-business—is best left for newspapers and magazines. A book deals most appropriately with underlying concepts and patterns that evolve more slowly, and that offer a method for organizing and understanding rapidly moving events. This chapter, therefore, attempts to address these organizing issues: the broad classes of functions to which mutual fund companies can profitably apply e-business techniques and the challenges and opportunities e-business presents in each of these classes.

Definitions

Industry observers have uniformly predicted that e-business would drastically reshape the consumer financial services landscape over the next few years, particularly Internet-based e-business. In 1999, Morgan Stanley Dean Witter, for example, projected a compound annual growth rate of at least 34 percent for consumer financial services on the Internet over the following four years. [3] Many other research and consulting firms have made similar predictions. Proper evaluation of these forecasts, however, requires that we first establish a few definitions.

E-Business and E-Commerce

Varying definitions of e-business can be found in both the popular press and academic literature. Many e-business definitions are synonymous with the Internet, or imply that e-business is a result of, and impossible without, the Internet. While the Internet has certainly intensified the interest in e-business, and added enormously to the range of e-business possibilities, they are not one and the same. E-business is much broader in scope: it is *improving business performance through electronic connectivity*. Many observers have asserted that it's only a matter of time until the term e-business disappears, since any business that hasn't transformed itself into an e-business will not have survived. In the interim, however, e-business can be broadly defined as the use of electronic linkage to facilitate or transform business function. If something about this electronic exchange has added value, then e-business has occurred.

Some observers use the term *e-commerce* synonymously with e-business. Strictly speaking, however, e-commerce refers to a subset of e-business: selling products (and perhaps providing customer service) via electronic channels, most notably via the World Wide Web. E-business encompasses *any* interaction between a business and *any* entity—supplier, service provider, customer, distributor, regulator—with which it interacts. If that interaction can be effected via electronic means, it is potentially e-business.

Categories of E-Business

E-business can be divided into two major categories:

- **Business-to-customer (B2C)**. This subset of e-business corresponds most closely to what many term e-commerce. It has attracted much media attention because it is so visible, being the world of Amazon, E*Trade, and the other dot-coms. It has been an area of rapid growth, and an area in which further rapid growth is expected. Forrester Research, for example, estimated that B2C e-business would grow from about $4 billion in sales in 1999 to over $100 billion in 2003.[4] The mutual fund industry has embraced B2C e-business enthusiastically, creating web sites to serve a variety of functions, including marketing, sales, and customer service.
- **Business-to-business (B2B)**. Less visible, but potentially much more important, is the connection of industry back offices in B2B e-business. In 1999, Forrester forecast business-to-business activity to increase from $45 billion per year to over $1.5 *trillion* per year in 2003. Lou Gerstner, IBM's CEO, described this as a "storm—a real disturbance of the Force," compared to business-to-customer e-business, which he termed merely "fireflies before the storm."[5] As we will see, B2B opportunities loom large for the mutual fund industry as well.

E-Business and Mutual Fund Functions

Figure 1 illustrates the interactions among components of the mutual fund industry categorized according to the roles they play. The industry comprises a set of functions, such as portfolio management, trading, trade settlement, securities accounting, marketing, client service, and so on. Different organizations carry out different subsets of this universe of functions, depending on their market strategy. For example, some sub-advisers carry out all the functions involved in investment management, but limit their marketing or client service functions to those required to deal with a few institutions. At the other end of the spectrum are the distribution or service specialists—the third-party transfer agent that provides customer service, for example. Of course, many players do it all. As PricewaterhouseCoopers' *Tomorrow's Leading Investment Managers* study indicated, choosing which among this set of functions to perform represents one of the most critical components of any mutual fund company's (or, indeed, any investment manager's) business strategy.[6]

Figure 1: The Mutual Fund Industry: Major Players and Relationships

Each of the arrows on the diagram in Figure 1 indicates an interaction that can be transformed via e-business. E-business opportunities match up well with functions within the industry. For example, whoever manages a fund's investments, internal adviser or external sub-adviser, for load or no-load funds, for retail or institutional distribution, will need to communicate trade settlement instructions to counter-parties. The e-business opportunity presented by straight-through processing (STP) requirements applies equally in any case. Similarly, anyone seeking to distribute mutual funds (or, for that matter, any type of financial service product) to individual consumers faces the same business-to-customer e-business challenges. This book, therefore, categorizes e-business opportunities in the mutual fund industry into two major groups according to the major functions they address—distribution and service versus manufacturing.

E-Business in Fund Distribution and Customer Service

As discussed in Chapters 8 through 10, distribution encompasses all of a fund company's sales and marketing-related activities aimed at securing new shareholders and new assets for their funds. Customer service comprises that set of functions the fund company provides to shareholders (and their intermediaries) who have already purchased into the fund. Often, however, nothing distinguishes those features and functions oriented toward distribution from those oriented toward service. For example, the ability to order an exchange transaction on a fund's web site provides a service, both by delivering a desired function to the client and by reducing the cost of providing the functionality. It also has a marketing effect, by making the fund more attractive to a certain type of investor. Many other mutual fund web site functions serve these dual purposes. Therefore this discussion treats e-business for distribution and service support as a single category.

Funds on the Web

Mutual fund groups have rapidly established their presence on the Internet. In 1997, about 180 fund groups had web sites. By 1998, the number had grown to over 300. Surveys suggested that by the end of 2000, all but the smallest among the 600+ fund families in the United States would be represented on the Web.[7] While a few fund groups had online interactions with their customers via proprietary links as early as 1990, these have all been superseded by Internet access. For the mutual fund segment, B2C e-business means Internet e-business conducted through their web sites.

The degree of penetration and success these fund companies have achieved with their web sites has varied widely. In 2000, the large, directly marketed funds had achieved the most visible success. Vanguard, for example, had succeeded in getting 37 percent of its shareholders to use the Web to get information or make transactions. Vanguard claimed that it saved money through these online facilities. Because there was no channel conflict involved, the larger, directly marketed funds offered shareholders the widest range of online facilities. Most of the broker-distributed funds, on the other hand, still wrestled with what functions they could offer their investors via e-commerce without alienating their distribution network.

Late 1999 and early 2000 saw a period of dueling commentators and surveys on mutual fund success with the Web. FRC stated in 1999 that "so far the Internet has been primarily a means for investors to gather information, not a distribution channel."[8] Forrester Research found respondents in a 1999 survey it conducted split almost evenly on whether the Internet would significantly impact how much mutual fund investors traded.[9] A late 1999 survey conducted by Putnam actually found very few investors (less than 1 in 10) using e-commerce to invest directly.[10] "Self serving," sniffed one observer, who termed Putnam's results "an obvious defense mechanism for a firm tied to intermediary sold funds."[11] But American Century, a directly marketed fund with no such ax to grind, found in its 1999 survey more or less the same thing—less than 10 percent of mutual fund investors doing transactions via the Web.[12] And Cerulli Associates backed this up in the study it released in March 2000, which claimed to find no hard evidence that the Web had boosted fund sales.[13] Schwab, on the other hand, released its study projecting that 70 or 80 percent of all mutual fund trades would soon be done online.[14] Another study predicted that 19 percent of all fund sales would be conducted over the Internet by 2005.[15] In mid-2000, the issue was far from settled.

The worth of the Web for client service has generated less controversy. Traditionally, fund groups handled customer service through representatives answering the mail and the telephone. The Internet offers funds a significant opportunity for cost avoidance in client service by migrating both investors and intermediaries to online self-service. Repeated studies have indicated that the marginal cost of an activity performed online is a fraction of the cost of the same activity with manual intervention involved. But it's not that simple, others have argued. A Vanguard spokesman, for example, stated in early 2000 that the fixed costs of providing Internet functions matched or outweighed the marginal savings obtained from capturing transactions via the web site.[16]

Types of Fund Web Sites

Several studies of mutual fund web sites have enumerated and classified features and functions these sites provide, but such feature and function lists become stale quickly. PricewaterhouseCoopers has developed a life cycle model of e-business into which historical mutual fund efforts can be mapped, and likely future approaches projected. This scheme, illustrated in Figure 2, identifies four distinct stages along the e-business life cycle into which a firm's web efforts can be categorized.[17]

1. *Presence*. The presence site is generally the entry point to being on the Web, and is a stage through which many fund companies had already passed by 2000. Firms use presence sites to tell the Internet-using public about themselves. Since the presence site typically contains mostly one-way communication, similar to advertising and literature fulfillment, presence sites, especially ones maintained by mutual funds, have often been termed "brochureware" sites.

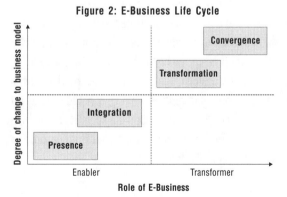

Figure 2: E-Business Life Cycle

The functions found on mutual fund presence sites typically include:

- an array of fund information, including prospectuses and applications for display and download, fund summaries, prices and dividend schedules, and often interviews with portfolio managers;
- investor education that can be both broad and deep (Vanguard's Learning Center is frequently cited as an example of this);
- interactive investment analysis tools, such as fund selection, retirement planning, or cost calculators; and
- general company facts and contact information.

These functions can become quite sophisticated. For example, some fund groups conduct web-based forums for investors, brokers, advisors and wholesalers. Participants may listen to a streaming audio file from a portfolio manager, watch a synchronized slide presentation, and then type in questions for response during such a forum.

In mid-2000, most mid-size broker-distributed fund groups offered presence sites. A visitor to one of these sites could get information about the funds, but could not do any business with the funds via the site other than download a prospectus and application. To open an account, an investor still had to fill out and submit a paper application, and to order transactions, the shareholder still had to go through a broker or the transfer agent. The fund groups in this category that were approached to provide an example of a presence site for this chapter all refused to do so, out of embarassment that their sites were not more sophisticated.

Presence sites return limited benefits to the fund group, but they likewise limit the group's risk. Since they do not interact with the transfer agent system, or other internal systems, they can be isolated into separate, specialized hardware/software environments. Fund groups can and did experiment with their fund presence sites at relatively low cost. In 1997, for example, when many funds were first appearing on the Internet, a fund company could establish a presence site comparable to those of its peers for a few tens of thousands of dollars.

2. *Integration*. At this stage, fund companies integrate the Web into their service offerings. They give investors and intermediaries access to personal financial information, such as balances and transaction history. They also allow their customers to do business with the fund by direct transaction entry. However, these sites still do not transform the basic business model—by and large, what investors can do on these integration web sites resembles what they could already do via an interactive voice unit, or on the telephone with a CSR. The functions they provide are valuable, and appreciated, but not revolutionary. By 2000, all the large directly marketed fund companies, and a few broker-sold fund groups, had moved at least to this stage.

In addition to providing all the information found on presence sites, integration sites typically add:

- access to shareholder personal financial information, including account balances and valuations, option selections, and transaction history;
- financial transaction order entry, including exchanges, liquidations, and, less frequently, purchases;
- account maintenance transaction entry such as dividend option changes; and
- in a few cases as of early 2000, the ability to open new accounts directly online without having to complete and submit a paper application.

These functions enable shareholders to perform self-service, which attracts both customers (many of whom prefer self-service) and fund companies (who see this as a cost reduction opportunity). Interestingly, however, several fund groups that have succeeded in getting their customers to use their web site functions have found that this stimulates increased traffic via other channels.[18] This may have been a transient effect—many of the calls were to check up on a transaction that the customer had just done on the web site—that should decrease as investors become more comfortable with using the Web.

In mid-2000, Neuberger Berman, a directly marketed fund group that managed about $14 billion in its open-end funds, showed the range of functions typical to integration sites. Figure 3 shows the site map for Neuberger Berman. This site featured a rich array of fund and investing information, but also allowed Neuberger Berman shareholders to view and manipulate many aspects of their accounts. Shareholders could look at their account balances, values, or transaction histories; set up purchase transactions to be paid by ACH funds transfer; order redemptions to be paid by ACH or check; and exchange from one fund to another.

These account access functions require links between the web site and the firm's legacy systems, particularly the transfer agent system. This raises the level of risk: customers become exposed to the frailties of internal systems, and security, reliability, and integrity become much more important than they are for presence sites. Because of this, a fund company moving from a presence to an integration site often found it had to dramatically increase its spending on Internet technology and development.

3. *Transformation.* Fund companies achieve transformation with their web sites when they use them to significantly change the way they relate to their customers. They do things that otherwise wouldn't be done. They allow the customers to tailor the site according to their preferences, creating for the fund company a one-to-one relationship. They provide content that ranges far beyond the mutual fund investments that the fund company offers. They strive to become the investor's preferred site for entering the Internet. The leading edge fund groups in terms of Internet capabilities—roughly 6 percent of the total—had reached this point by 2000.[19] Not surprisingly, Fidelity, which has been

Figure 3: Neuberger Berman Site Index

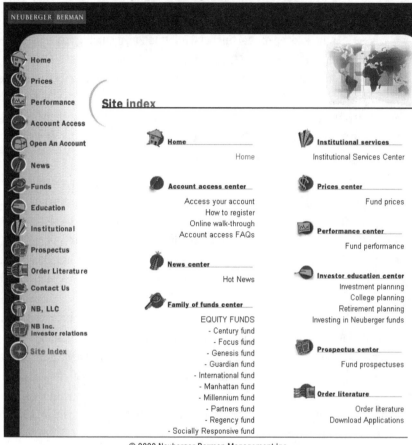

© 2000 Neuberger Berman Management Inc.
Used with permission.

spending heavily for many years on its Internet facilities, has often been cited as a leading example of a transformation web site. Figure 4 illustrates one aspect of Fidelity's site that brings it into the transformation stage—the ability Fidelity gives each individual user to customize the site to suit his or her particular preferences. As Figure 4 shows, Fidelity provides access to far more than its mutual fund family. And although Figure 4 doesn't reveal it, Fidelity, like other groups at this stage, features an enormous range of fund and investment information and transaction capabilities on its site.

Fidelity has achieved measurable results: about one third of its mutual fund trades came over the Internet by late 1999, and it had actually started to see a decline in call volumes, a phenomenon it attributed to Web use.[20] Achieving this took time, investment, and hard work, however. Fidelity had had a web site for five years, and transaction capabilities for three years before it saw the Web start to reduce call volumes. And industry watchers generally believe that Fidelity has spent tens if not hundreds of millions of dollars building and maintaining its web sites. For example, the industry press reported that one single subset of Fidelity's overall web capabilities, the set of functions aimed at brokers and advisors who sell Fidelity funds, cost the firm $20 million to deploy.[21]

4. *Convergence.* The life cycle model predicts that ultimately cross-industry networks of supply chains and markets will emerge. Consumers, including investors, will want to use sites that integrate offerings from multiple providers, sites that provide value in and of themselves by making it easier for consumers to find the goods or services they seek. Morgan Stanley Dean Witter suggests that to be successful on the Web, companies, including fund companies, will evolve toward one of two models.

Figure 4: Fidelity's Web Site Customization Facility

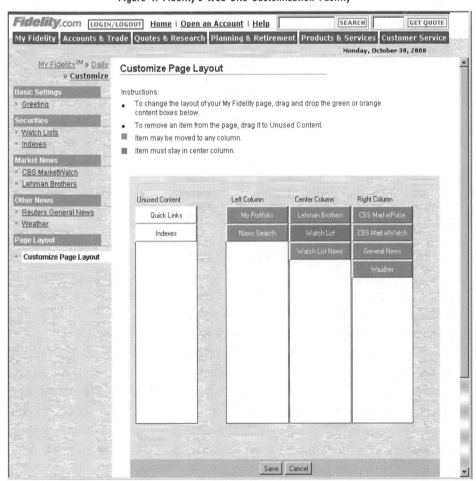

Some will be *specialty manufacturers*, supplying best-in-breed products to the primary distribution points on the Internet.[22] Others will become *vertical portals*, described as "a web site devoted to a particular topic that is a destination for cybersurfers to buy and/or get information on a variety of different products that share the site's focus."[23] The term "portal" stems from the way many web surfers use these sites as their entry points to the Internet. A financial services vertical portal might offer brokerage services, banking, insurance, mutual funds, and bill payment, all in one place. It might include products and services from multiple banks, insurers, fund companies, and so on. Figure 5 illustrates how these types of sites might relate to each other.

Figure 5: Specialty Manufacturers and Vertical Portals

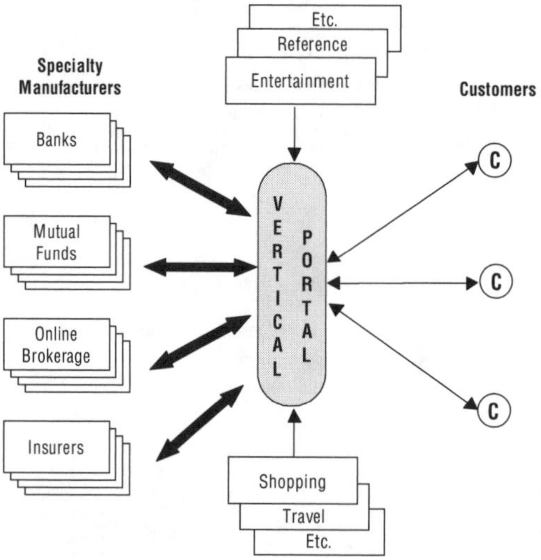

While a mutual fund management company might evolve its web site to become a vertical portal (and companies like Fidelity, Schwab, and American Express were showing signs of doing so in 2000), mutual funds could also appear on portals run by other types of firms. Morgan Stanley Dean Witter, among others, has speculated that such Internet powers as AOL, Yahoo!, and Microsoft might get into the business of distributing mutual funds via their portals. In late 1999, two fund groups (ING and Berger) started in this direction by making agreements with more than fifty Web retailers, through which a percentage of what a shopper spent with these merchants (on toys or books or whatever) would be invested for the shopper in one of two mutual funds.[24] Mid-2000 saw the appearance of firms that attempted to address some of the infrastructure needed for operating a successful vertical portal. For example, a firm called VerticalOne was developing a capability to integrate and present on a single web site the information a subscribing individual might have in multiple discrete accounts with many different businesses.

By mid-2000, most fund companies were still in the presence or integration stages with their web sites, with only a small percentage having moved beyond integration. How quickly and in what particular sequence they would move further forward still inspired intense and wide-ranging speculation.

E-Commerce at AIM Management

In late 1999, Internet consulting firm Kasina announced its list of the top twenty mutual fund web sites, according to its proprietary, multi-dimensional rating scheme. Among these was the web site (http://www.aimfunds.com) for AIM, a large load fund family that had been pushing the envelope for web site features and functions for several years. The survey commented:

> AIM's Web site effectively serves its shareholder base by offering visually appealing design, easy navigation, and a wealth of information. AIM's brand image of discipline and professionalism are clearly defined; its ongoing innovations help the site remain among the best, with excellent design, top-notch investor education, and shareholder services.

Perhaps more important was the evaluation that AIM had "done an exceptional job in aligning their online efforts with their business strategies."[25] Nor was Kasina the only observer that found AIM's site impressive—a month earlier, mutual fund industry research firm DALBAR had found AIM's web site to be the best it had evaluated among broker-sold fund groups. AIM's experience in getting to this point illustrates many of the issues and challenges of e-commerce strategy and tactics in the mutual fund industry.

AIM Management's founders started the firm in 1976, with little more than "a table, two chairs, and a telephone," along with some ideas about managing investments.[26] AIM was reasonably successful through the 1980s, but its explosive growth came during the 1990s, when it went from $13 billion under management at the beginning of 1990 to almost $160 billion at the end of 1999. Some of that growth came from the acquisition of the GT Global funds in 1998, but the vast majority resulted from strong investment performance coupled with astute marketing, mostly in the non-proprietary broker channel. In 1997, AIM merged with Invesco PLC to form AMVESCAP, a global asset manager offering both retail and institutional products.

AIM launched its first web site in November 1996, after a period of intense research on technology options, investor and intermediary needs, and competitive offerings. "We wanted to be competitive right out of the box," explained Margaret Reilly, AIM's director of Electronic Commerce. "We skipped the brochureware-only phase, and gave our shareholders account inquiry capability on the first version of our site, something no other load funds were doing at the time." This set the tone for AIM's web site development over the next three years— continual, aggressive expansion of capabilities for both investors and intermediaries. "For the next couple of years, we waged an all-out features and functions war with our competitors," said John Deane, AIM's chief information officer. "We kept track of the fifteen load fund groups and fifteen no-load fund groups that we believed were worth watching and made sure we kept up with or surpassed them."

As it developed its web site functions, AIM also evolved the organization with which it supported electronic commerce. For the first years, Internet development belonged to an interdisciplinary group drawn from the

Figure 6: AIM Funds Home Page

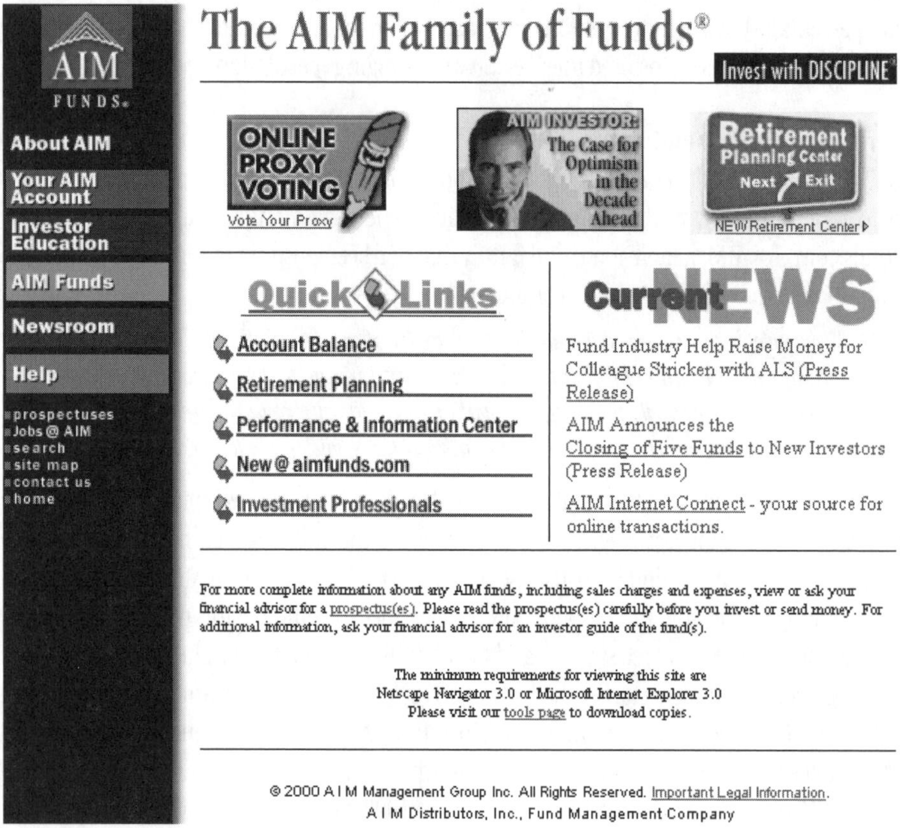

sales, marketing, customer service, IT, legal, and compliance departments. This group reported directly to AIM's president to ensure that the new initiative got the senior management attention it needed. Once the function was well established, AIM divided this group into two parts: e-commerce and e-commerce technology. E-commerce was "pushed back to the business," as Deane described it. This e-commerce group, headed by Reilly, reported to AIM's head of marketing; the e-commerce technology group became part of the IT function. In early 2000, about 20 staff worked in the e-commerce technology group, with a dozen more in the e-commerce group. Deane predicted that the evolution would continue: "Eventually these will both disappear as separate groups. E-commerce will become something every business department does as a normal matter of course, and e-commerce technology will become just another part of IT's toolset."

One of the keys to AIM's success, Reilly believed, had been the active e-commerce steering committee that had been put in place at the start. This group met regularly to review e-commerce initiatives, and make resource allocation and trade-off decisions when needed. "No one individual, not me, not anyone, can decide which of the various initiatives across the different departments contribute most value to the firm, and should get attention and funding. The steering committee, however, with all the groups represented, can. I'm sure that one major reason some fund groups' web sites are so mediocre or off-target is that they're the product of a single, big-ego web master, working without the guidance we get from our steering committee."

In early 2000, this strategy had given AIM perhaps the single most functional web site of any load fund family. AIM's seven million shareholders could browse a large selection of news and educational materials; retrieve information such as prices, yields, and commentary about the funds; order prospectuses, reports, forms, and other documents; check the status and value of their accounts; use financial planning tools to evaluate investment needs and options; vote on proxy questions; and order transactions to their accounts. Intermediaries had their own segment of the site with additional functions designed for and restricted to them. For example, they could download the letters of approval AIM had received from NASD on its sales materials that the brokers need before they could use the materials. Intermediaries could also check on the activity and balances within their clients' accounts, contact AIM transfer agent operations if they had questions, and view a large selection of sales support information.

In early 2000, AIM continued to add new features at a fast clip. It had, for example, recently added a segment to the site designed specifically to provide information for the back-office personnel at the dealer firms that distributed AIM funds. And the list of web site enhancements in various stages of development, planning, or envisioning contained at least thirty entries. "This is where the steering committee is really valuable in deciding which of these we do, and in what order," Reilly said.

Also in early 2000, AIM supported its web sites on hardware running at its Houston data center. Sun hardware, running the Solaris operating system and Netscape Enterprise Web server software, hosted the sites. These servers connected to the Internet via fault tolerant, redundant, high capacity circuits into multiple first-tier Internet service providers. This internal network lay behind firewalls configured to provide a single point of entry—all traffic entering or leaving the web site network had to flow through one. To achieve maximum security, AIM took the approach of "denying all except what was allowed;" that is, restricting activity on the network to only that which was deemed safe and, therefore, explicitly permitted by the firewall. AIM's IT staff constantly monitored network activity, taking steps to add resources whenever any component hit 70 percent of its capacity.

The AIM site had become quite busy by early 2000, with a volume of almost 400,000 visits per month. The majority of these visits were by shareholders, checking fund prices and account balances, or by investors gathering information. Intermediaries accounted for about one-fourth of this volume, much of it to order literature. Most intermediary activity came from registered investment advisers and brokers from smaller firms, since brokers in the big wirehouses and regional firms tended to use their own internal systems instead. And a few shareholders used the web site to execute financial transactions, a feature that many load fund groups had so far refused to put on their web sites.

"We had to get over a philosophical hurdle within the firm to offer shareholder transactions," Deane admitted. Many people within AIM and other load fund groups worried that giving shareholders the ability to perform transactions themselves via the web site would alienate the brokers by threatening their control of their clients. In the event, Deane pointed out, this turned out not to be an issue. "First, we allow only subsequent purchases, redemptions, and exchanges, things a shareholder could do by mail or telephone anyway. Second, we pay the brokers the normal commissions on any subsequent purchases their clients make. And finally, there aren't that many transactions, less than a thousand a month, and they tend to be the little ones—for $5,000 or $10,000 or so. The brokers want to know when their clients do these, but they don't particularly want to handle them. So our brokers haven't felt threatened at all."

According to Deane and Reilly, the ultimate net effect of the Internet on AIM remained to be seen. "We've spent millions of dollars, but it would be virtually impossible to compute a hard ROI on that," Deane admitted. "Nevertheless, you absolutely have to do it to be credible today. Everyone expects a major fund group to have certain things available via their web site, and if you don't have these, you aren't going to be taken seriously. It's a cost of doing business."

Second, they pointed out, AIM wanted to be well positioned, so that when Internet use took off, they could take advantage of it. Ultimately, Deane said, the web site should help AIM reduce costs as shareholders and brokers serviced themselves, but that had not happened so far. "We see people doing things they wouldn't otherwise have done without the web site, such as checking their balances 20 times per month. Before, when they had to call in, they might do it once per month, or not at all. In the short run, the web site probably adds to the cost of service."

Nevertheless, AIM's senior management believed that the Internet could become a major factor that would influence competition in the mutual fund industry. AIM's Internet strategy reflected this belief. The firm worked to aggressively expand its web site functions, building as it did so expertise in both foundational and evolutionary Internet technologies. If and when the Internet and e-commerce revolutionized mutual funds, AIM would be ready.

Distribution Chain Linkage

In addition to the producer-distributor linkages involved in convergence on the Web, the mutual fund industry's back-office distribution activities also benefit from e-business connectivity. The evolution of both the fund industry, particularly driven by Rule 12b-1, and the financial services industry in general (e.g., the growing popularity of defined contribution plans and fee-based financial advisors) has increased the complexity of mutual fund distribution. Funds today are marketed/distributed to investors through various channels, including:

- fund management companies (direct);
- broker dealers (traditional load channels and via supermarkets and wrap programs);
- defined contribution pension plans;

- bank trust departments;
- financial advisors and planners of all sorts, from individual proprietorships to large corporations; and
- insurance agents (both funds directly, and funds supporting variable annuities).

This evolution is likely to continue, with more organizations adding mutual funds to their product line, and individual fund groups expanding the range of distribution channels they use.

The mutual fund industry has long done much distribution-related B2B e-business, but it has depended on expensive, hard to establish, proprietary links, and has been fragmented with several competing standards. Where fund companies interacted electronically with their major distributors, they used established, third-party facilities, such as Fund/SERV, as much as possible. These existing links, classic EDI (electronic data interchange), presume that big players will conduct large volumes of business on them, thus justifying the high fixed cost of set-up. As the industry has evolved toward more diffuse distribution channels, these existing EDI links have come under pressure to change.

In addition to many proprietary EDI links created to connect a particular fund group with a particular intermediary, there were three industry-wide links or groups of links in use in 2000.

1. *NSCC Fund/SERV.* The NSCC has provided fund-to-distributor connectivity since the late 1980s, and in 2000, connected all the major broker-distributed fund groups with the major brokerage firms. In recent years, both no-load fund groups, such as Vanguard, and other types of distributors, such as banks, had joined Fund/SERV to automate interactions. NSCC provided a wide range of mutual fund functions, discussed in Chapter 8, including account setup and maintenance; order entry and confirmation; commission payments; reconciliation of account information between fund and broker; and net settlement of cash flows between funds and brokers.

   In 1999, NSCC's use of the Internet for mutual funds was limited to newsletters, operational notices, and member statistics. The majority of NSCC Fund/SERV users continued to use traditional EDI links. However, beginning in February 2000, NSCC planned to give mutual fund companies the option to provide Mutual Fund Profile System (MFPS) data via its PCWeb Direct Internet service. (MFPS disseminates such information as fund prices, investment objectives, portfolio manager names, and distribution rates and dates.)

   A small number of firms, which the NSCC has referred to as "trade consolidators," had already established NSCC connectivity and were contracting with smaller players whose activity they processed into and from Fund/SERV. Much of the information was directed back to the smaller firms through web browser screens. One firm began selling software in 1999 that performs file transfers between core record keeping systems (401(k) or trust accounting systems) and NSCC. Northern Trust, for example, used this method to connect to Fund/SERV, avoiding the high development cost in creating its own interface. The software could be used by a broker, a trust, or a third-party administrator.

2. *Defined Contribution Plan Links.* Mutual funds provide one of the most common investment vehicles for defined contribution pension plans. Defined contribution pension record keepers process participant and plan sponsor transactions—contributions, distributions, transfers—and translate them into trades in the underlying funds. These trades must then be communicated to the funds' transfer agents for execution. In addition, the pension record keeper must receive information from the fund and transfer agent to ensure that its records are reconciled to those kept by the fund.

     Several proprietary networks have connected pension record keepers to mutual fund transfer agents. SunGard and PFPC each operated such a network, designed to supplement the record keeping software and services they provide. NSCC entered this arena in 1998 with its Defined Contribution Clearance and Settlement (DCC&S) system, created to provide the retirement community with a set of functions similar to those provided by Fund/SERV. As of 2000, this system was still in the early stages of adoption.

3. *Financial Advisor Linkage.* Financial advisors have taken on an increasingly important role in mutual fund distribution, in many cases, trading their clients' accounts directly. DST, the largest third-party transfer agent in the United States, created a file transfer system (Financial Advisor Network Mail) that electronically supports broker dealers, branch offices, and individual financial representatives and advisors. FAN Mail transmits customer account information on a daily basis, providing reps, planners, and advisors with current account information, and eliminating the need for manual data entry of printed confirmations and statements. Originally developed in 1996 on a proprietary network, the service was moved to the Internet in November 1997.

The common thread running throughout mutual fund distribution is connectivity, particularly via the Internet. In the B2C arena, fund companies seek the best way to bind their customers to them with their web offerings. In the B2B arena, fund companies seek to make themselves attractive to distribution partners by using connectivity to make themselves easier to deal with.

E-Business in Mutual Fund Manufacturing

As exciting as e-business developments in mutual fund distribution and service are, their potential impact is overshadowed by that of e-business in mutual fund manufacturing. Ask anyone in the industry what sells mutual funds. The exact answers will vary, but they will all fall along a continuum bounded at one end by "nothing but performance," and at the other end by "performance and (something else)." Performance, in this context, means more than just spectacular return numbers—it means successfully achieving the fund's investment objective. Thus Vanguard's index funds achieve excellent performance when they closely match their benchmarks with little cost drag, just as American Century's aggressive equity funds achieve excellent performance when they post big annual returns. However one defines fund performance, it is universally recognized as the key variable in fund sales. And it is in fund manufacturing that e-business transformations can affect this all-important performance variable.

Manufacturing, in the mutual fund context, encompasses all the functions required to make investment decisions, purchase and sell securities, and maintain and service portfolios—the topics of Chapters 5 through 7. This fund manufacturing component offers three major opportunities to benefit from e-business practices. First, as we saw in Chapter 5, analysts and portfolio managers for actively managed funds constantly gather and sift information as they search for investment opportunities. Electronic connectivity, especially via the Internet, is transforming the way researchers gather data, and fund managers must keep abreast of these developments or risk putting their analysts at an information disadvantage. Second, investment managers execute their portfolio management decisions by making trades. E-business practices, represented by the growth of electronic trading venues, are transforming the U.S. securities markets, threatening to severely penalize managers who cannot effectively keep up with the change. Finally, investment managers must collaborate with brokers, exchanges, custodians, clearing and settlement agents, and regulators as they complete the trade and settlement processes. By automating and streamlining the interactions required for this collaboration, e-business practices offer opportunities to affect the cost of the investment management back office.

E-Business in Investment Management Research and Analysis

Investment managers have been early adopters of electronic distribution methods for the delivery and receipt of research materials. One of the early features of Bloomberg's widely-used proprietary network facilitated the delivery of research notes and news from brokerage firms to their selected clients. By 2000, the typical manager tapped into multiple electronic sources to gather economic, political, and company-specific data to support internal research and portfolio decision-making. These electronic sources included:

- the Internet, which delivered integrated market data applications, such as Open Bloomberg and BridgeChannel, along with company web sites, market news and analysis sites, media sites, and broker sites;
- proprietary research distribution networks such as First Call, Research Direct, and Multex;
- proprietary market data services such as Reuters; and,
- internal research networks, based on groupware such as Lotus Notes or intranet technology.

By 2000, most brokers made their proprietary research available directly to clients through electronic means. This included services such as immediate e-mail alerts to research/news specifically requested by a client and online communication between a fund's manager and a broker's industry analysts. In 1999, Meridien, a research firm, noted that some investment managers were pushing this even further, demanding access to the underlying models used by analysts to forecast earnings.[27] This would allow the fund's analysts and portfolio managers to manipulate the models and test their own assumptions.

In 2000, some investment managers were experimenting with highly customized web-based software that filtered news feeds and charts, delivering to a manager only the information relating to his or her portfolio's holdings. While this type of product clearly addresses the information overload problem aggravated by the Internet's enormous reach, users still grappled with the challenge of designing filters that included valuable information while excluding noise. The firms that succeed in doing this, however, would put their analysts at the center of a vast electronic web of information sources.

Executing Trades

The growth of order management systems and automated trading has provided the richest illustration of e-business in the investment management manufacturing cycle. In the late 1990s, software developers were rapidly networking portfolio management and trading software programs through electronic messaging, data, and Internet links. The new links connected money managers electronically to broker dealers, alternative trading systems, custodians, clearinghouses, and others.

As Chapter 5 discussed, the execution of an investment decision begins when the portfolio manager submits an order to the firm's trading desk, which is responsible for managing the book of orders placed by the various portfolio managers. Traditionally, the portfolio manager submits the order ticket via telephone or a manually documented instruction. Introducing a trade order management system dramatically changes the investment decision execution process.

Using a trade order management system, portfolio managers generate an order ticket online based upon modeling, "what if?" scenarios, cash balance requirements, or other factors. Depending on the product being traded and the complexity of the order, the system can run a pre-trade compliance check and electronically deliver the ticket to the internal trading desk, which uses the system to help select the optimal trading venue. The system supports the trading desk's decision by revealing available markets, bids and offers, liquidity, and other information. Once the optimal venue has been selected, the order may be electronically submitted for execution. For example, Putnam has done this and has been described as "paperless up to the trader's desk."[28] (The Invesco Funds case described in Chapter 5 likewise featured the use of a trade order management system.)

In 1999, the Tower Group estimated that "about 50 percent of the buy-side industry . . . uses a paper-based method of trading and managing orders." They forecast this percentage to drop dramatically over the next few years, projecting that close to 70 percent of money managers would have implemented trade order management systems by 2002.[29] This has significant implications for e-business, since an asset manager must first automate its own internal trade order processes to facilitate connecting to counterparties. For the industry to achieve next day settlement of securities as projected in 2002, any asset manager with significant trade volume would have to have installed automated trade order management systems.

Equity securities trade in several venues, including exchange markets, electronic markets, over-the-counter markets, and alternative trading systems. Electronic communications networks (ECNs) for equity trading attracted much attention in the late 1990s, because of the potential advantages they offer, and because of the pressure they have put on the New York Stock Exchange and NASDAQ to change the way they do business. However, the trade execution cycle for most U.S. equity securities already relies almost entirely on electronic solutions. The NASDAQ Stock Market revolutionized securities trading in 1971 when it introduced the first electronic trading market for over-the-counter equity products. The New York Stock Exchange launched the Designated Order Turnaround (DOT) system in 1976. The system was enhanced to SuperDOT in 1984 and by 1998 handled about 80 percent of the orders sent to the exchange (equating to 48 percent of share volume).[30] The average order through SuperDOT was transmitted, executed, and reported back to the originating firm in 22 seconds.

Fixed-income securities were traded in a much more manual way in 2000. Depending upon the product, a fixed-income security could be traded over the counter, on an exchange, or via an alternative trading system. The usage of e-business solutions by these trading spaces varied substantially, but, in general, players in the industry were looking for more automation. In late 1999, several major institutional bond investors, such as Putnam, Alliance, and J.P. Morgan, joined forces to urge Wall Street firms to ease the currently thin trading conditions then affecting most sectors except Treasuries.[31] This group claimed to be actively exploring ways to shift a significant amount of their bond trading to online services, some of which already allowed large investors to trade directly with each other. Alliance, for example, did about 30 percent of its Treasury trades via TradeWeb, an electronic multi-dealer system that gave buy-side institutions access to the inventory of many dealers simultaneously.

The challenge in 2000 was to automate the trading of complex securities, such as swaps and other derivatives. In early 2000, the Tower Group described this situation: "In past years, the rate of straight-through processing has been inversely related to the sophistication of the traded asset. While processing of equity and simple fixed-income trades has improved considerably, automation rates of more complex instruments like derivatives and mortgage-backed securities have remained much lower."[32] Ultimately, however, the industry must move to electronic trading of all but the most unconventional issues.

In mid-2000, the exact shape of the upcoming transformation of the U.S. securities market forced by electronic trading remained unfathomable. That there would be a transformation, however, few questioned. Almost everyone's projected scenarios included widespread use of electronic trading networks, although the details of these scenarios varied widely. All would give investment managers increased control over the execution process. The buy-side trader would be able to select an online execution service based upon available liquidity, the timing of execution, and other factors. Compared to historical trading patterns, the new configuration would feature low cost, fast, and anonymous executions. The SEC has come down firmly on the side of this evolution—it has pushed the New York Stock Exchange to open its markets to electronic networks, and in 2000 began to investigate why the mutual fund industry hadn't already directed more order flow through ATSs.

Clearing and Settling Trades

Chapter 6 discussed the settlement process for fund managers. In 2000, many fund managers still performed parts of this process manually—they faxed trade information to their custodians, confirmed trades by examining reports and entering confirmations into a DTC terminal, and/or reconciled positions with the custodian by matching printed reports. In general, the more manual intervention this process requires, the greater the cost, and the higher the risk of error.

Several factors—the need to control costs, error reduction, and the move to T+1 settlement—have already pressured fund managers to install technologies to automate these post-execution processes. Fund managers have increased their use of electronic trade confirmation services (ETC), such as those offered by Thomson Financial's Oasys and Global Oasys products or DTC's TradeSuite product to communicate allocations (i.e., which funds get which fractions of a trade's total quantity) to broker dealers. To communicate with custodian banks, some money managers used electronic solutions based upon industry-standard protocols, such as SWIFT or ISITC.* Many firms, however, still used proprietary software unique to the custodian, requiring the investment manager to maintain a separate interface for each custodian bank with which it does business. As the twentieth century ended, the industry still had much opportunity to standardize and streamline these connections.

In 2000, the anticipated move to T+1 settlement was beginning to force many investment managers to install more automation of these post-trade processes, sooner rather than later. Although the SEC had not issued any firm deadline for the move by mid-2000, many in the industry believed that it could come as early as mid-2002. By that time, a fund manager of any size would have to be fully connected with e-business links to all its counterparties on the manufacturing side to be viable.

Opportunities and Challenges

The e-business revolution has presented both opportunities and challenges for all organizations wanting to compete in the investment management industry. Morgan Stanley Dean Witter summarized this good news/bad news phenomenon:

> *"In the end, not all asset management companies will survive...[but] for firms that have built a 'culture of excellence' over the years, have segmented their customers efficiently, built brand, and delivered performance, the ongoing opportunities to take market share have never been more significant."[33]*

While observers have generally agreed that the Internet and e-business connectivity will induce sea changes in the industry, they have reached no consensus about the exact strategies firms must pursue to be winners

---

* The SWIFT (Society for Worldwide Interbank Financial Telecommunications) protocol is used primarily for communications between brokers and custodians. The ISITC (Industry Standardization for Institutional Trade Communications Group) protocol is used primarily between asset managers and brokers.

instead of losers in the e-business economy. In mid-2000, argument and even controversy swirled around a number of major questions, such as:

- How large a role would financial portals and aggregators play in mutual fund distribution?
- To what extent would retail mutual fund investors move online for transactions?
- Would new technologies, such as wireless computing, change the degree and nature of investors' interactions with the funds' web sites?
- Could investment advice be effectively delivered electronically, and, if so, how? Would that help disintermediate retail mutual fund distribution?
- Would altogether new players (e.g., Yahoo!, Microsoft) win significant share of the mutual fund market?
- How quickly would alternative trading systems gain liquidity and offer viable alternatives to exchange markets?
- Would the industry succeed in its attempt to create universal standards and utility functions to automate trade and post-trade processing interactions?

While some commentators claimed to have answers to some of these questions, the vast majority of players in the industry recognized the fundamental uncertainties that remained. Other industries faced similar uncertainty. For example, observers of the retail products distribution industry watched eagerly to see whether the Amazon.com model (be huge and sell everything), the E-toys.com model (be super-specialized and be very good at it), or some combination of these would prevail.[34]

The mutual fund companies, by and large, have done the only thing they could do under the circumstances. They have experimented and tried various e-business approaches, different fund groups choosing different goals and paths to those goals. The industry has focused both attention and resources on e-business: a NICSA survey in late 1999 showed that 96 percent of fund companies would be increasing their Internet emphasis and spending in the next year.[35] While the patterns that would ultimately prove most successful remained to be established, most participants in the mutual fund industry were convinced that discovering those patterns was only a matter of time and effort.

CHAPTER 15
Going Abroad: Open-End Funds Outside the United States

Investors throughout the world share many of the same basic needs and goals as U.S. investors: a comfortable retirement, higher education for their children, and improved living standards. Like their U.S. counterparts, foreign investors are turning to mutual funds as a way to participate in growing securities markets in a diversified manner.

— *Investment Company Institute (1997)* [1]

The open-end mutual fund was an American invention, and it is within the U.S. financial services sector that open-end funds have played their greatest role, becoming the preferred method of savings for Americans. Since this book has focused on the U.S. fund industry, the term "mutual fund" in all the preceding chapters has meant the U.S. version—an open-end investment company registered with the SEC under the provisions of the Investment Company Act of 1940 and operated in accordance with that Act and its subsequent regulations. Mutual fund industries, however, have developed outside the United States as well. This chapter broadens the view of mutual funds, considering the open-end pooled investment vehicles that are managed and sold in other countries—what they have achieved and where the opportunities for further growth lie.

In the 1990s, open-end investment funds began to make significant inroads in many countries, although not to the degree or at the speed they did in the United States. Figure 1 shows the growth of mutual fund assets both in the U.S. and in the rest of the world during the seventeen years ending in 1999. During most of this period, the U.S. generally accounted for half or more of the world's total assets in open-end

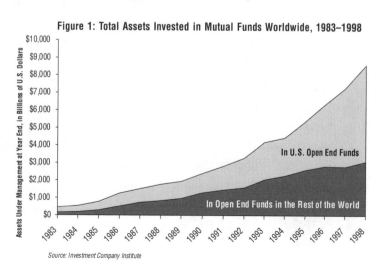

Figure 1: Total Assets Invested in Mutual Funds Worldwide, 1983–1998

In U.S. Open End Funds

In Open End Funds in the Rest of the World

Source: Investment Company Institute

funds, a proportion that grew to approach two-thirds in 1999. But the U.S. did not account for anything close to two-thirds of the world's investable assets—that figure was actually less than 20 percent in 1999. Mutual funds have been much more successful in capturing this investable wealth in the United States than in other countries.

This success has prompted a growing interest among U.S. mutual fund managers (and among big financial services firms in other nations, as well) in expanding to international markets. Today, many nations have the financial wherewithal to make large mutual fund investments, and, therefore, to generate significant revenues for firms managing, distributing, or servicing funds. Since mutual fund-like investment vehicles have not penetrated the financial markets of these nations to nearly the degree they have the United States, these markets are less saturated and offer more growth potential. And regulatory constraints on selling and operating mutual funds in various countries have been easing recently, at the same time that demographics have been raising the need for increased investment effectiveness, especially for retirement savings. Juxtaposed against a U.S. mutual fund market that many worry is rapidly approaching maturity, these factors—high potential, low penetration, and easing constraints—make foreign markets appear particularly attractive.

Areas of Opportunity

Not every part of the world presents a mutual fund opportunity. If individuals and institutions are to invest in mutual funds, they must first have assets available to invest. Resources available for investing vary widely across the globe. Figure 2 shows one measurement of this uneven distribution—the net domestic savings (NDS) for the year 1997. NDS measures how much of a year's economic output the inhabitants of a country or region have available to save or invest. It is calculated as the gross domestic product (GDP) minus consumption, including the consumption imputed in the depreciation of fixed capital. Since each country's net domestic savings relative to that of other countries changes slowly, the figures for 1997 are representative of most recent years. As Figure 2 shows, the wealth available for investing is concentrated among a few regions and countries.

- *Europe.* Wealth in Europe is concentrated among the developed nations of Western Europe, most of which are members of the European Monetary Union. The 23 percent of worldwide NDS that Europe represented in 1997 came mostly from seven countries: Germany, Italy, France, the United Kingdom, Spain, the Netherlands, and Belgium accounted for almost 85 percent of the European total.

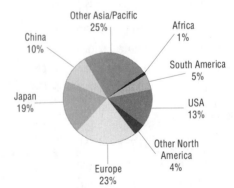

Figure 2:
Distribution of World Net Domestic Savings in 1997

Other Asia/Pacific 25%
China 10%
Japan 19%
Africa 1%
South America 5%
USA 13%
Other North America 4%
Europe 23%

- *The Asia/Pacific Region.* Two nations within the Asia/Pacific region—Japan and China—accounted for over 68 percent of the region's NDS in 1997. As in Europe, a handful of developed nations accounted for most of the remainder. Adding six more countries—South Korea, Indonesia, Thailand, India, Singapore, and Malaysia—accounts for over 90 percent of the region's total 1997 NDS.

- *South America and the Caribbean.* This region accounted for only 5 percent of the world's NDS in 1997, and two-thirds of that came from two countries, Brazil and Argentina. No other country in the region achieved an NDS in 1997 that constituted even one-half of 1 percent of the world total.

- *North America.* Within North America, the United States accounts for the lion's share of the savings—over 75 percent of the total among that continent's nations in 1997. Most of the rest was divided about equally between Canada and Mexico.

- *Africa.* Africa as a whole accounted for only slightly over 1 percent of the world's NDS, and no individual nation within Africa represented more than a few one-hundredths of a percent of the world total.

Other measures of wealth might change the relative positions of regions and countries slightly, but they would paint the same general picture. The United States, Japan, Western Europe, and a handful of developed countries elsewhere hold most of the world's investable wealth—and the potential for mutual fund investing. (China has wealth, as Figure 2 shows, but its Communist government makes it an unfriendly place for mutual funds, at least for the present.)

Figure 3 shows that the distribution of mutual fund assets does not track the distribution of wealth as measured by net domestic savings (and using other measures of investable wealth would show the similar patterns). The United States accounts for a far greater proportion of the world's open-end fund investments than its relative wealth would indicate. This reflects the particular popularity that mutual funds have enjoyed among American investors since the early 1980s. This also identifies the potential opportunity for mutual fund growth. What if the mutual fund industries in the other countries with significant wealth played as large a role as they do in the United States? The difference between the actual size of the industry and what it would have been at U.S. penetration rates forms the "mutual fund gap." Figure 4 shows one view of this gap for the most promising countries, using 1997 NDS as the normalizing factor.

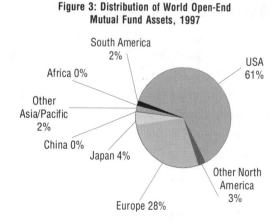

Figure 3: Distribution of World Open-End Mutual Fund Assets, 1997

South America 2%
Africa 0%
Other Asia/Pacific 2%
China 0%
Japan 4%
Europe 28%
USA 61%
Other North America 3%

Figure 4 dramatically illustrates what makes executives in U.S. fund firms so interested in global opportunities. If you believe that market saturation in the United States threatens the continuation of the amazing growth the U.S. industry has enjoyed over the past eighteen years, then the prospect of moving to less saturated markets is very attractive. And world financial markets appear far from saturated with mutual funds by U.S. standards.

Figure 4:
Estimate of Potential Additional Mutual Fund Penetration for Selected Countries

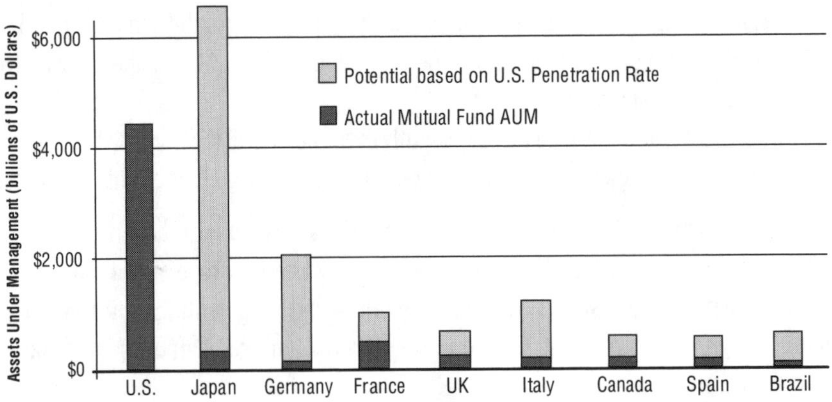

Note: Estimate of potential AUM based on 1997 assets and net domestic savings

Source: Investment Company Institute, World Bank

Open-End Funds Outside the U.S.

As Figure 1 shows, open-end funds outside the United States have grown in parallel with the U.S. industry. However, that growth has been concentrated in a relative handful of countries. Figure 5 shows the assets held in open-end funds at the end of 1998 for all those countries in which fund assets as measured by the ICI totaled the equivalent of at least US$100 billion. These nine countries accounted for over 90 percent of the world's total mutual fund assets under management.* A discussion of the eight countries outside the United States that account for most mutual fund assets illustrates the range of similarities and differences among non-U.S. mutual funds.

---

* Luxembourg in 1998 also had a robust mutual fund industry, but it was mostly in *offshore funds*; that is, funds intended for distribution in countries other than Luxembourg (which itself had a population of less than a half million).

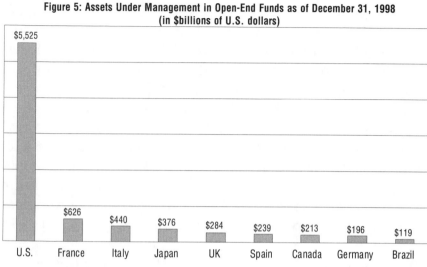

Figure 5: Assets Under Management in Open-End Funds as of December 31, 1998
(in $billions of U.S. dollars)

Source: Investment Company Institute

Europe

The developed countries of Western Europe, taken collectively, represent a pool of wealth that exceeds that of the United States. As of 2000, however, Europe remained a collection of smaller markets, rather than a single large market. The European Community has made efforts to establish a common market for mutual fund-like investments. In 1985, it passed the Undertakings on Collective Investments in Transferable Securities (UCITS) directive, permitting investment companies that register in one European country to sell shares in other European countries. In 2000, the European Parliament amended this directive to liberalize the rules about what types of securities UCITS could hold, making more funds eligible for cross-border sales.

These regulations, along with the introduction of the euro as a common currency, have fueled an expansion of cross-border fund sales, but in 2000 these remained small by comparison to fund sales within particular countries. Cross-border mutual fund sales were still inhibited by marketing issues (differing advertising regulations, for example), country-specific tax and reporting rules, and the difficulty of getting into closed distribution channels controlled by national banks and insurance companies.[2] To understand the European mutual fund market, one must examine it country by country.

- *France.* France has for some time had the second largest mutual fund industry in the world, trailing only the United States. Open-end funds first appeared in France in 1964 (although closed-end funds, never very popular, had been launched as early as 1945), with laws that created SICAVs (*societes d'investissement capital variable*). These correspond most closely to U.S. open-end funds—they are corporations with directors and shareholders, they continually issue new shares as needed, and they are bound to redeem upon demand. In 1967, France added a second type of fund, the FCP (*fonds communs de placements*), which was originally used only to support employer-sponsored plans, but later opened to direct investment by individuals. While the two types of vehicle provide essentially the same thing to investors, their structure and regulation differ, and in 1999 SICAVs were still much more popular, accounting for all but a few percent of the French total.[3]

Total assets at the end of 1998 totaled US$626 billion. As in the United States, French fund sales have responded strongly to conditions in the financial markets. Flows of money into funds were strong in the early 1990s as high short-term interest rates made money market funds attractive; languished in the mid-1990s as interest rates fell and the bond market crashed; and regained strength in the late 1990s as the capital markets recovered. Historically, the French tastes in funds have tended toward fixed-income investments—in 1998, the French fund industry's assets comprised 32 percent money market funds, 26 percent bond funds, 25 percent balanced funds, and only 18 percent equity funds.

Fund distribution in France lies primarily in the hands of the French banks. In 1998, 74 percent of French fund sales occurred through banks. The French Post Office, insurance companies, and independent asset managers each shared similar proportions of the remaining 26 percent.

- *Italy*. In a 1999 assessment, State Street Corporation's Global Strategy & Development department characterized Italy as "the hottest place in Europe for mutual funds."[4] In the previous year, the Italian industry had grown at the rate of 100 percent, doubling to the equivalent of almost US$440 billion under management. State Street also forecast that Italy's very high net savings rate of 14.7 percent of gross disposable income would fuel continued mutual fund growth at over 20 percent per year for the next few years. In 1999, this produced a net inflow of about US$100 billion, compared to about $350 billion of net flows to U.S. open-end funds for that year.

  Italy also has two types of open-end funds. FCIs (*fondo comune di investimento*) resemble the French FCPs, but in Italy these are the most common fund structure. An FCI must be managed by an SGR (*societa di gestione collettiva del risparmio*), a company organized and authorized to manage collective savings, and the Italian equivalent of the U.S. management company. Italy also allows SICAVs (in Italian, *societi di investimento a capitale variabile*), which, like their French counterparts, are corporations formed solely to hold transferable securities, resembling U.S. registered investment companies.

  Banks dominate the distribution of funds in Italy even more strongly than they do in France, with Italian banks accounting for about 90 percent of fund sales. Foreign firms attempting to enter the Italian market have had to work through these banks via joint ventures, alliances, or acquisitions. Italian investors resemble French investors in their preference for fixed-income products—in early 1999 the investment allocation for Italian funds was approximately 55 percent in bond funds, 18 percent in money market funds, 8 percent in balanced funds, and only 19 percent in equity funds.

"WHAT'S IN A MUTUAL FUND'S NOM, NAMEN, NOMBRE?"
by Stephen Garmhausen, American Banker, December 18, 1998

Psssst. Wanna buy a *beleggingsmaatschappij*? You might if you lived in the Netherlands, where the term means "mutual fund." If you were Greek, you might sock some of your money away in an *amivea kefalea*. French? You'd put your francs in a—take a deep breath—*societe d'investissement collective a capital variable* (SICAV, for short).

Spurred by the privatization of pension systems, the era of retail mutual funds is dawning in Europe, just as the region's march toward political and economic union kicks into high gear. But as Europeans warm to mutual funds, they have discovered a little problem: The region has even more terms to describe the things than it has languages. Calling Europe a mutual fund Tower of Babel might be overstating it—but probably not by much.

"A lot of people get terribly confused, because there is a lot of loosely used vocabulary," said Diana Mackay, whose job as European business development director for Lipper Analytical Services requires her to try to keep the Euro-fund lexicon straight.

The list is rife with terms that are so long and complicated that they must be crunched into acronyms such as SICAV (France), OEIC (the United Kingdom), and FIAMM (Spain).

The good old American term "mutual fund" is widely understood in the old countries. But the Europeans, ever protective of their national identities, stubbornly cling to their own terms. The results can be embarrassing.

Take the term OEIC (open-ended investment company). Adopted in the United Kingdom in the early 1990s, it describes a new kind of mutual fund designed to be sold throughout Europe. The problem is that the word—pronounced kind of like the noise pigs make—is also a slur used to dismiss a person of no importance. Investment companies tried to change the term to "investment fund," but backed down after an outcry from Britain's investment trust industry, which thought the term was too close to its own. (Investment trusts in the United Kingdom are what Americans know as closed-end mutual funds.)

Thus, OEIC appears to be here to stay. Also likely to be around for a while: the Italian *fondo comune di investimento*, or FCI. The Spanish commonly refer to a *fondo de inversion mobiliaria* as a FIM, unless of course they are referring to a money market mutual fund, which is a *fondo de inversion mobiliaria en activos del mercado monetario*, or FIAMM.

The German penchant for creating long, difficult words by smooshing smaller ones together is evident in their mutual fund terminology: *Investmentfonds* encompasses mutual funds aimed at big institutional buyers (*spezialfonds*) and at individual *volk* (*publikumsfonds*).

U.S. fund companies vying for a piece of the action in Europe say finding the words that will ring a bell with the locals is half the battle.

"You have to get the terminology 100% correct in each country," said Jan Nyholm, a Luxembourg-based executive with Fidelity Investments, which has $8 billion in assets under management in Europe. "Otherwise people will not know what you are talking about."

That is likely to change over time as a handful of terms gain wide currency. Because France has Europe's longest tradition of mutual funds, the French SICAV is widely recognized throughout the region. The term "unit trust" registers particularly well with English speakers. Another important term is UCITS, or, if you have some time on your hands, "undertakings for collective investments in transferable securities." UCITS are funds that adhere to rules laid down in 1985 by the European Commission so that they can be sold throughout Europe.

Most of the region's 15,500 mutual funds now have this "European passport" structure. Sadly, even those without the passport are often referred to incorrectly as UCITS. (By the way, if you guessed that an OEIC is, in fact, a UCIT, there may be a job for you across the pond.) But when it comes down to the individual countries, nationalistic impulses are likely to keep terms like the Greek *amivea kefalea* around for a long time. That may prove perilous. After all, a slight misspelling of that particular term will change its meaning from "mutual fund" to "open-ended big nose."

Reprinted with permission from American Banker.

- *The United Kingdom.* Unit trusts and OEICs (open-ended investment companies) make up the U.K. equivalents of U.S. mutual funds. A unit trust is simply a pooled investment vehicle that operates similarly to a U.S. open-end fund—its investors hold shares in the trust that must be redeemable on demand. (Closed-end fund equivalents in the U.K. are called investment trusts.) In 1997, the U.K. passed legislation that created OEICs, a version of the open-end fund that meets the European Union's UCITS rules, and that uses the corporate structure common to U.S. and Continental European funds.

  The key difference between OEICs and unit trusts from the investor's point of view is single pricing. Most unit trusts have a buying (or offer) price and a selling (or bid) price with a spread of about 5 percent between them, analogous to U.S. load funds' NAV versus public offering price. OEICs are quoted at a single price (NAV), and any purchase or sale charges (i.e., commissions) are shown separately.[5] The net effect for the investor is much the same. As of the end of 1999, however, OEICs had only grown to account for 14.5 per cent of U.K. funds. As in the United States, investors may purchase these as after-tax investments, or may use them as the investments in tax-incented savings plans, notably PEPs (personal equity plans) and ISAs (individual savings accounts). These tax-advantaged plans accounted for about a quarter of U.K. funds at the end of 1998.[6]

  By late 1999, unit trusts and OEICs held the equivalent of almost US$300 billion under management, making the U.K. the fifth or sixth largest market for mutual funds in the world—depending on how you count Luxembourg. The industry is much more fragmented than in France and Italy—independent asset managers, banks, insurers, and brokers all participate in fund management and distribution. The top ten managers control only 40 percent of the market, and almost thirty organizations each have at least a 1 percent market share. During the late 1990s, about 20 percent of fund sales were made directly by the fund company to the investor, with various intermediaries, including financial advisers and brokers, accounting for most of the rest.

  British investors' tastes in funds run very heavily toward equities, with almost 84 percent of the value of fund assets at the end of 1999 being held in equity funds. Bond funds represented about 8 percent of the industry total, and mixed or balanced funds held most of the rest. U.K. money market fund assets were negligible, accounting for less than 1 percent of assets under management. Investors in the U.K. have viewed mutual funds primarily as long-term investment vehicles.

- *Germany.* Germany displays one of the largest gaps between wealth and actual mutual fund penetration of all countries. This can be attributed to the strong conservatism of German investors, who have traditionally favored savings instruments such as CDs and passbook accounts. It also reflects the fact that the German government has provided no tax-advantaged savings vehicle with which mutual funds could be used, i.e., nothing like U.S. IRAs or 401(k)s or UK PEPs and ISAs. As a result, the total in German open-end funds only approached US$300 billion at end of 1999, plus another US$100 billion in Luxembourg-domiciled funds owned by German investors.

  German retail mutual funds, or *publikumsfonds*, are managed by investment management companies, most of which are the subsidiaries of banks or insurance companies. Banks dominate fund distribution, with a 95 percent market share. About half of the 1999 *publikumsfonds* assets were in equity funds, with 22 percent in bond funds, 13 percent in money market funds, and the remainder in mixed funds. Offshore funds, primarily Luxembourg domiciled, distributed in Germany broke down similarly among asset types.[7]

Some reports of collective funds in Germany also mention *spezialfonds*, or institutional funds. These funds, which held almost US$500 billion in assets at the end of 1999, resemble not U.S. institutional mutual funds so much as they do bank trust funds or insurance company separate accounts. They are not sold to individuals, but are mostly used as the investment vehicles for pension plans.

- *Spain*. Spain's mutual fund landscape shares many of the features of France and Italy: domination by banks which account for 90 percent of the market; a strong taste for fixed-income investments (less than 30 percent in equity funds); and rapid recent growth of 27 percent annually between 1994 and 1998.[8] In late 1999, Spanish funds held the equivalent of U.S. $171 billion under management.

Spanish open-end funds are called FIMs (*fondos de inversion mobilaria*) and come in several flavors, depending on the mix of assets they hold in their portfolios. Funds holding 100 percent bonds are *renta fijas*, those holding mostly equities are *renta variables*, and there are two intermediate stages as well. Money market funds are known as FIAMMs (*fondos de inversion en activos del mercado monetario*). As in most countries, closed-end type funds exist, but command only a fraction of the assets that open-end funds do.

Japan

Japan represents the single greatest plum in the eyes of the world's mutual fund managers. With the second largest economy in the world, and a population conditioned to save as much as 20 percent of its income as compared to under 4 percent for the United States, Japan has enormous potential for mutual fund investment. As of 2000, actual mutual fund penetration was miniscule—about US$500 billion, or less than 4 percent of personal financial assets as compared to 23 percent in the United States.[9] A Japanese mutual fund industry that was as successful as the U.S. industry in capturing share of wealth would be a giant.

A variety of reasons may account for this minor role the Japanese mutual fund industry has played so far. The considerable problems of the Japanese economy and stock market in the 1990s have clearly contributed, as evidenced by the increases in mutual fund sales once the economy began to rebound in the late 1990s.[10] Distribution has played a role. Until recently, only securities companies—that is, brokers—could distribute funds in Japan. This inhibited fund sales because of the limited networks these companies could muster, and because of Japanese investors' generally negative perceptions of brokers.[11] Finally, there is the "Mrs. Watanabe" factor as described by *The Economist*:

> The usual explanation for this lack of adventure is that Mrs. Watanabe, the archetypical house-wife who holds the family purse strings, has been averse to risk, especially since the stock market bubble burst in 1990.[12]

The results have been a track record of incredibly low returns for the Japanese saver, and a Japanese mutual fund industry best described as anemic.

The Japanese fund industry began in 1951 with the passage of the Securities Investment Trust Law. This act authorized the creation of investment trusts, structures similar to UK unit trusts, which were formed under a trust contract and had a limited lifespan. This legislation was tuned from time to time over the following forty-nine years, most notably as part of the "Big Bang," the reform of the Japanese financial services industry in the late 1990s. In 1998, the Securities Investment Trust Law was amended to provide for a number of reforms, including, among other things, a fund structure similar to the U.S. registered investment companies, the EU SICAVs, and the UK OEICs—the corporation that exists solely to be a pooled investment vehicle. As of mid-2000, however, funds of this structure were too new to have tallied any appreciable assets.

The Big Bang reforms also changed the rules for distribution of Japanese funds. Until this change, only securities firms could sell investment trusts, so distribution was limited to networks of brokers. The reforms opened up the distribution channels and liberalized rules concerning investment managers as well, opening the door for foreign firms to play a larger role in the industry. Like Germany, Japan has had no tax-advantaged savings vehicle with which investors could use mutual funds, but this was expected to change once the Diet approved the introduction of a 401(k)-like savings plan, perhaps in 2001.

Japanese investment trusts fall into two broad categories: stock investment trusts that can hold both stocks and bonds and bond investment trusts that can hold only bonds and other fixed-income securities. Seventy percent of trust assets were held in bond trusts in early 1999, but the bias toward fixed-income securities was even stronger than this proportion indicates. Of the securities held by all Japanese investment trusts at that time, only 13 percent were equities—even the stock investment trusts held over 50 percent fixed-income securities, reflecting the extreme conservatism of Japanese investors.[13]

Canada

Canada exemplifies, even more than the United States, how a mutual fund industry can be driven by retirement savings. At the end of 1999, about 70 percent of the US$250 billion in Canadian mutual funds was held in RRSPs (Registered Retirement Savings Plans), which resemble U.S. 401(k) plans. As a result of this heavy use of mutual funds as a retirement savings vehicle, 40 percent of Canadian households owned mutual funds, a figure second only to the United States at 48 percent[14] Canadian investors shared the conservatism of European and Japanese investors, however. Despite the heavy use of mutual funds for retirement savings, equity funds represented less than half (48 percent) of the total assets under management, with bond funds at 40 percent and money market funds at 12 percent of the total.

While there were over ninety fund companies in Canada in 2000, the top ten accounted for about 60 percent of the market. The majority of the industry's assets were managed by independent companies, with bank-associated fund groups in second place. These independent companies typically distributed via networks of brokers and personal financial planners, sometimes proprietary. Investor's Group, for example, the largest

Canadian fund company with US$26 billion under management at the end of 1999, deployed a force of almost 4,000 representatives to sell its products. Banks sold their funds primarily through their branch networks, and these two channels accounted for the lion's share of fund distribution.

Brazil

The Brazilian mutual fund industry expanded rapidly in the 1990s to crack the US$100 billion mark in 1996, and hit US$120 billion in 1999. Brazilian funds have been offered primarily by banks to relatively affluent individual investors ("Group A," the 5 percent of Brazil's population who earned more than US$45,000 per year). In 1999, only 8 percent of the value of Brazilian fund industry's assets were held in equity funds, with 60 percent in bond funds, 25 percent in mixed funds, and 7 percent in money market funds. In reality, however, these Brazilian funds were almost all money market funds by U.S. standards, whatever their nominal label. The maturity of the funds' fixed-income holdings of all types all averaged 60 days or less. Because of Brazil's experience with very high inflation rates in the past, all bonds were short term—long-term financing instruments simply did not exist.[15] Mutual funds for Brazilians have been largely a means of earning higher returns on short-term investments, the only type considered reasonably safe given Brazil's history of inflation.

While several dozen other countries have more or less well developed mutual fund industries, none are as big as the ones described here, and none exceeded US$100 billion in 1999. Collectively, the world mutual fund industry totaled just under US$9 trillion in assets under management at the end of 1998, of which the United States plus the eight countries discussed above accounted for slightly over $8 trillion.

The Opportunities and Challenges for U.S. Fund Companies

Given the two big pools of wealth in Europe and Japan, and the relative underpenetration of mutual funds into each, it is no wonder that many U.S. fund industry leaders believe that the best growth opportunities in the early twenty-first century lie abroad. Demographic and financial trends have combined to motivate investors worldwide to change their approach to savings and investment. As *The Wall Street Journal* put it, "falling bond yields, the realization that aging populations make pension cuts inevitable, high profile privatizations, and a bull market chugging along in the background," all have been pushing investors to include more equities in their mix, often via mutual funds.[16]

The literature discussing global opportunities frequently features assessments that the fund industry in Japan, Western Europe, or in some other country, currently stands where the U.S. industry stood ten, fifteen, or twenty years earlier.[17] Perhaps the single biggest factor prompting this comparison has been the growing realization in many parts of the world that individual savings must play a much larger role in the future in funding retirements. This shift began to occur in the United States in the 1980s, and IRA and defined contribution plan investments have fueled much of the expansion of the U.S. mutual fund industry. Many believe that the retirement savings gap will precipitate a similar impetus to mutual fund investing in other countries during the first five to fifteen years of this century.

Figure 6 illustrates this retirement savings gap for selected countries. Actuarial calculations show the assets that should currently be on-hand to produce the income needed to fund the country's retirements, given demographic trends, projected returns on investments, and standards for retirement income needs, e.g., annual retirement income should equal 60 percent of the average of the last five years' income. This calculation gives a figure of almost $19.5 trillion for the United States, for example. As Figure 6 shows, in no country do public and private institutionalized retirement plans come near to covering this need. Social security plans—that is, government provided pension plans (whatever their labels in each country)—all have negative present values, meaning that they would require additional infusions of capital just to fund existing commitments. Private plans—for example, corporate plans—cover only a fraction of this total requirement. That leaves the retirement savings gap.

Figure 6: The Retirement Gap in 1998 for Selected Countries (Figures in U.S. $billions)

	U.S.	Japan	Germany	France	U.K.	Canada
Assets Required to Fund Retirement	19,479	15,300	6,851	4,244	3,015	1,235
Sources of Retirement Income:						
Net Value of Social Security	(409)	(1,458)	(1,333)	(1,239)	(317)	(446)
Private Pension Assets	5,200	3,100	310	95	1,015	599
Retirement Gap	**14,688**	**13,658**	**7,874**	**5,388**	**2,317**	**1,082**
Household Savings	16,208	4,717	2,446	2,095	1,691	269
Coverage of Gap	110%	35%	31%	39%	73%	25%

Source: Bernstein Research

In the United States, this gap was more than covered in 1998 by the $16 trillion pool of household savings, of which mutual funds constituted about one-quarter. In no other country shown does household savings cover the gap. Historically, citizens of Japan, Germany, France, the U.K., and many other nations have devoted their personal savings to conservative, fixed-income vehicles because they counted on their employers and governments to provide the foundation for their retirement needs. Demographics—specifically, aging populations that make social security-like schemes almost impossible to finance—are forcing governments around the world to recognize that individual, private savings must become part of the solution. As a result, many countries—Japan and Germany, for example—have recently adopted or are in the process of adopting tax-advantaged schemes resembling 401(k) or IRA programs.

Were the citizens of the five countries shown in Figure 6 to use mutual fund investments to close their retirement gap to the same extent that the United States has done, this would represent an immediate demand for almost US$1.5 trillion additional in funds. In light of this, the assessment of one Scudder Kemper executive appears easily justified: "It's in the international markets, for all the companies, where the growth opportunities lie. That's where everyone is putting a stake in the ground."[18] But that still leaves two big questions—where and how to best drive that stake?

The Opportunity Question—Europe or Japan?

No one disagrees that Europe and Japan constitute the two greatest areas of opportunity for mutual fund growth over the next decade. Industry commentators do disagree, however, on where the most promising immediate opportunity lies. In a nutshell, the argument goes something like this. Japan possesses, in a single, homogeneous market, an enormous pool of wealth that might be converted to funds, but cultural and structural impediments may make that conversion a long, slow process. Europe's market, while slightly smaller, and still fragmented across multiple countries, may be easier to penetrate in the near term, especially for outsiders.

- *Japan.* Japan's great attraction stems from the huge pool of wealth currently invested in low-interest deposit accounts and certificates of deposit. In 2000 and 2001, for example, over US$1 trillion of that pool held in ten-year Postal Savings certificates was due to mature, facing Japanese investors with the need to reinvest it in an environment in which current deposit interest rates top out below 1 percent.[19] In early 2000, both current and prospective players in the Japanese fund industry awaited with great anticipation the disposition of this *tsunami* of money.

   In addition, several factors that have inhibited the Japanese fund industry in the past were being mitigated in 2000. Big Bang regulation had broken the securities dealers' monopoly on fund distribution and eased the sale of foreign funds in Japan. In 1999, the Japanese stock market appeared to be finally recovering after a ten-year period of dreadful performance, making equity investing, a driver of mutual fund investing, more attractive to Japanese citizens than it had been since the days of the "Bubble Economy" in the 1980s. And the Japanese government was close to giving the public a tax-advantaged retirement savings vehicle, similar to the U.S. 401(k) that has had such a large effect on the American mutual fund industry. Some saw in these factors a parallel to the United States in the early 1980s and projected a Japanese reallocation of wealth into mutual funds similar to that of the U.S. experience.[20]

   In 1999 and 2000, mutual fund executives, consultants, and researchers worried about how long it would take before this might happen. The cultural reluctance of Japanese investors to try something that they perceive as risky and unfamiliar could make mutual fund penetration to U.S. levels a fifteen to twenty year process. The industry consulting firm Cerulli, in particular, has been bearish on Japanese opportunities for U.S. fund companies. In Cerulli's view, the innate conservatism of Japanese investors will be overcome only slowly, and a fund manager attempting to penetrate the Japanese market must be prepared to make an expensive, long-term commitment to investor education.[21] Nevertheless, such fund powers as Fidelity, Goldman Sachs, Invesco, and Merrill Lynch were by 1999 aggressively and successfully pursuing fund sales in Japan.[22]

- *Europe*. Europe in 2000 taken as a whole approached Japan—and the United States—in terms of wealth available for fund investing, but for fund investing, Europe could not yet be taken as a whole. Despite the euro, the UCITS laws and the EU's efforts to foster cross-border trade, as of 2000 European country borders had not yet become transparent to fund marketers. Different countries still displayed different approaches to distribution, usually dominated by local financial institutions, e.g., the banks in Germany and Italy. Different countries' populations still displayed cultural differences in their approach to investing, such as the French preference for money market investments versus the British preferences for equities. And there was still the matter of taxes.

  Historically, European tax laws have put offshore funds at a disadvantage relative to funds managed by firms within the particular country. In short, the investor in a given country was likely to pay more in taxes, either directly (e.g., in the form of income tax on dividends) or indirectly (e.g., in the form of differential tax levied at the fund or investment level) on an offshore fund than he or she would pay on a domestic fund pursuing the same investment strategy. For example, Italy levies taxes on income and capital gains distributions from offshore funds but not on those from domestic funds held by its residents.

  PricewaterhouseCoopers, commenting in 1997 on European mutual fund tax laws, summed up the situation: "If one were to generalize (and we hesitate to do so) on post tax yields delivered by funds, it would be that local funds are rarely beaten where they are locally invested."[23]

  These cultural, distribution, and tax differences have inhibited the cross-border sales of mutual funds. Fund companies have not been able to attack the European market simply by setting up offshore funds in Luxembourg or Ireland and selling them to investors in Germany, France, Italy, the U.K., and so on. Nor could the manager of a fund in one of these countries—for instance Italy—readily sell that fund to investors in another country, such as Germany. While there has been some success with offshore funds, as of 2000 most sales went to funds organized and managed within the countries in which their investors lived. For the fund companies, this fragmentation reduced the economies of scale and the profitability they might otherwise have achieved. In 1998, for example, the average European fund was one-eighth the size in assets under management of the average U.S. fund.[24] While many observers believe that the EMU and euro will reduce the cross-border barriers, the question remains as to how long this might take.

  Despite these challenges, many believed in 2000 that Europe stood on the brink of a fund explosion. Assets under management in funds in Western Europe had doubled during five years from 1992 to 1997, and Morgan Stanley Dean Witter forecast in 1998 that US$13 trillion would flow into the European equity markets, much of it via mutual funds, by 2010.[25] The head of FEFSI, the European equivalent of the ICI, has wagered his ICI counterpart that the European fund industry will eclipse the U.S. industry within twenty-five years.[26] And U.S. fund managers have flocked to Europe—by 2000 virtually every large U.S. fund manager had established a presence ranging from distribution agreements with local firms to on-the-ground organic operations.

The Strategy Question—Organic Growth, Alliance, or Acquisition?

Once a fund company has decided to attack a particular foreign market, it must decide on the strategy to pursue in doing so. It has three basic options.

1. *Establish its own presence in the market and strive for organic growth.*

   The most conservative organizations attack a market by setting up shop themselves in that market and then growing as circumstances permit. This allows them to make expenditures as they feel the market potential justifies and relieves them of dependency upon any partner. Not surprisingly, Vanguard has pursued this route exclusively as it has moved into Australia and Europe in the late 1990s and early 2000s.

   This approach does not appeal to an organization in a hurry, however. Penetrating distribution channels dominated by local firms, e.g., banks in Europe and securities dealers in Japan, means a slow, difficult process of chipping away to grow market share. Fidelity, for example, spent $100 million in advertising alone in Europe during the 1990s, but still had only a fraction of the European fund market, and its European fund assets were still dwarfed by those of its U.S. funds.[27] A Fidelity director described the notion that American companies could quickly establish themselves and become dominant in Europe as "naivete."[28]

2. *Establish an alliance with a local player.*

   Establishing an alliance represents something of a compromise between the slow but controlled organic growth strategy and the quick but risky acquisition. An alliance can mean anything from an agreement to cooperate in marketing, distribution, or other operations, to a formal joint venture between two firms that creates a new legal entity. The different approaches that Alliance Capital Management and Putnam took to penetrating the Italian market illustrate this range of choices. Alliance entered into an agreement with the Eptaconsors banking consortium to sell Alliance products under the Epta brand name. Putnam established a joint venture, of which it owns 20 percent, with banking firm Gruppo Bipop to distribute Putnam funds in Italy. Putnam's approach took longer and cost more, but Alliance lost the ability to sell under its own brand name.[29]

   While alliances can get a firm into a market quickly, they do have their drawbacks. For one thing, when a manager from one country strikes an agreement with an established distributor in another, the lion's share of the revenue may end up going to that distributor, an arrangement unsatisfying over the long term. And the partners may change their business strategy over time—especially if one of them is acquired—invalidating the assumptions that originally underlaid the alliance. A Cerulli study of cross-border joint ventures noted that "a joint venture is like a dating arrangement that will either end in marriage or separation," with more than half of the ventures they studied ultimately being dissolved.[30]

3. *Acquire a firm already established in the target market.*

Acquiring an established firm may be the fastest way for a fund manager to gain a foothold within a given market, and it certainly controls many of the uncertainties associated with joint ventures. This strategy has two negative aspects, however: expense and risk. The expense drawback is straightforward—the acquiring firm must produce cash or equity up front to effect the transaction. And all acquisitions run the risk that they will fail, to a greater or lesser degree, to realize the results intended, often as a result of inability of the acquiring and acquired organizations to come together effectively. As an illustration of this, consider the case of Investment Advisors, Inc. (IAI). In 1985, Dain Rauscher sold Minneapolis-based IAI to a British firm, which, after further merger and acquisition, ended up being Lloyds TSB Group PLC, a leading U.K. bank. Everything was fine until early 1997, when IAI's CEO decided to retire and Lloyds mishandled the succession. Lloyds' management in London hesitated for a year to either confirm the outgoing CEO's choice or impose their own, during which time "people took sides and built grudges," according to former employees.[31] Over the next three years both talent and clients eroded steadily as Lloyds unsuccessfully tried different approaches to settle the waters, including four different CEOs over one eight month period.[32] As a result of these troubles, IAI's assets under management declined from a high of $17 billion (about $2 billion in mutual funds) in 1997 to less than $3 billion ($400 million in funds) in 2000, a staggering erosion of over 80 percent.[33] And by the end of 2000, IAI was dead—the remaining fragments sold piecemeal to various parties. While IAI is an extreme case, it is not unique. Cautionary examples abound to illustrate how difficult it can be to successfully manage an investment management company acquisition, especially a cross-border one.

These three strategies are not mutually exclusive. In its *Tomorrow's Leading Investment Managers* study, PricewaterhouseCoopers found that many of the participating firms planned hybrid strategies, taking different approaches in different countries.[34] Figure 7 shows the distribution of these strategies. Alliance Capital Management, for example, has pursued a variety of strategies in addition to distribution agreements with local partners such as the Italian banking consortium. At the end of 1998, Alliance offered funds in developing

Figure 7: Distribution of Intended Strategies for International Expansion among Asset Management Firms

Strategy	America	Europe	Asia
Acquisition	34%	30%	20%
Startup Development	63%	53%	40%
Alliance	61%	57%	50%
Hybrid	40%	40%	40%

Source: *PwC Tomorrow's Leading Investment Managers Study*, 1999

countries such as Brazil, Egypt, and Turkey through subsidiaries, some wholly-owned and some joint ventures. In other countries, such as the U.K., Singapore, Japan, and Luxembourg, Alliance had established its own operations. Alliance's CEO described their strategy as one of establishing their own operations where feasible, entering joint ventures "where we think we're incapable of doing it on our own, or where the cost of doing it on our own looks too steep," and making acquisitions when the right opportunity came along.[35]

These opportunities are not limited to U.S. fund managers looking abroad. While this discussion has mostly focused on opportunities from the U.S. point of view, the street goes both ways. John Bogle, in a 1999 speech at an International Bar Association meeting, pointed out that the U.S. market has been fair game for foreign asset managers as well:

> *However, it is hardly a takeover of the rest of the world's investment managers by the powerhouse firms in the United States. To the contrary, some of the very largest acquisitions turn that idea upside down: the takeover of Bankers Trust by Deutsche Bank (a combined $380 billion of assets managed); of Wells Fargo Nikko by Barclays Global Investors ($600 billion); of Kemper/Scudder by Zurich ($280 billion); and of Brinson by Swiss Bank Corp. ($380 billion). Total assets managed by these four merged firms alone approach $2 trillion. For better or worse, we are truly living in the age of the giant global manager.[36]*

Ultimately, the mutual fund industry may follow the path of many older industries, becoming dominated by multinational firms that both manufacture and distribute across the globe.

CHAPTER 16

Going Forward: Issues and Challenges

The mutual fund industry has won the war for the hearts, minds, and monies of the vast investing public, but now the occupied territory must be defended, and the fronts are immense.

— *Bernstein Research (2000)*[1]

This final chapter examines a handful of key issues and challenges that the mutual fund industry faces as it moves into the twenty-first century. Previous chapters have touched at least obliquely on these—the question of industry maturity, the continuing debate about the level of fees, and the fundamental disagreement over the value of active management and why investors pursue it. This chapter addresses each of these issues directly, attempting to assess what impact they might have on the industry's future. Of course, they all require the passage of time before definitive answers arrive, but their consideration today should contribute to an understanding of how the industry might evolve.

The Mutual Fund Industry in the Life Cycle

In mutual fund industry conferences and publications in 1999 and 2000, speakers and writers repeatedly raised the specter of industry maturity as a threat looming over the prosperity that fund companies had enjoyed over the past twenty years. "Signs of mutual fund fatigue are popping up everywhere," said the *New York Times* in January 2000.[2] "Investors are losing their appetite for mutual funds," began a *Business Week* story the same month.[3] The fund business "is heading quickly toward middle age," said *Barron's* three months later.[4] Speakers at ICI and NICSA conferences around the same time predicted slowing sales, consolidations, and even layoffs in the near- to intermediate-term future.[5] All these observations and predictions shared a common theme—the mutual fund industry, after twenty glorious years of unparalleled growth, was about to mature, and therefore enter a period of permanently slower growth.

These claims that the mutual fund industry was maturing implicitly referred to a model of the life cycle through which an industry progresses. Figure 1 shows the general form of this cycle, in its normal depiction as a pattern of sales volume over time. The cycle comprises five distinct stages:

1. *Development.* A new product emerges and a handful of firms try to develop a market for it. The firms in this market are mostly entrepreneurial, privately held, and financed with founders' money. Sales volumes, both for individual firms and for the industry as a whole, are low.

2. *Growth*. The product catches on with its targeted consumers. Sales grow at an increasing rate, and, because supply is still limited as compared to demand, profit margins are high. This makes the market for the product attractive enough to start drawing an increasing number of new firms into it. Firms in the industry become attractive to investors.

3. *Expansion*. The sales growth rate remains high, although not as high as during the growth phase. The rate of entry of new firms levels off. A few large firms begin to dominate the market. Products, prices, and profits become stable.

4. *Maturity*. The product has achieved full penetration within its target market, and the growth rate of sales becomes comparable to that of the gross domestic product or broad market indices such as the S&P 500. The number of firms in the industry declines as weaker competitors are driven out. Price competition becomes important as the product becomes a commodity.

5. *Decline*. Substitute products emerge and take market share. Sales growth becomes flat or negative.

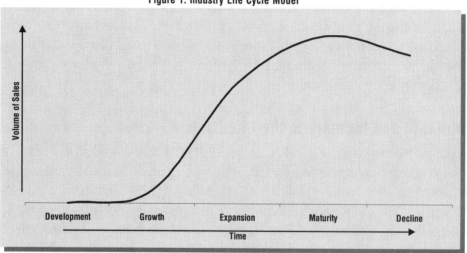

Figure 1: Industry Life Cycle Model

Source: Frost & Sullivan

The U.S. mutual fund industry spent a long time in the development phase of this cycle, starting as early as the 1920s, when the first open-end funds were introduced. It remained in this phase until about 1980, growing unevenly. From 1940 to 1960, assets under management, and accompanying revenues, in the very small industry grew at an average annual compound rate of around 16 percent. From 1961 to 1977, however, the average compound annual growth rate dropped to below 6 percent. (In fact, things got so bad during the bear market of the early 1970s, with fund assets values declining dramatically, that a *Business Week* article in 1973 predicted that "the fund industry as we know it today is likely to disappear.")[6]

Of course it didn't disappear. Instead, it survived and entered the growth phase of the life cycle around 1980, once investors who had been driven into money market funds by the effects of Regulation Q began to find equity and bond funds attractive as well. From 1978 to 1999, the growth rate in assets varied from year to year, but averaged over 30 percent per year. Growth in net new sales averaged around 15 percent for the same period.

Figure 2 shows mutual fund industry asset and sales figures for the period from 1980 to 2000, during which time the industry may have transited the growth phase into the expansion phase. (Not every version of the life cycle model differentiates between growth and expansion phases.) Figure 2 clearly shows the take-off in sales volume that marks the transition from development to growth. The question remains, however, whether the downturn in sales in 1998 and 1999 is the sign marking the transition to expansion, the transition to maturity, or just another transient turndown such as the ones in 1986–7 or 1993–4.

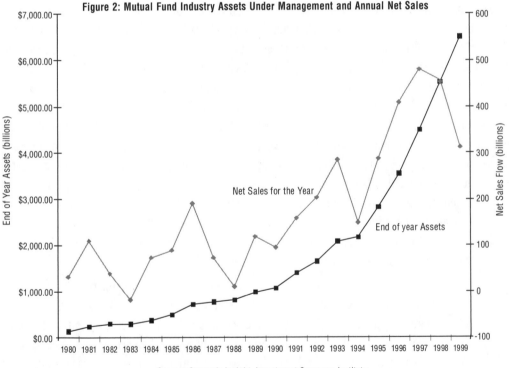

Figure 2: Mutual Fund Industry Assets Under Management and Annual Net Sales

Source: Strategic Insight, Investment Company Institute

This analysis is complicated by the fact that sales do not equal revenue in the mutual fund industry, as they do in many other industries. For mutual fund management companies, revenue derives from assets under management, whether they result from sales during the current year or sales made twenty years earlier. Thus the revenue curve for the industry would parallel the total assets curve in Figure 2, ascending sharply and smoothly without any sign of a downturn. This characteristic of fund economics helps account for the total absence of another typical indication of industry maturity—increasing concentration. Despite a few claims to the contrary, generally based on anecdotal evidence, the mutual fund industry in 2000 had shown no inclination so far to concentrate by erecting substantial barriers to entry and shaking out weaker competitors.

The U.S. Department of Justice uses a measure of concentration known as the Herfindahl-Hirschman Index (HHI) to evaluate the concentration of an industry or market sector—for example, to analyze the implications of a proposed merger. The HHI is calculated as the sum of the squares of the percentage market share of each competitor in the industry. Theoretically, it ranges from a maximum of 10,000 (one monopolist with a market share of 100 percent) down to a minimum of below one (many competitors none of which has even 1 percent of the market). In practice, Justice Department guidelines categorize an industry as unconcentrated if its HHI value is less than 1,000. The Department views an industry as moderately concentrated if the index value falls between 1,000 and 1,800 and highly concentrated if it is over 1,800. These guidelines also call for any proposed merger or acquisition to be challenged if it would result in a reduction of 100 points in the index value (50 points if the industry or sector is already highly concentrated).[7] For example, the Federal Trade Commission argued against a proposed merger of Staples and Office Depot, claiming that the HHI value after the merger for the office supply superstore market in forty-two metropolitan areas would exceed 5,000.[8]

Figure 3 shows the HHI values for the U.S. mutual fund industry for the period between 1982 and 1999. Figures from 1982 through 1987 come from the 1990 study of the industry conducted by Baumol, *et al*;[9] this author calculated the HHI values since then based on Strategic Insight data. Each management company represents one competitor, and its market share is calculated by dividing the year-end value of assets in its fund family by total open-end fund assets at year end. (The HHI is based on share of industry revenue, but for mutual fund management companies, revenue is approximately proportional to assets, so calculating the HHI on assets yields equivalent results.) Clearly, the U.S. mutual fund industry, with HHI values bouncing around in the 300–400 range for most of the 1980s and 1990s, was neither concentrated nor moving in the direction of concentration in early 2000. Several factors combine to the explain this:

- The barriers to entry to the industry have always been low. Establishing the fund itself requires less than $200,000. Nor does a fund manager have to commit to large expenditures to establish a support infrastructure. Third-party service organizations can handle any aspect of a fund's operations that the manager does not wish to undertake. An organization that already manages assets—such as a bank, an insurance company, a brokerage firm, or a pension manager—can add mutual funds to its product line at a small marginal cost. Additionally, the development of fund supermarkets in the early 1990s had the effect of further lowering barriers to entry by making effective distribution available at a low fixed cost.

  The large number of very small asset managers that have established funds reflects these low barriers to entry. For example, at the end of 1999, no fewer than 157 different managers each had fund groups with total assets of $50 million or less. Another 225 companies managed fund assets totaling between

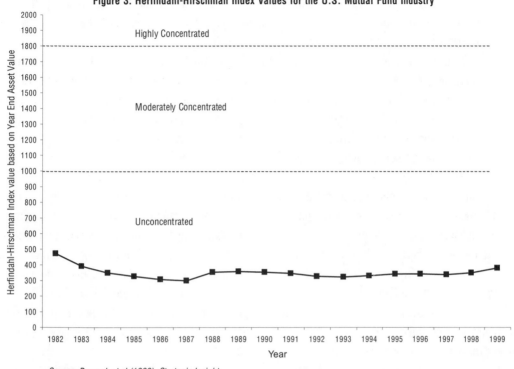

Figure 3: Herfindahl-Hirschman Index Values for the U.S. Mutual Fund Industry

Source: Baumol, et al (1990), Strategic Insight

$50 million and $1 billion each. While some of these have been acquired or otherwise gone out of business each year, enough new ones have entered to keep the HHI value for the industry relatively stable.

- The fact that revenue derives from assets under management, not new sales, gives fund groups a way to weather periods when their style is out of favor, their performance is unattractive, their marketing is ineffective, or some other factor depresses sales. Revenue changes much less quickly than does net sales. Thus a fund company can endure longer periods of low or even negative net sales than can any company for which revenue depends directly on new sales.

- Investors can and do easily switch from one fund family to another, particularly when investing new money. Investors may be slow to move the money once invested, especially if they have paid a sales charge to get into a fund. However, nothing prevents the investor from placing new investments with a different family, and, as a result, investors will readily invest in fund families other than the ones they already hold, particularly to chase performance. This is why it is misleading to equate concentration of sales flows for a given year with industry concentration. As Strategic Insight has pointed out, sales flows have always been concentrated, but as the years go by, the list of firms gathering the flows changes.[10] In the 1990s, for example, the list of firms that made it to the top twenty in net new sales at least once during the decade includes 46 separate fund companies. Some names appear in the list repeatedly; others appear for only a year or two.

- The bull market of the late twentieth century has combined with the baby boomer generation's increasingly urgent need to save for retirement to provide plenty of assets (and, therefore, revenue) for weaker as well as stronger competitors. As many in the industry are fond of saying, this rising tide did indeed lift everyone's boat. Even the weaker competitors, some of which experienced flat or negative net sales for several years running, still saw their revenues rise as the rising market increased the value of assets under management and annual management fees.

Nor did industry profitability appear to decline, to the extent that this could be determined in an industry in which many players are either privately held, e.g., Fidelity and American Century, or are components within a larger organization, e.g., Putnam and AIM. Strategic Insight's annual review of publicly held fund company financial results indicated that the average 1998 pre-tax operating margin for the 18 companies it examined was 35 percent.[11] This figure had been 30 percent in 1994 and had risen steadily since then. Furthermore, the group was uniformly profitable—with the exception of Pioneer, which had suffered losses in its European activities, all the companies in 1998 were at 30 percent or greater pre-tax margins. (Strategic Insight's preliminary figures for 1999 indicated that the pre-tax operating margins within their sample, again excepting troubled Pioneer, ranged between 28 and 46 percent.)

The question, therefore, is not so much whether the industry had yet matured at the end of 1999—clearly it had not—but rather whether maturity, with its slowing growth, shake outs, and reduced profitability, lurked in the near future. Those who believed that maturity was near in 2000 argued their case along four lines.

Saturation

The saturation argument holds that the industry has reached the point where just about every American who has the means and inclination to own mutual funds already does. One industry executive described the situation in 2000: "In the U.S. market we have reached pretty full penetration of eligible households. [The rate] might go from 40 percent to 45 percent, but it's not going to 60 percent."[12] The ICI estimated that 48 million households held funds in 2000, a figure that exceeded the number of households that had at least $20,000 of wealth to invest. Fund companies would not find much new money in the households that they had not already penetrated.

Nor was there much to be gained by further capturing assets Americans had placed in bank accounts, since the mutual fund industry in 2000 already held assets more than 1.6 times the size of the banking industry. The only significant potential source of new money for fund purchases within the United States in 2000 was the huge pool of wealth (over $7 trillion) that Americans held in individual securities. Much of this wealth would be transferred between generations over the next ten to twenty years as its owners died. How their heirs would dispose of it remained the 7 trillion dollar question. On the one hand, some observers believed that the baby boomer generation, which had embraced mutual funds as its preferred investing vehicle, would move at least some significant portion of this wealth into funds as they received it. Other observers were less sanguine, noting that the top 6 percent of wealthy households owned 90 percent of this total.[13] Investors at that level of wealth tended to be less attracted to mutual funds, instead preferring to hold individual securities, perhaps in privately managed accounts.

Of course, foreign markets offered another potential source of new money to fuel fund sales. As we saw in the preceding chapter, while many industry participants were actively pursuing that route in 1999 and 2000, they had varied expectations for the rate at which it might pay off. Similarly, the privatization of Social Security could conceivably open a vast new source of funds, should it occur, and occur in a way that would allow individuals or government units to direct investments to funds. In 2000, however, the public debate over this issue was just beginning, and no one could foresee the ultimate outcome.

Slowdown in Product Introduction and Firm Entry

The increase in the number of funds during the industry's growth/expansion phase had been dramatic, as shown in Figure 4. (In Figure 4, each fund is counted only once, no matter how many share classes it may have.) Some observers noted the drop in the number of new funds introduced in 1999, and interpreted it as a sign of industry maturity.[14] As with net sales, the question remained whether 1999 actually marked a fundamental turn in the curve or just one more annual variation in a pattern that varied quite a bit anyway. Similarly,

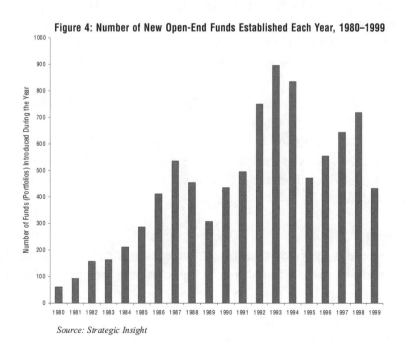

Figure 4: Number of New Open-End Funds Established Each Year, 1980–1999

Source: Strategic Insight

some observers wondered whether the number of firms entering the industry might be starting to tail off. As Strategic Insight put it in early 2000 "our data clearly shows a marked slowdown in the number of new managers entering the business and showing noticeable growth early on."[15] However, this reduction in the number of companies entering the industry had not yet had any significant effect on the HHI measure of industry concentration. Nor could anyone in 1999 predict whether this was a permanent change in the rate of entry, or merely an annual variation.

Changing Investor Needs

Mutual funds, some argue, best suit the smaller investor whose wealth is not great enough to achieve adequate diversification economically using individual securities. As investor wealth increases, a privately managed portfolio becomes more attractive for several reasons. It can be tailored specifically to the particular needs and objectives of the investor—for example, assembling a portfolio of fixed-income securities with a specific maturity to match an expected life event. It can be managed at a lower cost than many actively managed mutual funds, since it can dispense with much of overhead required for the 1940 Act, publicly offered funds. And it can be managed to control tax consequences for the investor, disposing of positions and generating capital gains and losses to meet the individual investor's specific needs.

For private portfolio management to be feasible and cost effective, the investor must have substantial wealth to invest—traditionally, at least a quarter to a half million dollars. At the beginning of 2000, an increasing number of investors, particularly members of the baby boom generation, who had been purchasing mutual funds over the past ten to twenty years, had in fact progressed to this stage of wealth accumulation. And these investors were precisely the mutual fund companies' best customers, the ones that contributed most to fund company profitability. And Internet folios, a form of private investment management sold via the Web, were driving this threshold down. Strategic Insight estimated in mid-2000 that these might be attractive to investors with as little as $40,000.[16]

Certainly fund management companies could participate in this business, but it presented certain challenges. As Strategic Insight put it, fund companies would have to "understand the nuances and differences . . . and ensure the right incremental services and investment processes to meet the needs of managed account representatives and clients."[17] Whether the fund companies could offer products to meet the needs of these increasingly affluent investors would determine at least in part how the industry's cycle would proceed as the twenty-first century unfolded.

Alternative Products

The late 1990s saw the emergence of products that some observers thought might displace mutual funds, even for smaller investors who would not be candidates for private investment management. Two vehicles in particular had gained notoriety and some popularity by early 2000: individual securities traded cheaply online and a group of instruments known as basket securities.

- *Individual Securities Traded Online.* The Internet revolution had at least two direct and significant effects for individual investors—it made trade execution a relatively cheap commodity, and it provided easy access to a vast array of information. Investors in 2000 could go online and look at data from literally hundreds of sources about investment possibilities. They could find data from public records such as EDGAR; from corporations via their web sites; from information providers like Motley Fool, Hoover, and Morningstar; and from each other via bulletin boards, chat rooms, etc. Once an investor had made a decision, he or she could execute a trade with an online discount broker for a flat rate of a few dollars, or even for free under certain circumstances. Millions of investors flocked to these facilities, and the number of online trading accounts with Schwab, E*trade, and others soared in the late 1990s.

  Some observers argued that this combination of access to information and cheap trading reduced the utility of mutual funds.[18] The investor could make his or her own decisions just as well as a fund manager could with the information now available. Trading had become so cheap that institutions such as funds no longer had any cost advantage over individual traders. Why incur the overhead of a fund, they asked, when you could invest more economically and effectively by buying securities yourself?

  These arguments flew in the face of reality along two dimensions. First, the trend among investors in the late 1990s swung hard toward seeking advice, not avoiding it. As investment options became more complex, and the amount of wealth at stake became higher, investors sought out professional help in the form of brokers and planners, who often still steered them to funds. Second, evidence began to accumulate that merely having access to all that information was not enough. In a fascinating study of six years of activity by over 1,600 Schwab investors who switched from telephone to online trading, two University of California professors found that the same investors who had beaten the market by 2 percent before going online lagged it by 3 percent after having become online traders. The study concluded that the "increase in trading and reduction in performance of online investors can be explained by overconfidence augmented by self-attribution bias, the illusion of knowledge, and the illusion of control."[19] Clearly there was still a role for professional management, perhaps bigger than some investors cared to admit.

- *Basket Securities.* Sometimes called exchange-traded funds, basket securities reflect pre-assembled portfolios that model some composite benchmark, but which an investor can buy in a single transaction. For example, Standard & Poor's Depository Receipts (SPDRs) mirror the S&P 500, World Equity Benchmarks (WEBs) mirror a single country's stock market, Cubes (NASDAQ: QQQ) mirror the NASDAQ 100 index, and the list goes on. Each basket security resembles an index fund for a given benchmark. Unlike open-end index funds, however, these basket securities are traded on the exchanges like stocks.

  This brings both advantages and disadvantages. Investors can buy and sell basket securities anytime during the day, at a price dependent on the current value of the benchmark. (Open-end funds in

2000 still calculated prices once per day, although there was some movement on the part of Fidelity and a few others to price some of their open-end funds more often.) They can buy these securities on margin, like common stocks. Since these securities are unmanaged, their expense ratio is low, although the basket securities established by early 2000 had no systemic cost advantage over the least expensive index funds, especially when commissions were considered. On the other hand, the investor had to pay a brokerage commission on each purchase or sale transaction for one of these basket securities.

Basket securities appeared in 1993 when the SPDR was created, and in 1999, Strategic Insight estimated that these instruments captured $16 billion in net cash inflows, as compared to over $350 billion for open-end funds.[20] Some mutual fund companies were at least studying the possibility of offering similar instruments, or even exchange-traded versions of their actively managed funds.[21] Noting that these instruments appealed primarily to market timers, Vanguard introduced ETF versions of some of its funds as a means of drawing the market timers out of the open-end funds. One such exchange traded fund is VIPERS – Vanguard Index Participation Equity Receipts.[22]

In early 2000, some believed that these instruments would become tremendously popular, and that many fund companies would begin to offer them.[23] Others, such as FRC, concluded that they might draw new cash into the markets, but were unlikely to divert assets from open-end funds.[24] Whether exchange-traded funds would ultimately capture a large share of the assets that would otherwise go to open-end funds remained to be seen.

Increasing price competition and generally declining price levels provide another standard signal of the onset of maturity in the industry life cycle. For example, when electronic calculators were in their development phase, a few competitors—the long-dead Bowmar, for example—sold them for hundreds of dollars per unit. As chip technology advanced and the calculator industry matured, basic calculators became a commodity and prices plummeted to a few dollars per unit, which drove Bowmar out of business. In the mutual fund industry, price to the investor means some combination of management fees and sales charges. How have these evolved over the years, and what can they tell us about the phase of the industry? The answer is not straightforward—indeed, debate still raged in 2000 about whether prices (fees and loads) for mutual funds had gone up or down in recent years.

The Fee Debate Revisited

On September 29, 1998, ICI President Matthew Fink testified before a congressional subcommittee that was holding hearings on improving price competition for mutual funds. Discussing fund costs, he said

Because of the sheer number of competitors, stringent government regulation, clear disclosure, low barriers to entry, and high scrutiny by the media, the mutual fund marketplace provides a

near textbook example of a competitive market structure. … Several independent studies dem- onstrate that overall, the total cost of investing in mutual funds has steadily declined.[25]

Not everyone agreed with this assessment. In the very same hearings, an economics professor who had published a number of studies of the industry stated "…the total expenses paid by investors have not fallen over the past decade… the success of the mutual fund industry has not produced price competition."[26] A co-founder of The Motley Fool, an online financial information service, also testified "…mutual fund fees are too high. It's certainly not obvious that investors are getting value for their fees."[27] John Bogle, who was drafting his 1999 book on mutual funds at about this time, produced a chart that showed average equity fund expense ratios climbing almost uninterruptedly from 97 basis points in 1981 to 155 basis points in 1997.[28] And Morningstar echoed this, asserting that average annual equity fund expense ratios had climbed from 125 basis points in 1985 to 153 basis points in 1999.[29]

How could such knowledgeable and informed observers come to such dramatically different conclusions, especially over something that was a matter of fact, not conjecture? After all, mutual fund expenses were a matter of public record, documented for anyone to see in prospectuses, SAIs, and financial reports. The ICI, Strategic Insight, Morningstar, Lipper, various universities, and others had assembled extensive databases of fund figures that could support research on fees. And analyses abounded, produced by academic researchers, the ICI, industry observers, and fund companies. But they came to conclusions that, on the surface at least, appear surprisingly inconsistent.

In fact, the diversity in conclusions rested on at least three areas of disagreement within the approach to fee analysis: what things got counted as fees, what was the proper definition of "average," and whether the question was what expenses *should be* or what they actually were. Varying combinations of opinions on each side of each of these questions resulted in a confusing tangle of conflicting claims.

The Definition of Fund Expenses

Everyone agreed that considering fund expenses used to be simpler. In the early 1980s, investors incurred two kinds of costs associated with mutual funds, each distinct from the other. All shareholders paid a management fee, calculated as so many basis points on fund assets. An investor who purchased a load fund paid a front-end sales commission, calculated as so many percentage points on the cash invested. This sales commission was really the price of getting investment advice from a broker, so the true cost of owning the fund was the management fee, both for load and no-load fund investors. Then Rule 12b-1 made it all much more complicated.

As funds began to use Rule 12b-1 to pay for marketing and distribution, they were able to reduce explicit front-end loads. These declined significantly—for example, the ICI pointed out that the average maximum front-end load for equity funds was 7.8 percent in 1982, but had gone down to 5 percent in 1998. And while some of this was offset by 12b-1 fees, overall selling costs declined during the 1980s and 1990s. For example, the ICI calculated that the average distribution cost ratio for equity funds (calculated as the 12b-1 fee plus the load, converted to an annual basis) had declined from 149 basis points in 1980 to 61 basis points in 1997.[30]

But the fact that the 12b-1 was an annual fee, like the management fee, clouded the formerly clear-cut distinction between costs of distribution and costs of management for some observers. Some shareholders ended up paying 12b-1 fees when they were not, in fact, getting investment advice from anyone, so that this fee truly added to cost of the fund.

So there were two different definitions of "fund expenses" in use by different commentators and analysts. One group, of which the ICI was a leading member, considered the total cost of ownership, which included both management fees and distribution expenses—loads and 12b-1 fees. This group typically found that this total cost of ownership had declined throughout the 1980s and 1990s. The second group, which included John Bogle and other industry critics, focused on management fees alone, and generally asserted that average management fees had not declined. But that brings us to the second question—what exactly does "average" mean?

The Definition of Average

Another reason that the studies differ is that they base their conclusions on different definitions of average expense. Those who claim that expenses have been rising typically use a simple average, calculated by adding the expense ratios of all the funds in the sample, and then dividing the result by the number of funds. Those who claim that expenses have fallen typically use an asset-weighted average, multiplying the expense ratios by total assets for the fund, then summing these results, and dividing the sum by the sum of total assets. The difference in approaches leads to diametrically opposed conclusions about the trend in expenses.

Management fees calculated as asset-weighted averages have generally declined over the past 20 years, for several reasons.[31] Many individual investors have put a great deal of money into low cost funds, including the index funds that have been so successful during this period. The funds used by defined contribution plans, another source of industry growth, often are institutional or other low-fee funds. In addition, increasing asset size has triggered breakpoint clauses in many funds' management agreements, resulting in lower fee schedules. Morningstar found that management fees calculated on an asset weighted basis declined by about 25 percent from 1984 to 1999.[32]

Management fees calculated as simple averages have not declined, since the number of funds has been growing rapidly, and many of the newer funds are more expensive funds. Global funds, many of which are relatively recent, tend to have higher fees than domestic funds. Conversely, relatively few money market funds, with their generally lower fee levels, were opened in the 1990s. And newer funds tend to be smaller, with asset levels below the breakpoint triggers. All of this makes a difference—for example, Strategic Insight pointed out that asset-weighted total expenses for funds in 1998 averaged about one-half of simple average total expenses.[33] At the same time that *Fortune* was claiming that "average" equity fund fees were 143 basis points (in 1998),[34] Strategic Insight calculated an average annual fee for these funds of 54 basis points. Clearly, "average annual fees" meant different things to different people.

The Effects of Economies of Scale

Some fund industry critics argue that mutual fund fee levels, whether or not they actually went up or down over the past fifteen to twenty years, *should have* gone down significantly as a result of the industry's dramatic growth. They point out that fund management should enjoy definite economies of scale—that it doesn't take twice as many portfolio managers, twice as much research, twice as many trades, and so on, to manage a fund when it grows from $1 billion to $2 billion. Yet management fees, which are largely pegged directly to asset value, may grow directly in proportion to assets. Many funds have tiered management fee structures, but many do not, and even the tiers do not reflect the true economies of scale, critics charge.

Defenders of the industry point out that it is simplistic to equate industry growth with fund growth. ICI President Matthew Fink, for example, wrote in a letter of rebuttal to a *Business Week* article:

> *The article's most fundamental error was to assume that industry-wide growth should lead to industrywide economies of scale. But economies of scale do not occur industry-wide; they occur fund by fund. For example, if the industry grows solely because of the entry of many new funds, virtually no economies of scale would be realized.*[35]

In fact, the industry has grown by both entry of funds and growth of individual funds, as Table 1 shows. The data do not support either side of the argument conclusively. On one hand, the median fund in 1985 managed $71 million in assets; in early 2000, the median fund managed $120 million, hardly a change that would lead to significant economies of scale. On the other hand, only two funds in 1985 had over $10 billion in assets, while eighty funds occupied this megafund category in 2000, accounting for almost 40 percent of industry assets. Yes, these funds had lower expense ratios than smaller funds, but critics charged that they were still far from what they would have been had economies of scale resulting from this enormous size been passed on to the shareholders.

Other critics maintain that it is not actually fund by fund that the economies occur; rather it is fund complex by fund complex. As the assets managed by a complex such as Fidelity (or Janus, or Putnam, or

Table 1: Funds, Assets, and Expense Ratios—1985 and 2000

| Size of Fund AUM ($millions) | Funds this size as a percent of the industry | | | | Average Expense Ratio* in 2000 w/o marketing costs (basis points) | |
| | Nbr. of Funds | | Total Assets | | | |
	1985	2000	1985	2000	Simple	Asset-Weighted
Below 100	53.2	42.1	5.2	1.7	113.5	100.0
Between 101 and 500	30.6	32.4	20.5	8.4	87.0	86.1
Between 501 and 1,000	8.6	9.6	17.4	7.3	77.7	77.7
Between 1,001 and 10,000	7.6	14.3	51.0	43.0	71.0	66.9
Over 10,000	0.0	1.6	5.9	39.6	56.3	54.3
All Funds					92.7	64.5

*This figure reflects the total net expenses of a mutual fund with the exception of the marketing or sales component.
Source: Strategic Insight SimFund Database, April 2000

whomever) grows by one or two orders of magnitude, these critics argue, the complex does not need to grow its staffing levels proportionately. And certainly the leading fund complexes grew enormously during the 1980s and 1990s. Table 2 shows average expense ratios for funds as of early 2000, broken down by the overall size of the fund complex. While Table 2 does show some patterns of decreasing expense ratios associated with increasing fund complex size, many believe that the decrease in fees should be much steeper.

These fee disputes continued to rage in early 2000, as they had for years. Some disgruntled investors took their arguments to court, suing fund groups such as Fidelity, Prudential, and T. Rowe Price for what they claim was the failure of independent directors to prevent the management companies from charging unreasonable fees. As of mid-2000, none of these suits had succeeded (some had been decided, others were still in progress). Nor did the SEC show much inclination to intervene. "We don't feel that it's our mission to set fees. We feel that's best left to competition and the marketplace," said a spokesman for the SEC's division of investment management.[36]

Evidence suggests that many shareholders are not upset about, or even aware of, the levels of fees mutual funds charge.[37] Nevertheless, the lack of consensus on such a seemingly simple question as whether prices were going up or down troubled some members of Congress. In 1999, Representatives Dingell and Oxley urged the General Accounting Office to conduct an inquiry into price competition in the mutual fund industry. As *Barron's* put it, "Widespread confusion and conflicting studies on whether mutual fund fees have been rising or falling" prompted the request for investigation.[38]

The GAO issued its report[39] to Congress in June, and to the public in July 2000. Most observers on both sides found it to be disappointing. On the question of fund fee levels, the GAO punted, saying that lack of data made it impossible for them to determine overall industry profitability, or whether any opportunity to reduce fees existed. The GAO further drew widespread industry criticism with its proposal to require fund companies to provide shareholders with individualized fee breakouts in dollars and cents. The ICI, the SEC, NASD, and many fund groups pointed out that mutual fund shareholders already receive more than adequate information on fees, and that the GAO had presented no compelling argument to support its disclosure proposal.[40]

Table 2: Average Expense Ratios* in April 2000, by Size of Fund Complex

Total AUM in funds within the complex (billions)	Simple Average Expense Ratio			Asset-Weighted Average Expense Ratio		
	Equity	Long-Term Fixed Income	Money Market	Equity	Long-Term Fixed Income	Money Market
Below $1	151	86	66	121	73	53
Between $1 and $10	119	71	54	106	69	50
Between $10 and $50	110	70	48	89	62	42
Between $50 and $100	115	76	42	89	70	36
Over $100	100	65	48	65	53	40

*This figure reflects the total net expenses of a mutual fund with the exception of the marketing or sales component.
Source: Strategic Insight SimFund Database, April 2000.

One Last Time—the Active vs. Passive Debate

We have several times visited the debate between proponents of passive management, as implemented via index funds, and those of active management, as practiced by most fund managers. Previous discussions have focused on specific implications of each position—e.g., on portfolio management, trading, and taxes—without going very far into the debate itself. This chapter pays one final visit to this debate and attempts to show that both sides are right—but by their own, differing standards of judgement, reconciliation of which may never occur.

A significant body of academic research has focused on this issue, and the majority concludes that investors chase a will-o'-the-wisp in attempting to choose active managers.[41] (There are a few exceptions, such as Walker,[42] but they are in the distinct minority.) These studies point out that very few active managers outperform the relevant benchmarks for their funds, especially over any period longer than a few years. Some researchers subscribe to the belief that market efficiency makes it impossible for the active portfolio manager to succeed, except by random chance. Others merely point out that whatever the theoretical underpinnings, the actual data show that most active portfolio managers underperform their benchmarks by about the amount of their expenses. The end result is the same, and Nobel laureate Paul Samuelson summarized it bluntly: "A respect for evidence compels me to the hypothesis that most portfolio managers should go out of business."[43]

Active fund managers measuring themselves against a specific benchmark certainly start out with a handicap in the form of their expense ratio. The size of this handicap has itself been the subject of study and controversy, with different researchers finding different values, depending on how market effects and trading costs are counted. Even the most conservative observers, however, admit that actively managed domestic equity funds typically cost the investor between 100 and 200 basis points each year. Thus the active manager must outperform the relevant benchmark by at least this much, just to get back to the starting point. Passively managed index funds suffer much less of an expense handicap because of their lower expense ratios.

Furthermore, even if some active managers do overcome the cost handicap and outperform the relevant benchmark, most research indicates that investors cannot identify, ahead of time, which ones will do so. For example, even though several hundred funds achieved spectacular returns in 1999, most research concludes that no data available to an investor in 1998 would have enabled him or her to identify which funds were going to do it. The best the investor can do, these studies say, is to avoid those funds that have had execrable performance, since poor performance does tend to persist.[44] A really bad fund today will probably be a really bad fund tomorrow. Conversely, funds that outperform today are likely to regress towards the mean in the future. Thus, the researchers typically conclude, the only rational decision an investor can make is to choose funds that track, with as little expense burden as possible, the benchmarks appropriate to their investment objectives. While they don't often say it explicitly, these researchers are recommending a choice that will maximize the *expected monetary value* (EMV) of the investor's risk-adjusted return. An EMV represents the outcome of a decision weighted by its probability. For example, consider the situation represented by the decision tree in Figure 5. It assumes an investor who wishes to invest in a large cap domestic equity fund and can choose between an indexed fund with total expenses of 50 basis points annually and an actively managed fund with total expenses of 150 basis points. For both funds, the relevant benchmark is the S&P 500.

No uncertainty attends the performance of the indexed fund relative to the benchmark—it will be the S&P 500 performance minus the fund's expenses. Choosing the actively managed fund, on the other hand, leads to a range of possibilities, from substantially underperforming to substantially outperforming the benchmark. To calculate the EMV of this choice, the investor must first identify an appropriate set of possible outcomes and then assign a probability to each. Research into investment performance indicates that the only reliable basis for these probabilities is historical statistical distributions. How likely, for example, is a particular large cap growth fund to outperform the S&P 500 by two percentage points? Ask how frequently large cap growth funds in general have outperformed by that margin in the past over the appropriate time period. The frequency distribution of past performance of the class of funds provides the only basis for constructing a probability distribution of future performance of a particular fund of that class.

Figure 5's decision tree embodies a hypothetical example of such a distribution. Multiple studies of active fund management have indicated that an actively managed fund will most likely track the benchmark, minus expenses, but the possibility of performing quite well or quite poorly is also distinct, if less probable. (Four branches are used in Figure 5 to represent this distribution, but more outcomes and probabilities could have been added if they were needed to describe the situation adequately.)

Figure 5: Example of a Decision Tree for an Active versus Passive Fund Choice

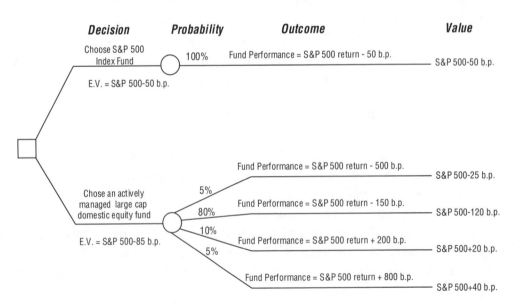

When each possible outcome associated with a decision is multiplied by its probability, and the results summed, that sum is the expected monetary value of the decision. Thus, in our example, the EMV of the indexed fund choice is 35 basis points better than that of the actively managed fund choice. Viewed in this context, the arguments made by indexed fund proponents boil down to two major points:

1. Repeated analyses of actual fund results show that the EMV of choosing an actively managed fund will always be inferior to the EMV of choosing an indexed fund that tracks the same benchmark but at lower costs.

2. Maximizing EMV is the rational and proper criterion for evaluating investment choices.

But investors, by and large, continue to put the majority of their money into actively managed funds—clearly the theory advanced by most academics does not connect with the actual practice of most investors. The disconnect lies in two areas. First, many investors persist in believing that they can, in fact, distinguish between funds that will outperform their benchmarks and those that will not. Thus, they reject the probabilities based purely on historical distributions, and assume probabilities that favor their actively managed fund choice. (And some research suggests that they simply misunderstand fund performance history altogether.)[45]

The overwhelming body of research on fund performance patterns suggests exactly what all the prospectuses say—that "past performance does not guarantee future performance." Investors cannot with any degree of reliability predict the future performance of a particular fund, except in terms of a probability distribution. Nevertheless, hope springs eternal, so many investors (and their advisers) study the analyses and charts produced by Morningstar, Lipper, The Motley Fool, and others, believing that they can pick the fund that is going to outperform. Critics such as John Bogle point out that many industry participants promote this belief that performance can be predicted, since it is in their self-interest to provide investors help with their data, ratings, charts, newsletters, advice, etc.

Second, even when they believe the historical probabilities, people often deliberately choose *not* to base their decision on maximizing expected monetary value. Edward Chancellor, in his study of the history of financial speculation, describes the mindset underlying this phenomenon:

> *In a democratic society, such as the United States, where wealth is the ultimate determinant of status, there lingers a constant fear of being left behind materially. We may say that the guiding principle of American society is not to grow richer in absolute terms, but to avoid becoming poorer in relative terms. And nothing makes a man feel poorer than being a passive bystander during a bull market.*[46]

Chancellor advances this argument to explain why people participated in the speculative excesses of the Roaring Twenties. It works equally well to explain why many investors today view index funds with disdain. The stock market of the 1980s and 1990s in the United States has largely been a bull market. Many funds have turned in, at one time or another, spectacular returns, most notably those triple-digit figures over one hundred funds hit in 1999. In choosing an index fund, an investor necessarily foregoes any chance of participating in this sort of excess return, however remote that chance might be.

At the same time, the bull market of the 1980s and 1990s made the downside risk associated with choosing an actively managed mutual fund over an indexed fund palatable to the investor. Funds that didn't hit the spectacular figures still, by and large, did pretty well. After all, the average equity fund's annual return during the 16-year period ending in 1998 was 16.5 percent, an attractive performance figure indeed, even if it did miss the Wilshire 5000 index's performance by a couple of percentage points.[47] So for many investors, the issue was one of taking a small risk of picking an actively managed fund that ends up somewhat underperforming its benchmark in the hope of achieving a large reward (picking a fund that ends up shooting the lights out). In our example in Figure 5, the investor taking this approach would decide to accept the 35 basis points penalty to get the chance at the 800 basis point outperformance.

Some would simply term this approach gambling, and it is true that if people always based their decisions on maximizing expected monetary value, gambling (at least in its institutionalized form in the United States) would cease to exist. Decision theorists, however, recognize that real human beings make decisions in messy, emotion-laden situations, in which information is incomplete and problem structure is ambiguous, using a variety of approaches. Decision theory textbooks describe dozens of such approaches, many of which are much simpler than maximizing EMV.[48] For example, "maximax" rule followers simply pick the alternative that could lead to the best possible outcome, ignoring probabilities. Some approaches include non-economic considerations. For example, a decision maker taking the "minimax regret" approach chooses the alternative that minimizes the chance that he or she could be second-guessed later. The list goes on and on. Many individuals simply are not coldly rational EMV maximizers.

So the argument will most likely continue unabated. The followers of Burt Malkiel and John Bogle will continue to produce analyses to show that EMV-maximizing investors cannot do better than to put their money into indexed funds. Investors will continue to make decisions in a variety of ways, some informed, some uninformed, some based on analysis, some based on hunches, wishes, or marketing. But as long as the bull market continues, many different approaches will yield satisfying results.

And Finally—The State of the Market

A common theme runs through the analysis of all these mutual fund industry issues—things could be very different if the long bull market of the 1980s and 1990s gave way to a sustained bear market. Fund companies have clearly benefited from this bull market, as market appreciation has increased their fund management revenues independently of their sales activity. During the 1990s, approximately half of the industry's growth in assets came from market appreciation, and the other from new sales. What the market gives, however, the market can take away. As Lawrence Lasser, chief executive of Putnam, put it, "growth in this business has become increasingly market-based. . . we are much more vulnerable to matters outside of our business control."[49]

So the single factor that would most impact the health and progression of the U.S. mutual fund industry as it proceeded into the twenty-first century was the one over which it had no control—the market itself. Continuing market appreciation would most likely mean business as usual for the nation's 600+ fund families. A market downturn, on the other hand, that significantly reduced assets and revenues over a sustained period (similar, for example, to the experience of the 1970s), could trigger massive change. Revenues that had been boosted by continually rising asset values would stagnate or fall, squeezing profits, shaking out weaker competitors, fostering price competition, and pushing the industry toward all the characteristics associated with maturity. Investor ignorance of, or tolerance for, current fee levels could be replaced by a sharper focus on cost, if plummeting securities prices brought fund returns closer in magnitude to fund costs. This in turn could change the way investors approached their fund selection decision. The low cost ratios of indexed funds might play a much larger role in an investor's decision process if average returns were near zero or even negative.

But while the golden times of 15 to 20 percent growth might well end, in 2000 it was hard to imagine the mutual fund industry continuing as anything but a major player in the U.S. financial services landscape, come bull or bear market. As Putnam's Lasser pointed out, "If the markets are down, people probably need to save more. The basic demographic, cultural, and economic underpinnings of this business are very strong."[50] Despite the shortcomings claimed by many critics, the industry had delivered on its basic promise of professional money management and risk diversification at a reasonable price. Nothing suggested that the public's need for that service would disappear anytime soon, nor that another product would replace the open-end fund as a vehicle for satisfying it.

Appendix

Prospectus

and

Statement of Additional Information

for

C/Funds Group, Inc.

Taken from the information in the 485BPOS filing of July 17, 2000,
and formatted for better legibility.

C/Funds Group, Inc.

February 28, 2000

The Series Funds

**C/Fund
C/Growth Stock Fund
C/Government Fund
C/Community Association Reserve Fund**

Prospectus

C/Funds Group, Inc. (the "Company") is a diversified, open-end, regulated investment company, incorporated in Florida and registered under the Securities Act of 1933 and the Investment Company Act of 1940. It offers four series Funds (the "Funds"), each with its own purpose, investment objectives, and associated risks as described in this Prospectus.

This Prospectus contains information, which you should know about The Company and its Funds before you invest. Please keep it for future reference.

C/Funds Group, Inc.
P. O. Box 622
Venice, Florida 34282-0622
Voice: 941-488-6772 • Toll-Free: 800-338-9477 • Fax: 941-496-4661
A No-Load Fund Group

Table of Contents

C/Fund

Investment Objective

Seek to maximize shareholder's total returns by investing in securities that offer the potential for capital gains, both realized and unrealized, and that produce dividend and/or interest income. When gains and income are added together, the total can be calculated as a percentage of the amount invested, producing a "total" return in percentage terms. This percentage then allows investors to fairly compare the performance of C/Fund with investment sectors, funds or securities having similar risk and financial traits.

Principal Investment Strategies

The C/Fund portfolio invests in stocks and fixed-income securities in proportions designed to meet its investment objectives while minimizing the risk of net asset value decline. The mix between stocks and fixed investments changes at times in response to market conditions while maintaining some balance within these two major categories most of the time.

While equity markets appear favorable, the Fund buys and holds a reasonably balanced percentage of its assets in:
- Regularly traded common stocks,
- convertible preferred stocks, and
- investment grade convertible bonds issued by listed public companies

The Fund's primary policy is to invest most often in issues such as those traded on the New York Stock Exchange and NASDAQ. However, to take advantage of investment opportunities, it may still invest in equities that may trade over the counter. The Fund is registered and managed as a diversified mutual fund.

When the market experiences major weakness, the Fund reduces equity investments in favor of fixed-income investments to protect asset value. At such times, it would most often invest in the fixed-income investments, such as short term investment grade securities. These investments include:
- U.S. Government issues, or
- Money market investments.

For additional restrictions that the Fund has imposed upon itself, please see the appropriate section in the Fund's Statement of Additional Information. It is on file with the Securities and Exchange Commission and is available to you free at your request placed to the telephone number or address shown on the cover of this Prospectus.

Principal Investment Risks

Investor Profile

A conservative investor who wants a fair current income plus potential for appreciation.

Risks

As with all marketable securities, risk of price declines of Fund securities is unavoidable. During times when the Fund is substantially invested in securities, its value can be adversely affected by a market decline. While shifted to fixed income investments, the fund is subject to interest rate risks associated with investment maturities. In its efforts to match or exceed returns produced by the popular market averages such as the Dow Jones Industrial Average and the Standard and Poor's 500 Average the Fund attempts to minimize the risk of asset value declines. It seeks to do this by being less exposed to equities during periods when the general market is weak and being more exposed to equity risk when the general market is strong. Even though that is a Fund objective, there is no assurance that it can be achieved. Correct timing of movement from one type of investment to another is critical but difficult to accomplish successfully at all times.

Risk/Return Bar Chart and Table

The following bar chart and table provide an indication of the risks of investing in C/Fund. The bar chart shows changes in the Fund's performance from year to year over a 10-year period. The table shows how the Fund's average annual returns for one, five, and ten years compare to those of a broad-based securities market index. Remember that how the Fund has performed in the past is not necessarily an indication of how it will perform in the future.

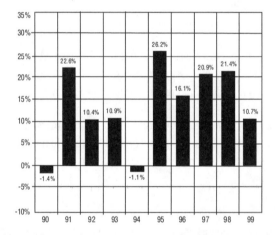

During the period shown in the following bar chart, the highest return for a quarter was 17.1% (quarter ending December 31, 1998) and the lowest return for a quarter was −9.7% (quarter ending September 30, 1990).

Average Annual Total Returns (for the periods ending December 31)	Past 1 Year	Past 5 Years	Past 10 Years
C/Fund	10.7%	19.0%	13.3%
S&P 500*	19.5%	26.2%	15.3%

* This is the Standard & Poor's Composite Index of 500 Stocks, a widely recognized, unmanaged index of common stock prices.

Fees and Expenses of the Fund

This table describes the fees and expenses that you may pay if you buy and hold shares in the Fund.

Shareholder Transaction Expenses (fees paid directly from your investment)	
Sales Commissions to Purchase Shares	None
Commissions to Reinvest Dividends	None
Redemption Fees	None

Annual Fund Operating Expenses (expenses that are deducted from Fund assets)	
Investment Advisor's Fee	1.00%
12b-1 Fees	None
Other Operating Expenses	.75%
Total Operating Expenses	1.75%

Examples:

This example assumes that you invest $10,000 in the Fund for the time periods indicated and then redeem all of your shares at the end of those periods. This example also assumes that your investment has a 5% return each year and that the Fund's operating expenses remain the same. Although your actual costs may be higher or lower, based on these assumptions your costs would be:

1 year	3 years	5 years	10 years
$178	$551	$949	$2,062

> Expenses shown in these examples do not represent actual past or future expenses. Actual expenses may be more or less than those shown. The assumed 5% return is hypothetical, and is not a representation or prediction of past or future returns, which may be more or less than 5%.

Financial Highlights

This financial highlights table is intended to help you understand the Fund's financial performance for the past 5 years. Certain information reflects financial results for a single Fund share. The total returns in the table represent the rate that an investor would have earned (or lost) on an investment in the Fund (assuming reinvestment of all dividends and distributions). This information has been audited by Gregory, Sharer and Stuart, whose report, along with the Fund's financial statements, are included in the Company's Annual Report, which is available upon request.

	1995	1996	1997	1998	1999
Net Asset Value Beginning of Period	$13.95	$16.83	$17.71	$20.61	$23.79
Net Investment Income (Loss)	.21	.19	.24	.28	.19
Net Realized and Unrealized Gain (Loss) on Investments	3.42	2.56	3.50	4.12	2.35
Total Income (Loss) From Investment Income	3.63	2.75	3.74	4.40	2.54
Dividends From Net Investment Income	(.21)	(.19)	(.26)	(.72)	(.19)
Distributions from Net Realized Capital Gains	(.54)	(1.58)	(.58)	(.50)	(1.52)
Returns of Capital	—	(.10)	—	—	—
Total Distributions	(.75)	(1.87)	(.84)	(1.22)	(1.71)
Net Asset Value at End of Period	16.83	17.71	20.61	23.79	24.62
Total Return[1]	26.18%	16.15%	20.95%	21.39%	10.66%
Net Assets at End of Period (000s)	$4,352	$5,423	$7,137	$8,860	$9,788
Ratio of Expenses to Average Net Assets	1.85%	1.90%	1.79%	1.68%	1.75%
Ratio of Net Income to Average Net Assets	1.36%	1.05%	1.24%	1.27%	.77%
Portfolio Turnover Rate	5.46%	11.38%	10.28%	17.58%	39.65%

[1] *Computed based on audited figures.*

C/Growth Stock Fund

Investment Objective

Maximum principal appreciation with dividend income a secondary consideration while investing substantially all of the Fund's assets in stocks at all times.

Principal Investment Strategies

The C/Growth Stock Fund portfolio invests substantially all of its assets, regardless of market conditions, in the common stocks or equivalents (such as convertible preferreds or bonds) of more rapidly growing companies. Some Fund assets are invested in large capitalization companies, but a major portion may be invested in medium to small capitalization companies having a total capital value of $1billion or less. The advisor makes investment selections by identifying companies that have above average growth prospects, regardless of capitalization or annual sales volume. Substantially all of its assets are invested all of the time in stocks. Liquid assets in the Fund that are awaiting investment in stocks are held in short term money market accounts or in short term U.S. government securities having maturities of less than one year.

Stock selections are made using a variety of research sources, including proprietary analytical methodology that produces quantitative, computer-generated analyses of corporate financial information. These sources and analyses help identify companies whose management appears to understand how to build shareholder wealth regularly and systematically, and manages to that end. The advisor's research indicates that understanding the importance of regularly maintaining or increasing corporate returns on invested capital ultimately creates a positive impact on the market value of the targeted company's outstanding shares. The advisor believes this is largely due to the company earning a return on invested capital that is consistently higher than the "cost" of its invested capital. When this takes place, shareholder wealth increases as a result of the rise in share price.

Principal Investment Risks

Investor Profile

The investor who wants potentially rapid principal value appreciation and who is willing to assume a higher degree of risk and more net asset value volatility.

Risks

The characteristics of securities selected for this Fund include the possibility for rapid growth and appreciation. However, they also commonly possess greater risk of price declines and in some rare cases, even corporate insolvency when less seasoned companies and management teams are unable to compete successfully in their respective businesses. The aggressive approach taken in this Fund can result in greater price volatility with attendant above average fluctuations in net asset value per Fund share, including a loss in value during periods when shares of stock of smaller companies lose favor with investors.

The advisor does not consider portfolio turnover a constraint when deciding to take profits or losses or to re-employ assets in investments better suited to meeting Fund objectives. Accordingly, the Fund can have higher turnover compared to funds with longer term orientations. This can cause the Fund to frequently realize capital gains or losses, which it distributes to shareholders annually for inclusion in their personal income tax return. (See the "Federal Income Tax Status" section on page 21 for more information about capital gains tax status.)

Risk/Return Bar Chart and Table

The following bar chart and table provide an indication of the risks of investing in C/Growth Stock Fund. The bar chart shows changes in the Fund's performance from year to year since its first full year of operation. The table shows how the Fund's average annual returns for one and five years and since inception compare to those of a broad-based securities market index. Remember that how the Fund has performed in the past is not necessarily an indication of how it will perform in the future.

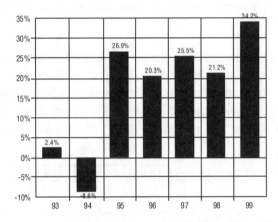

During the period shown in the bar chart, the highest return for a quarter was 25.7% (quarter ending December 31, 1998) and the lowest return for a quarter was −11.9% (quarter ending September 30, 1998).

Average Annual Total Returns (for the periods ending December 31)	Past 1 Year	Past 5 Years	Since Inception (07/12/92)
C/Growth Stock Fund	34.3%	24.7%	15.2%
S & P 500*	19.5%	26.2%	18.4%

*This is the Standard & Poor's Composite Index of 500 Stocks, a widely recognized, unmanaged index of common stock prices.

Fees and Expenses of the Fund

This table describes the fees and expenses that you may pay if you buy and hold shares in the Fund.

Shareholder Transaction Expenses (fees paid directly from your investment)	
Sales Commissions to Purchase Shares	None
Commissions to Reinvest Dividends	None
Redemption Fees	None

Annual Fund Operating Expenses (expenses that are deducted from Fund assets)	
Investment Advisor's Fee	1.00%
12b-1 Fees	None
Other Operating Expenses	.74%
Total Operating Expenses	1.74%

Examples

This example assumes that you invest $10,000 in the Fund for the time periods indicated and then redeem all of your shares at the end of those periods. This example also assumes that your investment has a 5% return each year and that the Fund's operating expenses remain the same. Although your actual costs may be higher or lower, based on these assumptions your costs would be:

1 year	3 years	5 years	10 years
$177	$548	$944	$2,052

> Expenses shown in these examples do not represent actual past or future expenses. Actual expenses may be more or less than those shown. The assumed 5% return in hypothetical, and is not a representation or prediction of past or future returns, which may be more or less than 5%.

Financial Highlights

This financial highlights table is intended to help you understand the Fund's financial performance for the past 5 years. Certain information reflects financial results for a single Fund share. The total returns in the table represent the rate that an investor would have earned (or lost) on an investment in the Fund (assuming reinvestment of all dividends and distributions). This information has been audited by Gregory, Sharer and Stuart, whose report, along with the Fund's financial statements, are included in the Company's Annual Report, which is available upon request.

	1995	1996	1997	1998	1999
Net Asset Value Beginning of Period	$9.34	$11.28	$12.38	$13.65	$15.84
Net Investment Income (Loss)	.02	(.05)	(.10)	(.06)	(.13)
Net Realized and Unrealized Gain (Loss) on Investments	2.13	2.24	3.20	2.96	5.49
Total Income (Loss) From Investment Income	2.15	2.19	3.10	2.90	5.36
Dividends From Net Investment Income	(.02)	—	(.15)	—	—
Distributions from Net Realized Capital Gains	(.19)	(1.08)	(1.68)	(.71)	(3.91)
Returns of Capital	—	(.01)	—	—	—
Total Distributions	(.21)	(1.09)	(1.83)	(.71)	(3.91)
Net Asset Value at End of Period	11.28	12.38	13.65	15.84	17.29
Total Return[1]	22.81%	20.30%	25.48%	21.25%	34.25%
Net Assets at End of Period (000s)	$2,080	$2,212	$2,541	$3,082	$3,647
Ratio of Expenses to Average Net Assets	1.85%	1.90%	1.81%	1.68%	1.74%
Ratio of Net Income to Average Net Assets	.20%	(.45%)	(.68%)	(.45%)	(.78%)
Portfolio Turnover Rate	16.46%	4.26%	51.11%	88.47%	118.73%

[1] Computed based on audited figures.

C/Government Fund

Investment Objective

Seek to earn and pay out to shareholders a regular income return above that produced by money market portfolios while also minimizing net asset value volatility and credit risk.

Principal Investment Strategies

This Fund invests substantially all of its assets in obligations of the U.S. government or one or more of its agencies which offers the opportunity to minimize price change and uses yield curve timing and maturity step-laddering. It only seeks the higher yields available on issues with maturities longer than a year when the attendant net asset value fluctuations appear to be at a minimum due to a lower probability that interest rates in general will rise.

The Fund buys seasoned issues below or above par or face value and step-ladders the portfolio so that issues usually mature at regular intervals, creating reinvestment opportunities in varying interest rate environments. While there are no restrictions on maturities or terms of purchased issues, the advisor typically invests in issues with under 10 year maturities. Maturities may change from time to time according to the Fund advisor's views on future interest rate trends. Volatility of the Fund's share NAV is minimized if the manager is successful in shortening the duration of its bond portfolios when rates appear to be likely to rise, and lengthening duration or the average maturity of the Fund's securities when inflationary influences and expectations appear to be on the wane, thus increasing the probability that interest rates will hold near current levels or even decline during periods ahead.

Typically, all available monies are invested in government issues to the extent practical, economical, and warranted by the then-existing interest rate climate as it relates to the Fund's objectives. When any monies are uninvested, they are automatically swept overnight into a short term money market which the advisor considers a permanent portfolio investment class or sector.

Principal Investment Risks

Investor Profile

The investor who wants income and principal safety with minimum net asset value volatility, but who also seeks a higher return than that which is available through money market or bank savings accounts.

Risks

The advisor tries to minimize net asset value changes by adjusting the portfolio from time to time, and to reduce share price risk through various portfolio management techniques. But, shareholders should know that fluctuations will likely occur in line with any changes in the government issues held. Longer maturities afford higher yields but contribute to price fluctuation. This risk of price decline is always present and investors in Fund shares should be aware that the Fund will not always be able to achieve its objective of minimum price fluctuations.

Risk/Return Bar Chart and Table

The following bar chart and table provide an indication of the risks of investing in C/Government Fund. The bar chart shows changes in the Fund's performance from year to year its first full year of operation. The table shows how the Fund's average annual returns for one and five years and since inception compare to those of a broad-based securities market index. Remember that how the Fund has performed in the past is not necessarily an indication of how it will perform in the future.

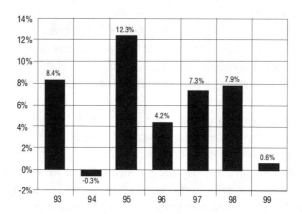

During the period shown in the bar chart, the highest return for a quarter was 5.1% (quarter ending September 30, 1998) and the lowest return for a quarter was -0.5% (quarter ending March 31, 1997).

Average Annual Total Returns (for the periods ending December 31)	Past 1 Year	Past 5 Years	Since Inception (07/12/92)
C/Government Fund	0.6%	6.4%	5.6%
Merrill Lynch 1-10 Year Treasury Index*	0.6%	7.0%	6.0%

This is a widely recognized index of U.S. Government securities with maturities of 1 to 10 years.

Fees and Expenses of the Fund

This table describes the fees and expenses that you may pay if you buy and hold shares in the Fund.

Shareholder Transaction Expenses (fees paid directly from your investment)	
Sales Commissions to Purchase Shares	None
Commissions to Reinvest Dividends	None
Redemption Fees	None

Annual Fund Operating Expenses (expenses that are deducted from Fund assets)	
Investment Advisor's Fee	.50%
12b-1 Fees	None
Other Operating Expenses	.49%
Total Operating Expenses	.99%

Examples

This example assumes that you invest $10,000 in the Fund for the time periods indicated and then redeem all of your shares at the end of those periods. This example also assumes that your investment has a 5% return each year and that the Fund's operating expenses remain the same. Although your actual costs may be higher or lower, based on these assumptions your costs would be:

1 year	3 years	5 years	10 years
$101	$315	$547	$1,213

> Expenses shown in these examples do not represent actual past or future expenses. Actual expenses may be more or less than those shown. The assumed 5% return in hypothetical, and is not a representation or prediction of past or future returns, which may be more or less than 5%.

Financial Highlights

This financial highlights table is intended to help you understand the Fund's financial performance for the past 5 years. Certain information reflects financial results for a single Fund share. The total returns in the table represent the rate that an investor would have earned (or lost) on an investment in the Fund (assuming reinvestment of all dividends and distributions). This information has been audited by Gregory, Sharer and Stuart, whose report, along with the Fund's financial statements, are included in the Company's Annual Report, which is available upon request.

	1995	1996	1997	1998	1999
Net Asset Value Beginning of Period	$9.44	$10.02	$9.87	$10.01	$10.23
Net Investment Income (Loss)	.54	.56	.57	.54	.50
Net Realized and Unrealized Gain (Loss) on Investments	.58	(.15)	.14	.22	(.44)
Total Income (Loss) From Investment Income	1.12	.41	.71	.76	.06
Dividends From Net Investment Income	(.54)	(.56)	(.57)	(.54)	(.50)
Distributions from Net Realized Capital Gains	—	—	—	—	—
Returns of Capital	—	—	—	—	—
Total Distributions	(.54)	(.56)	(.57)	(.54)	(.50)
Net Asset Value at End of Period	10.02	9.87	10.01	10.23	9.79
Total Return [1]	12.34%	4.12%	7.35%	7.89%	0.55%
Net Assets at End of Period (000s)	$3,972	$4,737	$4,543	$9,983	$8,944
Ratio of Expenses to Average Net Assets	.99%	1.02%	1.01%	.96%	.99%
Ratio of Net Income to Average Net Assets	5.54%	5.60%	5.74%	5.55%	5.00%
Portfolio Turnover Rate	124.70%	59.95%	22.05%	0.00%	99.20%

[1] *Computed based on audited figures.*

C/Community Association Reserve Fund

Investment Objective

Seek to earn a regular income return that is greater than can be earned on a money market type investment while minimizing fluctuations in the Fund's NAV.

Principal Investment Strategies

This specialty Fund is specifically designed and managed as a repository for reserve funds of Florida "Community

- A higher return than is available from other forms of eligible investments, and
- Net asset value safety and stability.

The Fund qualifies as an eligible investment for association reserve funds under Florida law and invests solely in obligations of the U.S. government or its agencies. It invests in short to intermediate term issues, most often having an average maturity of under 5 years. While fluctuations may be greater with maturities greater than one year, the Fund advisor manages the portfolio to meet its objectives while seeking to minimize share price volatility. Mathematical comparison of price risk potential to intermediate duration yields information that the advisor uses to assess whether investing in higher interest paying issues of longer maturity is profitable enough to justify or offset the added risk of price fluctuations. The advisor also uses portfolio management techniques, which may include, among others, yield-curve timing and portfolio maturity step-laddering to achieve Fund goals. Lengthening the Fund portfolio's average maturity or duration during periods of easing inflation and interest rates and shortening during periods of rising inflation fears, helps the Fund achieve its objectives.

Principal Investment Risks

Investor Profile

"Community Associations" that want to invest reserve funds safely while earning a higher return than is available on bank deposits or money market accounts with minimum net asset value fluctuation. This Fund is solely for Florida "Community Associations" which are registered and operating under the regulation of the State of Florida Bureau of Condominiums.

Risks

The advisor tries to minimize net asset value changes by adjusting the portfolio from time to time, and to reduce share price risk through various portfolio management techniques. However, associations investing reserve funds in this Fund should be aware that it is unlikely that the Fund will be successful in every instance when it seeks to minimize volatility or price declines in the Fund's NAV. The longer the maturity of issues held the larger the percentage of price change when interest rates change, both up and down. The Fund seeks to minimize price declines by shortening maturities of issues held prior to an actual rise in interest rates rather than waiting until an actual rise takes place. This tends to reduce returns to shareholders when an incorrect assessment has been made about interest rates but reduces the volatility of Fund shares due to the smaller price changes inherent with shorter term maturity issues.

Risk/Return Bar Chart and Table

The following bar chart and table provide an indication of the risks of investing in C/Community Association Reserve Fund. The bar chart shows changes in the Fund's performance from year to year since its first full year of operation. The table shows how the Fund's average annual returns for one and five years and since inception compare to those of a broad-based securities market index. Remember that how the Fund has performed in the past is not necessarily an indication of how it will perform in the future.

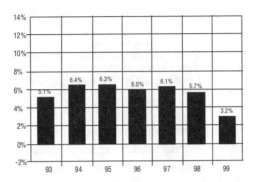

During the period shown in the bar chart, the highest return for a quarter was 2.6% (quarter ending December 31, 1997) and the lowest return for a quarter was 0.5% (quarter ending September 30, 1997).

Average Annual Total Returns (for the periods ending December 31)	Past 1 Year	Past 5 Years	Since Inception (07/12/92)
C/Community Association Reserve Fund	3.2%	5.4%	5.4%
Merrill Lynch 1-10 Year Treasury Index*	0.6%	7.0%	6.0%

* This is a widely recognized index of U.S. Government securities with maturities of 1 to 10 years.

Fees and Expenses of the Fund

This table describes the fees and expenses that you may pay if you buy and hold shares in the Fund.

Shareholder Transaction Expenses (fees paid directly from your investment)	
Sales Commissions to Purchase Shares	None
Commissions to Reinvest Dividends	None
Redemption Fees	None

Annual Fund Operating Expenses (expenses that are deducted from Fund assets)	
Investment Advisor's Fee	.50%
12b-1 Fees	None
Other Operating Expenses	.52%
Total Operating Expenses	1.02%

Examples:

This example assumes that you invest $10,000 in the Fund for the time periods indicated and then redeem all of your shares at the end of those periods. This example also assumes that your investment has a 5% return each year and that the Fund's operating expenses remain the same. Although your actual costs may be higher or lower, based on these assumptions your costs would be:

1 year	3 years	5 years	10 years
$104	$325	$563	$1,248

> Expenses shown in these examples do not represent actual past or future expenses. Actual expenses may be more or less than those shown. The assumed 5% return in hypothetical, and is not a representation or prediction of past or future returns, which may be more or less than 5%.

Financial Highlights

This financial highlights table is intended to help you understand the Fund's financial performance for the past 5 years. Certain information reflects financial results for a single Fund share. The total returns in the table represent the rate that an investor would have earned (or lost) on an investment in the Fund (assuming reinvestment of all dividends and distributions). This information has been audited by Gregory, Sharer and Stuart, whose report, along with the Fund's financial statements, are included in the Company's Annual Report, which is available upon request.

	1995	1996	1997	1998	1999
Net Asset Value Beginning of Period	$10.00	$10.00	$10.00	$10.00	$10.03
Net Investment Income (Loss)	.60	.58	.56	.52	.50
Net Realized and Unrealized Gain (Loss) on Investments	—	—	.04	.03	(.18)
Total Income (Loss) From Investment Income	.60	.58	.60	.55	.32
Dividends From Net Investment Income	(.60)	(.58)	(.60)	(.52)	(.50)
Distributions from Net Realized Capital Gains	—	—	—	—	—
Returns of Capital	—	—	—	—	—
Total Distributions	(.60)	(.58)	(.60)	(.52)	(.50)
Net Asset Value at End of Period	10.00	10.00	10.00	10.03	9.85
Total Return[1]	6.29%	5.95%	6.08%	5.70%	3.18%
Net Assets at End of Period (000s)	$430	$548	$854	$724	$811
Ratio of Expenses to Average Net Assets	[2] —	[2] —	.14%	.96%	1.02%
Ratio of Net Income to Average Net Assets	5.96%	5.83%	6.21%	5.28%	4.99%
Portfolio Turnover Rate	41.35%	9.61%	52.64%	14.20%	70.99%

[1] *Computed based on audited figures.*
[2] *Expenses and fees were absorbed by the Advisor.*

Fund Performance Discussion

Management's discussion of Fund performance is contained in the Company's Annual Report and in the Investment Letters produced monthly by its Custodian, Caldwell Trust Company and mailed to all shareholders. Both the Annual Report and these Investment Letters are made a part of this Prospectus by reference. To receive a free copy of the Annual Report, call or write the Company at the telephone number or address shown on both the front and back covers of this Prospectus. To review or print the Annual Report and Investment Letters via the internet, go to http://www.ctrust.com.

Management and Capital Structure

Investment Advisor

Omnivest Research Corporation
250 Tampa Ave. West
Venice, FL 34285
Voice: (941) 493-4295
Toll-Free: (800) 338-9477
Fax: (941) 496-4660

The Company's Funds retain **Omnivest Research Corporation** ("ORC") as investment Advisor under annual contracts with each Fund. ORC is registered under the Investment Advisors Act of 1940 and with the Florida Division of Securities, Tallahassee, Florida. As such, it periodically files reports with both agencies, which are available for public inspection.

ORC is a Florida corporation wholly owned by **Trust Companies of America, Inc.**, a holding company controlled by Roland G. Caldwell and his family. It has provided services to, and has had experience with, the management of investment companies since 1984. Its investment management history, and that of its principal, Roland G. Caldwell, includes serving as portfolio manager and/or investment advisor to corporations, individuals, retirement accounts, charitable foundations, and insurance companies. As of the date of this Prospectus, the sole business and activity of ORC is to provide investment management and advice under contract to the Company's Fund series.

Roland G. Caldwell and Roland G. Caldwell, Jr. are the primary investment professionals and Fund managers within ORC. The senior Mr. Caldwell has been active without interruption since 1958 in the field of investment research and portfolio management, both privately and as an officer of large domestic and foreign trust and banking institutions. Mr. Caldwell, Jr., who is President of ORC, has worked in the financial services industry since 1988 in trust account administration for individual investors as well as investment company and investment advisor management.

As Advisor to all Fund series, ORC receives the following fees:

- 1% per annum of the average daily market value of the net assets of **C/Fund** and **C/Growth Stock Fund**, and
- .5% per annum of the average daily market value of **C/Government Fund** and **C/Community Association Reserve Fund**.

Although 1% of assets may be higher than fees paid by some other equity mutual funds, the Advisor believes it to be comparable to those charged by other advisors to funds with similar objectives. The fee also takes into account that the Advisor pays costs of administering the Company's Fund series portfolios, including accounting record maintenance and shareholder ledgers.

Under terms of the advisory agreement, total expenses of each Fund series have been voluntarily limited to no more than 2% of Fund net assets in any one year. If actual expenses ever exceed the 2% limitation, the Advisor reimburses the Fund for such excess expenses and fully discloses to Fund shareholders in financial statements in accordance with generally accepted accounting practices.

ORC has its registered offices at 250 Tampa Avenue West, Venice, Florida, 34285. C/Funds Group, Inc., shares facilities, space and staff with both its custodian and with ORC.

Presently, the Company leases mutual fund software from C/Data Systems which is wholly-owned by **Trust Companies of America, Inc.** *(For additional details, please refer to the Investment Advisory and Other Services section in the Statement of Additional Information).*

Capital Structure

Organized October 24, 1984, the Company and its entire capitalization consists solely of 5 million shares of authorized common stock with a par value of $.001 each. When issued, each full or fractional share is fully paid, non-assessable, transferable and redeemable.

Shareholder Information

Introduction

As a shareholder, you vote your Fund series shares at each annual or special meeting on any matters on which you are entitled to vote by law or under provisions of the Company's articles of incorporation. All shares are of the same class, and each full share has one vote. Fractional shares (issued to three decimal places) have no voting rights.

You also vote to elect corporate directors and on other matters that affect all Fund series. As a holder of a particular Fund series, you vote on matters that exclusively affect that Fund series. For example, you would vote on an investment advisory agreement or investment restriction relating to your Fund series alone.

As holders of a particular Fund series, you have distinctive rights regarding dividends and redemption, which are more fully described, later in this Prospectus and in the Statement of Additional Information. The Board of Directors, at its discretion, declares dividends for each Fund series as often as is required for the Company to maintain qualification under Sub-Chapter M of the IRS code.

Direct all shareholder inquiries to the Company at the address and telephone number listed on the cover page of this Prospectus.

Pricing of Fund Shares

The Company calculates the Net Asset Value ("NAV") each day at the last known trade price on or after 4:00 p.m. NY time, and on such other days as there is sufficient trading in the Company's portfolio of securities to materially affect its NAV per share. It ordinarily values its portfolio of securities based on market quotes. If quotations are not available, it values securities or other assets by a method which the Board of Directors believes most accurately reflects fair value.

The formula for calculating the NAV per share is:

Total market value of all assets, cash and securities held, *minus*
Any liabilities, *divided by*
 The total number of shares outstanding that day.

Purchasing Shares

The Company requires no minimum to open an account or to make subsequent investments. After opening an account, you can make purchases in person or by mail. To open an account:
- Complete and sign the application enclosed with each Prospectus,
- Return it personally or by mail to the Company at P. O. Box 622, Venice, FL 34282-0622, along with a check payable to the name of the Fund in which you are investing.

Your check for an initial or subsequent investment does not have to be certified. If your check does not clear, the Company will cancel your order(s) and you may be liable for losses or fees incurred, or both.

On the business day the Company receives your completed application and check, the Company purchases shares for your account at the NAV per share of the Fund you selected, as calculated that same day.

The Company opens a separate account for you for each Fund you purchase. It credits each account with, and holds in it, all shares that you purchase or that are issued to you, such as automatic dividend reinvestments and capital gains distributions. The Company allocates fractional shares for purchases (and redemptions), including reinvested distributions. For example, if you purchase $1,000 at a NAV of $11.76 per share, the Company will credit your account with 85.034 shares. Remember that for voting purposes, fractional shares are disregarded.

If you want dividend or capital gains distributions in cash rather than additional shares, or want share certificate issued, you can make a written request containing all documentation that the Company requires. Call the Company at **1-800-338-9477** or write to the address shown on the front cover of this Prospectus to find out about the documentation the company requires for such requests.

To accommodate IRA investments and IRA rollovers, which are often odd amounts, the Company allows all IRA participants to invest or rollover such IRA monies in Fund shares in any amount that is eligible or allowed under current Internal Revenue Service rules.

The Company reserves the right to reject new account applications or additional purchases for an existing account. It also reserves the right to terminate the offering of shares made by this Prospectus if the Board of Directors determines that such action is in the interest of shareholders.

Redeeming Shares

The Company will redeem, with no redemption fee, all or any portion of your shares in any Fund on any day that a NAV is calculated for that Fund. The price paid to you will be the NAV per share next determined after the Company receives your redemption request.

To redeem shares, you and any other owner of the affected account must sign a written request in the exact same way that the shares are registered as shown on the original application you submitted which the Company holds in its records.

If you hold a share certificate, to redeem it you must deposit it with the Company along with all necessary legal documentation. That documentation includes, but is not necessarily limited to, a written and signed redemption request with the signature guaranteed by an official of a commercial bank, trust company, or member firm of the New York Stock Exchange.

The Company normally pays for redeemed shares on the next business day immediately following the redemption date. The Company reserves the right, however, to withhold payment for up to seven (7) calendar days if necessary to protect the interests of the Company or its shareholders. Redemption proceeds are mailed to the shareholder's current mailing address.

If you purchase shares and then request redemption within 15 days, you are not eligible to receive payment until the Company determines to its satisfaction that the funds you used to make the purchase have cleared and are available for payout.

No minimum amount is necessary to keep an account open, except that the Company reserves the right to request that small accounts be redeemed and closed if the cost of activity in the accounts is unjustified. The Company will provide prior notice of not less than 60 days to shareholders before closing an account as an opportunity for additional funds to be invested. No automatic redemptions will be made in accounts solely due to the amount of money invested.

The Company reserves the right to refuse or discontinue share sales to any investor who, in its opinion, is or may disrupt normal Company operations or adversely affect the interests of the Company or Fund shareholders by engaging in frequent or short-term purchase and redemption practices or by other actions.

Share redemptions, whether voluntary or involuntary, may result in your realizing a taxable capital gain or loss.

Dividends, Distributions, and Tax Consequences

The Company intends to remain a qualified "regulated investment company" under Sub-Chapter M of the Internal Revenue Code and qualify for the special tax treatment available by adhering to strict, self-imposed restrictions.

Distributions to you as a shareholder of a particular Fund come from interest and dividends that the Fund receives and net capital gains realized during the tax year. Whether received in cash or as additional shares, distributions of interest, dividends, and short-term capital gains are normally considered as taxable in most instances as ordinary income when received. Distributions of long-term capital gains are taxable at the appropriate rate. Under tax rules, individual taxpayers must report 100% of all income earned on shares owned with no deduction allowed for certain fees and expenses incurred. In short, all distributions of dividends, interest, and capital gains realized are normally subject to tax.

Early each calendar year, the Company will give you the information you need to correctly report the amount and type of dividends and distributions on your tax return. To avoid the Company having to withhold a portion of your dividends, you must provide needed information, including a valid, correct Social Security or Tax Identification Number.

IRA and Retirement Accounts

If you are eligible to open and/or make deposits to an Individual Retirement Account ("IRA") including a Roth IRA, or Self-Employed IRA ("SEP-IRA"), you can use the Company as custodian to hold Fund shares, but no other form of investments, securities, or assets. You must use a trust company or other eligible custodian to hold any non-Fund related securities or investments. Caldwell Trust Company, the Fund's custodian, is eligible to serve as custodian for such purposes. It can and will serve as custodian for any Fund shares on request. *(For more information regarding such services and fees, please call or write Caldwell Trust Company directly or the Company at the address and telephone number shown on the front page of this Prospectus).*

If you have or open an IRA or SEP-IRA account and want to invest all or portion of your deposits in shares of any Fund series, you can do so by opening a "Self-Directed" IRA or SEP-IRA account with the Company. To obtain copies of the forms needed to open an account, write or call the Company. Retirement plans and other "rollovers" are eligible to be rolled into an IRA or SEP-IRA account with the Company, as are rollovers from most other types of qualified retirement accounts. The Company makes no charge of any kind to open, maintain or close an IRA account invested 100% in shares of any Fund series.

You can also invest funds deposited into other types of profit-sharing, pension or retirement plans, including Keogh accounts in shares of any Fund series. However, the qualification and certification of such "Plans" must first be prearranged with a pension or tax specialist who is qualified to assist and oversee plan compliance requirements. Although the Company retains an expert to help you establish such plans, it neither offers nor possesses the necessary professional skills or knowledge regarding the establishment, compliance or maintenance of IRS-qualified retirement plans. The Company recommends that you retain professional counsel for such purposes

Financial Information

Highlights

Financial highlights for each Fund for the past five years, or since inception if less, are included in the discussions of each Fund. This information has been audited by Gregory, Sharer & Stuart whose report, along with the Fund's financial statement, are available upon request.

To review this information for:

- C/Fund, go to page 3.
- C/Growth Stock Fund, go to page 7.
- C/Government Fund, go to page 11.
- C/Community Association Reserve Fund, go to page 16.

Shareholder Reports

The Company's latest annual financial statement is a part this Prospectus by reference. If an interim financial statement with a later date is available, it is incorporated by reference also. These reports include:

- Statement of Assets and Liabilities,
- Statement of Operations,
- Statement of Changes in Net Assets,
- Schedule of Fund Investments,
- Per Share Tables,
- Notes to financial statements, and
- Any applicable supplementary information.

You receive the most recent annual statement and interim statement if applicable, along with this Prospectus. Existing shareholders are the exception, because they receive their statements earlier. You can request a free copy of the most recent financial reports by contacting the Company at the address on the cover of this Prospectus.

Custodian, Auditor, and Distributor

Custodian

Caldwell Trust Company, 201 Center Road, Suite Two, Venice, FL, 34292, serves as custodian of the Funds' assets. Under an agreement as agent for the Company, it is empowered to:

- Hold all assets, securities and cash for each separate series. It may do so in the trust company's name or in its nominee name (or names). It accounts to each Fund regularly for these holdings.
- Accept instructions for the purchase, sale or reinvestment of all Fund assets from the Company's president or from the
- Disburse funds for authorized shareholder redemptions.

Auditor

Gregory, Sharer & Stuart, CPAs, 100 2nd Ave. S., Suite 600, St. Petersburg, FL 33701, Certified Public Accountants, serves as the independent public accountant and auditor for the Company and its Funds. Neither the firm nor any of its principals or staff holds any financial interest directly or indirectly in the Company or in any of its Funds.

Distributor

The Company acts as distributor of all shares of its Funds and maintains its own shareholder register by Fund, acting as transfer agent for all common shares outstanding.

The Statement of Additional Information for C/Funds Group, Inc. contains more information about the Company and its Funds. The Company's Annual Report and its Semi-Annual Report if applicable (which are incorporated into this Prospectus by reference) also provide additional information. In the Annual Report, you will find a discussion of the Funds' performance during its last fiscal year.

The Statement of Additional Information, Annual Report, and Semi-Annual Report if applicable are available to shareholders without charge. To request a copy of any of these documents, call or write C/Funds Group, Inc. at the telephone number or address shown below.

Information about the Company and its Funds can be reviewed and copied at the Securities and Exchange Commission Public Reference Room in Washington, DC. Information on the operation of the Public Reference Room can be obtained by calling the Commission at 1-202-942-8090. Reports and other information about the Company and its Funds are available from the EDGAR Database on the Commission's internet site at http://www.sec.gov and copies of this information may be obtained, on payment of a duplicating fee, by electronic request at publicinfo@sec.gov or by writing the Commission's Public Reference Section, Washington, DC 20549-0102.

C/Funds Group, Inc.

Investment Company Act File Number 811-04246

P. O. Box 622 • Venice, Florida 34284-0622 • 941-488-6772 • 800-338-9477

http://www.ctrust.com/cfunds.htm

C/FUNDS GROUP, INC.

P. O. Box 622
Venice, Florida, 34284-0622
Voice: 941-488-6772 • Toll-Free: 800-338-9477 • Fax: 941-496-4661

February 28, 2000

C/FUNDS GROUP, INC. ("the Company") is an open-end diversified investment management company that operates a series of funds in four portfolios ("the Funds") under the names C/FUND, C/GROWTH STOCK FUND, C/GOVERNMENT FUND, AND C/COMMUNITY ASSOCIATION RESERVE FUND.

This Statement of Additional Information is not a Prospectus. You should read it in conjunction with the Prospectus dated the same date. To receive a free copy of the Prospectus, write or call the Company at the address or telephone numbers shown above.

Table of Contents

Statement of Additional Information

Fund History

Date and Form of Organization

C/Funds Group, Inc. was incorporated in the State of Florida on October 24, 1984 under its original name, Caldwell Fund, Inc. In 1992, the corporation changed its name to C/Funds Group, Inc.

The Fund and Its Strategies and Risks

Classification

C/Funds Group, Inc. is a diversified, open-end, regulated investment company registered under the Securities Acts of 1933 and 1934 and the Investment Company Act of 1940.

Investment Strategies and Risks

Overview of the Funds and Their Objectives

Each Fund series has its own investment objective as briefly described below.

- **C/Fund** is a "total return" fund that seeks growth and income. It buys and owns both common stocks or equivalents, and fixed-income obligations in any proportion that its Adviser deems appropriate at any given time.
- **C/Growth Stock Fund** invests substantially all of its assets in common stocks or equivalents at all times as it seeks maximum growth of net asset value with only minor concern for volatility.
- **C/Government Fund** invests substantially all of its assets in fixed-income obligations issued by the U.S. Government or one or more of its Agencies for safety of principal and income.
- **C/Community Association Reserve Fund** is a specialized fund offered only to qualified community associations in the State of Florida for investment of association reserve funds. It invests in U.S. Government or Agency obligations for safety and income.

Total Return Concept

The Adviser believes that the "total return" concept is an all-important, though not well understood, factor affecting all investors and asset managers in contemporary times. The goal of maximizing portfolio returns with a minimum of risk is now a universal maxim within the investment community. The Adviser further believes that most, if not all, asset managers either knowingly or unknowingly use the concept in their attempts to maximize returns, regardless of the type of investment used.

The risks of value loss due to price change or to a deterioration in the issuer's financial health are vitally important influences in selecting investment types and specific securities within each type. Accordingly, the Adviser invests or reinvests fund assets in varying proportions in either fixed investments or equity investments according to the Adviser's view of the immediate outlook for each category.

The Company's original fund, then called the Caldwell Fund, now called C/Fund, was established with "total return" as its investment objective. The basic outline of that strategy applies in some respects to each Fund series, constrained mainly by the types of investments each series is permitted to acquire and hold. An edited and updated version of the original description for C/Fund is provided here for reference and information.

"The Fund and its Adviser think that high total returns are mathematically achievable over time if a portfolio can:
- Minimize decline in investment value during periods of sustained stock price weakness by reinvesting largely in fixed-income investments; and
- Achieve average or better stock appreciation (as measured against such popular market averages as the Dow-Jones Industrial and Standard and Poor's 500 averages) during periods of rising prices.

There is, of course, no assurance that the Adviser can achieve this objective.

When investment appreciation is the goal, the Adviser invests most fund assets in securities of widely-held, well-known companies. Such investments are mostly common stocks and other securities, whose prices tend to rise or fall similarly to stocks, that are equivalent to or convertible into an equity investment. When asset value protection is most important, the Adviser most often invests in highest quality investments with maturities selected to achieve its goals in such a market environment. Such investments would include Treasury or Government Agency issues, money market investments, and other investments of similar quality.

With fixed-income securities, market prices fluctuate with changes in interest rates, generally the longer the maturity the greater the percentage change. As such, investing in fixed-income securities provides an opportunity to make capital gains. To maximize total return, from time to time the Adviser may also invest in fixed-income securities, doing so for appreciation from capital gains rather than for value protection or current income maximization. The Adviser would confine its fixed-income investment purchases to bonds rated A or better by Standard & Poors (see Appendix).

Flexibility is key to achieving "total return" in a portfolio. Smaller investment companies have the advantage of being able to add or remove total positions without substantially or adversely influencing the market value of individual issues traded. In today's markets, the share position size that can be traded without disrupting the market for the issues involved appears to be expanding. Should this trend continue as anticipated, constraints that might today limit the size of the Fund's portfolio because of its desire to retain trading flexibility, will become less a factor.

The Fund, like all registered investment companies, reserves the right to limit the size of its assets by discontinuing sales of Fund shares at any time. Its Board of Directors could decide to do so at any time if they feel it would be in the best interests of the Company and/or Fund shareholders to maintain adherence to its objective which requires that it be able to sell and buy total security positions.

The Adviser deems the most important portions of a portfolio's total returns to be income from interest and dividends and appreciation in share value. Appreciation is viewed as a form of repayment for the risks of price change that cannot be avoided when owning securities such as common stocks whose prices constantly change.

Recognizing that interest and dividends are important in enhancing returns sometimes results in shareholders incurring federal, state and/or local income taxes on a significant portion of their annual distributions. Shareholders should understand that such tax considerations are secondary to maximizing the Fund's total returns when the Adviser makes investment decisions.

This policy is partly based on the Adviser's belief that such taxes and tax rates have only an indirect bearing on any single company's attractiveness as an investment and partly because the Adviser believes that tax rates in general are, and should be, of declining importance to the investment decision-making process, viewed in a widest sense. Non-taxed portfolios, such as Individual Retirement Accounts, Keogh and other pension plans, are ideally suited for investing in one or more Fund series of the Company for these and other reasons."

Common Stocks or Equivalents

These investments, "equities," represent either a residual share ownership interest in a publicly-traded for-profit enterprise, or are preferred shares or fixed-income obligations of an issuer that can be converted into its common stock. In broad terms, the Adviser categorizes for-profit enterprises into two basic groups: seasoned large capitalization entities; and, newer smaller capitalization entities. The features that help determine which category best fits any given enterprise are:

- Annual sales volume and the rate of growth being experienced in sales;
- Market value of all shares outstanding;
- Amount of debt owed;
- Profitability of the enterprise;
- Length of time it has been successfully in business; and,
- Kind of business in which it specializes or is seeking to participate.

Usually the applicable category for an enterprise is obvious. General Motors, AT&T, IBM, General Electric, and American Home Products are large, seasoned, widely-held enterprises with long records to analyze. Conversely, an enterprise that has been in business only three to five years when it first offers its shares publicly is clearly an unseasoned enterprise, probably with relatively small annual sales volumes and small market capitalization. Less obviously, companies that have been in business for many years, yet still have relatively small market capitalizations and annual sales volumes, may owe considerable debt as a percentage of total capital, or have unseasoned management, or offer a less well-defined or understood product or service.

Because equities normally are not required to pay a dividend unless declared, and have no maturity date when repayment in full of an initial investment is due, their market price tends to fluctuate with the issuer's changing prospects and market conditions. This open-ended nature makes equity investments more risky by definition and accordingly inappropriate for some investment purposes.

Similarly, because common stocks have no fixed-income component (convertible preferreds and fixed obligations excluded from this definition because of their hybrid nature), investment value can either advance or decline depending on the issuer's success. This potential can attract those who are prepared to accept the risks in exchange for the prospect of investment price appreciation and/or dividend stream, as compared to other types of investments.

The Adviser believes equities or equivalents are the most attractive type of investment available based on a superior long term equity performance record, today's marketplace liquidity, and the favorable longer term prospects for most enterprises in the current economic environment. Accordingly, for those investors who can afford the risk of price fluctuation or total investment loss in the most extreme case, the Adviser expects that common stocks and equivalents will continue to be the primary form of investment in Fund portfolios allowing such investments.

In making investment decisions, the Adviser considers all of these criteria as well as commonly accepted financial data like per share figures, return rates on capital, etc. Further, the Adviser uses computer-generated data which provides information that helps to determine whether the management team of an enterprise, regardless of size, understands the need to add to shareholder wealth and knows how to do it on a regular and sustained basis. This computerized analysis uses inputs that are proprietary to the Adviser and its sources, including an enterprise's "cost of capital" and its rate of return on invested capital. The Adviser believes that shareholder wealth is created when return on investment exceeds cost of capital. Both current and past experience are important indicators of whether an enterprise is succeeding on this basis, which in turn the Adviser sees as evidence of its management's capabilities in this important regard.

Fixed-Income Obligations
The U. S. Treasury, federally authorized Agencies and other governmental bodies, public enterprises, and state, local and municipal authorities all issue many kinds of fixed obligations including Bills, Notes, Bonds, Indentures, First Mortgage Obligations, Participation Certificates, and others. Each of these kinds of obligations has unique characteristics and terms which are complex and awkward to describe in detail individually. Before making a fixed-income investment purchase, the Adviser examines all known relevant data regarding term, rate of interest, call features, conditions of repayment, collateral, guarantees, etc.

In the current environment, U. S. Government obligations dominate the fixed-income market and interest rates on most fixed-income obligations are related or pegged in some way to rates on similar government obligations. In such an environment, the Adviser believes there is less need to invest in non-government related fixed-income investments.

Further, investors in general have become more risk-averse in recent years creating a favor for fixed-income investments that have some form of insurance or government guarantee or backing. Because the borrowing needs of the U. S. Treasury and other U. S. Government Agencies have created substantial growth in the size of the government-related securities market, interest rates being paid on such issues are no longer significantly lower than the rates on high quality privately-issued fixed-income obligations.

Strategies in Practice in the Funds
Generally, the Investment Adviser to the Company's Funds invests **C/Fund** assets mostly in shares of larger, more

seasoned enterprises and **C/Growth Stock Fund** mostly in shares of smaller, less seasoned enterprises. When the Adviser believes an enterprise is an appropriate investment for a Fund, it makes a purchase decision regardless of how others in the investment field might categorize the enterprise as a particular class size by capitalization. In general, however, the Adviser adheres to a practice of favoring seasoned issues in the more conservative funds, and issues that appear to have faster growth prospects, regardless of size, in the more aggressive funds.

Because of the factors discussed above at "Fixed-Income Obligations" and for other reasons, the Adviser favors purchasing government-related obligations, mostly Notes and Bonds, for all Funds, most particularly those in which principal safety and income are primary objectives such as **C/Government Fund** and **C/Community Association Reserve Fund**. Although acquiring corporate fixed-income obligations in **C/Fund** as part of its fixed-income component from time to time is not prohibited, the Adviser favors and intends to continue to favor government-related issues, which are more marketable than all other forms of fixed-income securities. (See the Appendix for a further definition of quality as defined by a major fixed-income rating agency.)

Fund Policies

Under the terms of the By-laws of the Company and its Registration Statement pursuant to the Investment Company Act of 1940, the following investment restrictions were adopted. These restrictions can only be fundamentally changed or amended by majority approval by vote of all outstanding shares of all Funds, both individually and of the Company in total, as set forth in Company By-laws and the Investment Company Act of 1940.

Accordingly, all Fund of the Company will **not**:

A. Invest in the direct purchase and sale of real estate.

B. Invest in options, futures, commodities or commodity contracts, restricted securities, mortgages, or in oil, gas, mineral or other exploration or development programs;

C. Invest in foreign-based issuers that would exceed 10% of the value of its net assets at market value at the time of acquisition, except for issues widely traded on exchanges or in markets domiciled in the U.S., which may be held in any amount permitted registered investment companies;

D. Borrow money, except for temporary purposes, and then only in amounts not to exceed in the aggregate 5% of the market value of its total assets taken at the time of such borrowing.

E. Invest more of its assets than is permitted under regulations in securities of other registered investment companies, which restricts such investments to a limit of 5% of the Company's assets in any one registered investment company, and 10% overall in all registered investment companies, in no event to exceed 3% of the outstanding shares of any single registered investment company.

F. Invest more than 5% of its total assets at the time of purchase in securities of companies that have been in business or been in continuous operation less than 3 years, including the operations of any predecessor, except for direct investments made in custodian banking entities serving one or more of the Company's Fund series;

G. Invest or deal in securities which are not readily marketable.

H. Own more than 10% of the outstanding voting securities of any one issuer or company, nor will it, with at least 75% of any Fund's total assets, invest more than 5% in any single issue, valued at the time of purchase. This restriction shall not be applicable for investments in U.S. government or agency securities, which are permitted to constitute 100% of the assets of any Fund of the Company at any time.

I. Invest 25% or more of its total assets in a single industry or similar group of industries, except U.S. government securities.

J. Maintain a margin account, nor purchase investments on credit or margin, or leverage its investments, except for normal transaction obligations during settlement periods.

K. Make any investment for the purpose of obtaining, exercising or for planning to exercise voting control of subject company.

L. Sell securities short.

M. Underwrite or deal in offerings of securities of other issuers as a sponsor or underwriter in any way. (Note: The Company may be deemed an underwriter of securities in some jurisdictions when it serves as distributor of its own shares for sale to or purchase from its shareholders.)

N. Purchase or retain any securities issued by an issuer, if any officer, director, or interested party of the Company or its Investment Adviser is in any way affiliated with, controls or owns more than 1% of any class of shares of such issuer, or if any such described persons as a class beneficially own or control more than 5% of any class of securities of such issuer.

O. Make loans to others or issue senior securities. For these purposes the purchase of publicly distributed indebtedness of any kind is excluded and not considered to be making a loan.

Regarding **Item E** above, the Company uses computerized cash management sweep services offered by custodians. These services presently include reinvesting overnight and short term cash balances in shares of a money market whose primary objective is principal safety and maximum current income from holding highly liquid, short-term, fixed investments, principally U. S. Government and Agency issues. The Company only invests in such funds temporarily for convenience and efficiency as it tries to keep short term monies invested at interest only until it can make more permanent reinvestments in the ordinary course of business.

Further, **Item N** above does not apply to C/Growth Stock Fund which is free to buy and invest in permitted percentages in shares of companies in which a significant or majority ownership is owned or held by or for the beneficial interest of an officer, director or interested person of the Company or any of its Fund series. C/Growth Stock Fund has ever purchased such shares nor does it intend to do so in the foreseeable future.

Temporary Defensive Position

Each fund series seeks to achieve its objectives by adhering to its investment approach as outlined in the Prospectus. When equities are the principal investment sector, each fund manager maintains short term money market balances in order to earn interest on all cash balances until stocks are selected and purchased. Likewise, fixed income funds retain all cash in short term money market balances until security selections are determined. In view of the modern investment environment of low inflation and low interest rates, all fund managers now consider money market balances as a permanent investment sector when avoidance of price change on fixed investments is considered consistent with fund objectives. As a total return fund, carrying large money market balances at any given time for any length of time is fully consistent with the objective of the C/Fund series.

Portfolio Turnover

The Company's policy is to limit each Fund's portfolio turnover to transactions necessary to carry out its investment policies and/or to obtain cash for share redemptions. Portfolio turnover rates, which vary from period to period depending on market conditions, are computed as:

> The lesser of either total purchases or total sales, on an annualized basis, ***divided by***
> The average total market value of the assets held.

For equity Funds, the portfolio turnover rate tends to be higher than normal during formative years. Afterward, it is the Advisor's goal to minimize turnover by buying and holding rather than trading securities to the extent that it remains consistent with the Fund's investment objectives. For government securities purchases and sales, turnover is calculated if the securities mature beyond one (1) year from date of purchase. This tends to increase the portfolio turnover percentages, which are reported for each Fund series in the financial statements incorporated into this Statement of Additional Information by reference.

Turnover rate differences from 1998 to 1999 were not significant for C/Fund and C/Growth Stock Fund given their investment objectives and market conditions during the period. Increases in turnover rate in the C/Government Fund and C/Community Association Reserve Fund reflect response to rising market interest rates and are not abnormal for bond funds with similar maturities. It is anticipated that in the upcoming year changes in turnover rates for the various Funds will fluctuate driven by the same investment objectives as they are pursued in the market environment that occurs.

Management of the Fund

Board of Directors

Under the By-Laws of the Company, the Board of Directors have control and management of the business of the Company. Also, subject to the laws of the State of Florida and the Company's Certificate of Incorporation, they may do all those things and exercise all those powers that are not required by law or by the Certificate of Incorporation to be done or exercised by the shareholders.

The members of the Board of Directors have the power to appoint and remove officers or employees, determine their duties, fix and change their compensation, and, in an officer's absence, to grant his or her powers to another officer. They may also fix and change any compensation paid to members of the Board. By resolution, they may designate committees that can exercise the powers of the Board in management of the business and affairs of the Company.

Officers and Board of Directors

Following are the names, duties, and affiliations of the Officers of the Company and the members of the Company's Board of Directors, as elected by shareholders at the latest Annual Meeting of Shareholders.

Name and Address	Position with the Company	Past Five Year Business Affiliations and Primary Occupation	Age
Roland G. Caldwell, Jr.* 3320 Hardee Drive Venice, FL 34292	Director and President	President, Trust Companies of America, Inc.; Vice President, Secretary and Trust Officer, Caldwell Trust Company; President, Omnivest Research Corp.	32
William L. Donovan 627 Padget Court Venice, FL 34293	Chairman, Board of Directors	Retired. Investments & Real Estate. Former VP Gately Shops, Inc., Grosse Pointe, MI.	79
D. Bruce Chittock 19625 Cats Den Road Chagrin Falls, OH 44023	Vice Chairman, Board of Directors	Industrial Engineer, Equipment for Industry, Inc., Cleveland, OH.	65
Emmett V. Weber 3411 Bayou Sound Longboat Key, FL 34228	Director	Capt. (ret.) USAir, Pittsburgh, PA; Real Estate.	68
Deborah C. Pecheux* 1911 Oakhurst Parkway Sugarland, TX 77479	Director and Sister of President	VP CareVu Corporation; Former Sr. Project Engineer Ferranti, Intl., Houston, TX.	43
Lyn B. Braswell 542 Silk Oak Venice, FL 34293-4311	Secretary and Fund Administrator	C/Funds Group, Inc.; Former commercial banking professional.	48

* Interested persons as defined under the 1940 Act.

Compensation

All persons who hold positions with the Company and perform duties for the Funds are employees of Trust Companies of America, Inc. ("TCA") and are compensated by TCA. Expenses of "interested" directors are and will always remain the responsibility of the Investment Adviser to the Company and its Funds, Omnivest Research Corporation ("ORC").

The non-interested directors of the Company are the **only** persons receiving compensation from the Company which has no retirement plan. Compensation paid by the Company to non-interested directors as of fiscal year end 1999 is as follows:

Name of Non-interested Director	Aggregate Compensation From Each Fund					Total Compensation From Company and Funds Paid to Directors
	C/Fund	C/Growth Stock	C/Govern-ment	C/Community Association Reserve	(1) Adams Equity	
William L. Donovan	$2,981.09	$907.33	$1,219.85	$91.76	$99.97	$5,300.00
D. Bruce Chittock	$2,981.09	$907.33	$1,219.85	$91.76	$99.97	$5,300.00
Emmett V. Weber	$2,981.09	$907.33	$1,219.85	$91.76	$99.97	$5,300.00

(1) *Fund closed November 29, 1999.*

Code of Ethics

The Company and the Investment Advisor have adopted a Code of Ethics under which covered persons and members of their immediate family may not purchase or sell a security within prescribed periods before or after the purchase or sale of the same portfolio security by the Fund. Nor, within the prescribed periods, may such persons purchase or sell any security into which a portfolio security is convertible or with respect to which a portfolio security gives its owner an option to purchase or sell the security.

Control Persons and Principal Holders

Control Persons

Omnivest Research Corporation ("ORC"), the Investment Advisor to the Company and its Funds, is a wholly owned subsidiary of Trust Companies of America, Inc. ("TCA"). Shares of TCA, a corporation registered in the State of Florida, are owned by approximately 140 shareholders. Voting control of TCA is held by the Caldwell family.

Neither ORC nor TCA has control over the voting rights of Fund series shareholders. No shareholder holds a controlling interest (more than 25%) of the total assets of the Funds.

Principal Holders

No individual shareholder either directly or beneficially owns 5% or more of the shares of C/Fund. Following is principal holder information for C/Growth Stock Fund, C/Government Fund, and C/Community Association Reserve Fund.

C/Growth Stock Fund:

Account Holder	Address	Percentage
Jean L. Docster	4601 Las Brisas Ln., Sarasota, FL 34238	5.16%
Wilson-Wood Foundation, Inc.	7188 Beneva Rd., S., Sarasota, FL 34238	11.95%
The Cumberland Companies, Inc.	6300 S. Syracuse Way, Englewood, CO 80111	14.82%

C/Government Fund:

Account Holder	Address	Percentage
E. V. Babcock, III	1510 S. Tuttle Ave., Sarasota, FL 34239	5.26%

C/Community Association Reserve Fund:

Account Holder	Address	Percentage
Terra Cove Homeowners Assn.	250 Tampa Ave., W., Venice, FL 34285 [1]	5.90%
South Creek Owners Assn., Inc.	250 Tampa Ave., W., Venice, FL 34285 [1]	6.79%
Beach Manor Villas South, Inc.	250 Tampa Ave., W., Venice, FL 34285 [1]	8.30%
Fiddler's Green	250 Tampa Ave., W., Venice, FL 34285 [1]	14.76%
Holiday Travel Park	250 Tampa Ave., W., Venice, FL 34285 [1]	16.58%
Mission Lakes of Venice Condo Assn.	250 Tampa Ave., W., Venice, FL 34285 [1]	23.99%

[1] *Each of these community associations uses their association management company's address as their mailing address.*

The officers and directors as a group own less than 1% of the total assets of the Funds. Ownership percentage in C/Fund is 1.4%, and in C/Growth Stock Fund an C/Government Fund is less than 1%.

Investment Advisory and Other Services

Investment Advisors

The Investment Adviser to the Company and its Funds is Omnivest Research Corporation ("ORC") *(formerly Caldwell & Co.)*. ORC is a Florida corporation, presently registered and practicing as an "Investment Advisor" under the Investment Advisors Act of 1940 with the Securities and Exchange Commission and with the Florida Division of Securities. ORC is a wholly-owned subsidiary of Trust Companies of America, Inc. ("TCA"), a privately held company whose majority ownership is controlled by the Roland G. Caldwell family. TCA was formed mid-1995 to serve as parent to all operating subsidiaries and divisions, each of which provides a specific trust or financial service to the general public under its own identity.

ORC was incorporated October, 1969, and has been continuously offering investment advisory services since the date of its formation. Until 1995, ORC's principal activity was to provide investment advisory services, primarily under contract to the Company, to banks and other financial institutions, and to individual clients generally located in the service area in and around Sarasota County, Florida. In mid-1995, ORC ceased all Advisory activities except to the Company, which is now its sole advisory client. In July, 1997, Roland G. Caldwell, Jr., who is President of the Company, was elected President of ORC.

Roland G. Caldwell serves as director of ORC and its principal investment professional. He has been actively employed and/or in practice as a securities analyst, portfolio manager and Investment Adviser since 1958, mainly managing trusteed accounts and similar types of client portfolios for bank trust clients. He has held key managerial investment responsibilities at trust/banking companies with assets under administration at each ranging in size from approximately $80 million to over $1 billion. These trust/banking companies were located in both the U.S. and abroad. Mr. Caldwell was born November 10, 1933, and is a graduate of Kent State University, 1958, holding a Bachelor of Science Degree in Business Administration/Accounting.

ORC provides services to the Company and all its Funds under contracts which are non-assignable by ORC. Those contracts provide for payment of a fee, calculated daily and paid monthly, at the rate specified in each contract and based on the daily market value of the Fund's net assets. For C/Fund and C/Growth Stock Fund, that rate is 1%. For the C/Government Fund and C/Community Association Reserve Fund, that rate is .5%. These contracts, which shareholders and the Board of Directors approve as required, are terminable upon 30 days written notice, one party to the other.

Management fees paid to ORC by the Company for the last three fiscal years are shown below.

Year Ended	Amount
1999	$179,947
1998	$176,602
1997	$139,453

Services Provided by Advisor and Fund Expenses Paid

Total direct operating costs of the Company are voluntarily restricted to 2% of net assets of each Fund, primarily because this is the maximum permissible percentage permitted by some states. Expenses in excess of this 2% limitation are the responsibility of ORC under the terms of the investment contract with the Company. In compliance with standard accounting practices and rules and laws governing regulated investment companies, investment research costs and/or allowed expenses of the Company are included for purposes of calculating the 2% limitation.

During its fiscal year ended December 31, 1999, expenses of the Company did not exceed 2% of net assets of the Company, and no reimbursements were required or made by ORC to the Company for any Fund series. The Company does not expect the expenses of any Fund series to exceed 2% of net asset value in any fiscal year.

Expenses of "interested" directors and losses incurred by the Company as a direct result of any purchase fails shall always remain the responsibility of the Investment Adviser. ORC and its parent company TCA have been providing administrative and shareholder services to the Company since inception.

No part of the expenses of the Company or its Funds is paid by any other party.

Service Agreements

Since 1987, the Company became responsible for lease payments for software to operate the Company's Fund series. Software lease payments were paid to C/Data Systems (*formerly C/Data Systems, Inc.*), a division of Trust Companies of America, Inc. ("TCA"), to lease "C/MFAS," a mutual fund accounting system trademarked and owned by C/Data Systems. TCA is controlled by the family of Roland G. Caldwell. As of the date of this Statement of Additional Information, lease payments being paid to C/Data Systems are at the rate of $500 per month under a contract approved by the Board of Directors of the Company and of TCA, which contract is cancelable by the Company on 30-days written notice.

Other Service Providers

Transfer agent

C/Funds Group, Inc. serves as its own Transfer Agent under the Securities Act of 1934 and as its own dividend paying agent. The Company makes no charge to any of the Fund series for these services.

Custodian

The custodian for the Company and all its Fund series is Caldwell Trust Company, 201 Center Road, Venice, Florida 34292. Caldwell Trust Company ("CTC") is an independent trust company chartered in the state of Florida and is a wholly-owned subsidiary of Trust Companies of America, Inc. ("TCA"). TCA is a privately held company whose majority ownership is controlled by the Roland G. Caldwell family.

The custodian performs customary custodial services under its Custody Agreement with each of the Company's Funds. Among those services are handling the purchase and sale of investments and managing securities deliveries through the custodian's relationship with the Depository Trust Company. The custodian also collects income on the property it holds under its custodial agreements, pays expenses and remittances, and reinvests income as instructed by the Company. The Company compensates the custodian as they mutually agree from time to time. Currently the fee paid to CTC by the Funds is calculated as .3% of the market value per year for each fund.

Accountant

The independent accountants for the Company and all its Fund series is Gregory, Sharer & Stuart, 100 Second Avenue South, St. Petersburg, Florida 33701-4383.

Brokerage Allocation and Other Practices

Brokerage Transactions and Commissions

Orders to purchase and sell portfolio securities are made under the control of the President of the Company, subject to the overall supervision of the Board of Directors. All orders are placed at the best price and with the best execution obtainable. Buy and sell orders are placed according to the type, size, and kind of order involved and as each condition may demand, to secure the best result for the Company and its shareholders, all factors considered.

The Company is permitted to use broker-dealer firms that: (1) charge low commission rates; (2) have demonstrated superior execution capabilities; and (3) provide economic, corporate and investment research services. In the opinion of the Advisor, the Company, and its Board of Directors, selections based on such criteria serve the best interests of the Company and Fund shareholders.

Following are the aggregate commissions paid to these firms during the last three fiscal years. The changes from year to year are normal and consistent with normal Fund growth and portfolio turnover.

| Year | Fund | | | | | Total |
	C/Fund	C/Growth	(1) Adams Equity	C/Govern- ment	C/Community Assoc- Reserve	
1999	5,637	16,664	7,662	283	417	30,663
1998	2,190	18,442	6,804	1,008	167	40,957
1997	2,554	7,982	9,077	281	680	22,140

(1) *Fund closed November 29, 1999.*

Brokerage Selection

The Company's policy is to allocate brokerage business to the best advantage and benefit of its shareholders. The President of the Company and its Investment Advisor are responsible for directing all transactions through brokerage firms of its choice. All securities transactions are made so as to obtain the most efficient execution at the lowest transaction cost.

From 1986 to the end of 1999, the Company made all securities transactions through large, non-retail brokerage firms specializing in providing financial institutions and others with low cost security transactions, third-party generated research services, and certain specialized services for the direct benefit of shareholders of regulated investment companies. At the end of 1999, the Company began using a direct electronic link to an institutional broker that charges $.03 per share for most trades and that does not provide the Company with research services.

Capital Stock

The only securities authorized by the Company are 5,000,000 capital shares at $.01 par value.

Purchase, Redemption, and Pricing of Shares

Purchase of Shares

Initial Purchases

Investors can purchase common shares of the Company with no required minimum investment and no sales charge by filling out an application form, signing it correctly, and delivering it by mail or in person to the Company's principal office in Venice, Florida. A copy of the application is inserted as a part of the Prospectus and is available by request to the Company, which is the sole distributor of Fund shares.

The purchase price will be at the next net asset value per share that the Company determines after receiving a valid purchase order. The date on which the Company accepts the application and the net asset value that is calculated at the close of business on that date determines the purchase price and will normally be the purchase date for shares. Payment for shares purchased must be by check, which need not be a certified check, or receipt of good funds by the Company.

The Company reserves the right to withhold or reject requests for purchases for any reason, including uncollectable funds. If a purchase is canceled due to uncollectable funds, the purchaser is liable for all administrative costs incurred and for all other losses or charges for the invalid transfer and/or purchase.

IRA accounts and other pension accounts can purchase shares of the Company at any time for any eligible amount.

Subsequent Purchases

Subsequent purchases of shares by a registered shareholder can be made by mail to the Company at its current address and/or telephone number. All subsequent individual and other non-IRA purchases can be made in any amount with no minimum required and with no sales charge. Such amounts are due and payable to the Company in good funds on the purchase date.

Reinvestments

The Company automatically reinvests all dividend distributions to shareholders in additional shares of the Company at the net asset value determined as of the close of business on the dividend distribution payment date, unless the shareholder instructs otherwise in writing before the distribution record date.

Fractional Shares

When share purchases or redemptions are made or when a shareholder requests cash, shares will be issued or redeemed accordingly, in fractions of a share, calculated to the third decimal place. (Example: $1,000 invested in shares at a net asset value of $11.76 per share will purchase 85.034 shares.)

Issuance of Share Certificates

The Company does not issue share certificates to registered shareholders unless they specifically request issuance in writing to the Company. All such requests must be signed exactly as the share registration appears on the shareholder register kept by the Company as its own Registrar and Transfer Agent. However, due to the additional work involved with issuing certificates and the added costs, shareholders are encouraged to have all shares held in an account maintained by the Company itself, as is rapidly becoming the custom within the mutual fund industry.

Redemption of Shares

Shareholders can sell back all or a portion of their shares to the Company on any day that the Fund's net asset value ("NAV") is calculated. Such share redemptions will be made as described in detail in the Prospectus dated this same date and are subject to the terms and conditions stated in this document. The Company makes redemptions at the next NAV calculation after it receives and accepts the redemption request. Although the Company can withhold payment for redeemed shares until it is reasonably satisfied that all funds for any purchases have been collected, payment will normally be made the next business day immediately following redemption date. However, the Company reserves the right to hold payment up to seven (7) calendar days if necessary to protect the interests of the Company and its shareholders.

If the New York Stock Exchange is closed for any reason other than normal weekend or holiday closings, if trading is halted or restricted for any reason, or if any emergency circumstances are determined by the Securities and Exchange Commission, the Company's Board of Directors of have the authority and may suspend redemptions or postpone payment dates.

Under circumstances the Board of Directors may determine, they may, like with most other mutual funds, elect to make payments in securities or other Company assets rather than in cash, if they deem at the time that such payment method would be in the best interest of the shareholders of the Company. Such payment in kind, if ever necessary, would involve payment of brokerage commissions by the shareholder if and when securities so received are ever sold.

No minimum amount is necessary to keep an account open, except that the Company reserves the right to request that small accounts be redeemed and closed if the cost of activity in the accounts is unjustified. The Company will provide prior notice of not less than 60 days to shareholders before closing an account as an opportunity for additional funds to be invested. No automatic redemptions will be made in accounts solely due to the amount of money invested. IRA and pension accounts may retain a balance in their accounts without regard to any minimums.

All share redemptions, regardless of the reason, give rise to a "completed sale" for tax purposes when made and shareholders will normally realize a gain or loss at that time. Such gain or loss is customarily determined by, and is usually equal to, the difference between the original purchase price of redeemed shares compared to the dollar amount received upon redemption of the same shares.

Shareholders who hold share certificates and want to redeem their shares must deliver those certificates to the Company in person or by mail in good form for transfer before redemption can occur. Signatures on all certificates to be redeemed must be guaranteed by an officer of a national or state bank, a trust company, federal savings and loan association; and/or a member firm of the New York, American, Boston, Mid-West, or Pacific Stock Exchanges. Any such guarantee must be acceptable to the Company and its transfer agent before any redemption request will be honored. The Company will not accept signatures guaranteed by a Notary Public.

The Company has the right to refuse payment to any registered shareholder until all legal documentation necessary for a complete and lawful transfer is in its or its agent's possession, to the complete satisfaction of the Company and its Board of Directors.

Pricing of Shares

Net asset value per share is computed by dividing the aggregate market value of the net assets of each Fund of the Company, less that Fund's liabilities if any, by the number of that Fund's shares outstanding. Portfolio securities are valued and net asset value per share is determined as of the last known trade price on or after the 4:00 p.m. close (NY time) of business on the New York Stock Exchange ("NYSE") on each day the NYSE is open, and on any other day in which enough trading in portfolio securities occurs so that value changes might materially affect the current net asset value. NYSE trading is closed weekends and holidays, which are listed as New Year's Day, President's Day, Good Friday, Memorial Day, Independence Day, Labor Day, Thanksgiving, and Christmas.

Portfolio securities listed on an organized exchange are valued on the basis of the last sale on the date the valuation is made. Securities that are not traded on that day, and for which market quotations are otherwise readily available, and over-the-counter securities for which market quotations are readily available, are valued on the basis of the bid price at the close of business on that date. Securities and other assets for which market quotations may not be readily available or which might not actively trade will be valued at fair value as determined by procedures that will be established by the Board of Directors. It is the belief of the Board that such procedures result in price determinations that more closely reflect the fair value of such securities, particularly for tax-exempt fixed income securities, which often have only limited trading activity.

Money market instruments are valued at cost which approximates market value unless the Board of Directors determines that such is not a fair value. The sale of common shares of the Company will be suspended during periods when the determination of its net asset value is suspended pursuant to rules or orders of the Securities and Exchange Commission, or when the Board of Directors in its sole judgment believes it is in the best interest of shareholders to do so.

Taxation of the Fund

The Company has qualified for and has elected the special treatment afforded a "regulated investment" company under Subchapter M of the Internal Revenue Code. In any year in which it qualifies and distributes substantially all of its taxable net investment income (NII), the Company (but not its shareholders) is required to pay Federal income taxes only on that portion of its investment income that is undistributed. Otherwise, the Company would be taxed at ordinary corporate federal and state income tax rates on *any* NII not distributed to shareholders at least annually.

The Company intends to remain qualified under Sub-Chapter M of the Internal Revenue Code by:
- Distributing to each shareholder at least 90% of the aggregate NII of each Fund at least annually,
- Investing and reinvesting so that no more than 30% of aggregate Fund NII is derived from gains on the sale of securities held less than three months; and
- Investing its portfolios so that 50% or more of Fund assets are invested in stock issues, no one of which exceeds 5% of the value of Fund aggregate assets at purchase price.

Dividends paid to shareholders are in effect distributions of the Company's NII which are normally taxable to shareholders when received whether in cash or as additional shares. Distributions to shareholders of any realized capital gains are also taxable under existing tax laws at ordinary income tax rates, whether distributed in cash or as additional shares.

For a shareholder who sells shares back to the Company as a redemption, the tax treatment will depend on whether or not the investment is considered a capital asset in the hands of the shareholder. In most cases this would be true, and in that event, a sale of shares will be treated as a capital transaction to be taxed depending upon the tax treatment afforded such transactions by tax laws existing at the time of sale. Advice from shareholder's own tax counsel is recommended regarding the taxability of distributions. For tax purposes, the Company will endeavor to notify all shareholders as soon as practicable after the close of the calendar year of all amounts and types of dividends and distributions paid out during the year just ended, generally in accordance with tax laws in place at the time of payment.

Changes or interpretations of rules made from time to time by the Internal Revenue Service may serve to temporarily or permanently alter existing tax treatment of Fund distributions to shareholders. The Company makes every effort, with the assistance of its tax advisors and independent public accountants, to act in the best interest of its Fund shareholders at all times. Such changes and/or delays in IRS rules make it difficult for regulated investment companies and their shareholders to be certain as to all interpretations at all times.

Performance Calculation

The Company may advertise fund performance in terms of average annual total return for 1, 5, and 10 year periods, or for such lesser periods as a fund has been in existence. For funds that invest primarily in bonds, the Company may quote 30-day yields. Total return is computed as of the close of business on the last business day of the year. Yields are computed as of the close of business on the last business day of the month. The calculation formulas are show below.

Total Return
$$P(1+T)(n) = ERV$$

Where:

P = a hypothetical initial payment of $1,000
T = average annual total return
N = number of years
ERV = ending redeemable value of a hypothetical $1,000 payment made at the beginning of the 1, 5, or 10 year periods at the end of the year or period

30-Day Yield
$$Yield = 2[((a-b)/(cd)+1)^6 - 1]$$

Where:

a = Dividends and interest earned during the period
b = Expenses accrued for the period (net of reimbursements)
c = The average daily number of shares outstanding during the period that were entitled to receive dividends
d = The maximum offering price per share on the last day of the period

Financial Information

The Company's audited Annual Report, and its Semi-Annual Report if applicable, are incorporated into this Statement of Additional Information by reference. Investors may request a free copy by calling or writing the Company at the telephone number or address shown on the cover page of this document.

For financial highlights for each Fund series, see the section of the Prospectus describing each Fund. For information regarding the compensation of Company officers and directors, see the "Compensation" topic in this Statement of Additional information on page 8.

Statement of Additional Information Appendix

Bond Rating Categories as Defined by Standard & Poor's are quoted in part and inserted herein for the information of potential investors in the Company as a reference as follows:

A S&P's corporate or municipal debt rating is a current assessment of the creditworthiness of an obligor with respect to a specific obligation. This assessment may take into consideration obligors such as guarantors, insurers or lessees.

The debt rating is not a recommendation to purchase, sell or hold a security inasmuch as it does not comment as to market price or suitability for a particular investor.

The ratings are based on current information furnished by the issuer or obtained by S&P's from other sources it considers reliable. S&P's does not perform any audit in connection with any rating and may, on occasion, rely on unaudited financial information. The ratings may be changed, suspended or withdrawn as a result of changes in, or availability of, such information, or for other circumstances.

The ratings are based, in varying degrees, on the following considerations:

I. Likelihood of default-capacity and willingness of the obligor as to the timely payment of interest and repayment of principal in accordance with the terms of the obligation;

II. Nature of and provisions of the obligor;

III. Protection afforded by, and relative position of, the obligation in the event of bankruptcy, reorganization or other arrangement under the laws of bankruptcy and other laws affecting creditors rights.

AAA. Debt rated AAA has the highest rating assigned by S&P's. Capacity to pay interest and repay principal is extremely strong.

AA. Debt rated AA has a very strong capacity to pay interest and repay principal and differs from the highest rated issues only in small degree.

A. Debt rated A has a strong capacity to pay interest and repay principal although it is somewhat more susceptible to the adverse effects of changes in circumstances and economic conditions than debt in higher rated categories.

BBB. Debt rated BBB is regarded as having an adequate capacity to pay interest and repay principal. Whereas it normally exhibits adequate protection parameters, adverse economic conditions or changing circumstances are more likely to lead to a weakened capacity to pay interest and repay principal for debt in this category than in higher rated categories.

BB,B,CCC,CC,C. Debt rated BB,B,CCC,CC, and C is regarded, on balance, as predominantly speculative with respect to capacity to pay interest and repay principal in accordance with the terms of the obligation. BB indicates the lowest degree of speculation and C the highest degree of speculation. While such debt will likely have some quality and protective characteristics, these are outweighed by large uncertainties or major risk exposures to adverse conditions.

CI. The rating is reserved for income bonds on which no interest is being paid.

D. Debt rated D is in default, and repayment of interest and/or repayment of principal are in arrears.

NR. Indicates that no rating has been requested, that there is insufficient information on which to base a rating, or that S&P does not rate a particular type of obligation as a matter of policy."

Notes

Chapter 1

1. In testimony before the Permanent Subcommittee on Investigations, Committee on Governmental Affairs, United States Senate, 1997.

2. The source for all mutual fund statistics is the Investment Company Institute, unless otherwise noted.

3. Strategic Insight, "A Commentary on Selected Events and Developments during 1998," November 1998.

4. John D. Rea and Brian K. Reid, "Total Shareholder Costs of Bond and Money Market Mutual Funds," *Investment Company Institute Perspective*, Vol. 5, no. 3, March 1999, and "Trends in the Ownership Cost of Equity Mutual Funds," *Investment Company Institute Perspective*, Vol. 4, no. 3, November 1998.

5. *Ibid.*

6. Dreyfus, Jack, *The Lion of Wall Street*, Washington: Regnery, 1995.

7. Bogle, John C., *Common Sense on Mutual Funds: New Imperatives for the Intelligent Investor*, New York: Wiley, 1999.

Chapter 2

1. William A. Campbell, "The Investment Act of 1940: Reasonable and Intelligent," *Friends of Financial History*, Fall, 1994.

2. Bullock, Hugh, *The Story of Investment Companies*, New York: Columbia University Press, 1959, p. 2.

3. Max Rottersman and Jason Zweig, "An Early History of Mutual Funds," *Friends of Financial History*, Spring, 1944.

4. Bullock, *op. cit.*

5. Rottersman and Zweig, *op. cit.*

6. Bullock, *op. cit.*

7. *Ibid.*

8. Natalie R. Grow, "The 'Boston-Type Open-End Fund'—Development of a National Financial Institution: 1924–1940," Doctoral Thesis, Harvard University, April 30, 1977.

9. Baumol, William J., *et al*, *The Economics of Mutual Fund Markets: Competition Versus Regulation*, Boston: Kluwer Academic Publishers, 1990.

10. *Ibid.*

11. Campbell, *op. cit.*

12. Rottersman and Zweig, *op. cit.*

13. Griffeth, Bill, *The Mutual Fund Masters*, Chicago: Probus Publishing, 1995, p. 63.

14. Diana Henriques, *Fidelity's World*, New York: Simon & Schuster, 1997.

15. *Investment Company Act of 1940*, sec. 1(b).

16. Henriques, *op. cit.*

17. Dreyfus, Jack, *The Lion of Wall Street*, Washington: Regnery Publishing, Inc., 1996.

18. Henriques, *op. cit.*

19. Ashley Dunn, "The 50: People who Most Influenced Business this Century," *The Los Angeles Times*, October 25, 1999.

20. "Benham Group Founder Leaves 25-Year Legacy; James M. Benham Retires from American Century," *Business Wire*, December 23, 1997.

21. Peter Fortune, "Mutual Funds, Part I: Reshaping the American Financial System," *New England Economic Review*, July/August 1997.

22. Bernstein Research, *The Future of Money Management in America*, 1997 edition.

Chapter 3

1. Fortune, *op. cit.*

2. These figures are for open-end funds as of July 1999, as stated in the testimony of Matthew P. Fink, President of the Investment Company Institute, before the House Committee on Banking and Financial Services, July 21, 1999.

3. Investment Company Institute, *1999 Mutual Fund Fact Book*.

4. Gordon Altman Butowsky Weitzen Shalov & Wein (New York), *A Practical Guide to the Investment Company Act*, St. Paul: Merrill/Magnus Publishing Corporation, 1996.

5. Mindy Rosenthal, "Vanguard Moves to Cut Costs," *Fund Directions*, May 1998.

6. Investment Company Institute, *The Organization and Operation of a Mutual Fund*, June 1997.

7. Burks *vs.* Lasker, 441 U.S. 471, 484-85 (1979).

8. "A Quick Q&A with Warren Buffett," Morningstar web site (www.morningstar.net), May 6, 1998.

9. Arthur Levitt, "Keeping Faith with the Shareholder Interest: Strengthening the Role of Independent Directors of Mutual Funds," delivered at the Mutual Funds and Investment Management Conference, Palm Springs, CA, March 22, 1999.

10. Mike Garrity, "Director's Pay Rose in 1999, Study Finds," *Mutual Fund Market News*, May 15, 2000.

11. Strategic Insight, *Money Management Financial Comparisons, 1998*, April 1999.

12. Carolyn K. H. Ing, *Mutual Fund Accounting: Full and Remote Service Providers*, The Tower Group, January 1997.

13. Kenneth Gilpin, "Nudging Out Middlemen With a Chip," *The New York Times*, August 1, 1999.

14. Miles Livingston and Edward S. O'Neal, "Mutual Fund Brokerage Commissions," *Journal of Financial Research*, June 1, 1996.

15. Bogle, John. *Bogle on Mutual Funds*.

16. Livingston and O'Neal, *op cit.*

17. John M. R. Chalmers, Roger M. Edelen, and Gregory Kadlec, "Transaction-Cost Expenditures and the Relative Performance of Mutual Funds," Working paper 00-02, The Wharton School, University of Pennsylvania, November 23, 1999.

18. Russ Werners and Tobias J. Moskowitz, "Mutual Fund Performance: An Empirical Decomposition into Stock-picking Talent, Style, Transactions Costs, and Expenses," *Journal of Finance*, August 1, 2000.

19. U.S. Securities & Exchange Commission, *Inspection Report on the Soft Dollar Practices of Broker-Dealers, Investment Advisers and Mutual Funds*, September 22, 1998.

20. John D. Rea and Brian K. Reid, "Trends in the Ownership Cost of Equity Mutual Funds," *Investment Company Institute Perspective*, Vol. 4, no. 3, November 1998, and "Total Shareholder Cost of Bond and Money Market Mutual Funds," Vol. 5, no. 3, March 1999.

21. Henriques, Diana, *Fidelity's World*.

22. Investment Company Institute, 1998 Annual Report.

23. LaCrisha Butler, "Lobbyists Say New Rules Won't Change the Way They Do Business," Gannett News Service, May 10, 1996.

24. Elizabeth MacDonald, "New Rule Requires Growing Concerns to Immediately Write Off Start-Up Costs," *The Wall Street Journal*, April 9, 1998.

25. Mike Garrity, "With Reserves Up, ICI Cuts Member Dues," *Mutual Fund Market News*, June 21, 1999.

26. "The Work of the SEC," Office of Public Affairs, Policy Evaluation and Research, United States Securities and Exchange Commission, June 1977.

27. Cheryl Winokur, "SEC Fund Chief Hits the Ground Running," *American Banker*, June 25, 1999.

28. Gordon Altman, *et al*, p. 7-1.

29. "Chairman Levitt Forces the Pace of an Expanding Regulatory Agenda," *Fund Action*, UMI Company, May 17, 1999.

30. Matthew P. Fink, testimony before the Telecommunications and Finance Subcomittee, U.S. House of Representatives on the "Capital Markets Deregulation and Liberalization Act of 1995," October 1995.

Chapter 4

1. Joe Queenan, "Rocker Elvis or Vegas Elvis: Niche Funds Emerge for Every Fad and Fancy," *Barron's*, July 27, 1992.

2. Ake, *et al*, *Registration of Mutual Funds*, R.R. Donnelly Financial, 1999. This document, available for download via the Internet (http://www.rrdfin.com), contains an exhaustive discussion of Form N-1A requirements.

3. "SEC Says Yes To Plain English," *Financial Planning*, March 1, 1998.

4. Robert Tie, "Plain English, Please," *Investment Dealers' Digest*, November 17, 1997.

5. Katerina Simons, "Risk-Adjusted Performance of Mutual Funds," *New England Economic Review*, September/October, 1998.

6. Jerry Morgan, "Mutual Funds / How to Measure Risk? You Can Count the Ways," *Newsday*, April 28, 1996.

7. "Prospectuses Would be Read If They Could be Understood," *Buffalo News*, October 22, 1996.

8. Livingston and O'Neal, *op. cit.*

9. Lori Pizzani, "Profile prospectus receives tepid reception," *Mutual Fund Market News*, October 12, 1998.

10. Stephanie Rosen, "The Right Cut: As the number of mutual funds approaches 10,000, classification systems struggle to stay relevant," *Bank Investment Marketing*, April 1, 1999.

11. Dan DiBartolomeo and Erik Witkowski, "Mutual Fund Misclassification: Evidence Based on Style Analysis," *Financial Analysts Journal*, September 1, 1997.

12. Rosen, *op. cit.*

13. Karen Damato, "Grading Lipper's New Report Card: Data Firm's Category System Disturbs Some Fund Managers, But Investors Should Be Pleased," *The Wall Street Journal*, October 4, 1999.

14. Griffeth, *op. cit.*

15. Karen Damato, "Morningstar Edges Toward One-Year Ratings," *The Wall Street Journal*, April 6, 1996.

16. Walecia Konrad, "Power Brokers: The SmartMoney 30," *SmartMoney*, September 1, 1997.

17. Burton Malkiel, *A Random Walk Down Wall Street*, multiple editions, the latest being W. W. Norton, 1999.

18. Marten Gruber, "Another Puzzle: The Growth in Actively Managed Mutual Funds," *Journal of Finance*, July 1, 1996.

19. See, for example, W. Scott Simon, *Index Mutual Funds: Profiting from an Investment Revolution*, Camarillo, CA: Namborn Publishing Company, 1998. Simon refers to all the major research work that supports the passive management school of thought.

Chapter 5

1. David Whitford, "Where Have All the Geniuses Gone?" *Fortune*, October 11, 1999

2. "Crabbe Huson's Contrarian Investment Process," on http://www.contrarian.com/contrarians/view.html, October 15, 1999.

3. Scudder Micro Cap Fund Prospectus, January 1, 1999.

4. Goldman Sachs Domestic Equity Funds Prospectus, April 30, 1999.

5. Massachusetts Investor Trust prospectus, May 1, 1999, p. 1.

6. Will Daley, "Legg Mason Skirts the Style Issue," *Ignites.com*, October 25, 1999.

7. Brett Johnson, "Why Aren't the GE Funds More Successful?" *The Wall Street Journal*, October 11, 1999.

8. Neuberger Berman Income Funds Prospectus, August 16, 1999.

9. Seligman High Yield Bond Series Prospectus, June 1, 1999.

10. Leland Montgomery, "Bond Voyage: Pacific Investment Management's Bill Gross Hunts Out Big Profits in Cheap Bonds," *Financial World*, June 25, 1991.

11. Anne Kates Smith, "A Mutual Fund Tells All on the Web. Is that Wise?" *U. S. News and World Report*, October 18, 1999.

12. Lewis Braham, "Funds With the Personal Touch," SmartMoney.com, July 1, 1999.

13. John Treuschel, "Analytical Tools for U.S. Equity Managers," Tower Group, November 1997, and Sylvia Chou and John Tresuchel, "Fixed Income Analytics: Case Study of a Top Mutual Fund Company," Tower Group, July 1998.

14. Investment Company Institute, "Distribution of Mutual Fund Assets in Equity, Hybrid, and Bond Funds," *1999 Mutual Fund Fact Book*.

15. "ECN Evolution: Moving Toward a Central Order Book," *Securities Industry News*, November 29, 1999.

16. Ian Domowitz and Benn Steil, "Automation, Trading Costs, and the Structure of the Trading Services Industry," Department of Finance, Penn State University, unpublished paper, November 1998.

17. "1999 Full-Year Statistical Report," *Securities Industry News*, February 7, 2000.

18. Pui-Wing Tam, "Bond Traders Seek More, Better Online Services," *The Wall Street Journal*, October 25, 1999.

19. Hal Lux and Jack Willoughby, "May Day II: Technology and Regulatory Reform are Turning the Over-the-Counter Market on its Head," *Institutional Investor*, February 1999.

20. Lynnley Browning, "Who Runs Your Fund? Often, It's Rent-a-Manager," *The Boston Globe*, December 6, 1998.

21. Mike Garrity, "Best Execution Practices Face Pressures," *Mutual Fund Market News*, September 13, 1999.

22. "Soft Dollar Arrangements," Exchange Act Release No. 23170, April 23, 1986.

23. Jack Willoughby, "A Hard Line on Soft Dollars," *Institutional Investor*, April 1, 1998.

24. Aaron Lucchetti, "SEC Probes Funds' Commissions," *The Wall Street Journal*, September 16, 1999.

25. Strategic Insight, *Flow Watch, Executive Summary*, November 1998.

26. Lux and Willoughby, *op. cit.*

27. Emily Harrison, "If I Can Make It Here...," *SmartMoney*, June 1, 1998.

28. "Gabelli Takes in More than $42 Million in 98—Leading Pack of CEOs in Pay," *Fund Action*, July 12, 1999.

29. Pui-Wing Tam, "Fund Managers Get Raises for So-So Showings," *The Wall Street Journal*, July 20, 1999.

30. Carol J. Clouse, "Investment Firms Show Pros the Money," *Investment Management Weekly*, August 2, 1999.

31. Linda Sakelaris, "Who Makes What: Compensation Story is in the Incentives," *Pensions & Investment*, May 3, 1999.

Chapter 6

1. Carol E. Curtis, "BISYS Thrives Behind the Scenes," *USBanker*, February 1999.

2. Herzberg, Frederick. *Work and the Nature of Man*. London: Staples Press, 1968.

3. Jill M. Considine, Keynote Address delivered to the Securities Industry Association 26th Annual Operations Conference, May 12, 1999.

4. Steven Goldstein, "Error Correction," *Compliance Reporter*, December 21, 1998.

5. Investment Company Institute, *Introductory Guide for Investment Company Directors*, 1995.

6. Michael Siconolfi, "Financial Firms Prefer to Pay Rather Than Fight Investors," *The Wall Street Journal*, August 25, 1994.

7. U.S. Securities and Exchange Commission, *Administrative Proceeding File No. 3-9704*, September 15, 1998.

8. *Ibid.*

9. Lewis Braham, "SEC to Fund Companies: Keep Managers in Line, or We Will," *Financial Planning*, October 1, 1997.

10. Deborah Williams, "Risk for the Investment Manager," Meridien Research Brief, March 1999.

11. G. Bruce Knecht, "Piper Reaches $70 Million Pact to Settle Suit," *The Wall Street Journal*, February 16, 1995.

12. "Worth Bruntjen's Biggest Gamble / Will His Bad Bet Continue to Soak Investors?" *Minneapolis Star-Tribune*, October 10, 1994.

13. Tim Quinson, "Investors in Piper Fund to Get Day in Court Today," *Minneapolis Star-Tribune*, December 8, 1995.

14. Jill J. Barshay, "U.S. Bancorp Agrees to Buy Piper Jaffray," *Minneapolis Star-Tribune*, December 16, 1997.

15. Bruce G. Leto, "Portfolio Manager Sanctioned for Government Income Fund Investments," *Mondaq Business Briefing*, June 6, 1999.

16. Strategic Insight, *Money Management Financial Comparisons, 1998*, April 1999.

17. Katherine Fraser, "State Street Cuts Fees 40% to Retain Calpers Contract," *American Banker*, June 24, 1996.

Chapter 7

1. James M. Storey and James M. Clyde, *Mutual Fund Law Handbook*. Little Falls, NJ: Glasser LegalWorks, 1998.

2. Charles A. Jaffe, "Not Always as Simple as 1, 2 3," *The Boston Globe*, November 16, 1997.

3. "The Alphabet Soup of Share Classes," *Mutual Fund Cafe* (http://www.mfcafe.com), October 5, 1998.

4. *Vanguard Tax-Managed Funds Prospectus*, August 18, 1999.

5. Charles Gasparino, "'Fair-Value' Pricing for Shares In Funds to be Reviewed by SEC," *The Wall Street Journal*, November 3, 1997.

6. Andy Dworkin, "Some Investors Left to Wonder About Numbers," *The Dallas Morning News*, October 30, 1997.

7. Deborah Lohse, "Too Little Coverage: How General American Got Fancy in Investing, Lost its Independence," *The Wall Street Journal*, September 3, 1999.

8. "1998 Fund Accounting Survey," PricewaterhouseCoopers, November 1998.

9. Strategic Insight, *Money Management Financial Comparisons, 1998*.

10. Stanley J. Friedman, "Obligations of Directors of Money Market Funds," *Review of Banking and Financial Services*, January 15, 1992.

11. Strategic Insight, *Money Management Financial*

Chapter 8

1. Vlae Kershner, "Three Ways to Run a Mutual Fund Company," *The San Francisco Chronicle*, June 27, 1986.

2. "Pilgrim SmallCap Opportunities Fund Will Close to New Investors," PR Newswire, December 22, 1999.

3. Strategic Insight Simfund data as of November 1999.

4. Rule 12b-1(a)2 under the Investment Company Act of 1940.

5. Robert Slater, *John Bogle and the Vanguard Experiment*. New York: McGraw-Hill, 1997.

6. Karen Slater, "Critics Say Brokerage Firms Hide Fees on Their New 'No-Load' Mutual Funds," *The Wall Street Journal*, August 8, 1985.

7. Laura A. Walbert, "Babies and Bathwater (Mutual Fund Distribution Fees)," *Forbes*, October 3, 1988.

8. Scott Burns, "No-Load Funds Disguise Expense Burdens," *The Dallas Morning News*, April 2, 1985.

9. Laura R. Walbert and Christopher Power, "Careful, It's Loaded. (Mutual Funds Which Cheat the Investor)," *Forbes*, September 16, 1985.

10. Michael K. Ozanian, "Fee Jungle (Mutual Fund Charges)," *Financial World*, February 9, 1988.

11. Based on Simfund data as of the end of 1999.

12. Timothy Middleton, "Load? No-load? Who Knows?" *Houston Chronicle*, November 25, 1996

13. Stephen Garmhausen, "Fund Firms Struggle to Fill Bank Wholesaling Positions," *American Banker*, September 11, 1998.

14. "Selling to Intermediaries Roundtable," *Fund Marketing Alert*, November 1, 1999.

15. Cheryl Winokur, "Franklin Templeton to Double In-House Wholesaler Staff," *American Banker*, November 1, 1999.

16. Rochelle K. Plesset and Diane E. Ambler, "The Financing of Mutual Fund 'B Share' Arrangements," *Business Lawyer*, August 1, 1997. Also see Christopher O'Leary, "Latest Fodder for Securitization: Mutual Fund Fees," *Investment Dealers Digest*, December 20, 1999.

17. Jerry Morgan, "Level Loaded Mutual Funds Are Loaded," *Newsday*, December 4, 1994.

18. Ilana Polyak, "They Sell C Shares for Revenue Stream: Load Fund Investors Don't Mind Paying More Over the Long Term," *Investment News*, October 18, 1999.

19. "Prudential Investments Begins Breaking Proprietary Mold," *Registered Representative*, January 30, 1999.

20. "Proprietary Funds Consider Outside Sales Channels," *Registered Representative*, June 30, 1999.

21. Gavin Daley, "MSDW Offering Brokers New Payouts to Push Proprietary Funds," *Ignites.com*, January 14, 2000.

22. Edward S. O'Neal, "Mutual Fund Share Classes and Broker Incentives," *Association for Investment Management and Research*, September/October 1999.

23. Richard Todd, "Who Has An Ax to Grind," *The CPA Journal*, May 1, 1998.

24. Gavin Daly, "NASD Cautions Firms on Inappropriate Sales of B, C Shares," *Ignites.com*, July 26, 2000.

Chapter 9

1. The Economist Intelligence Unit, *Tomorrow's Leading Investment Manager*, research report, 1999.

2. Lee Barney, "Direct Marketing is Not Always so Direct," *Mutual Fund Market News*, June 3, 1999.

3. Charlie Bevis, "New Playing Field for Mutual Fund Firms, *National Underwriter Life & Health—Financial Services Edition*, March 22, 1999.

4. *Ibid.*

5. Donald Jay Korn, "Super Market Share: Schwab Remains the Supermarket Where Most Financial Planners Take Their Clients Shopping," *Financial Planning*, November 1, 1999.

6. Michael Schneider, "Investment Services," *Standard & Poor's Industry Surveys*, April 15, 1999.

7. *FRC Views on the News*, January 3, 2000.

8. Lee Barney, *op. cit.*

9. Jenny Anderson, "The All-Purpose Wrap," *Institutional Investor*, December 1, 1999.

10. "Mutual Fund Outlook for 2000," *Strategic Insight Overview*, October 1999.

11. Barton Crockett, "U.S. Trust Taking Over Affinity Specialist's Funds in Exchange for Marketing," *American Banker*, March 10, 1995.

12. Virginia Munger Kahn, "How We Diversified Our Business: A Conversation with American Century's Bill Lyons," *Mutual Fund Cafe* (http://www.mfcafe.com), March 1998.

13. Interview with the author, April 14, 2000.

14. Stephen Garmhausen, "American Century's Sales Through Banks Climbing," *American Banker*, August 23, 1999.

15. Mercedes Cardona, "American Century Pitch Sells Values," *Advertising Age*, March 13, 2000.

16. Eric Palmer, "Private Business Revenue Keeps City on Famed Forbes 500 List," *The Kansas City Star*, January 18, 2000.

17. Peter Fortune, "Mutual Funds, Part I: Reshaping the American Financial System," *New England Economic Review*, July/August 1997.

18. Melanie Waddell, "Muscling in on the Money Wars," *Bank Investment Marketing*, November 1, 1999.

19. *Ibid.*

20. Kenneth Kehrer and Kevin Crowe, "Diminishing Distinctions," *ABA Banking Journal*, November 1, 1999.

21. Niamh Ring, "More Banks in Fund Big League But Further Rise May Be Tough," *American Banker Online*, February 11, 2000.

22. Yankelovich Partners/Mutual Fund Forum survey cited in "Overview of Distribution Trends with a Focus on Direct Distribution Developments," *Strategic Insight*, March 1998.

Chapter 10

1. Andrew Fraser, "Mutual Funds Find Magic of Marketing," *Chicago Sun-Times*, March 26, 1998.

2. 15 U.S.C. §17b(10)

3. "Protecting Investors: A Half Century of Investment Company Regulation, United States Securities and Exchange Commission, Division of Investment Management, May 1992.

4. Natalie R. Grow, *op. cit.*, p. 381.

5. 17 C.F.R. §230.134

6. Michael Ellison, "Anger as Superman Appears to Walk: Actor Christopher Reeve, Paralysed Five Years Ago, Accused of Misleading Disabled People With Role in TV Commercial," *The Guardian*, February 3, 2000.

7. "Protecting Investors," SEC Division of Investment Management, 1992.

8. Bruce Ingersoll, "SEC Staff Warns Mutual-Fund Industry About Advertised Performance Figures," *The Wall Street Journal*, November 11, 1985.

9. "New SEC Fund Mutual Funds Tips Reminds Investors to Look at More Than Short-Term Performance," http://www.sec.gov/news/press/2000-7.txt.

10. Ron Carrick, "Lies, Damned Lies, Statistics, and Fund Ads," *The Globe and Mail*, February 3, 2000.

11. J.R. Brandstrader, "Sesame St., Wall St.: In Tough Times, Marketers Widen Net," *Barron's*, February 11, 1991.

12. Michael Fritz, "Just Another Can of Peas: What Are Funds to Marketers?" *Investment News*, February 9, 1998.

13. Mike Garrity, "How the Mutual Fund Industry Got Its Wings," *Mutual Fund Market News*, June 17, 1999.

14. Laura Saunders Egodigwe, "U.S. Mutual Funds Get Advertising Fever," *The Wall Street Journal Europe*, April 9, 1998.

15. "Winning In An Uncertain World: A Study of Mutual Fund Distribution Costs and Strategy," Financial Research Corporation, 1999.

16. Barry Henderson and Sandra Ward, "All Stars: A Look at the Fund World's Heaviest Hitters," *Barron's / Lipper Mutual Funds Quarterly*, January 10, 2000.

17. Mark A. Hoffman, "At 25, ERISA Has Compiled a Mixed Record of Success: May Have Caused Eclipse of Defined Benefit Pensions," *Business Insurance*, May 10, 1999.

18. "Defined Contribution Plan Investments in Mutual Funds," *Strategic Insight Overview*, August 1999.

19. Michael Goldstein and Igor Krutov, "The Future of Money Management in America: Challenges Facing the Mutual Fund Industry," *Bernstein Research*, February 4, 2000.

20. Interview with the author.

21. "Winning In An Uncertain World: A Study of Mutual Fund Distribution Costs and Strategy," Financial Research Corporation, 1999.

22. "The Sources of Mutual Fund Growth in 1998," *Strategic Insight Overview*, July, 1999.

23. *Ibid.*

24. "The Continuing Evolution of the Mutual Fund Industry," Goldman, Sachs & Company, 1995.

25. Garrity, *op. cit.*

26. John Bogle, *Common Sense on Mutual Funds: New Imperatives for the Intelligent Investor*, New York: John Wiley & Sons, 1999.

27. Lee Barney, "Fund Ads Miss Mark, According to Study," *Mutual Fund Market News*, March 8, 1999.

28. Ken Schachter, "Alliance Funds Grab Nearly Quarter of Broker Sales," *Ignites.com*, February 9, 2000.

29. Charles Gasparino and James S. Hirsch, "How Scudder's Missteps Made It a Takeover Candidate," *The Wall Street Journal*, June 20, 1997.

30. "Winning In An Uncertain World: A Study of Mutual Fund Distribution Costs and Strategy," Financial Research Corporation, 1999.

31. Julie Carrick Dalton, "Mutual Fund Advertising Blitz," *Boston Business Journal*, April 28, 1997.

Chapter 11

1. Charles A. Jaffe, "Mutual Interest: Ask Questions When Your Mutual Fund Gets a New Transfer Agent," *The Milwaukee Journal Sentinel*, February 18, 1996, p. 4.

2. Meghan M. Burti, editor, *The 1999 Transfer Agent Service Guide*, Securities Data Publishing, Volume XIV, Issue 1, 1999.

3. "American Transtech Acquires Advanced Information Services Company," PR Newswire, December 22, 1988.

4. Strategic Insight, *Mutual Fund Industry Fee and Expense Benchmarks Updated for 1998*, April 1999.

5. American Century Investments, *Prospectus: Growth Fund, Ultra Fund, Select Fund, Vista Fund, Heritage Fund*.

6. Barry P. Barbash, "Remembering the Past: Mutual Funds and the Lessons of the Wonder Years," speech delivered to the 1997 ICI Securities Law Procedures Conference, Washington, D.C., December 4, 1997.

7. Carolyn K. H. Ing, "Mutual Fund Shareholder Servicing Systems and Transfer Agents," The Tower Group, Report 012:008, July 1997, p. 10.

8. Conversation with the author.

9. Gordon Powers, "Report on Mutual Funds: Uncle Sam Scoops Up Funds," *The Globe and Mail*, January 20, 1994.

10. Barton Crockett, "Servicing Giant First Data Poised to Get Bigger," *American Banker*, January 4, 1995, p. 15.

Chapter 12

1. Investment Company Institute, "The Service Quality Challenge: Understanding Shareholder Expectations," Autumn, 1994.

2. "Eleventh Annual Shareholder Service Survey Report of Findings," Transfer Agent Committee, National Investment Company Service Association, June 1999.

3. Humberto Cruz, "Switch to E-Mail Could Pay Off for Vanguard, Shareholders," *Ft. Lauderdale Sun Sentinel*, July 12, 1998.

4. Kathy Brogan, Geoff Bobroff, and Mike MacMillan, "How Fund Companies Are Using the Internet to Strengthen Customer Relationships and Cut Costs," *Mutual Fund Cafe*, (http://www.mfcafe.com), August, 1998.

5. Mark Casady, quoted in Pui-Wing Tam, "Scudder Turns to the Internet to Boost its Sales Effort," *The Wall Street Journal*, June 30, 1999.

6. Hafner, Katie and Lyon, Matthew, *Where Wizards Stay Up Late: The Origins of the Internet*. New York: Simon & Schuster, 1996.

7. "Vanguard Tops E-Mail Response Survey," *Fund Action*, June 11, 1998.

8. "Fidelity Investments Launches Online Account Statements; First Discount Brokerage Firm to Offer Real-Time Statements Online," *Business Wire*, June 21, 1999.

9. Investment Company Institute, "Mutual Fund Transfer Agents Trends and Billing Practices 1997," 1998.

10. "Toward an Increased Focus on Customer Retention," *Strategic Insight Overview*, March 1998.

11. Allen R. Myerson, "The Voice is Friendly, the Job Hectic," *The New York Times*, April 3, 1993.

12. Joanna Bean, "Baltimore-Based T. Rowe Price to Open Colorado Springs, Colo., Center," *The Colorado Springs Gazette*, March 30, 1999.

13. Mike Garrity, "Telephone Centers Wrestle With Hiring," *Mutual Fund Market News*, February 22, 1999.

14. Slater, Robert. *John Bogle and the Vanguard Experiment*. New York: McGraw-Hill, 1997.

15. *Ibid.*, p. 185.

16. Thomas S. Mulligan, "In Case of Emergency...Vanguard is Ready," *Los Angeles Times*, March 1, 1998.

Chapter 13

1. Augustus De Morgan, *A Budget of Paradoxes*, 1872.

2. PricewaterhouseCoopers internal documents.

3. Vanessa O'Connell, "How'ya Doing? Many Investors Don't Know," *The Wall Street Journal*, February 2, 1996.

4. "Your Money: Levitt Seeks Fund Statement Change," *Los Angeles Times*, April 21, 1998.

5. "Liberty Funds Allow OnLine Proxy Votes," *Ink Spot News*, October 13, 1998.

6. Maureen Goggin, "For States, a Hidden Bonanza," *The Boston Globe*, April 30, 1996.

7. *Ibid.*

Chapter 14

1. Harvey Golub, Chairman of American Express, in a discussion with analysts, July 7, 1999.

2. Michael L. Goldstein and Igor Krutov, "The Future of Money Management in America: Challenges Facing the Mutual Fund Industry," Bernstein Research, February 4, 2000.

3. Morgan Stanley Dean Witter, Equity Research North America, *The Internet and Financial Services*, August 1999.

4. James B. Punishill, *et al*, *Net Investing Goes Mainstream*, Forrester Research, March 1999.

5. Steve Lohr, "Big Blue Casts Itself as Big Brother to Business on the Web," *The New York Times*, September 22, 1999.

6. The Economist Intelligence Unit and PricewaterhouseCoopers, *Tomorrow's Leading Investment Managers*, 1999.

7. Bridget O'Brien and Mara Der Hovanesian, "How Surfing the Web Is Next Big Fund Wave," *The Wall Street Journal*, April 5, 1999.

8. FRC, *FRC Views on the News*, Volume 5, Issue 3, September 7, 1999.

9. James P. Punishill, *et al*, *op. cit.*

10. Ken Schachter, "Putnam Poll: 9 of 10 Don't Invest Direct via 'Net," Ignites.com, October 22, 1999.

11. *Ibid.*

12. Andrew Greene, "Technology Seen as Transforming," *Annuity Market News*, February 1, 2000.

13. Joe Morris, "Web Hasn't Panned Out for No-Load Sales: Study," *Ignites.com*, March 7, 2000.

14. Larry Rulison, "Online Trading May Be Wider Than Suspected," *Mutual Fund Market News*, July 19, 1999.

15. "Fund Sales Will Be 19 Percent Online by 2005, Survey Predicts," Mutual Fund Market News, March 27, 2000.

16. Jim Norris, in Danielle Fugazy, "Mutual Fund Growth Online Should Continue," *Web Finance*, January 17, 2000.

17. Ed Berryman, "Taking Another Look: Getting On with the Business of E-Business," *Insights & Solutions*, PricewaterhouseCoopers, 1999.

18. Danielle Fugazy, "Mutual Funds: Is the Internet Replacing Other Channels?" *Web Finance*, February 28, 2000.

19. Frank Byrt, "Technology Transforming Online Mutual Fund Trading," *Dow Jones News Service*, February 16, 2000.

20. Danielle Fugazy, "Brokerage — Fidelity: Phone Reps Decline as Web Presence Ascends," *Web Finance*, February 28, 2000.

21. Evan Cooper, "Street Talk — Fund Focus: Fidelity Spends $20 Million on Broker Tools," *On Wall Street*, January 1, 2000.

22. Morgan Stanley Dean Witter, *op. cit.*

23. *Ibid.*

24. Aaron Luchetti, "Shop and Save? E-tailers Allow Buyers To Add Fund Investments to Their Carts," *The Wall Street Journal*, December 21, 1999.

25. "Aimfunds.com Named Among Top Mutual Fund Web Sites," *Business Wire*, December 7, 1999.

26. "Corporate Profile for AIM Management Group Inc. Dated August 13, 1999," *Business Wire*, August 13, 1999.

27. Octavio Marenzi, "The Future of Internet-based Equity and Bond Research Distribution," Meridien Research, Inc., February 1999.

28. Edward Kountz, "Thinking Globally, Acting Locally—How Technology Shaped Putnam and Vice Versa," *Securities Industry News*, August 25, 1997.

29. Dushyant Shahrawat, "STP, Global Trading and Transaction Costs Spur the Popularity of Buy Side Order Management Systems," Tower Group Research Note 020:022, August 1999.

30. William A. Bautz, Senior Vice President and Chief Technology Officer, New York Stock Exchange, Speech at the Securities Industry News Second Annual Internet Technologies Conference, September 28, 1998.

31. Gregory Zuckerman and Pui-Wing Tam, "Bond Traders Seek More, Better Online Services," *The Wall Street Journal*, October 25, 1999.

32. "STP Trends and Progress Report for Investment Managers, Broker/Dealers, and Custodian Banks," *The Tower Group*, February 2000.

33. Morgan Stanley Dean Witter, *op. cit*.

34. George Anders, "Ante Up! Big Gambles in the New Economy — Different Strokes: Amazon, E-Toys Make Big, Opposing Bets; Which One Is Right?" *The Wall Street Journal*, November 2, 1999.

35. "96% of Mutual Fund Companies Will Be Increasing Their Emphasis on Internet Initiatives in the Year 2000," *Business Wire*, November 1, 1999.

Chapter 15

1. "International Mutual Fund Survey, First Quarter, 1997," *Investment Company Institute*.

2. Geoff Winestock, "Fund Borders Are Opening," *The Wall Street Journal Europe*, February 17, 2000.

3. "France: Europe's Largest Mutual Fund Market," State Street Global Strategy & Development Department, *The Mutual Fund Café*, (http://www.mfcafe.com/pantry99/wf_0699.html), June 1999.

4. "Italy – A Dynamic and Growing Market," State Street Global Strategy & Development Department, *The Mutual Fund Café*, (http://www.mfcafe.com/pantry99/wf_1099.html), October 1999.

5. Stuart Holah, "A Crash Course in OEICS: Forecasts Were That the Unit-Trust Industry Would Switch Rapidly to OEICS So Why Has Take-up Been Slow?" *Money Marketing*, June 11, 1998.

6. "UK: 'PEP's Dropped, but Market Still Has Pep,'" State Street Global Strategy & Development Department, *The Mutual Fund Café*, (http://www.mfcafe.com/pantry99/wf_0499.html), April 1999.

7. "Germany – Mutual Fund Segment," State Street Global Strategy & Development Department, *The Mutual Fund Café*, (http://www.mfcafe.com/world/wf.html), March 2000.

8. Margaret Boitano, "US Asset Mgmt Companies Poised To Tap European Market, Report Says," *Dow Jones News Service*, May 4, 1999.

9. Richard Chimberg, "Japan's Resurgence Bodes Well for Mutual Fund Firms," *The Orange County Register*, December 5, 1999.

10. Bill Spindle, "Making Waves: Japan's Investors Discover the Spirit of Mutual Funds," *The Asian Wall Street Journal*, December 2, 1999.

11. "Mutual Funds in Japan: Looking for a Second Chance," State Street Global Strategy & Development Department, *The Mutual Fund Café*, (http://www.mfcafe.com/pantry99/wf_0999.html), September 1999.

12. "Japanese Savings: Mrs. Watanabe Learns to Invest," *The Economist*, December 18, 1999.

13. "Investment Trusts in Japan 1999," The Investment Trusts Association, Japan (Skoken Toshishintaku Kyokai), Tokyo, Japan.

14. "Canada—Into the New Millenium," State Street Global Strategy & Development Department, *The Mutual Fund Café*, (http://www.mfcafe.com/pantry/wf_0100.html), January 2000.

15. "How Mutual Funds Work in Brazil," Interfund Research, (http://interfund-research.com).

16. Robert Bonte-Friedheim, "Review of Markets & Finance: Fund Managers See No Turning Back the Investment Tide," *The Wall Street Journal Europe*, January 2, 1998.

17. Larry Rulison, "Fund Companies Adding to Offshore Products," *Mutual Fund Market News*, November 9, 1998.

18. "U.S. Firms Spread Investment Gospel: Personal Investing Style: It's Becoming Clear Traditional Pension Plans Aren't Working," *National Post*, March 4, 2000.

19. Bill Spindle, "Japanese Economy Faces a Potential Bonanza As Nearly $1 Trillion in Savings Plans Mature," *The Wall Street Journal*, March 24, 2000.

20. "International Markets Said to Be Rewarding," *Mutual Fund Market News*, February 21, 2000.

21. Nancy Opiela, "Promise Is in Europe, Not Japan, Study Says," *Mutual Fund Market News*, June 10, 1999.

22. Natsua Nishio, "Goldman Sachs Bullish on Developing Mutual Fund Market in Japan," *Dow Jones Business News*, February 3, 1999.

23. "Taxation of European Retail Funds," PricewaterhouseCoopers, International Investment Management Tax Group, 1997.

24. David Franecki, "EMU to Fuel Growth in Mutual Funds in Europe," *The Wall Street Journal*, March 16, 1998.

25. "Morgan Stanley Forecasts Bright Funds Future," *Funds International*, August 1, 1998.

26. Richard Newell, "European Focus: Maintaining the Integrity of the European Ideal: Richard Newell Hears the Gospel According to St. Julian as the UK's Departing Head of FEFSI Assesses Progress Made in the Funds Sector," *International Money Marketing*, June 19, 1998.

27. Cheryl Winokur, "Home Market Aging, U.S. Funds Eye Europe," *American Banker*, February 15, 2000.

28. *Ibid.*

29. Sara Calian, "European Mutual Funds—When in Rome," *The Wall Street Journal Europe*, July 13, 1999.

30. Sara Calian, "On the Buyside: Fund Firms Shun European Ventures: They're Too Risky," *The Wall Street Journal Europe*, March 30, 2000.

31. Linda Sakelaris, "Lloyds Exerts Control at IAI: Knelman Resigns CEO Post After Only Two Months," *Pensions & Investments*, August 10, 1998.

32. Jill J. Barshay, "Another CEO is leaving troubled IAI," *Minneapolis-St. Paul Star-Tribune*, January 29, 1999.

33. Jill J. Barshay, "Investment Advisers Quits Fixed-income Business," *Minneapolis-St. Paul Star Tribune*, February 8, 2000.

34. The Economist Intelligence Unit and PricewaterhouseCoopers, "Tomorrow's Leading Investment Managers," 1999.

35. Virginia Munger Kahn, "We Are a Risk-Oriented Investor: A Conversation with Alliance Capital's Dave Williams," *Mutual Fund Cafe* (http://www.mfcafe.com), February 1999.

36. John C. Bogle, "Globalization of Mutual Funds: Perspective, Prospects, and Trust," Keynote Speech before the International Bar Association Seminar, Bermuda, May 3, 1999.

Chapter 16

1. "The Future of Money Management in America: Challenges Facing the Mutual Fund Industry," Bernstein Research, February 4, 2000.

2. Daniel Akst, "Mutual Funds Report: When Ennui Replaces Infatuation," *The New York Times*, January 9, 2000.

3. Jeffrey M. Laderman and Amy Barrett, "Mutual Funds: What's Wrong: To Keep Pulling in Investors, Managers Must Lower Costs and Deliver the Goods," *Business Week*, January 24, 2000.

4. Michael Santoli, "Midlife Crisis: After Years of Spectacular Growth, an Industry Faces Hard Decisions," *Barron's*, April 10, 2000.

5. Lee Barney and Mike Garrity, "Conference Coverage: Fund Industry Said to Face Major Layoffs," *Mutual Fund Market News*, February 28, 2000.

6. *Business Week*, March 3, 1973, cited in Henriques, *Fidelity's World*.

7. U.S. Department of Justice and the Federal Trade Commission, "Horizontal Merger Guidelines," revised April 8, 1997.

8. Federal Trade Commission vs. Staples, Inc and Office Depot, Inc., Plaintiff's Memorandum of Points and Authorities in Support of Motions for Temporary Restraining Order and Preliminary Injunction, April 10, 1997 (available from www.ftc.gov)

9. Baumol, *et al*, *The Economics of Mutual Fund Markets*, 1990.

10. "1999 Mutual Fund Outlook," *Strategic Insight*, November 1998.

11. "Money Management Financial Comparisons, 1998," *Strategic Insight*, April, 1999.

12. Mark Casaday, in Santoli, *op. cit.*

13. "The Future of Money Management in America: Challenges Facing the Mutual Fund Industry," Bernstein Research, February 4, 2000.

14. Michael Santoli, "Midlife Crisis: After Years of Spectacular Growth, an Industry Faces Hard Decisions," *Barron's*, April 10, 2000.

15. "New Product Development: Themes and Recent Successes," *Strategic Insight Overview*, February 2000.

16. "Internet Folios: Threat to Funds of Just Another Brokerage Commodity?" Sionline.com, August 16, 2000.

17. Strategic Insight, "Flow Watch Executive Summary: Results for February 2000," April 2000.

18. Margaret Boitano, "Mutual Funds Lose Appeal to Day-Trading Enthusiasts," *Dow Jones News Service*, May 4, 1999.

19. Brad M. Barber and Terence Odean, "Online Investors: Do the Slow Die First?" unpublished paper, University of California-Davis, November 1999.

20. "Rapid Growth of Exchange Traded Programs," Sionline.com, March 27, 2000.

21. Sandra Ward, "New Spiders, New Webs" Fund Companies Consider Creating Their Own Exchange-Traded Replicas," *Barron's*, November 15, 1999.

22. Jerry Morgan, "VIPERSs to Keep Away Market Timers / Vanguard hopes 'serpentine' ETFs will shield its index funds, give traders an alternative," *Newsday*, May 28, 2000.

23. Andrew Greene, "Firms Are Wary of Exchange-Traded Funds," *Mutual Fund Market News*, April 24, 2000.

24. Joe Morris, "Study: ETF Threat No Biggie to Traditional Funds," *http://www.ignites.com*, May 31, 2000.

25. Mathew P. Fink, testimony before the Subcommittee on Finance and Hazardous Materials of the Committee on Commerce, U.S. House of Representatives, September 29, 1998.

26. Charles A. Trzcinka, testimony before the Subcommittee on Finance and Hazardous Materials of the Committee on Commerce, U.S. House of Representatives, September 29, 1998.

27. David Gardner, testimony before the Subcommittee on Finance and Hazardous Materials of the Committee on Commerce, U.S. House of Representatives, September 29, 1998.

28. John C. Bogle, *Common Sense on Mutual Funds*, New York: Wiley, 1999.

29. "Why Fund Fees Are So High," *Business Week*, (http://www.businessweek.com), July 16, 1999.

30. John D. Rea, Brian K. Reid, and Travis Lee, "Mutual Fund Costs, 1980–1998," *Perspective*, Investment Company Institute, September 1999.

31. Richard A. Oppel, Jr., "Fund Expenses: They're Going Down, Down, Down," *The New York Times*, July 4, 1999.

32. *Ibid*.

33. Strategic Insight, "A Perspective on Fund Opportunities and Misconceptions," June 1999.

34. Erin Kelly, "Fund Fees: How Much Is Too Much? Salt in the Wounds," *Fortune*, May 15, 2000.

35. Matthew Fink, in "Readers Report: An Unfair Poke at Mutual Funds," *Business Week*, September 13, 1999.

36. Mike Garrity, "Assessments of Fund Fees Anticipated," *Mutual Fund Market News*, May 29, 2000.

37. Karen Damato, "How Investors Failed to Note a Fund Benefit: A Cut in Fees," *The Wall Street Journal*, April 29, 1999.

38. Sandra Ward, "Fund of Information: The Feds Probe Funds—Congressional Inquiry Into Fees, Disclosure Under Way," *Barron's*, May 24, 1999.

39. United States General Accounting Office, "Mutual Fund Fees: Additional Disclosure Could Encourage Price Competition," GAO/GGD-00-126, June 5, 2000.

40. Stephen Garmhausen, "GAO Report Draws Fire from Fund Industry," Ignites.com, July 12, 2000.

41. See Simon, *Index Mutual Funds*, 1998, for a summary of this research.

42. Gary A. Walker, "Testing the Predictability of Mutual Fund Returns, *Review of Business*, June 22, 1997.

43. Larry Swedroe and Peter D. Fleming, "The Quest to Outperform," *Journal of Accountancy*, January 1, 2000.

44. W. N. Goetzmann and R. G. Ibbotson, "Do Winners Repeat? Patterns in Mutual Fund Return Behavior," *Journal of Portfolio Management*, January 1, 1994.

45. Aaron Lucchetti, "Investors Misjudge Performance of Funds," *The Wall Street Journal*, March 29, 2000.

46. Edward Chancellor, *Devil Take the Hindmost: A History of Financial Speculation*, New York: Farrar, Straus, and Giroux, 1999.

47. Larry Swedroe, "Is It a Search for the Holy Grail?" *Journal of Accountancy*, January 2000.

48. As, for example, W. J. Fabrycky, G.J. Thuesen, and D. Verma, *Economic Decision Analysis*, Upper Saddle River, NJ: Prentice Hall, 1998.

49. Chet Currier, "Top Mutual Fund Executives Fear End of Rising Stock Prices," *The Dallas Morning News*, November 28, 1999.

50. *Ibid*.

Index

For additional copies of this book,

contact The National Investment Company Service Association at

http://www.nicsa.org/textbook